Makers of
Modern Journalism

PRENTICE-HALL JOURNALISM SERIES

Kenneth E. Olson, Editor

Makers of
Modern Journalism

KENNETH STEWART · JOHN TEBBEL

Department of Journalism, New York University

New York   PRENTICE-HALL, INC.   1952

PN
4871
S7

To
Evelyn and Kay

Foreword

THIS BOOK IS A HISTORY OF AMERICAN JOURNALISM TOLD IN TERMS
of men and motives. It is a biographical history, intended to encompass the story of newspapers in America (and a few of the
significant magazine, radio, and television leaders) by means of
the interconnected lives and times of the men who have made,
and are making, the free press of this country.

Such a volume must necessarily have its limitations. It cannot
presume to be a definitive history of journalism in the United
States. Nor can the inevitable omissions and points of emphasis
be charged to anything but the judgment and viewpoints of the
authors. Much of the contemporary material is based upon the
authors' own experience and upon contacts and interviews with
the editors and publishers concerned, but that is not to imply
that those editors and publishers have in any sense authorized
the book's content. We have attempted a fair and factual survey
of American journalistic history from a somewhat different perspective than that of the conventional historian, and it is our
hope that we have provided a book which will make the story
live for readers.

KENNETH STEWART
JOHN TEBBEL

Contents

Makers of
Modern Journalism

The Editors of Revolt

THE NEWSPAPERS OF AMERICA BEGAN AS THE VOICE OF REVOLUtion, and in little more than two centuries they have accomplished the full swing from radical revolt to solid conservatism. In the process, however, they have retained the single dominant quality which has always distinguished the press in this country: a freedom of thought and action unsurpassed anywhere else in the world.

To make that kind of press possible, all kinds of men have dedicated their lives and fortunes. Some have exhibited the highest kind of integrity and courage; others have showed themselves to be the meanest of money-changers. Some have been idealistic, others, cynical. They are, in brief, human beings, not merely names on the mastheads of newspapers—human beings with the passions and prejudices, the virtues and failings, common to us all.

They have been considered dangerous men by those who crave absolute power and authority. For centuries it has been recognized clearly in every country that a printing press in the hands of a man who is bound in its use only by the voice of his own conscience is a threat to total government.

That is why the press remained the tool of government until the editors of colonial America demonstrated that it could be used as a powerful instrument of revolt, and thereby realized the worst fears of tyrants and dictators.

This momentous development in human affairs attained startling speed after it was under way, but it was painfully slow getting started. The settlers who first came to America from England were in revolt against religious tyranny, but it was religious freedom and not freedom of publication they sought in the new land—and then only freedom for their own religion.

Nearly seventy years of colonizing slipped away before the first feeble attempts to establish a newspaper were made. The stern New England elders were aware that publications not controlled by them might easily become the outlet for whatever dissension from the prevailing rule existed in the colonies. They intended to brook no such unholy nonsense.

The man who first defied them, however briefly, and thus made a place for himself in history as the first American journalist, was Benjamin Harris. He was hardly a man who deserved the honor.

Before he arrived in America in 1686, Harris had achieved a notoriety in his native London for his part in "exposing" the so-called Popish Plot, an entirely imaginary conspiracy in which, so thought its Whig instigators, the Catholics intended to kill London's Protestants and burn the evil city. As a bookseller, Harris had prepared for this inglorious portion of his career by publishing numerous attacks on the Catholics and Quakers from his shop in Bell Alley.

As the campaign against the Popish Plot reached its dismal conclusion, Harris paid for his sins of intolerance by first seeing his newspaper suppressed and then finding himself arrested for publishing a seditious pamphlet. A judge as scurrilous as the pamphlet sent him to King's Bench Prison in default of his fine, but he obtained an illegal discharge after he had served nine months' time and went back immediately to his old pursuit of Pope-baiting.

After a brief interlude in which he opened a coffee house and sold books, patent medicines, and playing cards with propaganda printed on their backs, another pamphlet got him into trouble with the authorities again, and he fled to Boston.

There he found the intellectual climate much more to his liking, since the authorities were as anti-Catholic as he. Harris quickly established himself as the foremost publisher and bookseller in the colonies. His list of authors included the Mathers, who dictated both the religion and the politics of the city. They were also among the patrons who frequented the London Coffee House which Harris opened in August of 1690, a place which rapidly became Boston's social center. Even women were permitted, though they could not enter an inn without loss of their reputations.

Emboldened by success, Ben Harris followed the opening of his shop a month later, on September 25, 1690, by the publication of the first newspaper ever printed in America. He called it *Publick Occurrences Both Foreign and Domestick,* filled it principally with local items, and announced he planned to publish monthly, or oftener, if the "Glut of Occurrences" warranted.

But the glut of authority ended *Publick Occurrences* after its initial issue. The Mathers were offended—primarily because it had been published without their license. They objected, in addition, to Harris's gossipy items concerning the indiscretions of the French King, not because the gossip impugned royalty, but because the details were immoral.

The Mathers were particularly aghast at one of Harris's lead items, which told of how the Mohawk Indians, at that moment the allies of the colonists, had mistreated in their customary manner certain French prisoners taken in the intermittent warfare between the colonies and Canada. The sanguinary habits of the Iroquois nations were doubtless common knowledge, but the authorities found it embarrassing and inconvenient to have the misdeeds of their allies related publicly.

Thus the indictment against Ben Harris's paper was sweeping. Not only was it suspended and its only issue called in, but anyone else was forbidden to publish a newspaper unless licensed.

It was fourteen years before anyone dared to repeat the experiment, and this time it was done under such conservative auspices that there was little danger of offense. The publisher was Boston's postmaster, a sour-visaged Scot named John Campbell, who had evolved as newspaper publisher through his practice of writing news-letters for a regular list of patrons, both in and out of Boston. His position made him an ideal candidate for the job, because he was at the center of whatever news came from abroad by ship, or was repeated in his shop, or came in by way of the post-riders he sent galloping through the other villages and cities of the colonies.

The front page of Campbell's *Boston News-Letter,* which appeared for the first time on April 24, 1704, was a key to the personality of the publisher and his paper. It proclaimed in large type, just under the flag, that it was "Published by Authority." That meant it was semi-official and therefore dull. The left-hand ear carried a sailing ship, which signified that most of the news was foreign. London news was four months old by the time it reached the *News-Letter,* and even New York events were at least a week in the past. The other ear depicted a galloping post-boy, soon to be a familiar symbol on the first pages of most colonial newspapers.

What followed in the news columns was respectable but soporific. Ben Harris might have cut a ridiculous figure at times, but he could write well and he recognized news when he saw it. John Campbell had neither of these attributes. He was more interested in advancing his business affairs, which eventually made him a citizen of some position, and the control of his newspaper passed into other hands in 1722.

Shortly before this transition, Campbell's successor as postmaster, William Brooker, had begun the *Boston Gazette* in competition with the *News-Letter.* This paper was successively edited by four other postmasters and then by its printers, all in a largely unimaginative way, before it passed into the hands of a pair of young firebrands who transformed it into one of the leading newspapers of the colonies.

Meanwhile, on August 7, 1721, another young Bostonian entered the scene with a paper he called the *New-England Courant,* and with its publication, the uncertain beginnings were over and American journalism began to flower.

The Bostonian was James Franklin, a brisk youngster of short temper who had served his apprenticeship by printing forty numbers of Brooker's *Gazette.* When the new postmaster took over the paper, he also took the printing of it away from Franklin, who at once embarked on what many of his friends thought was an ill-considered revenge by starting a third newspaper in a town which had shown itself hardly able to support two.

By a fortunate coincidence, however, the *Courant* emerged at the beginning of a new movement in Boston—a hardly discernible groundswell of revolt against authority, civil and religious, that would in time engulf the colonies. It was not a revolt against Mother England—not yet. The colonists still thought of themselves as Englishmen, as most of them were by birth, and they gave allegiance freely to their King. Their slowly burning rebellion was against the harshness of civil and ecclesiastic rule.

James Franklin found himself the spearhead of this new movement, arraigned with the Episcopalians and deists against the Congregationalist Mathers and the authorities who served them.

The *Courant* began with a crusade, in which it happened to be completely wrong and the Mathers, for once, correct. The first issue appeared during a hot summer in the midst of a smallpox epidemic. Cotton Mather had persuaded a physician friend to inoculate two of his own sons and a pair of slaves, and he urged others to do the same.

That touched off the smoldering resentment against the Mathers and all their works. A torrent of abuse and threats descended on the unfortunate divine and his doctor friend, and in the van of it was James Franklin's *Courant.* The young Boston wits rallied to his columns and amused themselves by shredding Mather's ponderous and supercilious replies.

The inoculation fight consumed nearly all of the first few numbers, until Franklin's new friends suggested he turn to other matters. The friends wrote under such names as Timothy Turnstone, Tom Penshallow, Ichabod Henroost, and Abigail Afterwit. What they wrote made the *Courant* the best-read paper in Boston, because it discussed ladies in a scandalously free manner, poked pins in Boston's pedantry and foppish ways, and satirized whatever authority it dared.

No wonder Cotton Mather called Franklin's paper "a wickedness that was never known before in any country, Christian, Turkish, or Pagan, on the face of the earth." He gave the *Courant's* writers a name they accepted delightedly: The Hell-Fire Club.

One of the contributors was James's sixteen-year-old brother, Ben, who wrote as "Silence Dogood." Apprenticed to James, who was nine years older, Ben had carried the first issues of the *Courant* through the streets.

Both the brothers were seized in June 1722 by the magistrates, who had been watching for some pretext to hinder the *Courant's* enterprising printer. The Council examined and released apprentice Ben with an admonishment, but James was committed to the stone jail. There he lay for a month, presumably repentant, or so he told the magistrates, until he was freed, whereupon he entertained the *Courant's* readers with a mischievous account of his imprisonment.

"It was no mitigation of my punishment to think that better men than myself had been in prison before me," he wrote. "I know the late Governor Dudley was confined in the time of the Revolution; but I never could perceive that the gaol stank a whit the less for him."

Ben had edited the *Courant* alone while his brother was in jail, and now the two young men resumed the attack together, centering it largely on the town's magistrates. Again the offended authorities struck back and forbade James to publish the

Courant or any other newspaper. James and his friends simply transferred the publisher's title to Ben, and the paper went on a little more discreetly, gaining circulation and influence.

By this time, however, the brothers were uncomfortable partners. Ben was still nominally an apprentice, bullied a little by his brother, and taken for granted, as a seventeen-year-old would be, by his elders. Yet his authorship of the much-admired Dogood papers had now been noised around, and praise had come to him which aroused James's jealousy. Ben was in reality the *Courant*'s publisher and easily its most brilliant contributor, but James, who was merely able where his brother approached genius, continued to treat the boy like an apprentice. Sometimes, in quick passion, he struck Ben with blows which, the boy modestly wrote later, might have been inspired because he was "too saucy and provoking."

Ben took the serious step of breaking his apprenticeship to his brother—serious, because the bond between apprentice and master was then regarded as almost sacred. Yet Ben was determined to do it, though he was conscious that James might try to detain him by force. He wanted to be his own man, and since he was of a more conservative nature than James, he did not relish being in bad repute with the "good" people of Boston, pointed at as an infidel and suspect by the authorities. With the connivance of a friend and the captain of a New York sloop, he slipped away quietly from Boston one night and sailed toward Philadelphia and a new fortune.

Three years later, James left the *Courant* to others and settled in a more congenial spot, in Newport, Rhode Island, bringing with him the first printing press the colony had seen. He became public printer and the publisher of the *Rhode Island Gazette*.

In Philadelphia, meantime, young Ben endured a few more vicissitudes before his sure and steady path to greatness found him, on October 2, 1729, the proprietor of the *Pennsylvania Gazette*.

"To publish a good newspaper is not so easy an undertaking

as many people imagine it to be," he warned in his first issue, and went on to point out that an editor should "be qualified with an extensive acquaintance with languages, a great easiness and command of writing and relating things clearly and intelligibly, and in few words; he should be able to speak of war both by land and by sea; be well acquainted with geography, with the history of the time, with the several interests of princes and states, the secrets of courts, and the manners and customs of all nations. Men thus accomplished are very rare in this remote part of the world."

They were, indeed, but Ben Franklin satisfied these severe requirements. He wrote most of the *Gazette* himself, both its foreign and domestic news, penned letters to the editor and answered them, and even turned out advertisements and short fillers.

As to policy, the *Gazette* was much more conservative in its dealings with religious and civil authorities than the *Courant* had been, yet Franklin had no intention of making his paper subservient. "If all printers were determined not to print anything till they were sure it would offend nobody, there would be be very little printed," he observed dryly.

Successful and notable as the *Gazette* became in the life of Pennsylvania and the other colonies, it could not wholly engage the attention of a man like Franklin. His "rich, flexible, dramatic" personality, as Carl Van Doren termed it, and his personal ambitions impelled him to assume many roles in his busy life, and in time he turned from the *Gazette* to other matters.

But the seeds of revolt against authority which he and James had sowed in Boston, and the solid foundation of independence he had built in Philadelphia, were not forgotten. They were forecasts of things to come—a clear warning to governors and their magistrates that a free press was rising in the colonies, a press controlled by men of ability and determination who had already become the spokesmen for a growing tide of discontent.

The *Courant* had been the first organ of the opposition, but the issue between press and Crown was not joined until 1734, when John Peter Zenger and his *New-York Weekly Journal* precipitated a crisis and brought into focus the elemental facts of what would become a great controversy.

Although Zenger is celebrated as one of American journalism's heroes, he was not actually a heroic figure. Other men went to jail—James Franklin, for one—because they dared to defy authority in print, but it happened that Zenger became the virtually helpless pawn in a violent New York political battle, and the issue raised by his trial was far more important than the man himself.

Zenger was a German Palatinate immigrant, who served his eight years of indenture to William Bradford, the Philadelphia printer. Both men later came to New York, where Bradford began, on November 8, 1725, the publication of the city's first newspaper, the *New-York Gazette*. In that same year, Zenger joined him in a short-lived partnership. Bradford was a man of considerable ability, but Zenger was an indifferent printer and a worse writer. The partnership split up within a year, after only one book under their joint imprint, and Zenger took himself to Broad Street, where he set up his own shop and printed several unimportant volumes.

Meanwhile, events were moving rapidly to elevate Zenger to a position of international importance. Governor William Cosby, the latest of a long succession of corrupt men sent by the Ministers in London to govern New York, had by 1733 succeeded in alienating everyone in the city outside his own clique. The people complained that they were taxed outrageously to provide ease and luxury for Cosby and his royal friends, who were openly drunken and wanton in their conduct.

The unendurable blow came when Cosby summarily removed a well-beloved old man, Lewis Morris, as chief justice and replaced him with young James DeLancey, son of a wealthy merchant in the governor's inner circle. That antagonized the lawyers among the population. The merchants had already been antagonized by high taxes, and the common people were vastly irritated by the whole situation, particularly by the re-

moval of Morris, whom they rightly regarded as a friend in a
high place.

The opposition sought a means of attack. William Bradford,
proprietor of the town's only newspaper, was out of the question. He was the official printer. Morris and his friends therefore turned to Zenger and set him up in business as editor of
an anti-administration paper. Zenger did little more than print
the paper, though he was courageously in sympathy with the
better-educated men who wrote the slashing attacks on the
governor's party which filled the *Journal*'s columns.

As publisher, however, Zenger was legally responsible for
these diatribes, and when Cosby reached the end of his patience
in the fall of 1734, it was Zenger and not his influential friends
who went to jail. For nearly ten months he edited the *Journal*
from his cell, passing through the hole in its door daily instructions to his wife, Anna, who conducted the business for him.

While the *Journal* appeared on schedule every Monday, and
the governor fumed and sputtered and wondered what to do
with this political hot potato, the opposition prepared for trial.
Zenger's friends persuaded Andrew Hamilton, nearing eighty
and perhaps the best lawyer in all the colonies, to make the
hard journey from Philadelphia and conduct the defense.

Never was a trial more rigged. At its first session, before
Hamilton had been secured, Zenger's two lawyers protested the
appointment of DeLancey and another of Cosby's puppets as
judges, and were promptly disbarred for their pains. When the
case came up again in August 1735, Hamilton found himself
blocked at every point. As a defense against the charge of
criminal libel, Hamilton attempted to cite the truth of the
alleged libelous statements, or at least to permit the jury to
examine the truth or falsity of the statements. This, young
DeLancey informed him curtly, would not be permitted, and
from a legal standpoint, he was correct in so decreeing, since
such examination was contrary to common-law doctrine.

Using the opposition as a weapon in itself, Hamilton skill-
fully created an atmosphere friendly to his cause, an art at

which he was an old hand. By jabbing at the supercilious Court with pointed questions and remarks, Hamilton led DeLancey to make clear in his own words that he and the entire Court were unalterably opposed to Zenger and completely subservient to the governor. Thus Hamilton succeeded in arousing to high pitch among jury and spectators the same animosity toward the Court that existed toward the governor.

In the course of a long and brilliant address to the jury, he exploited this feeling and gave the jurymen a sense of their rights. "A proper confidence in a court is commendable," he said, "but as the verdict (whatever it is) will be yours, you ought to refer no part of your duty to the discretion of other persons. If you should be of opinion that there is no falsehood in Mr. Zenger's papers, you will, nay (pardon me for the expression), you ought to say so; because you do not know whether others (I mean the Court) may be of that opinion. It is your right to do so, and there is much depending upon your resolution, as well as upon your integrity."

At the end he declared, his voice ringing powerfully in the courtroom, "The question before the Court and you, gentlemen of the jury, is not of small nor private concern, it is not the cause of a poor printer, nor of New York alone, which you are now trying. No! It may, in its consequences, affect every freeman that lives under a British government on the main of America. It is the best cause; it is the cause of liberty, and I make no doubt but your upright conduct, this day, will not only entitle you to the love and esteem of your fellow citizens, but every man who prefers freedom to a life of slavery will bless and honor you, as men who have baffled the attempts of tyranny, and, by an impartial and uncorrupt verdict, have laid a noble foundation for securing to ourselves, our posterity and our neighbors, that to which nature and the laws of our country have given us a right, the liberty both of exposing and opposing arbitrary power in these parts of the world at least, by speaking and writing truth."

DeLancey made an effort to counteract the obvious effect of

this plea by asserting that, inasmuch as Zenger had confessed the publication, the jury had only to decide whether the words were libelous, and since that was a question of law, they could safely leave it to the Court—in other words, a directed verdict.

The jury returned a verdict of not guilty, as it might have done in any event, since its members were scarcely in sympathy with either Cosby or DeLancey. Zenger was released to the tumultuous acclaim of the crowded room, and a subsequent celebration by most of the citizens.

The result did not, as so often asserted, immediately establish freedom of the press in America. Far from it. But it was the first major victory for a free press, it started a debate which ran like a woods fire through the colonies and leaped across the sea to Great Britain, and it established an important precedent which could be cited in the battles to come.

Zenger's verbatim account of the trial, published first in the *Journal* and then widely circulated as a separate publication, brought him momentary fame. He was rewarded by being made public printer for the colony in 1737, and for New Jersey the following year. Even these appointments were not sufficient to keep him solvent, however, and he died poor in 1746.

It is ironical that William Bradford should have been cast as villain in the Zenger drama—Bradford, whose earlier career in Philadelphia had cost him his official printing contract, and his type and paper as well, when he came into conflict with authority. Committed to house arrest, he argued his own case in court so eloquently, maintaining his right to challenge biased jurors peremptorily in a libel action and asserting the burden of proof as belonging to his prosecutors, that he obtained a hung jury after it had deliberated forty-eight hours. New York had set him up in business again as printer to the Crown, and he naturally felt grateful to the government, however bad it might be.

Nevertheless, at the time of Zenger's trial, so strangely had the times changed political labels, this same Bradford who had resisted Quaker censorship in Philadelphia and fought there for freedom of the press found himself charged as the enemy of freedom, and the man he had helped start in business was suddenly not only his business rival but his enemy as well. It is understandable that Bradford considered journalism an unprofitable line and retired from it in 1742.

The basic conflict between Crown and people, dramatized by the Zenger trial, gained momentum with every passing year. It was not diminished appreciably even by the Seven Years' War, when colonists and Crown were compelled to band together in order to prevent the French from overwhelming them.

This experience sharpened the struggle, if anything, because it brought the colonial assemblies into stubborn deadlock with the royal governors over the question of raising militia and supporting them in the field. The mutual contempt which these troops and the British regulars held for each other, even after they had fought side by side, did not help the general situation. Neither did the uneasy knowledge, recognized by some informed persons, that these regulars had saved the personal and political existence of the recalcitrant, faction-ridden, and shortsighted colonists.

When the war was over, the colonies moved rapidly to the Stamp Act crisis, in which the press showed clearly it was a powerful entity which the authorities could no longer manage. It promised to become the greatest single force for unity among Americans whose differences were many and deep.

Almost from the beginning, the colonial press was in the hands of patriots. It was a controlled propaganda medium, not particularly devoted to the truth. As early as 1766, an eminent Pennsylvanian complained in a letter to Ben Franklin that he could not find a printer who would publish his article on the Stamp Act. These printers, he charged, had "combined together, to print every thing inflammatory and nothing that is rational or cool."

Tories everywhere voiced the same feeling. The people, they said, heard only "what their leaders chuse they should hear." The Whig press had turned the whole country into a debating

society, and made its cause a popular crusade in which everyone could take part. The Tories deplored this fact too; they
thought the debate should be restricted to the highest echelons.
The *Boston Evening-Post*, although declaring itself impartial
in politics, protested in 1769 that "the peasants and their house-
wives in every part of the land were able to dispute on politics
and positively to determine upon our liberties."

The Tories were convinced, and correctly, that the people
believed what they read in their newspapers. Thus the fears
of those in power were realized. George Grenville rose in the
House of Commons, waved a copy of the *Boston Gazette* above
his head, and warned the members that subversive newspapers
were preparing the American people for open rebellion.

Nor was there anything that could be done about it. The
men who printed the newspapers were either Whig politicians
themselves, or enjoyed the protection of the party. In Massachusetts, the King's Attorney, in charge of all prosecutions, was
paid, not by the King, but by the people, and in any case, the
royal governors were well aware they would never get a conviction from a colonial jury. Beyond this, there was the sullen
threat of mob violence by the patriots if the law failed them.

The patriots had need of their overwhelming strength in the
press. After the repeal of the Stamp Act, a dangerous division
appeared in their united front, as the settlers who lived away
from the seaport cities drifted into isolationism. They could
not see at first hand what went on in Boston, New York, and
Philadelphia—the busy work of the King's tax collectors, and
the oppressive business of absentee rule operating in every
aspect of a citizen's life.

Here the seaport newspapers performed their most significant
service. They sent their editions into the hinterlands week
after week, hammering on the farmers' fear of taxation to keep
them aroused and united behind seaport leadership. They did
not hesitate to paint the most lurid pictures of how far the
British might go in their taxing. Even a girl's kisses given to
her suitor would be taxed, one paper darkly predicted.

Thus the colonial editors and their papers played a vital role in the great popular movement which led to the Revolution itself, and the papers recognized their own importance. "The Press hath never done greater Service since its first Invention," the *Maryland Gazette* exulted in 1766.

The men who accomplished that service were young, for the most part, and wildly partisan in their cause. They shouted that their papers alone were the organs of truth, but there was justification in the Tory complaint that the truth was often not in them.

Among the principal fire-eaters were Benjamin Edes and John Gill, proprietors of that *Boston Gazette,* which had so aroused Grenville. The Boston Tories called it the "Weekly Dung Barge."

Edes and Gill were aptly described as "men of bold and fearless hearts." Both were Charlestown, Massachusetts, boys who were only twenty-three years old in 1755 when they began to publish the *Gazette.* Its office at the corner of Court Street and Franklin Avenue quickly became a patriot resort, as the paper itself became the chief radical organ. It was in the hospitable *Gazette* offices, according to some historical reports, that the Boston Tea Party's members assembled to put on their Indian disguises.

When the British were besieging Boston, they were advised by their officers not to forget "those trumpeters of sedition, the printers Edes and Gill," and when the troops finally occupied the city, they arrested Gill and held him for a month or two. After the siege, he started a new paper by himself, but it was a colorless affair, relying mostly on clippings from other sheets.

Edes was apparently the stronger of the partners. After the two men dissolved their partnership hurriedly in the crisis of 1775, Edes escaped with the press and type and set up shop again in suburban Watertown. There he continued to print the *Gazette* until 1798, but its popularity diminished rapidly and it expired. Edes died five years later, in poverty, as Gill had done in 1785.

Obviously the *Gazette* was a child of the times, influential and powerful during the years of crisis and war, dying of inanition thereafter.

Of a different character was another youthful printer, Isaiah Thomas, a master craftsman who established a patriot paper called *The Massachusetts Spy,* in the spring of 1770. Like the *Gazette,* the *Spy* was absolutely fearless, and so successful in its fight for Whig liberties that the authorities tried every possible means to suppress it. Thomas escaped the British occupation by decamping during the night of April 16, 1775, with his press and type. He sent the equipment to Worcester and, backing his beliefs with arms, joined the Minute Men and fought at Concord and Lexington. After these skirmishes, he began once more to print the *Spy,* at Worcester.

Thomas experienced numerous difficulties in keeping afloat, but by the time the war ended, he was successful enough to publish books, and before long became the leading publisher of his time. Besides three magazines, his newspaper, and an almanac, he turned out such important books, beautifully designed typographically, as the first folio Bible printed in English in the United States, the first dictionary printed in America, Blackstone's *Commentaries,* and more than a hundred children's books. Franklin admired these and other works so much that he dubbed Thomas the "Baskerville of America," comparing him with the great English printer and designer.

Retiring rich in 1802, Thomas devoted his remaining years to scholarship. Probably the best product of those years was his *History of Printing in America,* still the primary authority on this subject.

The *Spy* was one of the few patriot papers to survive the years of the Revolution. When passions had subsided, it could be seen that papers like the *Boston Gazette* were much more propaganda papers than newspapers. Yet the exchanges between Tory and patriot publications provided much the same kind of public excitement that the sensations of the penny press were to give the people decades later.

Here, for example, are Edes and Gill describing a Boston incident of January 1775:

A little after ten o'clock this evening, two young men passing down Milk Street, near the entrance into Long Lane, they were accosted by an officer, not in the English, but as they supposed in another language, which they did not understand; they asked him what he meant; he replied he meant to tell them to go about their business. They had not gone far before the officer called to them to stop. They stopped till he came up to them, and angry words ensued. The young men, however, parted from him the second time, and went on their way towards their homes. The officer followed and overtook them near the head of the lane, and stopped them again, telling them he supposed they were stiff Americans; to which one of them said he gloried in the character. Here again words ensued, and the officer drew his sword, flourished it and struck one of the young men on the arm, who immediately seized him. At this juncture, three or four of the town watch, who were upon the patrol, came up and separated them, advising them to go home. The two young men did so, but the officer refused, saying he was prisoner of the watch and would go with them; they told him he was not their prisoner, but might go where he pleased, and if he desired it, they would see him safe home: but he insisted upon it that he was their prisoner. The watchmen went down the lane towards their head-quarters in King Street, where they had been going before, and the officer accompanied them. In the way they met with several persons, whom they took to be servants of officers, who, supposing the officer to be in custody of the watch, attempted to rescue him, but he insisted upon being a prisoner, and said the watchmen were his friends, and he *would* go with them. They then went forward, and in Quaker Lane, which leads into King Street, they were met and assaulted by more than twenty officers of the army, who took several of their watch poles from them, and wounded some of them.

This is the same incident, the "Other Side of the Question," as reported in James Rivington's *New-York Gazetteer,* a prominent Tory newspaper:

You have read in that fund of lies and sedition, Edes and Gill, of a "high-handed riot." There have been five field officers on a court of inquiry, to inspect into the conduct of the officers concerned on that occasion. It commenced by Lieutenant Myers, 38th Regiment, being, without the smallest cause, insulted by two townspeople, who not only called him a Tory, rascal, scoundrel, &c., but damned the king, governor, army, and every friend to government; the former he put up with, the latter resented, by knocking the person down. He was immediately surrounded by the watch; and though he immediately surrendered, and gave his sword to a Mr. Winslow, who came up at the time, (a private gentleman), and informed them, and this gentleman, of the cause of the quarrel, they treated him with every indignity possible; not only allowed the two men to knock him down in the midst of them, but they themselves kicked and beat him all the way to the watch-house, a little short of a quarter of a mile. The noise about the watch-house brought together a few officers, whom Mr. Myers requested not to interfere, concealed from them the cruel treatment he had met with, and insisted on remaining in custody. The insolence of the watch to those gentlemen occasioned a fresh riot, when the interposition of a party from the main guard prevented any bad consequences. Immediately after, Myers was released, by order from the governor. Complaints were immediately lodged against the officers, and bail is to be given to-morrow for their appearance. I cannot quit this subject without observing, that the high-flyers are much disappointed in the event of this riot; not only at the little mischief done, but at the ready submission of every officer concerned, to the laws of the country.

The spirit of the people here seems to subside a little; and we have every reason to believe, that, in order to keep it up, the vagabonds of the town are employed to insult the troops, which they do daily, in hopes of bringing about another massacre.

The man who wrote those words was hated more than any other Tory editor, but "Jemmy" Rivington was also colonial journalism's most colorful character. He was a fine-looking man in his prime—portly, and always dressed in the latest fashion, which in Revolutionary days included curled and powdered hair, a claret coat, underneath it a scarlet waistcoat trimmed with gold lace, and buckskin breeches and top boots below. He moved in the best society.

Son of a noted London publisher, he prospered in his father's business there, clearing ten thousand pounds profit alone on the publication of Smollett's *History of England*. Rivington lost a good part of his gains pleasantly, on the horses at Newmarket and in other forms of entertainment, before he departed for America in 1760 and set up as a Philadelphia bookseller. He advertised himself as "the only London book-seller in America" and lived up to the slogan by becoming the chief importer of English books.

In his expansive way, Rivington drifted from dazzling success to bankruptcy and back again, until in 1768 he settled in a shop at the lower end of Wall Street in New York, and there, after laying a foundation as a commercial printer, he launched his *Gazetteer* in 1773.

No one could accuse Jemmy of lack of vision. The *Gazetteer*'s subtitle proclaimed it as "the Connecticut, New Jersey, Hudson's River and Quebec Weekly Advertiser," and its publisher announced that it would serve every human interest.

Both claims were more or less realized. The *Gazetteer* may not have been an Advertiser for the whole Eastern seaboard, but in little more than a year, according to Rivington, it was circulating 3,600 copies "thro' every colony of North-America, most of the English, French, Spanish, Dutch, and Danish West India islands, the principal cities and towns of Great Britain, France, Ireland, and the Mediterranean." As for its service, Isaiah Thomas himself wrote of its editor that "few men, perhaps, were better qualified . . . to publish a newspaper," and of the *Gazetteer,* that "no newspaper in the colonies was better printed, or was more copiously furnished with foreign intelligence."

Rivington's announced editorial policy was blameless: "Never to admit any Performance, calculated to injure Virtue, Religion, or other public Happiness, to wound a Neighbour's Reputation, or to raise a blush in the face of Virgin Innocence." Further, he declared he would print both sides of every public question. Following this laudable policy, he found himself in trouble.

The Sons of Liberty were not interested in an impartial press. If a newspaper was not outspokenly for the Whigs, it must be considered against the patriot cause. Consequently, a party of Sons from Connecticut demolished Rivington's printing plant one November day in 1775.

Jemmy fled to England, but returned two years later with a new press and an appointment as the King's printer. He began publishing the *Gazetteer* once more, and this time, quite naturally, its policy was frankly Loyalist. As such, it became perhaps the leading Tory paper in the country, and one of the best of any persuasion in its editing and writing.

When the British finally evacuated the city in 1783, Rivington was allowed to stay in New York. He had apologized pro-
fusely, and it was said (a point still argued by historians) that
he had given secret help to Washington's spies.

But the people did not forgive him so readily. One patriot
beat him severely. He was thrown into debtor's prison, for
other people's debts. His business ultimately failed, and he died
poor—by an ironic coincidence, on Independence Day, 1802.

Rivington left behind a New York street named after him,
and an anecdote, often told but worth telling again in his own
words, which illuminate his character more than any formal
biography. The story concerns Rivington's postwar encounter
with General Ethan Allen, one of the rebel leaders who had
frequently encountered the sharp sting of Rivington's caustic
pen. The Vermonter swore he would "lick Rivington the very
first opportunity" he had, and after the war came to New York
to do it. Rivington wrote of their interview:

I was sitting after a good dinner, alone, with my bottle of Madeira
before me, when I heard an unusual noise in the street, and a huzza from
the boys. I was in the second story, and stepping to the window, saw a
tall figure in tarnished regimentals, with a large cocked hat and an enormous long sword, followed by a crowd of boys, who occasionally cheered
him with huzzas, of which he seemed insensible. He came up to my door
and stopped. I could see no more. My heart told me it was Ethan Allen.
I shut down my window and retired behind my table and bottle. I was
certain the hour of reckoning had come. There was no retreat.

Mr. Staples, my clerk, came in paler than ever, and clasping his hands,
said, "Master, he is come! . . . He entered the store, and asked if James
Rivington lived there. I answered, 'Yes, sir.' 'Is he at home?' 'I will go
and see, sir,' I said; and now, master, what is to be done? There he is in
the store, and the boys peeping at him from the street."

I had made up my mind. I looked at the bottle of Madeira—possibly
took a glass. "Show him up," said I; "and if such Madeira can not mollify
him, he must be harder than adamant."

There was a fearful moment of suspense. I heard him on the stairs, his
long sword clanking at every step. In he stalked.

"Is your name James Rivington?"

"It is, sir, and no man could be more happy than I am to see Colonel
Ethan Allen."

"Sir, I have come—"

"Not another word, my dear colonel, until you have taken a seat and a glass of old Madeira."

"But, sir, I don't think it proper—"

"Not another word, colonel. Taste this wine; I have had it in glass for ten years. Old wine, you know, unless it is originally sound, never improves by age."

He took the glass, swallowed the wine, smacked his lips, and shook his head approvingly.

"Sir, I have come—"

"Not another word until you have taken another glass, and then, my dear colonel, we will talk of old affairs, and I have some droll events to detail."

In short, we finished two bottles of Madeira, and parted as good friends as if we never had cause to be otherwise.

In a similar haze of good feeling engendered by the prospect of peace and prosperity, the enmities of the Revolution disappeared as the eventful century ended. Zenger, the Franklins, Edes and Gill, Thomas, Rivington, and others less noteworthy had played their parts and disappeared into the wings.

There was left an American press free at last of governmental domination, but unfortunately far from free of blind and bitter partisanship. It was passing slowly from the hands of printers into the clutches of politically minded editors who were acutely conscious of its demonstrated power. It was at once becoming valuable business property and a potent weapon in the hands of new rivals, new factions in the burgeoning American experiment.

2

Partisan Editors

AFTER THE REVOLUTION ENDED, THE AMERICAN PEOPLE FOUND themselves united as a nation but dangerously divided on the fundamental question of how that nation ought to be governed. In its simplest terms, the question was whether the government should be centralized under the control of an educated, aristocratic minority, or a government by the majority of the people. This division of opinion led to a bitter partisanship which plunged American journalism into a "dark ages," in which newspapers became the tools of the vigorous, powerful public men who fought out the issue.

Both factions were led by members of President George Washington's Cabinet. Alexander Hamilton, the Secretary of the Treasury, was the chief advocate of minority rule, and the President himself represented the triumph of the philosophy of Federalism which Hamilton had so brilliantly espoused.

The leader of the democratic opposition, who, paradoxically, called themselves Republicans—because of their avowed sympathy with the new-born French Republic, was the Secretary of State, Thomas Jefferson, a Virginia intellectual.

In this epic conflict between the principles of government by aristocracy and government by majority will, Washington was not a primary figure. The real contest lay between Hamilton and Jefferson: one the spokesman for "gentlemen of principle

24

and property," the other a firm believer in a government founded on the 90 per cent of Americans who were simple countrymen and villagers.

Both men rallied to their support the power of the printed page, which had proved its usefulness in the Revolution. The editors Hamilton and Jefferson called upon to speak for them were overshadowed in a sense by the principals in the argument, but they were also individuals in their own right—men who were editors, not simply master printers who happened to own the mechanical means of communication.

Hamilton made the first move in the journalistic struggle. In 1789, with a Federalist government under Washington firmly established, he lent his support to the founding of a newspaper, the *Gazette of the United States,* which presumably would consolidate public support behind his program, including a national bank, protective tariffs, credit mechanisms, and similar Federalist trappings.

The editor of the *Gazette* was a man of mediocre talents, whose chief virtue was a desire for dignity in the conduct of a newspaper, an aim he had little opportunity to achieve. John Fenno was a Bostonian who had received a genteel education in Samuel Holbrook's Writing School and employed the fine penmanship he learned there in keeping General Artemas Ward's orderly books during the Revolution. After the war, he went into trade, but in a few years he had demonstrated to the satisfaction of his creditors that he was no businessman.

Arriving in New York in 1789 to start over again as a printer, he proposed to publish a newspaper "for the purpose of disseminating favorable sentiments of the federal Constitution and the Administration." No prospectus could have pleased Hamilton more. He and other influential Federalists loaned Fenno money, an act of charity they would be called upon to repeat often, and helped him set up his *Gazette.*

It was a modest publication, three columns wide on a page only seventeen by twenty-one inches, and Fenno undoubtedly saw in it a safe, secure berth for himself, attended with all the dignity which surrounded the gentlemen of the government. Whatever it might lack in circulation, it promised to gain financially from the government printing Hamilton threw to his friend, the editor.

Jefferson, Madison, and other Republicans viewed this development with alarm. Soon after the government moved to Philadelphia in 1791, taking the *Gazette of the United States* with it, the Secretary of State and his friends approached Philip Freneau and suggested that he set up a rival paper to be called the *National Gazette*.

The offer came at a critical point in Freneau's varied life, and it was singularly appealing to this poet, sea captain, and fierce idealist whose whole career had been one of rebellion in the cause of human freedom. He came from a cultured, well-to-do Huguenot family in New York, and had been so well educated by private tutors that at fifteen he was able to enter the sophomore class at the College of New Jersey, later Princeton University, where he shared a room with Jefferson's friend, James Madison.

Freneau's patriotic idealism and his early discovered writing talents had found an outlet in the ferment of the first years of the Revolution. He wrote long poems, published in pamphlets, which satirized such British leaders as General Gage. Then, after a romantic interlude as a secretary to a planter on the West Indian island of Santa Cruz, where he turned to the non-political poetic lyricism which makes his name a landmark in American literature, he had come back to America. But soon he went to sea again, on a brig which was captured only a few days out of port by a British warship. Miserable months followed as a captive on British prison and hospital ships anchored in New York harbor.

Temporarily quieted by this experience, Freneau spent three years in Philadelphia as a post office employee, wrote more lyric patriotic verse, which earned him the title "Poet of the Revolution," then went to sea once more as master of a Jamaica-bound brig. He spent the next few years sailing the Atlantic and the

Caribbean, describing his ocean world in poetry with a singular realistic passion. Marriage brought him to land in 1789, and he started a new career as editor of the *New York Daily Advertiser,* a paper whose importance exceeded the money he was able to earn from it.

The proposition that Jefferson made to him, therefore, was doubly welcome. The new paper he was asked to edit would be a platform for his personal fight against the principles of Federalism—a platform he would never have been able to provide for himself—and there was the added inducement of a job as "clerk for foreign languages" in the State Department, at a salary of $250 yearly.

Thus, at one stroke, Jefferson provided himself with an able editor who would also, through his job in the department, have access to official papers, and to both foreign and domestic newspapers. All these would be grist to the *National Gazette*'s mill in its battle against Hamilton and the Federalists.

Later, when this move had proved so successful that Washington was compelled to intervene in the war between his two Secretaries and plead with them to desist for the sake of national unity, Jefferson denied his connection with the *Gazette.* Freneau made an affidavit to Philadelphia's mayor that the Secretary of State had never controlled him or written a line for the paper. In later years he swore the exact opposite and produced proof of Jefferson's connection. But no matter which time Freneau perjured himself, few historians doubt that Jefferson was well aware of everything that went on in the *Gazette* office.

For the two years Freneau spent as editor, his paper and "Johnny" Fenno's engaged in a head-on, headlong battle in which taste, propriety, and the truth itself were forgotten. Fenno's *Gazette* spoke warmly of the British form of government, was eloquent on the subject of Hamilton's extraordinary wisdom, and characterized all "Jacobins" in the harshest terms. Freneau's *Gazette* hacked away at Hamilton's character and

works, and ardently supported every Republican thought and
action which attacked any form of aristocracy.

In this struggle, Freneau was a clear victor, pitted as he was
against a much less able man. The Federalists knew it, and
they suffered under his incandescent attacks. Washington
fumed at "that rascal Freneau," and after one stormy session
with the President, Jefferson wrote that he was certain Washington meant him to do something about Freneau. "But I will
not do it," Jefferson added. "His paper has saved our constitution which was galloping fast into monarchy, & has been checked
by no means so powerfully as by that paper. . . ."

Exaggerated as this view may have been, there is no doubt
that the Federalists, from Washington on down, breathed more
easily in 1793 when the *National Gazette* was suspended because of the yellow fever epidemic. Freneau himself left the
scene soon after, coincident with Jefferson's retirement from
the Cabinet. Afterward, Freneau had a further brilliant career
as a New York editor before he retired to spend his time alternately at sea and on his New Jersey farm. In 1832, he lost his
way in a December blizzard and died in the storm.

But if one irritant had been removed by Freneau's departure,
another remained in Benjamin Franklin's grandson, Benjamin
Franklin Bache, who, at the brash age of twenty-one, had begun
publishing the *General Advertiser* in 1790.

They called Bache "Lightning Rod Junior," in tribute to his
grandfather, and his paper also acquired a nickname in 1794,
when its editor began to center "Aurora," the name of a popular London publication, above the title on the first page.

As the *Aurora*, Benny Bache's paper succeeded to the throne
Freneau's *Gazette* had held in Republican affairs. Its virtues
were its full accounts of proceedings in Congress and its extensive coverage of foreign affairs, but these were overshadowed by
the virulent campaign of personal abuse it directed against
Washington and the whole Federalist camp, a campaign remarkable even in a decade noted for its vituperative press. The
Aurora's publications were "outrages on common decency," de-

clared Washington, who had been accused in it of such crimes as overdrawing his salary and violating the Constitution.

Under a cloak of personal anonymity, Bache used the columns of the *Aurora* for every kind of assault, however low. He did not hesitate to reprint forged letters of Washington, which the British had circulated in 1776 to discredit the commander-in-chief. After John Jay had concluded his controversial peace treaty with the British in 1795, Bache printed a summary of its contents, complete with numerous inaccuracies, before Washington could make the text public and discuss it with Congress and the people. That stirred up the worst storm the Federalists had yet been compelled to weather.

The kind of language Bache used to attack Washington was composed of such words and phrases as "treacherous," "mischievous," "inefficient," "want of merit" and "spurious fame." When the President delivered that Farewell Address, which is so celebrated today, the *Aurora* wrote of its author:

> If ever a nation was debauched by a man, the American nation has been debauched by Washington. If ever a nation has suffered from the improper influence of a man, the American nation has suffered from the influence of Washington. If ever a nation was deceived by a man, the American nation has been deceived by Washington. Let his conduct then be an example to future ages. Let it serve to be a warning that no man may be an idol. . . .

Though this brand of press criticisms is regarded now as typical of the "dark ages," its persistence in American journalism can be judged by substituting the name of Lincoln or Franklin Roosevelt for Washington's, and for the *Aurora*'s name the titles of those newspapers which, during the Civil War and in our own time, did not hesitate to heap the worst invective on the head of the nation. Indeed, no President of the United States of any stature has escaped such abuse. Only the lesser figures have been given mild treatment.

Because of his aloof, dignified nature, Washington probably suffered more than the others. Jefferson thought the constant assaults made the President physically ill toward the end, and

Washington listed among the "varieties of reasons" which impelled him to quit public life "a disinclination to be longer buffeted in the public prints by a set of infamous scribblers. . . ."

The day after he retired from office in March 1797, Bache delivered a parting shot:

> If ever there was a period for rejoicing, this is the moment—every heart in unison with the freedom and happiness of the people, ought to beat high with exultation that the name of Washington from this day ceases to give a currency to political iniquity, and to legalized corruption.

It is understandable that Washington left Philadelphia a disillusioned man, as far as freedom of the press was concerned, and stopped several of his newspaper subscriptions when he got home to Mount Vernon.

John Adams, who succeeded him as President, was welcomed by Bache and other Republican editors with tentative approval. The honeymoon soon ended, however, and the *Aurora* returned to its former partisan tone. Unlike Washington, Adams made no reply to these attacks while he remained in office, but Bache suffered for them personally. Once a gang of Federalist hoodlums wrecked his shop. Another time he was beaten by a man he had slandered in his columns. In June of 1797 he was arrested for libeling Adams, but was soon released on parole. That same year he met Johnny Fenno on the street one day, and after hot words were exchanged, Fenno delivered an uppercut to Bache's face, which Benny countered by striking Fenno on the head with his cane.

Little more than a year later, both combatants were dead, victims of the recurring yellow fever. Bache's Danish wife, Margaret, picked up the paper's management and married its associate editor, William Duane, an enterprising Irishman who had once published a paper in Calcutta until he dared to criticize the influential East India Company and thereby brought about his own bankruptcy.

The Federalists did not mourn Bache's passing. "The Jacobins are all whining at the exit of the vile Benjamin Franklin

Bache," said *Russell's Gazette,* a Boston paper. "So they would do if one of their gang was hung for stealing. The memory of this scoundrel cannot be too highly execrated."

A few months later, however, the Federalists realized they had survived Bache only to take on a better man in Duane. Under Duane's direction, the *Aurora* became an even more powerful advocate for the party of Jefferson, who was the Irishman's idol. Duane had courage, audacity, an almost fanatical belief in his cause, and a rugged, hard-hitting style.

His application of these talents to the service of the Republicans made his life in Philadelphia one of danger and imminent disaster. Timothy Pickering, the Secretary of State, told Adams that the *Aurora's* columns were full of "an uninterrupted stream of slander of the American Government," and Adams agreed, observing of the issue Pickering submitted as proof, that it was imbued "with rather more impudence than is common to that paper."

The Federalists twice succeeded in indicting Duane, but the Irishman carried on with unabashed energy. In his few short years as editor, he did more than any other person to discredit the threatened war with France, to arouse the public against the injustices of the Alien and Sedition Laws, and finally to get his hero, Jefferson, elected to the Presidency in 1800. For all this, Duane expected to get the government contract for printing and stationery when Jefferson moved the capital to Washington after his election, but somehow the President failed to reward him, and Duane stayed behind in Philadelphia as editor of the gradually diminishing *Aurora* until he retired in 1822.

While Duane, Bache, Freneau, and their friends were lambasting the Federalist government, it must not be supposed that their victims had no voice to cry out for them in the wilderness of vituperative journalism. The chief crier—not only because of his ability to reply in kind, but because he fought the Republican press on its own ground in Philadelphia—was an English political refugee named William Cobbett, who had no love for his temporarily adopted land and even less for its dissident democrats.

Cobbett came to America in 1792, on the heels of a disastrous journalistic exposé he had engineered in London, involving a graft ring among British army officers. He was a naturally argumentative fellow, loving argument for its own sake, and was known as "the Contentious Man." The *Aurora* referred to him as "the celebrated manufacturer of lies, and retailer of filth." He called himself Peter Porcupine, and under that sobriquet launched his *Porcupine's Gazette,* a well-printed daily, in 1797.

"Professions of impartiality I shall make none," he declared in his first issue, and more than lived up to the promise in subsequent editions, as he showed his Republican rivals some new fashions in name-calling. Cobbett was good at it. He had a cutting, sardonic prose style, full of scintillating cleverness, which later earned him recognition in his own country as one of its great satirists.

Cobbett attacked Bache not only in his own person, but through Lightning Rod Junior's illustrious grandfather, whom he spoke of as a "crafty and lecherous old hypocrite . . . whose very statue seems to gloat on the wenches as they walk the State House yard."

Porcupine's Gazette was exactly the kind of product that might have been expected from a visiting Englishman who had been threatened with tar and feathers even before he launched it, when a year previously he had opened a bookshop whose windows were full of pictures of George III, Lord Howe, and other royal personages. The *Gazette* came out in its sarcastic fashion in favor of an alliance with England, the seemingly imminent war against France, and consignment to hell for the whole Republican movement. Philadelphia had never seen anything like it.

Cobbett's political enemies were constantly at his throat, and he narrowly escaped prosecution on numerous occasions. President Adams even considered deporting him. In the end, however, it was a nonpolitical onslaught which enmeshed the redoubtable Porcupine. He made the mistake of libeling one of Philadelphia's chief citizens, Dr. Benjamin Rush. At the beginning of the yellow fever epidemic which carried off Bache and Fenno, among hundreds of others, Cobbett launched a blistering attack on Dr. Rush's treatment for the disease, which consisted of plentiful bleeding and a violent instrument of torture called the mercurial purge.

However much Dr. Rush deserved it, he had unquestionably been libeled and he sued. It took two years for the case to come to court, before a hostile judge and jury, who gave the good doctor a $5,000 verdict and $3,000 costs. Having anticipated this result, Cobbett was already on his way. In New York he issued one more copy of the *Gazette* and five editions of a libelous sheet he named the *Rush-Light,* all devoted to further examinations of his enemy's character. Then he departed hurriedly for England.

While Cobbett carried on his one-man war, there were other Federalist editors, of more conservative stripe and removed from the chief arena of Philadelphia, who upheld the cause in a less sensational way. In Boston, for example, there was Major Benjamin Russell, whose *Columbian Centinel* had been founded in 1784.

Ben Russell had learned to set type in the office of Isaiah Thomas's *Massachusetts Spy.* He had run away from home to fight in the battle of Lexington when he was only thirteen. Thereafter, his irate father had apprenticed him to Thomas in Worcester, where the *Spy* had been removed. Young Russell gratified his urge to get into the army when Thomas was drafted and sent his apprentice as substitute. The apprentice returned a major, though he never fought an engagement, and a few years later set up for himself in Boston.

The *Centinel* argued for the adoption of the Federalist Constitution, backed Washington at every step, supported Adams, opposed Jefferson, and, in general, became New England's principal Federalist newspaper. It was a child of Federalism, and when the party began its decline, the child declined too.

Meanwhile, the government found a somewhat more intellectual voice in New York, where Noah Webster took five years out of his varied life to edit, with considerable distinction, the *American Minerva.*

Like Benjamin Franklin, Webster was a man of numerous talents. He not only compiled the dictionary for which he is best remembered today, but he was an able political writer, among his many other abilities, and it was this skill the Federalists persuaded him to employ in 1793 with the establishment of the *Minerva.*

The paper was started quite simply, as Webster himself remarked, "for the purpose of vindicating and supporting the policy of President Washington." Under the pseudonym of "Curtius," Webster wrote the best things that appeared in it, among them what was considered the most effective defense of Jay's treaty. Hamilton also wrote frequently for the *Minerva.*

Webster made two nonpolitical contributions to journalism. He began to run his editorial in the same prominent place every day, initiating what would later become the editorial page, and he launched a semi-weekly edition, the *Herald,* "for country readers," which may have been the first bulldog edition in journalism.

Disillusioned in 1798 with what he considered Hamilton's betrayal of Adams, Webster moved to New Haven and had less and less to do with the *Minerva,* until he sold both papers in 1803.

The election of Jefferson in 1800 began the decline of the Federalist party and its ultimate eclipse, at least in its Hamiltonian incarnation. With it went the more virulent editors of the party press. It might be supposed that the departure of these men would have signaled a new and enlightened era in newspaper publishing, but instead the press descended into another phase of its dark age, even worse than the preceding decade.

If the dominant figures in it were lesser men, on the whole, there was no lack of venom in them. The prime victim, ironically enough, was Jefferson, who had fought hard for that freedom of the press about which the Federalists had been so doubtful. Now, as President, Jefferson learned at first hand how Washington had felt under the lash of the Republican press. A tremendous campaign of vilifications against him emanated from every quarter. A time began in which blatant corruption and irresponsibility were the hallmarks of nearly every newspaper, and in which libel suits, assaults, and duels were the order of the day. National attention was centered for the moment on the new capital of Washington, and there the old war began anew, under different auspices.

Jefferson had prudently provided himself with a semi-official mouthpiece as soon as he came to Washington. It was a triweekly, the *National Intelligencer and Washington Advertiser*, edited by Samuel Harrison Smith, a minor Philadelphia publisher whom Jefferson had invited to follow the government southward.

Smith was not a fighter, and his relatively calm paper won it the contemptuous Federalist nickname of "Mr. Silky-Milky Smith's National Smoothing Plane." Smith was a man who understood good wine and good food, and his accomplished wife Margaret was an excellent hostess. Margaret was the Pearl Mesta of her day. Her weekly salons were frequented by Administration notables from Jefferson on down, and they were visited almost as often, to the amazement of some guests, by Federalists who were friends of that other devoted Federalist— Mrs. Smith.

At "Sidney," their country estate, where Catholic University now stands, the politically opposite Smiths entertained both parties royally, along with authors, musicians, editors, and other intellectuals. Nothing like it was seen again in Washington until the nineteen thirties and forties, when friend and foe alike sat down at Evalyn Walsh MacLean's hospitable "Friendship" table on Sunday nights.

Although the *Intelligencer* was an Administration organ, it remained less partisan than any of its contemporaries. Its mod-

erate tone was largely the result of Smith's old-line Philadelphia
conservatism, and presumably Margaret had something to do
with it too. Smith shared Jefferson's sympathy for the masses,
but he did not have the President's confidence in government
by the people.

Although ill health compelled Smith to sell the *Intelligencer*
in 1810, the pattern of enlightened conservatism he established
in the paper persisted for decades under other managements.
Changed to a daily in 1813, it remained until after the Civil
War as one of the best American newspapers, a dependable and
informative sheet in an era when these attributes were far more
rare than they are today.

Smith's only opponent of any stature in the journalistic arena
was the newspaper that Hamilton began in New York in 1801,
the *Evening Post.* It was often argued later that the *Post* was
no more "Hamilton's paper" than the *Intelligencer* was Jefferson's. However, it is certainly true that Hamilton and his
friends were the financial founders and backers of the *Post,* and
in its pages the ex-Secretary, now reduced to a minor role in
national politics by reason of Jefferson's ascendancy, criticized
his triumphant rival and wrote on such public questions of the
day as the acquisition of Louisiana.

The *Post* emerged on November 16, 1801. It was printed on
a hand-press, like the one Ben Franklin had used, and its
quarter-size sheets were distributed to a city whose population
numbered sixty thousand, concentrated in an area south of City
Hall. Beyond, along Broadway, were only country houses and
green fields.

Hamilton and his friends chose as editor of their paper a
Massachusetts lawyer, William Coleman, a big, handsome, robust man who loved pleasure, argument, and politics. He was
well read and considered scholarly, yet he was no esthete: one
evening in Massachusetts he had skated from Greenfield to
Northampton, a distance of twenty miles.

In the lead article of the first issue, signed with his initials,
Coleman made the usual lofty protestations of high moral pur-

pose. He declared that he abhorred "personal virulence, low sarcasm, and verbal contentions with printers and editors," and announced he was determined not to be swerved from "the line of temperate discussion."

It was not long, however, before the *Post* began attacking Jefferson with partisan vigor, and it was one of these attacks, written by Coleman, which resulted in the greatest blow struck for freedom of the press since Zenger's trial—and by a Federalist, at that.

Coleman had remarked in the course of an article that it had been said the "burden of the Federalist Song" was that "Jefferson paid Callender [James Callender, a contributor to the *Richmond Examiner*] for calling Washington a traitor, a robber, a perjurer; for calling Adams a hoary-headed incendiary and for most grossly slandering the private characters of men he knew well were virtuous. These charges not a democratic Editor has yet dared or ever will dare to meet in an open and manly discussion."

This somewhat roundabout assault on Jefferson was picked up and published by Harry Croswell, editor of the *Hudson* (N.Y.) *Wasp*. He was promptly prosecuted for libeling the President. Found guilty, his case was appealed. Hamilton appeared to argue for him, and made the most eloquent plea for freedom of the press the New York bar had heard since Andrew Hamilton's appeal to Zenger's jury. In spite of it, the conviction was upheld, but the plea had made so strong an impression that the New York Assembly passed a significant law which admitted the truth as evidence in a libel case, and provided that the jury must judge the law as well as the facts—the points old Andrew had pleaded in New York more than a half-century before.

It was the free press, by a choice irony, which led indirectly to Hamilton's untimely death. While he was in Albany for Croswell's trial, he made some derogatory remarks in conversation about his rival, Aaron Burr. These comments, duly retailed in the *Albany Register*, were read by Burr, who then challenged Hamilton to the historic duel, and killed him with a single shot on a July morning beside the Hudson, under the heights of Weehawken.

This was the most famous of innumerable incidents during Jefferson's two terms as President, when the warfare between Republican and Federalist newspapers reached an abysmally low point of scurrility. Yet Jefferson, the principal object of attack, continued to defend freedom of the press, even though freedom could scarcely be distinguished from license. When the Prussian minister to the United States picked up a Federalist paper from the President's table one day and inquired why he allowed such libels to continue, Jefferson made a reply which has as much meaning today as it did then.

"Put that paper in your pocket, Baron," he said, "and should you ever hear the reality of our liberty, the freedom of our press questioned, show them this paper—and tell them where you found it."

After Jefferson's administration, the conflict died down for a time. The opposition party all but disappeared, the principal actors left the stage, and those who came after did not provoke the strong emotions which had swirled around Washington, Jefferson, and Hamilton. Nor did any understanding new editors appear on the scene during those days of Madison, Monroe, and John Quincy Adams.

It was not until a popular democratic movement landed Andrew Jackson in Washington that the old quarrels were revived, and the party press flared anew. In the campaign of 1828, which elected Jackson, the shape of things to come was apparent in the newspaper tales that Jackson's mother was a Negro, and the counter charges that Adams was guilty of immoral conduct and that his mother was English, not American. There were other accusations much worse.

These accounts produced such bitterness that Jackson did not even pay Adams the usual courtesy call when he arrived in Washington. But having observed the power of the partisan press, the Tennessean was determined to use it to his own advantage, and this he did, better than any other President before him.

The man who aided him in this effort, and who shared with Jackson an intimacy no editor had ever enjoyed with a President and thus rose to unprecedented power and influence, was Francis Preston Blair.

Blair was a native Virginian, raised in Kentucky, who survived a delicate childhood and adolescence to plunge into the political wars of his state with fiery pamphlets which resulted in his editorship of the influential Frankfort (Kentucky) paper, the *Argus of Western America*. His predecessor in that job had been Amos Kendall, a Groton-educated lawyer, who also began life in poor health but lived to become the rugged editor of a newspaper whose influence was so strong that he had to carry a knife and a pistol to defend himself from its enemies.

It was Kendall's *Argus* which proved to be the chief spokesman for the wave of progressivism that elected Old Hickory. The Republicanism of Jefferson had languished sadly, and it had been virtually replaced in Washington by a Hamiltonian Federalism revitalized and given new meaning by the brilliant Henry Clay. Jackson's election meant the imposition of a radical reform program on this thriving conservatism, and Kendall found himself at the center of it as Jackson's speech writer and adviser.

Naturally, such a program invited violent opposition from anti-Administration papers, and to counter these blows, Jackson and his friends planned an organ of their own. Blair was invited to be its editor.

When he arrived in Washington, Blair looked like anything but the St. George delegated to kill any dragons threatening the President. One historian describes him as "an insignificant-looking man, weighing slightly over one hundred pounds, sandy-haired and hatchet-faced, with a black patch covering a head wound he had got when the stage overturned near Washington. . . . But a glance at Blair's clear, blue, unblinking eyes, and a few minutes of his keen and sensible conversation, wiped out the initial misgivings."

Kendall was no more prepossessing. He was "bent, near-sighted, badly dressed, with premature white hair, sallow complexion and a hacking asthmatic cough." Even on the hottest July days he wore a greatcoat made of white broadcloth, buttoned to the throat, and if he happened to have one of his blinding headaches, he wore a white handkerchief around his head. One Congressman remarked of him in a House speech: "Poor wretch, as he rode his Rosinante down Pennsylvania Avenue, he looked like death on the pale horse."

To this strange appearing duo was added a third—John C. Rives, a shaggy giant of a man, who became business manager of the new paper.

These three formed the famous "Kitchen Cabinet" of the Jackson administration. These were the men closest to Jackson, who advised and aided him every step of his difficult way. The paper they established to do it was the *Washington Globe,* which first appeared in December 1830.

Blair had never met Jackson before, but the two men were profoundly impressed with each other, and it was not long before Jackson's characteristic "Give it to Blair," when he wanted to talk to the people, would be followed by slashing editorials in the *Globe,* written at terrific speed by the editor, who kept two copyboys busy carrying his production to the typesetters.

Under the slogan, "The world is governed too much," Blair leveled the *Globe*'s heavy guns against the United States Bank and Clay's "American System," as the new Federalism was called.

Always Blair was close to the President, traveling with him on vacations, and he was often the first man Jackson saw in the morning, even before breakfast. His style, like those of the best partisan editors before him, was vitriolic. The *Globe* was "a radical paper," Blair's biographer remarks, "dogmatic, bold and defiant. At times the editor hesitated when it was politic to do so. His gift for satire played to his advantage and to the great discomfiture of the enemy. Blair's sarcasm bit like vipers, and friends and foes alike came to dread his editorial attacks."

Blair had need of his talents because, as Claude Bowers has noted, Jackson was opposed "by two-thirds of the newspapers, four-fifths of the preachers, practically all the manufacturers, and seven-eighths of the banking capital." Yet the *Globe,* under Blair's direction, became a potent arm of the government itself, and through it Jackson ruled the country.

During the President's second term, when the *Globe* was at the summit of its power, a struggling young journalist applied for a job as associate editor. "I should like such a position remarkably well," he wrote to a friend of Jackson's, adding that he thought he "would add a good deal of reputation and patronage to the *Globe.*"

James Gordon Bennett didn't get the job, and he had some difficult times ahead of him, but he was rapidly approaching the day when his *New York Herald* would mark the beginning of a new era in American journalism. It would put an end to the long rule of the partisan editors, and while far from impartial itself, it would establish a concept of news and newsgathering which is the foundation of the modern American newspaper.

3

The Bennetts
and Their "Herald"

THERE WAS NOTHING REMARKABLE ABOUT THE NEW MORNING paper that greeted New Yorkers on their way to work one May day in 1835. It was modestly printed on a double sheet of four pages, ten-and-a-half inches wide and fourteen inches long. The first word in its first item was a typographical error: "Ptblished daily by James Gordon Bennett & Co., office Number 20 Wall Street, basement story."

Nearly the whole first page was devoted to a "Biographical Sketch of Matthias the Prophet," and the remaining space was occupied by fillers with such intriguing heads as "Books," "Love for Shakespeare," and "Fashions for April." Even these failed to fill the page, and it concluded with a few lines of sententious advice to its readers: "He who loves to employ himself well can never want something to do."

The prospectus, on the next page, offered the same high-sounding promises that every newspaper had given an increasingly cynical public. "Our only guide," said Mr. Bennett, "shall be good sound practical common sense, applicable to the business and bosoms of men engaged in everyday life. We shall support no party, be the organ of no faction or coterie, and care nothing for any election or any candidate from President down to constable. We shall endeavor to record facts, on every public and proper subject, stripped of verbiage and coloring,

42

with comments suitable, just, independent, fearless and good-tempered."

Mr. Bennett concluded his first broadside with a few hopeful remarks about circulation: "There are in this city at least 150,000 persons who glance over one or more newspapers every day and only 42,000 daily sheets are issued to supply them. We have plenty of room, therefore, without jostling neighbors, rivals or friends, to pick up at least 20,000 or 30,000 for the Herald, and leave something for those who come after us."

If there were doubters who sneered at these brave words, they probably lived to regret it because James Gordon Bennett (see photograph 1), and the son who succeeded him, began with this issue a revolution in the newspaper business. Their *New York Herald* achieved an international reputation for getting the news. Bennett Senior revolutionized the whole business of newsgathering, and Bennett Junior made the exclusive story a *Herald* trademark. Between them they made the early edition of the *Herald* a newspaper no rival editor dared to go to bed without reading. In the public mind it stood for generations as the foremost newspaper in the world.

The man who started it was no printer or political hireling, but a born editor with considerable, though unsuccessful, publishing experience behind him. Scottish-born, he had emigrated to Halifax in 1819 and begun his new life by teaching school. He was poor, desperately poor. A shilling he found on the ground once saved him after two days of starvation.

He got a job at last in Boston, in the publishing house of Wells & Lillie, where he began a slow progress, improving himself with books and sermons after work. After a time, he moved to other jobs in New York and Charleston, and back to New York again in 1823, where he advertised a "permanent commercial school" of his own to teach elocution, algebra, geometry, history, political economy, English composition, commercial law, bookkeeping and other subjects as required.

Bennett advertised but never opened this school. He had no money to do it. The slow, grinding progress was resumed, but

this time on newspapers. While he was working for a Sunday
sheet called the *New York Courier*, he first attracted attention
to himself by a series exposing the activities of certain specu-
lators, and sharp practices among the city's businessmen. Some
of these men were indicted and he covered their trials.

When the associate editor of the *New York Enquirer* was
killed in a duel, Bennett got the job, though not the title. But
it was his first important position, and soon he found himself
Washington correspondent for the paper. In Washington,
he quickly leaped to prominence by writing a series of stories
in the style of Horace Walpole, profiling politicians and
hangers-on with a merciless, clever pen. The subjects squirmed
and fought back, but everyone read the pieces anyway.

Bennett supported Jackson in 1828. His paper became a
strong Administration backer, and he was made associate editor.
A short time before he had suggested to James Watson Webb,
the owner of the *Courier*, that the *Enquirer* be bought and
merged with it. When this deal was consummated through
Bennett's efforts, the result was a newspaper able to challenge
any in the country.

For the next three years, Bennett edited the *Courier and
Enquirer* with a shrewdness and vitality which displayed his
extraordinary talents for the first time. He might have gone on
to fame at once, but the paper changed its financial controls
and at the same time became a Whig journal. There was nothing else to do. Bennett resigned.

By that time he was thirty-seven, and not much richer except
in experience. With what little money he had accumulated, he
set up a paper he called the *New York Globe*. It lasted a
month. Then he bought an interest in a Philadelphia paper,
the *Pennsylvanian*, but when he tried to borrow money from
his former political friends to get control of it, they turned him
down. His own money ran out and he had to retire from the
Pennsylvanian after only a year.

Bennett was back in New York, broke and discouraged. He
had tried to get a job on Francis P. Blair's Washington *Globe*,

without success. He applied for a position on the amazingly successful *New York Sun,* but its editor, Benjamin H. Day, refused him.

Nonetheless, this new paper, which sold for only a penny, intrigued him. Ben Day was a New Englander who had learned the printing trade on Samuel Bowles's *Springfield Republican,* and after working as a compositor on several New York papers, had started a penny paper almost as an act of desperation during a depression in 1833, which foreshadowed the financial crash that came three years later. Three other penny papers, in Boston, Philadelphia, and New York, had already failed and the local sixpenny papers showed no signs of disintegration.

However, the *Sun* was an instant success. Day produced it virtually alone, and for the first time in journalistic history, it was a newspaper hawked on the streets by newsboys. Day had told his readers that he intended to lay before them "all the news of the day" at a price they could afford, and the citizens responded eagerly to this bargain. In little more than six months, the *Sun* had a circulation of eight thousand.

This was proof enough for Bennett that Day had the right idea. If Ben would not take him as an associate, he would be compelled to take him on as a rival, Bennett decided. His determination was practically his only stock in trade, besides a slim $500 in capital, all he had in the world. In the Wall Street cellar from which the first issue of the *Herald* appeared, Bennett was editor, reporter, proofreader, and business manager. His desk was a plank laid across two flour barrels.

Yet his paper, like Day's, was an immediate success. Not only because it, too, was a bargain, but because the editor performed the unprecedented feat of living up to his initial promise that he would give the people who read the *Herald* "a picture of the world."

He did just that. For the first time, people were provided with thorough, accurate coverage of local news, written in a dashing, entertaining, and often sensational style. The editorials were no dull pontifications about the state of the nation and the world, but short, penetrating comments on people and events written in Bennett's half-mocking style.

In these essays, the editor showed very little respect for anyone, particularly stuffed shirts of all varieties. Nobody was safe, whether churchman, politician, or merchant.

Always Bennett attacked the money-changers, and when one of them tried to pass off on him a piece of propaganda for a speculative venture, disguised as a news story, the editor wrote bluntly in his columns:

> Here is, now, some fellow in Wall Street who has a private object in view—the making of a few thousand dollars by speculation; and he asks us to help him to do so, at our own expense. If we refuse, he threatens to say "you are bought up." We tell this patriot, and every other patriot, that we have no sort of objection to publish his communications on being paid for them, as for any other advertisements. If "M.Q." will transmit $15 (for the article will occupy thirty squares), we shall publish them with as much fearlessness as we do "Loco Poco Matches," "Dancing Parties," "Dr. Moffat's Vegetable Life Pills," or "Dr. Brandreth's Vegetable Universal Pills."

One of the chief objects of Bennett's editorial probing was his former *Courier and Enquirer* associate, James Watson Webb. They had parted enemies, and Bennett's subsequent comments in the *Herald* on Webb's activities had led to a demand by the *Courier*'s editor that his name never be mentioned in his rival's paper again. Bennett blandly ignored these wishes. On a January day shortly after, the two men met in Wall Street and engaged in an unseemly scuffle, which Bennett duly reported in his *Herald*. In May, almost at the same spot, they met again and Bennett was attacked once more. He told his readers:

> My damage is a scratch, about three quarters of an inch in length, on the third finger of the left hand, which I received from the iron railing I was forced against, and three buttons torn from my vest, which any tailor will reinstate for a sixpence. His loss is a rent from top to bottom of a very beautiful black coat, which cost the ruffian $40, and a blow in the face, which may have knocked down his throat some of his infernal teeth for anything I know. Balance in my favor, $39.94.
> As to intimidating me, or changing my course, the thing cannot be

done. Neither Webb nor any other man shall, or can, intimidate me. I tell the honest truth in my paper, and leave the consequences to God. Could I leave them in better hands? I may be attacked, I may be assailed, I may be killed, I may be murdered, but I will never succumb. I never will abandon the cause of truth, morals, and virtue.

However doubtful Bennett's contribution to truth, morals, and virtue may have been, the people liked his newspaper. In fifteen months it had 40,000 circulation, and the editor felt justified in lifting it from the clamor of penny press competition by raising the price to two cents.

Part of the public was not amused by the *Herald,* however. In this era of mawkish refinement, Bennett insulted his virtuous contemporaries and shocked conventional morality by refusing to call a leg a limb. The *Herald* sometimes referred satirically to the "branches" of dancers. It also used "shirts" for the popular "linen," and "pantaloons" for what most people termed "inexpressibles." Occasionally irritated by the affectation of the times, Bennett would lash out savagely.

"Petticoats—petticoats—petticoats—petticoats—there—you fastidious fools—vent your mawkishness on that!" he wrote.

This kind of thing, and the jealousy of his fellow publishers, resulted in the famous "Moral War" against Bennett and the *Herald.* It was a virulent onslaught, emanating from the press, a part of the pulpit, and some of the more conservative citizenry. In its anxiety to demolish Bennett, the Moral War had little of morality in it. "Stigma on the city . . . vice and vulgar licentiousness . . . hypocrisy, ignorance and bloated conceit . . . double apostate and traitor in politics . . . half-crazy, uneducated wretch . . . immoral and blasphemous monstrosity . . . pest . . . villain . . . forger"—these were the kinds of barbs tossed at the *Herald* and its proprietor.

That Bennett had been reckless in his impudent, flippant, and often sensational columns, not even his best friends could deny. But he also gave the public a blunt, unvarnished, reasonably accurate and complete picture of the news of those days, in a raw metropolis growing too rapidly for its own good. This fact hurt his competitors far more than the Moral War hurt Bennett.

Meanwhile, he worked furiously to put the *Herald* beyond the reach of financial peril. Up at five in the morning, he wrote his lead editorials and much other material before breakfast, spent the day from nine to four in editing, writing, reading other papers, receiving visitors, and covering Wall Street in person. At four he ate dinner, then read proofs, attended to the business and advertising sides of the paper, and was in bed by ten o'clock. He held to this killing schedule for years, until he could afford to assemble an adequate staff.

In 1838 he went to Europe and there organized a six-man staff to cover the Continent, after which he returned home and bustled about the South, extending the *Herald*'s coverage on the national scene.

By opposing the powerful political alliance of President Van Buren and Governor W. H. Seward in the campaign of 1840, Bennett brought the Moral War against him roaring to a climax. He aided his enemies by such characteristic but damaging displays of bad taste as his public declaration of love in the *Herald* of June 1, 1840. He had met a handsome Irish girl named Henrietta Agnes Crean at a party, pursued her hotly, and soon announced his engagement to the amazed city under these headlines:

TO THE READERS OF THE HERALD—*DECLARATION OF LOVE—CAUGHT AT LAST—GOING TO BE MARRIED— NEW MOVEMENT IN CIVILIZATION*

I am going to be married in a few days. The weather is so beautiful; times are getting so good; the prospects of political and moral reform so auspicious, that I cannot resist the divine instinct of honest nature any longer; so I am going to be married to one of the most splendid women in intellect, in heart, in soul, in property, in person, in manner, that I have yet seen in the course of my interesting pilgrimage through human life. . . .

I cannot stop in my career. I must fulfill that awful destiny which the Almighty Father has written against my name, in the broad letters of life, against the wall of Heaven. I must give the world a pattern of happy wedded life, with all the charities that spring from a nuptial love. In a few days I shall be married according to the holy rites of the most holy Christian church, to one of the most remarkable, accomplished, and beautiful young women of the age. She possesses a fortune. I sought and found a fortune—a large fortune. She has no Stonington shares or Manhattan stock, but in purity and uprightness she is worth half a million of pure coin. Can any swindling bank show as much? In good sense and elegance another half a million; in soul, mind and beauty, millions on millions, equal to the whole specie of all the rotten banks in the world. Happily, the patronage of the public to the *Herald* is nearly twenty-five thousand per annum; almost equal to a President's salary. But property in the world's goods was never my object. Fame, public good, usefulness in my day and generation; the religious associations of female excellence; the progress of true industry—these have been my dreams by night, and my desires by day.

In the new and holy condition into which I am about to enter, and to enter with the same reverential feelings as I would Heaven itself, I anticipate some signal changes in my feelings, in my views, in my purposes, in my pursuits. What they may be I know not—time alone can tell. My ardent desire has been through life to reach the highest order of human excellence by the shortest possible cut. Association, night and day, in sickness and in health, in war and in peace, with a woman of this highest order of excellence, must produce some curious results in my heart and feelings, and these results the future will develop in due time in the columns of the *Herald*. . . .

And so they were married, and Mr. Bennett took his paragon to Niagara Falls, improving the time he was away from the paper by writing for it long descriptions of the country and the people.

When he came back to New York, he brought his bride to the Astor House, whereupon his enemies raised a great outcry and tried to high-pressure the proprietor, Charles Stetson, into refusing the hospitality of the establishment. Bennett correctly estimated the result of such attempts upon his good name. "These blockheads," he wrote, "are determined to make me the greatest man of the age. Newspaper abuse made Mr. Van Buren chief magistrate of this republic—and newspaper abuse will make me the chief editor of this country. Well—be it so, I can't help it."

Whether it was Henrietta's influence or his enemies', Bennett continued to prosper. He organized a Washington press corps, and conducted a successful campaign to get its members admitted to the galleries of Congress whenever they wished. He moved his offices to a fine new building at Fulton and Nassau streets, and from there began a period of uninterrupted progress which lasted two decades. No paper had the *Herald*'s news coverage. Bennett even kept a fleet of fast packets cruising off Sandy Hook to intercept incoming steamers and get the news from Europe first. When the telegraph was introduced, no paper used it to better advantage.

As the *Herald* and Bennett both grew rich, the editor found that he had more in common with the business community than he had supposed in his poor beginnings. It was this identity of interests, as it was with Horace Greeley, that led him to support Douglas against Lincoln. A civil war, highly unpopular with the commercial interests of New York, began to loom.

It was charged that Bennett's brief residence in the South had made him pro-Southern, but actually he conceived it to be in the best business interests of the North to let the seceding states go, another attitude he shared with Greeley. Once he even advocated reorganizing the republic under the South's new constitution, with the New England states left to their own devices.

Such a course was not calculated to make the *Herald* popular with patriots. A crowd gathered one day before the Herald Building and there was wild talk of burning it and dressing its proprietor in tar and feathers, but the rioters were dispersed before any damage was done.

Bennett stuck to his opinions stubbornly, however, until Fort Sumter was fired upon. Then he bowed to the flood of public opinion. He turned *Herald* policy to the cause of the Union, and as a proof of his good intentions, gave his yacht to the government and instructed his son to enlist in the Navy.

Thereafter, while the war endured, the *Herald* was a supporter, though often a lukewarm one, of Lincoln and Union. Ardent Northern patriots were sometimes given to calling it a Copperhead rag, but Bennett placed his paper solidly behind the President's bid for reelection in 1864.

As for the conflict itself, Bennett's newsgathering enterprise was never more evident than in the *Herald*'s war coverage, which was audacious, complete, and accurate. This effort cost the proprietor more than a half-million dollars but was well worth it in terms of circulation. One issue in 1864 sold more than 132,000. Only Greeley's *Tribune* competed seriously with the *Herald,* but it may be significant that it was the *Herald* that Lincoln himself read most constantly, in spite of its critical editorials.

By the end of the war, Bennett stood at the summit of his personal success. He had outfought his enemies. He was rich. Lincoln had offered to make him minister to France, but he had declined the honor. In 1867, he turned the management of the *Herald* over to his son and went into luxurious retirement.

When Bennett's florid-faced, commanding, six-foot figure stepped off the journalistic stage, he left behind him a vacant space far larger than most of his contemporaries had been willing to grant him. For this hard, calculating, strong-willed man, whose modest aspect in private was so out of keeping with his public brashness, had shown the newspaper business how to get news. In doing so, he had broadened the base of newspaper appeal, and led the way to a Jacksonian democratic revolution in publishing.

Yet he was no reformer. He sneered at the efforts of Greeley and others to correct or abate social evils. The world, he once wrote in an editorial, was not full of misery, suffering, and corruption, as Greeley and his friends insisted. Such conditions might occur, he admitted, "but the world of these gloomy enthusiasts has no existence in reality. The great mass of mankind, living in civilized society, are happy. The suffering and misery are only exceptions to the general condition. The world is an excellent world. It is a happy world. . . ."

Bennett's conception of his own role in this best of all possible planets was cast in the largest terms. "My ambition," he wrote, "is to make the newspaper Press the great organ and pivot of

government, society, commerce, finance, religion, and all human civilization. I want to leave behind me no castles, no
granite hotels, no monuments of marble, no statues of bronze,
no pyramids of brick—simply a name. The name of James
Gordon Bennett, as one of the benefactors of the human race,
will satisfy every desire and every hope."

This kind of bombast was exceptional even in a bombastic
era, but the name of Bennett was honored in spite of it, and
when he died in 1872, the quick death of the old animosities
against him was shown by the list of honorary pallbearers,
which included several of the men, including Greeley, who had
attacked him most virulently. And in spite of his failings, time
has given him a secure place in history—not exactly the noble
and lofty one to which he aspired, perhaps, but one that would
have made his newspaperman's soul happy.

The legacy Bennett left behind him was, aside from his substantial fortune, a newspaper of international reputation. A
few may have equaled it, but none surpassed "The Thunderer,"
as it was called, both affectionately and sarcastically. To Bennett's son, who bore his name, fell the unexampled opportunity,
when he was only twenty-six years old, to guide the destiny of
this great paper.

That the younger Bennett largely threw away his grand
chance, and at his death left the *Herald* only a dismal memory
of its former greatness is a fact often lamented and moralized
about. In some respects this is unfair, because young Bennett
performed spectacular and noteworthy deeds for his property
before his own character ruined him. His personal tragedy is
more understandable today, when the business world is full of
stories of sons who were called upon to fill the shoes of eminent
fathers who built great fortunes and reputations—sons who
found themselves unequal to the responsibility of inherited
wealth and influence.

There are gloomy parallels between the histories of many of
these unfortunate sons, and that of the younger Bennett. Most
of his early years were spent in Europe with his mother; she

hoped to shield him from the violence of his father's public life. He was at school in Paris when the Civil War broke out, and came home to be commissioned a lieutenant in the Navy as part of the patriotic conversion by which his father's business was saved.

After the war, he underwent a two-year internship in various *Herald* departments, became managing editor in 1866, and editor at his father's retirement the following year. Not much was expected of him, and such cynical estimates appeared justified when it was observed that he spent a good part of his time acting like the gay-young-bachelor-about-town, which he was. It was also evident that he was erratic, impulsive, prodigal with money, quick-tempered, and jealous.

But young Bennett had two valuable assets. One was a keen sense of news and a hardheaded understanding, inherited from his father, that newspapers paid off on news. The other was an ability to surround himself with editors and reporters who knew how to get news and, even more, how to make it. The father was a master at getting news; the son a genius at making it happen.

One of his first exploits in this direction was to send his star reporter, Henry M. Stanley, into unknown Africa to find and rescue a missing missionary, David Livingstone. Stanley had already covered General Hancock's expedition against the Indians and the British Army's foray against the Emperor of Abyssinia. Bennett gave him the Livingstone assignment when the two met in Paris in 1869. Stanley immediately fitted out an expedition in Zanzibar, and two years later he was able to report that most laconic of historic conversations:

STANLEY: Dr. Livingstone, I presume.
LIVINGSTONE: Yes.

Another of Bennett's roving correspondents, Aloysius Mac-Gahan, who had covered the Franco-Prussian War, the troubles in the Crimea and parleys in Geneva, enhanced his own and the *Herald*'s reputation in 1873 with the stories he sent from

Central Asia while he fought with the Russians against the tribesmen there.

Two years later, MacGahan was off on a Bennett-financed expedition to find a Northwest Passage, in the bark *Pandora*. The expedition failed in its mission, but Bennett marked it up as a journalistic success.

At home, Bennett fought the Panic of 1873 singlehandedly by opening soup kitchens in the slums, where he startled the palates of the poor by serving food brought downtown from famed Delmonico's.

Bennett could often be found in the forefront of charity. Probably his most charitable act was his founding of the *Paris Herald* in 1887, which was not a business decision but the result of his love affair with France—an impulsive, friendly gesture which he hoped would help maintain friendly relations with America. It accomplished that purpose, and in later years the paper served as a hospitable home for numerous great names in journalism, caught abroad without funds or stricken with a hopeless passion for Paris. In other respects, the Paris *Herald* was a financial liability as long as Bennett lived.

More difficult to understand was Bennett's support of the *New York Herald*'s afternoon edition, the *Evening Telegram*, which Oswald Garrison Villard once termed "that pink drab of lowest journalism." It drained the *Herald*'s profits for years. Once Bennett even decided to discontinue it, but in the end it proved a profitable charity because it reversed the situation and kept the *Herald* alive in that paper's declining years.

It is possible that Bennett, for all his personal peculiarities, might have stayed in New York and continued to build his paper's reputation for news enterprise if a mysterious incident had not occurred in 1877 which changed the entire course of his life.

Engaged to a Washington society girl, he had seemed well en route to the domestic bliss so feelingly described by his father, when the engagement was broken off suddenly for reasons which have never been adequately explained. The young lady's brother came up to New York, horsewhipped Bennett on the steps of the Union Club, and then fought a duel with him on the Delaware-Maryland border. There was no damage to either contestant.

This choice scandal rocked the city and provided a field day of speculation for the *Herald*'s enemies. Bitter and utterly disillusioned, Bennett gave up the fine old family home on Washington Heights, his Newport villa, and his town house at 37 West Forty-seventh Street, and, except for infrequent visits, lived the remainder of his life in Paris—not counting whatever time he might spend shooting from his "lodge" at Versailles, cruising on his yacht, the *Lysistrata,* with its hundred-man crew, or sunning himself in his villa at Beaulieu.

From all these places, at various times, he edited the *Herald,* by cable, by letter, and by conference with editors and writers peremptorily summoned across the Atlantic. But where this editing had once been brilliant despite its erratic character, now it was increasingly arrogant and eccentric. The eccentricity appeared to be in ratio to Bennett's alcoholic content at the time.

He made one more sensation with his financing, in 1879, of the ill-fated voyage to the Arctic of the ship *Jeanette,* under George Washington De Long. The *Jeanette* was crushed by the polar ice and sank with all hands.

Bennett's long-distance editing was made easier in 1883 when he helped John W. Mackay establish the Commercial Cable Company, and the laying of this transatlantic line, through its financial interlock with the *Herald,* enabled the paper to maintain its foreign coverage superiority.

But its expatriate editor became less and less a newspaperman, and more and more a fabulous international figure, "The Commodore," as he was familiarly known—a spender, a sportsman, a whispered-about participant in scandalous affairs, an unpredictable man whose attitudes were European rather than American.

The tales of his eccentricities were endless. Once he made a city editor out of the first reporter who climbed aboard to meet him in New York Bay on one of his occasional trips home. Another time, in Paris, he was restrained during a drinking bout from cabling to the *Herald* a story, one of his own, denouncing the Pope—and this from a man whose father was a good Catholic, and who had enshrined himself in the hearts of Irish-Americans by his enormous gifts to struggling Ireland.

Newspapermen laughed without much humor when they told how Bennett, admonished by his editor in New York that a man he had just fired was "indispensable," had cabled back, "Send me a list of all the men you consider indispensable," and had then ordered every one of them dismissed. He added sourly that he intended to have no indispensable men working for him.

It was a tribute to the solid character of the paper the elder Bennett had built that it survived so long under this kind of management. But in a perverse kind of way, it was the son's fondness for the unusual that helped the *Herald* in these later days. He was quite naturally the first editor to espouse the cause of the airplane and the automobile when they appeared, and his love of yachting made the paper preeminent in maritime news for generations. Moreover, his international outlook aided the *Herald*'s superiority in foreign news. It was a *Herald* man who stood by Dewey in Manila Bay and heard the Admiral's calm voice instructing Gridley to fire.

Bennett's tastes were reflected in other *Herald* specialties. No other paper gave such attention to owls, beloved of its editor, and its campaigns against vivisection, long predating those of the Hearst newspapers, were the result of Bennett's anxious preoccupation with dogs. In sports and the theater, too, the *Herald* had no rivals in reporting the news.

But these virtues were not enough to compensate for an absentee publisher who could not retain the able men he had gathered to work for him, and who had no faith in the virtues of an editorial page at a time when personal journalism was still the order of the day. These two factors were exceedingly serious in a period when new giants of the press were rising in

New York. The *World* was striding rapidly to the front ranks under Joseph Pulitzer, and Adolph S. Ochs had begun to breathe life into the *Times*. These men and Bennett were challenged by the sensational successes of young William Randolph Hearst, whose *Journal* had introduced a new phrase into the popular vocabulary—"yellow journalism."

Ochs hewed to the *Times* line and avoided troubles or comparisons with Hearst, but Pulitzer and Bennett made the same initial mistake of trying to out-Journal the *Journal*. The *Herald* looked more and more like the scandalous sheet it had been in the early days of the elder Bennett. In a desperate effort to bolster its steadily declining position, it enlivened its personal columns with items of a peculiarly personal nature. These were typical:

> YOUNG LADY, good figure, wants to pose for artists; references exchanged; positively no triflers.
>
> A CATHOLIC maiden (28) worth nearly $5,000, musical, refined, good appearance, would wed.—Rosalie
>
> A HANDSOME young girl desires copying or some other profitable work.—M.P.
>
> ANY person knowing of impending business failures or having other valuable information can make big money by communicating with smart lawyer.—Strict confidence.

These were the more refined personals. Others were far less disguised, and many under the subdivisions of "manicure," "massage," "medical," "financial," and "business opportunities" were, as one shocked contemporary historian reported, "full of snares, pitfalls, decoys, frauds and temptations."

On a Sunday morning in 1896, this historian goes on to report with horror, the *Herald* "scored a victory over its rivals" when it "printed an account of a prominent lady's linen with such detailed frankness that it may not be copied here."

By an adroit maneuver, Hearst converted this competition into an instrument to destroy it. The man who was credited with inventing yellow journalism blandly took the most righteous possible position and succeeded in getting Bennett, the *Herald* corporation, and its advertising manager indicted for violating the postal laws by using the personals column for immoral purposes. Henry L. Stimson, then in the Department of Justice, conducted the prosecution. There was no defense to be made. Humiliated and consumed with a profound hatred for Hearst, Bennett pleaded guilty and paid total fines of $31,000.

That was the beginning of the end. The remainder of Bennett's life was a *tour de force* of irony, a climax of contradictions. Long a bachelor, he married the widow of a French baron. At the same time, he left the faith of his father and joined the Protestant Episcopal Church. Three years later, he learned that the thirty million dollars he had drawn from the *Herald* and spent during his lifetime had so weakened the paper that it was being supported by its strident and wildly inaccurate sister, the *Telegram*.

After Bennett's death at Beaulieu from a heart attack, his will provided the final, and choicest, irony. In spite of his pledge to the old employees of the paper that the property would be left to them to conduct cooperatively, the *Herald* was placed in the hands of the executors. The will also provided that the greater part of the estate was to be used to establish a home in memory of his father as a shelter for poor New York newspapermen. But there was so little money left in the estate, so many obligations held against it, and so many persons provided with annuities, that the James Gordon Bennett Memorial Home remained only a pious good intention.

Bennett died in 1918. Two years later the *Herald*, with its proud tradition of newspapering, fell into the clutches of Frank A. Munsey, the grand high executioner, who cared nothing whatever for the news but only for the money the news would bring. There it languished until 1924, when its identity, if not its name, was finally lost forever by its merger with the *New York Tribune*, the newspaper founded by Horace Greeley, the man both Bennetts had fought.

It was a victory old Horace would have given his side-whiskers to see.

4

Horace Greeley

FOR A MAN WHO WAS AS MUCH A POPULAR LEGEND IN HIS OWN time as William Randolph Hearst was in ours, Horace Greeley (see photograph 2) has left remarkably little for Americans not in the newspaper business to remember him by. A Gallup pollster would almost certainly discover that Greeley can be identified today only by people able to associate him with a cliché he gave to the language: "Go West, young man, go West."

Few citizens know, for example, that Greeley took his own advice in the summer of 1859 and journeyed overland to California, pausing in Salt Lake City for a two-hour interview with Brigham Young, which, among other things, may have been the first time a newspaper interview was reported in direct question-and-answer form, instead of in the formal, indirect manner used until that time.

Readers of Greeley's *New York Tribune* not only got an amazingly frank report on the Mormon leader's religious and political views, but it was typical of the *Tribune*'s editor that he used the story as a potent weapon in his assault on those who opposed the rights of women. It was only three years later that Congress, in response to the pressure Greeley helped generate, outlawed polygamy.

That incident was typical of the restless, crusading spirit of the man who dominated American journalism of the nineteenth

century from 1830 to 1870, and whose voice, resounding in the
pages of the *Tribune,* was heard from coast to coast. Never
was there an American editor who spoke more directly to the
people who read his newspaper, who hoped and dreamed more
for those people, who so aspired to lead them to a better world,
and whose zeal for them led him to such political disaster.

Horace Greeley, it might be said, was the great showman, the
P. T. Barnum of American journalism. He looked like the
prototype of all the eccentrics and amiable medicine men who
ever wandered up and down the byways of our national life.
One of his biographers, William Harlan Hale, speaks of his
"moon-faced stare, his flopping trousers, his squeaky slang, his
sputtering profanities, his unpredictable oddities, and his general air of an owlish, rustic sage. . . ."

The eminent men of his time, at least many of them, viewed
this strange figure with disdain. James Fenimore Cooper, who
fought a one-man war against the press in general, thought
Greeley a vulgarian. Edwin L. Godkin, who founded the
Nation, and later became the distinguished liberal (though
highly opinionated) editor of the *Evening Post,* was openly
contemptuous of his more popular contemporary, and William
Cullen Bryant, the poet-editor who had preceded Godkin at
the helm of the literary and respectable *Post,* would not even
speak to Greeley.

It is easy to understand why these dignified and conservative
men so grossly underestimated "Uncle Horace," as the *Tribune*'s readers affectionately called him. In a personal sense,
they could make little of so ridiculous a figure, whom the critic
Vernon L. Parrington has perceptively characterized as strange
and childlike, "with his round moon-face, eyes blinking through
spectacles, and a fringe of whiskers that invited the pencil of
the cartoonist."

The spectacle of Greeley's frock-coated form, surmounted by
a white hat, hurrying around the country and talking endlessly
to the people, led more sober editors to suspect that their colleague was insane. They were sure of it when he had the

unimaginable temerity to run against General Grant for the Presidency of the United States, and Greeley himself obligingly confirmed their diagnosis by dying, out of his mind, only a few weeks after Grant had inflicted an overwhelming, heartbreaking defeat on all his hopes and ambitions.

They told endless stories about his eccentricities—how as an ardent vegetarian he could nevertheless be so absent-minded that he unthinkingly consumed a splendid steak under the illusion that it was Graham bread.

Again, it was whispered about New York how Greeley had sat at his desk listening to an irritable visitor and seeming not to hear the tirade directed against him until his irascible guest declared angrily that he had treated the editor like a gentleman, which, from all appearances, he was not. "Who in hell ever said I was?" Greeley protested mildly, looking up for the first time.

The New York editors and their friends elsewhere shook their heads in bewilderment at Greeley. They couldn't understand this man who kept a goat in his backyard on East Nineteenth Street in New York, and who forthrightly befriended the former Confederate president, Jefferson Davis—Greeley, who had been an ardent Abolitionist and a leader in the fight for the Union.

Nor was his defense of Davis apologetic. He called fellow members of the Union League Club who opposed him "narrow-minded blockheads," and he dared them to put him out of the Club's sacred precincts.

The men who worked for him and, under his editorial tutelage, rose to eminence in the profession often failed to understand him and appeared to absorb nothing of the Greeley personality beyond his editing genius. Henry J. Raymond learned his craft at the *Tribune* and went on to found the *New York Times,* which was also Republican but was opposed to the *Tribune*'s and Greeley's zeal to reform the world. Charles A. Dana, who later made the *New York Sun* as eminent as the *Tribune* had been, worked for Greeley but his newspaper re-

flected none of "Uncle Horace's" idealism and Dana himself
wound up a cynic, and an apologist for the practices which
Greeley had fought.

Probably the strangest of Greeley's employees was the London
correspondent he acquired in 1851, a young pamphleteer named
Karl Marx, who subsisted on his Republican boss's ten dollars
a week (later cut to five) while he worked on a book called *Das
Kapital.* Greeley and Marx were both socialists; both were
ardent advocates of the rights of labor. But the radical dogmas
of Marx were very far from the editor's Utopian idealism. If
Marx had ever understood Greeley, he must have been contemptuous of him.

Those who did understand Greeley, and loved him, were the
people. Not Marx's faceless "masses," but the individual Americans who recognized in Greeley a champion who would fight
for their rights in the revolution already taking place in the
United States—the surging upheaval which accompanied the
transition from an agrarian to an industrial economy.

Greeley may have been hopelessly idealistic in his ambition
to lead the American people by the hand to high ground where
they would be safe against the floodtides of savage materialism,
but the means by which he intended to save them were practical enough. There was a considerable gap between the high-
minded utterances in his books and his newspaper, nicknamed
"The Great Moral Organ," and the specific reforms which he
struggled all his life to bring about.

He summed up his philosophy in a volume titled *Hints Toward Reforms,* writing, in 1850: "The avocations of Life, and
the usages and structure of Society, the relations of Power to
Humility, of Wealth to Poverty, of master to servant, must all
be fused in the crucible of Human Brotherhood, and whatever
abides not the test rejected."

The road he traveled toward the fulfillment of that philosophy was unremittingly rocky from the beginning. He was
born a New Hampshireman, in 1811, the son of a farmer who
failed to wrest enough from the rocky New England soil to

stay out of debtor's prison. Horace's youth was cast in the mold later immortalized by Horatio Alger in a phrase, "rags to riches." Like Alger heroes, Greeley lived an exemplary boyhood, filled with hard work and devoted to such practical virtues as reading the Bible through before he was five and laboring as a printer's apprentice.

It was wholly in the Alger tradition that he should come to New York at twenty with only ten dollars to his name and his worldly goods slung, Ben-Franklinwise, over his shoulder in a bandanna handkerchief.

His first effort in journalism was a flat failure. He went into partnership with a Dr. H. D. Shepard, who intended to establish a penny daily to be sold on the streets, at that time a novel idea because dailies were presumably read only by merchants and were sold by the year. Their first issue of the *New York Morning Post,* priced at two cents on the insistence of the printers, appeared on New Year's Day, 1833, coincidentally with a blizzard which tied up New York and destroyed the initial sale.

When the storm cleared away, the customers were able to see that Dr. Shepard was an uninspired editor and the paper died within three weeks. Not even a reduction to one cent saved it.

Next year the undaunted Greeley started a Whig weekly, the *New-Yorker,* whose literary columns were enlivened by an editorial page so vigorous that it drew the attention of the New York State political boss, Thurlow Weed, who shrewdly hired young Greeley to edit some campaign papers for him. These were so successful that Horace was emboldened to start a daily penny paper of his own. He was only thirty years old. His total assets were a thousand dollars of his own, another thousand borrowed, and a thousand dollars worth of printing equipment. With these he launched, on April 10, 1841, the *New York Tribune,* a four-page, five-column-wide paper. In seven weeks, it had 11,000 circulation.

This was the vehicle on which Greeley rode to fame, and

which he made the most famous newspaper of its time. People spoke much of the *Tribune*'s "influence," and it is this attribute by which it is most remembered, but it must never be forgotten that its "influence" was a highly personal matter. The *Tribune* was Greeley. Without him, it would have had no influence, no character, and probably no existence.

From the beginning, the *Tribune* spoke with a voice of fire to the plain people of America. It was the voice of a Yankee who was profoundly disturbed by what he saw happening in the nation, who was determined to right the wrongs of an expanding society, and whose style was so persuasive that he swept his readers along with him, even when they were not quite sure where he was going.

It often appeared that Greeley himself was not sure. He was an explosive bundle of contradictions. "Uncle Horace" could always be found arguing the virtue of thrift; however, it was no secret that he not only failed to practice it but actually had the utmost disdain for money.

Similarly, Greeley and his *Tribune* were ardent in the conservative Whig cause while it was opposing slavery, but the party leaders were shocked and irritated to find their champion coming out with equal ardor for socialism. Greeley was a pacifist by nature and labored earnestly for peace, but the idealism that made him an abolitionist led him into helping bring about the Civil War. Then, during that war, he failed to agree with Lincoln and for a time it was difficult for his readers to decide whether "Uncle Horace" was about to ride to the front personally on a white charger, or whether he had concluded that the North had better give up while there was still time to save itself from ruin.

The founders of the Republican Party, of which he was one, counted him as among their own, of the inner circle, yet he had no hesitation in running against the party as a rebel, with Democratic support, when it failed to measure up to his ideas of what it should be.

Greeley led his readers whooping off down the streets on

crusades for labor unions and free homesteads, and with equivalent enthusiasm on behalf of vegetarianism and spiritualism. All manner of wizards, witch doctors, quacks, and panacea dealers gained his ear, and their spiels were rebroadcast in the persuasive voice of "Uncle Horace," speaking in the columns of the *Tribune,* and circulated from one end of the country to the other, to the frequent bemusement of his readers.

The *Tribune,* in fact, was unique among newspapers. Its dominance was not based on circulation; others were larger but not as influential. It often failed to get the news first; James Gordon Bennett's *Herald* many times beat it to the streets. It was on the unpopular side politically as often as not. Yet it flourished; and Greeley became perhaps the only editor in American journalism who ever made liberalism pay.

From Greeley on down through a brilliant staff, which included such names as George Ripley, Margaret Fuller, and Bayard Taylor, the *Tribune* was imbued with the purpose which its editor had proclaimed in the first issue, that this "New Morning Journal of Politics, Literature and General Intelligence" was intended to "advance the interests of the people, and promote their Moral, Political and Social Wellbeing."

For the forty years following this pronouncement, Greeley advanced the people's interests in several major crusades, aimed to lift the laboring class, as he put it, "out of ignorance, inefficiency, dependence, and want." To these crusades he brought the advantages of a vigorous, independent mind, able to express itself in language the average American could understand, and the disadvantage of a fierce idealism which compelled him to change his mind about issue after issue when the reforms for which he fought failed to come up to his exorbitant expectations.

A case in point was Fourierism, a briefly popular ideology imported from a French communist named Charles Fourier. By present standards of radicalism, this was a mild enough version of what would be called today the cooperative ownership of lands and homes. For five years Greeley went up and down the country preaching Fourierism, though, characteristically, he disagreed with Fourier on the communistic basis of the theory. There was considerable interest for a time in several states, and forty or more communities were attempted, but eventually Fourierism died of inanition, and not even a newspaper debate lasting six months, in which Greeley naturally defended the cause in his *Tribune,* could save it. Greeley lost interest in the idea, too, and hardly mentioned it again.

Much more lasting was the editor's strong advocacy of labor unions. As a printer himself, Greeley helped organize the New York Printers' Union and became its first president. But again, and typically, he gave the union movement more moral support than actual service.

Greeley and the *Tribune* were ever in the forefront of any movement designed to improve the morals of the population. A teetotaler himself, he argued for enactment of state laws prohibiting the sale of liquor, but the fervor he and others whipped up over this issue subsided in time. He was also busy opposing capital punishment, and there he had more success. The pressure exerted by the *Tribune* and other papers ended executions by hanging in several states.

The great moral issue of his time, of course, was slavery, and Greeley was undoubtedly the most active editor of them all in the abolition fight. Some historians even go so far as to say that he was the primary influence in bringing about emancipation, though this may well be doubted. However, there is not the slightest doubt that he was the principal mover in the historic fight for abolition.

Greeley might possibly have changed his mind even on so fundamental an issue if he had ever been in the South, since first-hand examination of a situation quite often persuaded him the other way. He traveled extensively in his lifetime, far from his native New England, but he never visited the South and he failed to understand that region politically as he understood the people and ideas in every other section of the United States.

Sometimes he campaigned in behalf of Whig Party principles for what Party leaders considered the wrong reasons. Thus, he supported the protective tariff, a fundamental plank in the Whig platform, but not because he wanted to uphold the interests of the industrialists who were its chief proponents. His interest lay in keeping the standards of American labor on a higher level than those of Europe, and he thought that could be done best by protecting the price of the worker's product. It is quite understandable how confused the Whig industrialists must have been to find their protectionist views supported in the same issue of a *Tribune* which might speak eloquently of the need for Socialism.

More important, however, was the fact that Greeley sold his tariff idea to the farmers of the nation, with whom the *Tribune* had extraordinary influence. It must be remembered that Greeley's paper was read, admired, and absorbed everywhere in the Middle West and West, as well as the East. The protectionist philosophy of the *Tribune* became a fundamental attitude among farmers, so firmly planted that it has persisted until the present day in a very large proportion of rural voters.

Greeley's reasoning in this matter was blameless, although he advocated a doctrine basically opposed to his Jeffersonian faith. He wanted to see America made strong internally. Many of his other crusades had their origin in this primary desire. For example, he opposed the Mexican War, along with other Whigs, not because he thought it would interfere with business but because he disapproved of such adventures, calculated to weaken the nation needlessly.

The "go West" slogan was also part of this pattern. Greeley preached westward expansion endlessly in the *Tribune*'s columns, advocating all the controversial items that went along with expansion, such as government help in the building of railways and telegraph lines to the West Coast, and a Federal homestead law which would encourage young men to take his advice and go out to develop the Western lands. By these means, he argued, the sorry state of the underprivileged would be improved at the same time, and many a mean and pinched New York life would find itself rescued from poverty if it could be transplanted to new and fertile soil.

Greeley often told his readers how superior the country and its residents were to the homes and ways of city dwellers. He practiced what he preached, first with a house at the end of a muddy lane in the Turtle Bay section of Manhattan, now a high-rent district a little south of the Queensboro Bridge. Later he moved his family out to a farm in Chappaqua, a long way indeed from town, considering that Turtle Bay was then in the country. Uncle Horace was no city farmer. He was genuinely interested in new agricultural methods, and he wanted to be next to the soil himself as much as he could.

It is plain, then, why it was that Greeley was so popular with the country's farm population, and why his crusading for agriculture and westward expansion, coinciding happily with mass migrations westward and the consequent resurgence of the farm, made both him and his paper popular over so much territory. It was said that Illinois farmers, for example, never made up their minds on public issues until they could read the *Tribune* and "see what Horace thinks."

These "causes" of Greeley's, viewed as a whole, take on significance. In the large sense, they show clearly what was always paramount in his mind: the protection of the honest worker from those who sought to exploit him, the finding of methods to give the producer of goods a fair return for his work and elevate him from poverty to well-being. He was intensely nationalistic—he might possibly have been an isolationist if he had lived in our own time. Unquestionably he would have been a zealous advocate of the large reforms of the Thirties, because it was his basic belief that *laissez-faire* was "suicidal" and could lead only to what has been termed "the anarchy of individualism," therefore government must exercise an intelligent control of the economic forces which produced it.

In this sense, Greeley would undoubtedly be considered radical in some quarters today, but most of the reforms for which he fought have been realized, and some have gone far beyond what he himself might have wished.

But it would be wrong to consider Greeley, as some have done, in no broader terms than as a social reformer, an eccentric whose political ideas were as confused and contradictory as the *Tribune*'s editorial columns sometimes made them appear to be. On the contrary, Greeley was a hard-working, enterprising, independent man in the Yankee tradition. His sympathies lay wholly with people like himself, who knew how hard and bitter life could be for the poor in an era when the onset and rapid development of the industrial revolution caused the national economy to gyrate rapidly between prosperity and panic. Therefore he was earnest in his support of the wage-earner and the farmer.

In the end, however, he did not let his sympathies carry him to the point of pure radicalism. He believed in the partnership of farm and factory, for the best interests of both and of the nation, with the government empowered to extend adequate but not hampering controls over the whole economy.

These beliefs excited as much violent opposition in Greeley's time as they have in our own, perhaps more, and he was constantly embattled with the upholders of *laissez-faire,* who argued for freedom of competition. Greeley agreed with them. He was also an advocate of competition, he said; he only wanted what he considered its evils corrected.

To attain the balance of forces he sought, Greeley put his trust in the fundamental goodness of humanity, in the free and unhampered mind, the essential human spirit, free of perversions by the institutions of civilization.

This romantic view accurately forecast that he would be a failure in politics. It was inevitable that such idealism would founder on the cold, hard rocks of political realism as embodied in parties and the men who controlled them. Greeley antagonized not only many industrialists, which was natural, but he also earned the enmity of middle-class Americans, who tended to side with their employers rather than with the farmers and

workers, with whom they felt they had much less in common.
Greeley was laughed at by so-called "practical" men.

   In all these turbulent cross-currents of an expanding America, Greeley remained his honest self—honest, always, right or
wrong. Because he took the world and its sorrows to his heart,
it was likewise inevitable that he should break his heart trying
to hurry the processes of social evolution and bring peace and
justice to a civilization that was decades, perhaps centuries,
from achieving them.

   One by one he saw the dreams of his lifetime dissipated. The
organizations he had helped to form got out of control, and
he perceived that the era of conflict was beginning, not ending.
He had helped to start and carry on a great moral revolution in
America, but the men who had raised their voices most effectively in his causes, men like Emerson and Garrison and Whitman, became tired old men and left him to fight alone.

   He was tired, too, but he had one major fight left in him. He
would go at last to the people who had always supported him
and the *Tribune* and ask them to send him to the White House,
where he could put into practice what he thought of as true
Republican principles, as opposed to the perversions of them
enunciated by his rival for the office, Ulysses S. Grant.

   It was the worst political mistake of a life which had been
full of them. He profoundly overestimated the concern of the
farmers for the wage-earners, and vice versa. They would not
give their votes to the man they had called "Uncle Horace," and
Grant was elected by more than three-quarters of a million
votes.

   The shadows closed in rapidly. A few days before the election
his wife Mary, who had long been ill, died. Five days later
Greeley wrote to a friend, "I am not dead, but wish I were. My
house is desolate, my future dark, my heart a stone. . . ." He
had nothing left but his *Tribune,* and he began to have the
delusion that his enemies were trying to take this, too, from
him, a fear which had a real basis in fact.

   He lay ill for a time in the house of a friend on Fifty-seventh

Street, writing feverish, despairing notes, fragments of wills, abject apologies to the Liberal Republican leaders, despairing confessions. "I stand naked before my God the most utterly, hopelessly wretched and undone of all who ever lived. I have done more harm and wrong than any man who ever saw the light of day. And yet, I take God to witness that I have never intended to wrong or harm anyone. . . . My total vice has been a readiness to believe and trust every flattering, plausible villain. . . ."

Finally he was taken to a private mental hospital in Pleasantville, a little Westchester town near Chappaqua, and noted brain specialists sought to cure him, but it was useless. Sometimes clear in his mind, sometimes raving, he lived a few more days, then sank into a coma and died on November 28, 1872.

Greeley had left behind him explicit and characteristically whimsical instructions for a simple funeral and burial. "Plant me in my favorite pumpkin arbor, with a gooseberry bush for a footstone," he had written.

Instead, he got a Fifth Avenue church funeral with three officiating ministers, the most prominent pallbearers and mourners, and in the funeral procession rode the new President of the United States.

That was the final ironic commentary on Greeley the reformer and politician—to be attended in death by his successful rival and the men who were even then fighting for control of his beloved *Tribune*.

It was a commentary lost on the silent, melancholy crowds who lined Fifth Avenue. They mourned Horace Greeley, the greatest editor American journalism had ever known.

Dana and Godkin

OF ALL UNCLE HORACE GREELEY'S BRILLIANT PROTÉGÉES WHO GOT their start on the *Tribune,* none has been more admired, particularly by his own profession, than Charles Anderson Dana. It was Dana's *New York Sun* that came to be known as "the newspaperman's newspaper," and Dana himself who was characterized by "Marse Henry" Watterson, the elegant founder of the *Louisville Courier-Journal,* as "the most scholarly and accomplished of American journalists."

Marse Henry was largely right when he remarked that what Dana "did not know about a newspaper was scarcely worth knowing," but at the same time it must be admitted that there is more to the making of a great newspaper than the gathering and writing of news, and Dana's contribution to the furthering of journalism's best ideals left something to be desired.

Few of his contemporaries got off to a more promising start. He shared, it is true, the early adversities of other noted editors —his country storekeeper father failed in business in Dana's native New Hampshire, his mother died when he was nine, he was sent to be a clerk in an uncle's store in Buffalo when he was twelve, and at eighteen he was cast into the world when the store went bankrupt. But fortunately he was equipped with an intellect which gave him a distinct advantage over less able men, and enabled him to survive these difficulties.

As a farm boy he had studied Latin by himself, and during long evenings in Buffalo, he had gone on with Greek and read voraciously in the classics, consequently he was able to get into Harvard without conditions at nineteen. Hard study nearly ruined his eyesight, and it was at this point, forced to retire from the university in despair after his junior year, that one of those fortunate incidents in the lives of great men occurred to him. The cooperative experiment in "plain living and high thinking" at West Roxbury, Massachusetts, known as Brook Farm, whose transcendentalist idealism had so intrigued Greeley, hired Dana to teach German and Greek.

An idealist himself at that stage of his life, Dana accepted eagerly and lived at the farm for five years, giving the experiment everything he had in time, talent, energy, and money. There he met Greeley, and there he began writing for Brook Farm's paper, the *Harbinger,* discovering in this activity where his interest really lay. When the great experiment ended in 1846, he naturally pursued his new-found interest and found a job in Boston as assistant editor of a Congregationalist organ called the *Daily Chronotype.*

As a denominational editor, Dana gave the Congregational cause the kind of support it might have expected from a strong Unitarian. While the editor was away, his young assistant shocked and astonished the *Chronotype*'s readers by coming out "mighty strong against hell," a Unitarian view which compelled the editor to apologize by letter to the state's Congregational ministers.

It was just as well, therefore, that Dana remembered his Brook Farm conversations with Greeley, and approached Uncle Horace for a job. He got one—as city editor of the *Tribune.* The salary scarcely matched the title; it was ten dollars a week, later raised to fourteen.

Thus began the first of three well-defined periods in Dana's extraordinary career. In the fifteen years he spent on the *Tribune,* becoming eventually its managing editor, he perfected his writing style—concise, a little on the pompous side,

and spiced with epigrams—and he acquired the encyclopedic
knowledge of the business that made him perhaps the best
manager of a newspaper property in his time. Certainly there is
little doubt that the *Tribune* was better run when Charlie
Dana was alone at the helm, during Greeley's frequent excursions at home and abroad. He made all the editorial decisions,
edited everybody's copy, including Greeley's, and kept the
business side of the paper in the same firm grip.

Although such experience was all-important to his later
career, it was another episode during this period that altered
his character and shaped him toward the man he was to become.
He chose one of the most critical times in world history, during
1846 and 1847, to make a long European trip, and in the turbulent capitals of the Old World he saw at first hand the
appalling results of power politics and political chicanery.

From a Continent swept by revolution and mighty tides of
unrest, he sent home comprehensive, informed reports to newspapers in New York, Boston, and Philadelphia. It was a superb
reporting performance; but in the letters began to appear signs
of the corrosive cynicism and disillusionment that so blighted
his later years. Under the impact of European politics, the
Brook Farm idealist was losing his idealism and replacing it
with the hard, practical principles of nineteenth century business management.

Still, his basic ideas remained more liberal than not, coinciding with Greeley's in advocating the building of a transconti-
nental railway and opposing any extension of slavery. Like
Greeley, he approved a high protective tariff, but on the other
hand, he was profoundly against labor unions.

The great question of the day, however, was the Union—slave
or free, divided or preserved—and on that Dana split for good
with Greeley. Before Fort Sumter, the two men were agreed on
permitting the Southern states to go quietly, if they wished, but
when the quarrel boiled over into violence, Dana's aggressive
nature led him sharply away from his boss's pacific temporizing.
The result was that Greeley asked for and got Dana's resigna-

tion in 1862, but not until the managing editor had given the *Tribune* its famous "Forward to Richmond!" battle cry and committed it to the war.

This kind of support had been warmly received in Washington, where Lincoln and his cabinet were happy to get the influential newspaper aid which was so seldom forthcoming. Secretary Stanton was quick to reward Dana, when he heard of the editor's resignation, by offering him a post in the War Department.

Thus began the second phase of Dana's career. His first assignment was his best—to join Grant's headquarters and provide Stanton with a daily report, which was also an estimate, of the general's activities. Ostensibly he was there as a special commissioner to examine the pay service.

Dana brought his talents for reporting and organization to this task, and the result was valuable both to Washington and to Grant. Through the perilous days of Vicksburg he labored day and night, collecting, sifting, and analyzing thousands of facts. Out of them emerged a picture of Grant as a superb general, bringing him into the proper focus for the President and Stanton, whose constant worry was the command problem. Grant himself appreciated Dana's daily report-writing; it relieved him of burdensome correspondence.

When Vicksburg fell, Dana was appointed assistant secretary of war and assigned to do a similar job of reporting and analysis on General Rosecrans' campaign against Bragg. His report advised that Rosecrans be removed.

As the Administration's personal reporter, so to speak, Dana went on with Grant and Sherman through other campaigns—Chattanooga, Missionary Ridge, Lookout Mountain—before he returned to Washington in 1864 and spent the remaining months of the war at a desk, except for field trips to Virginia. As long as he could be useful, he served, until July 1, 1865, when he resigned and departed from Washington.

For two years he marked time in Chicago, where he worked briefly as editor of the *Republican,* a dismal and unsuccessful sheet, which began to sink rapidly beneath him. Dana's thoughts were elsewhere. He dreamed of having a New York newspaper of his own. Fortunately, he had made the kind of friends who could help him now, men like the New York State political poobah, Roscoe Conkling, and wealthy investors like Cyrus W. Field, W. M. Evarts, Alonzo Cornell, and A. A. Low. With the financial help of these men, he was able to buy the *Sun* for $175,000, considered a bargain, and thus the third major phase of his career began.

The *Sun* had come into bad times since Ben Day made it the talk of the town in its penny press heyday. It had been taken over by Day's brother-in-law and bookkeeper, Moses Y. Beach, and later by Beach's two sons. The Beaches were excellent managers and mechanical experts, but they did not possess the editorial qualifications to keep up with the stiff pace set by Bennett's *Herald,* and the *Sun* lost its circulation leadership.

During the summer of 1860, Moses S. Beach, one of the sons, leased the plant and sold the *Sun*'s goodwill to a man named Morrison, who was both rich and intensely religious, perhaps as a result of the tremendous revival which swept America in 1858.

Under Morrison's direction, the *Sun* passed through a strange period during which prayer meetings were held in the city room at high noon and Union generals who read it found themselves urged not to fight on Sunday.

However laudable these pursuits may have been, they did not sell newspapers, and Morrison gave the paper back to Beach near the end of 1861, after which it reverted to character. But it languished and might have died if Dana's ambition had not coincided with Beach's search for a buyer in 1868.

When Dana took over, the *Sun* had 43,000 circulation and was sinking fast. Less than three years later it was leading the New York field once more with an average daily circulation of 102,870. Six years later, it was at its peak of 131,000.

The answer could be found in promises kept. In the first issue, Dana had declared his paper's intentions in words which became journalistic history. The *Sun,* he said, would "study condensation, clearness, point, and will endeavor to present its daily photograph of the whole world's doings in the most luminous and lively manner." Advertising in other newspapers in 1870, he asserted that the *Sun's* news was "the freshest, most interesting and sprightliest current, and no expense is spared to make it just what the great mass of the people want."

In its news content the *Sun* was much like Bennett's *Herald*: a little sensational, flip in its language, and leaning heavily to murder, scandal, gossip, and interviews. The difference was that the *Sun* did it much better than the *Herald,* which was handicapped by the idiosyncrasies of Bennett Jr.

Dana's method with news gave two clichés to the business. One was the "human interest story," which the *Sun* virtually invented, at least in its modern form. The other was the immortal admonishment to a young reporter by the paper's city editor, John B. Bogart: "When a dog bites a man, that is not news; but when a man bites a dog, that is news."

On the editorial page appeared the full flowering of Dana's cynicism, which amounted sometimes to little more than savage perversity. Apparently even association with Lincoln had given him no confidence in public office, and he made few attempts to curb his personal resentments, antagonisms, and prejudices.

Nor did he have much use for human loyalties. When his old friend Grant, whom he had so much admired during the war, sat in the White House, he turned on the general and attacked him with more severity than any other editor in New York, contributing the raucous campaign cry, "Turn the rascals out!" to the campaign of 1872. Yet, in this same campaign, he gave only lukewarm support to his own candidate, his other old friend, Horace Greeley, whose cause he hurt more than he helped by referring to him sardonically as "Dr. Greeley."

When Greeley died after this political failure, however, it was Dana who self-righteously and bitterly attacked the men he thought were responsible for the *Tribune* editor's tragic death.

Sometimes it seemed that no man in high office could satisfy Dana. In the disputed Hayes-Tilden election of 1876, the *Sun* took Tilden's side and refused to accept Hayes as anything but "the fraudulent president." In 1880, it was Garfield who stood before the *Sun's* onslaught, branded by Dana as scarcely better than a common thief. Garfield's Democratic opponent, General Winfield Scott Hancock, came off just as badly. For him Dana coined one of his biting, damaging phrases, describing him editorially as "a good man, weighing 240 pounds."

Worst of all was Dana's determined opposition to Grover Cleveland, for no better reason than the fact that Cleveland had refused to do him a political favor for a friend. But again, he had an even worse opinion of James Blaine, Cleveland's opponent, and found himself with no candidate at all to support except B. F. Butler, stalwart standard bearer of the Greenback Ticket, whose support was almost microscopic. This idiosyncracy cost him thousands in circulation.

Meanwhile, he continued to attack labor unions and strikes, denounced civil service reform, came out strongly for the annexation of Cuba, San Domingo, and Canada, and at home supported some of the most fragrant Tammany candidates ever to run for office. The one public act that met with Dana's unqualified favor was the McKinley tariff act, which, in the opinion of many historians today, was one of the most damaging pieces of legislation ever enacted. Dana thought it, as Allan Nevins notes, "the most scientific and valuable tariff the country ever had."

These views, which earned him the wholehearted condemnation of more honest and liberal editors, were expressed on an editorial page which, nevertheless, sparkled because of the pungent writing Dana and his able aides turned out. Whether humorous, political, or literary, *Sun* editorials were, in any event, highly readable. It was their moral content that was so sadly lacking.

Dana surrounded himself with first-rate writers. In the editorial writing sanctums were such men as Edward P. Mitchell, W. O. Bartlett, Henry B. Stanton, and Francis P. Church, who later wrote the famed "Yes, Virginia, there is a Santa Claus"

editorial. On the news side were Julian Ralph, David Graham
Phillips, Jacob Riis, and Richard Harding Davis. To all these
men, Dana was an omnipresent boss, but encouraging and
helping far more often than he condemned. He saved his
venom for his editorials. A man of dignified presence, he was
most at home and most human in the *Sun*'s offices, and he en-
deared himself to those who worked most closely with him.

In this post-Civil War period of change, Dana stood preeminent among the editors of his time. Raymond and Greeley
were dead; Samuel Bowles, who had made the Springfield
Republican not only the best provincial paper in the country
but also one of the most completely independent organs politically, had laid down his labors in favor of his son; Bennett,
Jr., was not considered first-rank competition.

There was only one man to challenge Dana—not in terms of
circulation, or news coverage, but as the foremost leader of
public opinion. Greeley had been that leader in his lifetime,
and now his role was taken up by a man Dana disdained as he
had disdained Greeley. The man was Edwin Lawrence Godkin.

William James wrote of Godkin: "To my generation, his was
certainly the towering influence in all thought concerning
public affairs, and indirectly his influence has assuredly been
more pervasive than that of any other writer of the generation,
for he influenced other writers who never quoted him, and
determined the whole current of discussion."

This man who achieved what Dana only aspired to was a
transplanted Anglo-Irishman, utterly devoted to his adopted
country, a college graduate, aloof from his professional colleagues and everyone else. Godkin was something new in
American journalism. Other editors before him were men of
the people who spoke to the people. Godkin did not mix with
the masses, had little real sympathy with them, and spoke
largely to intellectuals like himself. Yet he was the best and
most effective advocate of many liberal, progressive causes.
Even more, as Oswald Garrison Villard wrote later, "Almost

every one of the reforms in government of our day Godkin championed, and always by going to the root of the thing, by seeking the underlying principle and setting it forth."

The organs he chose for his work were most unpromising. From 1865 until 1899 he was editor-in-chief of the *Nation*, a brilliant but unprofitable publication which eventually became a weekly edition of the *Post*. The *Post* had come far since its founding by Alexander Hamilton. It had done best under the guidance of William Cullen Bryant, who had retired eventually to his own scholarly pursuits and left the paper in the hands of a succession of managing editors until 1881, when it was re-organized under the direction of three editors. Two of these were already noted in their own right—Horace White and Carl Schurz. The other was Godkin, who took over as sole editor in 1883 and continued in that post until the end of 1899.

In all this time, Godkin never reached more than 35,000 subscribers, including both papers, but his opinions penetrated to the farthest corners of the country through other newspapers, from ministers in their pulpits, out of the offices of college presidents, in the thoughts and speeches of public men, until they eventually reached the masses, who had never even heard of their author.

Governor David B. Hill of New York once remarked during the course of a battle in which Godkin was fighting the efforts of the Hill machine to railroad a man into office: "I don't care anything about the handful of Mugwumps who read it [meaning the *Evening Post*] in New York. The trouble with the damned sheet is that every editor in New York State reads it."

Godkin was not a great editor. He was an editorial writer of exceptional talent, an intellectual of extraordinary integrity, who boldly and fearlessly taught the country, as Henry Holt said, more than any other man in it. The instrument he used for the purpose was his prose style. Of it, Villard wrote:

His English was clear and straightforward, wonderfully powerful, free from all unnecessary verbiage. No one else, no Bowles, or Watterson, or

Raymond, has approached that style in our press except occasionally. For one thing, it was the writing of a completely educated man, polished by travel and the society of intellectual leaders everywhere, who wrote only with profound conviction, who till the last of his long career burned at injustice with the ardor of youth. To this he added a power of irony and sarcasm never equaled by anyone else, almost too great at times.

Godkin turned this wonderful instrument of his to oppose everything Dana stood for, not deliberately, but because his moral austerity was at the opposite pole from Dana's disillusioned cynicism. He was for civil service reform, against high tariffs, for sound currency, and against corruption of any kind in government.

Dana hurled his sarcasms and brilliant epigrams at politicians sometimes without reason and not often with much effect, but these same politicians writhed under Godkin's deadly pen. Like William Cobbett, Godkin was naturally combative and was not afraid of a possible libel, yet he had a remarkable versatility of style, a change of pace that made his writing continuously readable, combining "a lightness of touch and a weightiness of judgment," as Lowell remarked.

Such coldly witty irony, such penetrating devastation day after day was too much sometimes even for the intellectuals who comprised most of the *Post*'s readership. A wryly humorous story was circulated about the old lady who lived alone in the country but felt safe nevertheless, as she told her friends, because every evening at dusk the carrier threw her copy of the *Evening Post* on the porch, and "it just lay there and growled all night."

Perhaps no more appropriate example of Godkin's style could be cited than his public flaying of Jim Fisk, the stock gambler who looted the Erie Railroad in company with Daniel Drew and Jay Gould. On July 20, 1871, when Fisk was at the height of his fame as a gambler, financial manipulator, and man-about-town, Godkin attacked him in a *Nation* editorial titled "Notoriety." His words have a special application to our own time, read in the light of the Kefauver Committee hearings in 1951, which used television to expose the lives of latter-day big gamblers to public view.

Of Fisk, the editorial said in part:

This man came to New York a few years ago, a smart, impudent and ignorant pedlar, without morals or manners, and with a good deal of animal spirits, and in search of two things—physical enjoyment and notoriety. The physical enjoyment he might have had with a little money, but notoriety he could only get with the help of the newspapers, and this help they gave him to his heart's content.

He went incontinently to work to do strange, indecent, and outrageous things, and they went to work to chronicle them and denounce him for them. This was natural enough when he first showed himself on the scene as a swindler and blackguard, but when it was discovered that he was really indifferent to public opinion, that he had no shame and no sensibility, and really enjoyed his bad reputation, liked to be thought lewd and smart and knavish, the press at once began to treat him as a curious phenomenon, and laugh over him, chronicle his movements, record his jokes, give him pet names, and devoted an amount of time to the consideration of him as an entertainment simply, which proved the best advertisement any charlatan ever had, and gratified his dearest ambition. To be "in the papers" every day, to be thought smart by brokers and drygoodsmen and railroad men, are what he of all things most desires.

The treatment he received, too, helped all his speculations. It advertised his theatre (the Grand Opera House), his steamboats, and his railroads; it made the box in which he sat, and the carriage in which he rode with his strumpets, the objects on which all eyes were fixed. His fame, in short, filled the continent, and has now filled the civilized world.

At last, too, the jocose treatment of him resulted in making him look less disreputable than he was at the beginning; from laughing over him a good deal, people got to thinking him "not such a bad fellow after all"; and, finally, we came to see business suspended at midday in the principal thoroughfare of the commercial capital of the country, whose courts and legislature he had corrupted, in order to see him ride down as elected Colonel at the head of a regiment nine hundred strong, composed of respectable young Americans. As colonel of this regiment, he asked for a municipal invitation for himself and it from the city of Boston, and, amongst other things, expressed a desire to have "divine service" celebrated for his benefit on Boston Common. The newspapers, thereupon, took this up, and discussed it, and joked over it, and showed the absurdity of it in article after article, and paragraph after paragraph, as if Fisk was really trying to play the hypocrite, and was trying to pass himself off as a religious man, the fact being that he was merely gratifying a showman's love of making a sensation, and by the newspaper exposures of him as an impudent dog got all he wanted, and probably far more than he looked for. . . .

We cannot make Fisk a person of importance, and fill everybody's mind every morning with his doings and sayings, without making Fisk's career an object of secret admiration to thousands, and making thousands in their inmost hearts determine to imitate him. The newspapers ought to remember that, while for some offenders against public decency and security denunciation may be a proper and effective punishment, the only way of reaching others is not to mention them.

A year later, Fisk lay dying in the lobby of the Grand Central Hotel, shot by Edward Stokes, his rival for the affections of the actress Josie Mansfield.

It was such public attacks as these which earned Godkin his enormous reputation as a leader of opinion, while, at the same time, he failed to be any other kind of leader because of the curious blind spots in his character which prevented him from speaking directly to the people. He had the upper-middle-class Englishman's prejudice against the small merchant, and he failed utterly to understand the tidal rise of the labor union movement.

If Dana sneered that Godkin's political idealism was all theory without practical substance, it had to be admitted that there was some truth in the charge. Yet when the final assessment was made, it could be seen that Godkin was a powerful constructive force in the country through his newspaper, and Dana, by contrast, was only a man rich enough through the successful management of the *Sun* to afford the luxury of venting his prejudices and opinions in its editorial columns.

But Dana could point to the solid achievements of the *Sun* in its news columns, and as for his personal life, he took pride in intellectual and esthetic accomplishments of his own. Before he died in 1897, he had used the leisure of his later years to learn most of the European languages, and he conducted classes in Dante, raised rare foreign trees, shrubs, and flowers, considered himself a connoisseur of wines, and spent his time with writers, musicians, and artists.

His editorial enemies would not permit Dana to escape entirely into the pleasures of his old age. This caustic editorial appeared in the *New York Press,* a penny paper of no particular distinction.

HE LOVES THE FLAG, HE LOVES THE TREE

An antipathy to clergymen and a caressing tenderness for tigers [meaning Tammany] may coexist in one bosom with some of the finest emotions of which our mortal nature is capable.

We say this because we had always known that Mr. Dana loves the flag, and because we know now—having read "Garden and Forest"—that Mr. Dana loves a tree. We find therein that Mr. Dana has sniffed the balsamic air of the *Pinetum schoberianum* and that everything in it has his cordial and hearty support and approbation, from the *abies amabitis* to the *Cunninghamia sinensis.*

It is lucky for these trees that Mr. Dana loves them. Overburdened as they are with first names and last names, we don't see how they could survive the infliction of some of the weird and eerie middle names with which Mr. Dana is wont to christen the specimens of man that delight him not.

But what we want to pin attention to is that Mr. Dana's bosom is not all one savage gloat in this time of tigerish triumph. He loves the flag, he loves a tree; and on those two points he is habitually and nobly right.

When Dana died in 1897, the *Sun* carried no obituary. None was necessary to preserve his memory in the annals of journalism. Whatever his faults, he had made a newspaper that was a model in brilliance of writing and coverage of the news. The glow he gave to it persisted for many years after his death, until the fine traditions he established faded to ultimate extinction.

Godkin outlived Dana by only five years. His health broke in 1900, and in 1901 he sailed for his native England. There he spent a comparatively happy year, even contributing pieces to the *Evening Post,* written in his old, forceful style. But he failed in health and died in 1902, in a house beside the peaceful River Dart.

With the passing of these two men, the "good old days" of American journalism came to an end. In their last years, the New York newspaper world was turned upside down by the rivalry of Hearst and Pulitzer, and all over the country new forces were shaping the business of gathering and printing news.

Many of the changes were, eventually, for the better. But it was also true that, after the deaths of Godkin and Dana, the editorial pages of American newspapers never again spoke with so much conviction, strength, and authority, and never again were they so influential in shaping the opinions of the people who read them.

6

Joseph Pulitzer
and His "World"

THE MAN WHO DOMINATED TURN-OF-THE-CENTURY JOURNALISM
in America and left behind him a rich tradition which has survived the most noted of his two newspapers was Joseph Pulitzer
(see photograph 3), born in 1847 "a simple Jewish-Hungarian
immigrant of humblest origin," as Oswald Garrison Villard
once described him. This man wrote one of the proudest
chapters in the history of his profession.

Pulitzer started his career in America from scratch, but he
came of a good and reasonably well-to-do family in his native
Mako, Hungary. His father, Philip, had been a prosperous
grain merchant, a Jew of Magyar descent who had married a
Catholic girl, Louise Berger. Shortly after his retirement,
Philip died of a heart attack and his widow soon married another merchant.

Although the records are obscure, it appears that young
Pulitzer, at seventeen, found his stepfather not to his liking,
though he idolized his mother, and consequently decided to
leave home and make his own way. He had enjoyed the advantages of private schools and private tutors, but they had not
fitted him for anything in particular. One of his biographers
describes him as a "tall, scraggy youth with long, thick black
hair, large head, and oversized nose . . . about six feet two and

a half inches tall, ungainly in appearance, awkward in movement, lacking entirely in the art of human relations."

He had one quality that might have foretold his future—a well developed talent for asking questions and getting answers from people who didn't want to reply. At the moment, however, he had no aspirations for journalism. He wanted to be a soldier. But even in a world torn by wars and rumors of wars in 1864, it was no easy job for such doubtful material as young Pulitzer to find the military life he craved.

Austria seemed ready to cast its army into Bismarck's scheme to grab Schleswig and Holstein, and Joseph applied there first. He was rejected. The recruiters told him he had weak eyes and an unpromising physique. He went on to Paris then, hoping to join the Foreign Legion that Napoleon III was forming to seize Mexico while the Americans were fighting among themselves. The French thought no better of him than the Austrians.

Pulitzer swallowed his anger and disappointment and traveled across the Channel to London, where he applied for the British Army, then eager to get recruits for the Indian empire. Once more he was rejected, with the added comment that even if he qualified physically, he could not speak English.

It must have been a humiliating experience for a seventeen-year-old boy, and probably his mood was a black one as he turned toward home. On the way, he stopped in Hamburg and made a desperate effort to ship as a common seaman. The old salts only laughed at him.

At this juncture he fell in with an agent of the infamous Civil War draft system, by which a man called for service might hire a substitute to serve for him. These agents were abroad in Europe doing a lively business in hiring young men who wanted adventure and an opportunity to get to America. The recruit got his passage; the agent took the $500 bounty for himself.

There could have been no more willing victim than Joseph Pulitzer. He signed up at once, and took passage to Boston.

Pulitzer himself told several stories about what happened next (the man who was a perfectionist in the matter of accuracy was anything but accurate about the details of his early life) but the story commonly accepted, probably because it is the best one, relates that Pulitzer found out about the bounty scheme on the way over, jumped ship in Boston Harbor, swam ashore, and collected the $500.

In any event, he enlisted for a year in the First New York (Lincoln) Cavalry, which had been organized by an earlier immigrant who was to win journalistic renown, Colonel Carl Schurz. The army life was not what the eager recruit had thought it would be. To a man who was an incorrigible question-asker and who despised anyone in authority who withheld information, it was nearly intolerable. Pulitzer fought four skirmishes in the field and innumerable others in barracks and on the parade ground. Once he narrowly escaped court-martial when he struck a noncommissioned officer.

Discharged at last in 1865, he spent a miserable few months, working at anything that would hold body and soul together, trying to learn English, and sitting in City Hall Park. Across its clipped lawns, along Park Row, stood the offices of the *Times,* the *World,* the *Tribune,* the *Herald,* and the *Sun.* But Pulitzer had no yearning at the moment to join the company of Dana, Greeley, and the elder Bennett. He wanted most to live where he could learn the language of his adopted country. A practical joker told him the best place to learn it was St. Louis—St. Louis, which had one of the largest concentrations of Germanic immigrants in the country.

Pulitzer took the advice seriously, and so he came to the city where he launched his newspaper career. After three years of touch-and-go existence, during which he worked once more at anything he could get, he got a job on the *Westliche Post,* the city's leading German daily, then under the direction of its owner, Pulitzer's old cavalry commander, Colonel Schurz.

Judging from contemporary accounts, Pulitzer's impact on the newspaper business was startling, at least to the other St.

Louis reporters. They had never seen a reporter like the lank, dark young man who burst on a story with the furious energy of a Kansas tornado, button-holed everyone in sight, and asked more questions in five minutes than the ordinary reporter could think of in an hour.

The others made fun of Joe Pulitzer's strange appearance and behavior (no novelty in his life), but they could hardly laugh off his accomplishments. In less than a year, he was by far the town's leading reporter. He excelled particularly at political reporting, and his fearless, vivid accounts of what went on in the State House caught public attention and attracted the notice of professional politicians, who concluded that he ought to run for the State House of Representatives. By this time, of course, he had learned English and obtained his certificate of naturalization.

Even in a legislature not especially noted for its decorous behavior, Pulitzer was a fireball. The climax of his legislative career came only a year after he was seated, when he shot and wounded a well-known lobbyist. His admirers, who by that time were numerous, financed his fine and court costs.

For a time it seemed that he might be headed for a political career. He became one of the city's three police commissioners, worked ardently for the Liberal Republican movement, and helped nominate Greeley in 1872. With Greeley's failure, the movement failed too, and the disappointed Pulitzer turned to the Democrats and was thereafter a lifelong member of the party.

Meanwhile, he had acquired a part interest in the *Westliche Post*. With the same talent he had shown for reporting and politics, he maneuvered a series of financial transactions in which he sold his *Post* interest at a profit, bought the bankrupt *Staats-Zeitung* for next to nothing, and sold its AP franchise to the *Daily Globe,* again for a substantial profit.

With these monies, he was able to finance his study of law and politics. By this time Pulitzer was able to write English far better than most native Americans, and his knowledge of

American history and institutions exceeded that of most politicians. Moreover, he had become a magnificent public speaker.
The combination of these qualities made his voice a potent
force in the Missouri constitutional convention of 1875 and in
the campaign for Tilden. The District of Columbia admitted
him to the bar, and a remote cousin of Jefferson Davis's, Kate
Davis, admitted him to matrimony.

Joe Pulitzer could easily have become a career politician,
possibly a great one, in 1878, but he chose instead to buy a
newspaper, and from that moment his life was pointed in a
single direction.

His purchase, which cost him $2,500, was the *St. Louis Dis-
patch.* It was $30,000 in debt and its sole asset of any value was
an Associated Press franchise. Pulitzer put aside $2,700 (his
total resources) as running expenses for the paper, and his managers told him they thought the sheet could operate for seventeen weeks on that sum.

Before the $2,700 was gone, the *Dispatch* had turned the
corner for good. Its recovery was substantially aided by its
merger with the old *Post*. This was a joint ownership at first,
but Pulitzer acquired sole control within a year, and in three
years the *Post-Dispatch* was earning $45,000 annually.

Pulitzer could not forget politics. He used the paper in his
old, fearless manner to attack corruption from the first day
he owned it. Twice personally assaulted by the people he exposed, Pulitzer printed names and facts about rich tax-dodgers,
unmasked a public utility's franchise extortion, and broke up a
gambling ring which had flourished with police protection.
The gambling fight was the toughest. It took three years, but
the victory justified one of the editor's prime contentions:
"Never drop a big thing until you have gone to the bottom of
it."

He took a final personal fling at politics. In 1880, he was
both a delegate to the Democratic national convention and an
unsuccessful candidate for Congress. That was his last personal
participation except for the odd, anti-climactic episode five

years later, when he was actually elected to Congress from New York, but resigned after a few months, in utter disgust with what he was expected to do and be as a national legislator.

Pulitzer might have remained in St. Louis, rooting out corruption and consolidating his interests, except for two personal shortcomings. One was his hypersensitivity to criticism; the other was his increasingly bad health. The latter was at least partly the result of a body, badly equipped from the start, being subjected to the exorbitant demands of a driving mind. Pulitzer's insatiable curiosity, his feverish zeal for hard work, his complete disregard for his own physical capabilities, laid the groundwork early in life for the ills which made his later adult years so tragic.

As for the criticism, Pulitzer learned to fight attack with attack when he took on men like Dana and Hearst, but in the earlier St. Louis days he was hurt and dismayed by the public anger directed against him and the *Post-Dispatch* when his chief editorial writer killed a well-known lawyer in an argument over the paper's attack on the victim's law firm. The fact that Pulitzer's man escaped prosecution, on a self-defense plea, stirred up a tempest of public resentment.

Seeking to escape it and searching another outlet for his restlessness, Pulitzer started on a trip to Europe. While he tarried in New York, en route, representatives of Jay Gould, the noted financier, approached him, and after considerable negotiation, sold him the *New York World,* which had struggled for survival virtually since its founding as a penny religious daily.

The price of the *World* was $346,000, to be paid in installments. Pulitzer could afford it: the *Post-Dispatch* by that time was netting him $85,000 a year. (Today its operating expenses alone amount to more than $15,000,000 annually.)

Though this abrupt move left the St. Louis paper without the physical presence of its owner, it never, except for a brief period, lost the dominating force of his personality behind it. That personality had been stamped ineradicably on the paper and the city. When Pulitzer departed for New York, the *Post-*

Dispatch told its readers that he would still be its editor and proprietor, and promised that it would "continue to be a faithful and untiring chronicle of events, expanding with its own force and growing with its surroundings." It did exactly that during Pulitzer's lifetime, and after his death, it carried on his ideals.

Pulitzer bought the *World* on May 10, 1883, and almost from that moment, it became not only commercially successful, but a prime factor in American journalism.

Under the masthead on the editorial page, Pulitzer proclaimed the purposes of his newspaper in a statement that remains today one of the finest expressions of journalistic idealism. The *Post-Dispatch* still carries it on its own editorial page. This was what it said:

An institution that should always fight for progress and reform, never tolerate injustice or corruption, always fight demagogues of all parties, never belong to any party, always oppose privileged classes and public plunderers, never lack sympathy with the poor, always remain devoted to the public welfare, never be satisfied with merely printing news, always be drastically independent, never be afraid to attack wrong, whether by predatory plutocracy or predatory poverty.

In addition, the *World* announced a ten-point platform. It would, said Pulitzer, advocate taxing luxuries, inheritances, large incomes, and monopolies. It would fight for the abolishment of all special privileges possessed by corporations. It favored tariffs for revenue only. It called for civil service reform, and severe punishment for corrupt officials, particularly those who bought votes. It asked punishment, too, for employers who attempted to coerce their employees in elections.

Such a platform invited conservative denunciation, and Pulitzer heard himself called a demagogue, a socialist, and a dangerous radical. On the other hand, the new paper was joyously received by workingmen, who were referred to in its pages as the true American aristocracy, "the aristocracy of labor."

Shrewdly, Pulitzer aimed the news content of his paper directly at these aristocrats, about whose tastes in reading matter he had no illusions. Taking a leaf from the elder Bennett's book, he revived and improved upon the sensational methods by which the *Herald* had leaped to infamy. Deliberately he played to the appetites of the masses with sensational headlines, explicit coverage of crime and sex, and plenty of pictures, until the upholders of Bennett's journalism were shocked, and the *World* was barred from New York's "refined" homes and clubs.

This approach, however, combined with Pulitzer's natural genius for newspaper management, enabled the *World* to earn a $500,000 profit within three years. In October 1887, Pulitzer established the *Evening World,* which was even more successful in the long run than its morning partner.

Along with crime and sex in the news columns, Pulitzer carried out the promise of his platform by embarking on a series of crusades in the public interest, attacking mercilessly every evidence of greed, privilege, and corruption he could find, as he had in St. Louis.

Between the news pages and the editorial page there was a vast intellectual gulf. The editorials were brilliant, accurate, and high-minded. They were also extremely effective in the fashioning of liberal opinion. Thus, the *World* appealed to two different classes of readers, and in this split personality were embodied its serious defects.

Pulitzer wanted the *World* to be the workingman's paper, and to maintain its broad mass appeal, he was willing to be as lowbrow as possible in the news columns, even to the extent of using cheap paper and ink when the paper could have afforded to look much more respectable. But the editorial page, with its highbrow, intellectual liberal appeal, was not read by most of the *World's* audience, and more important, was not read by the middlebrows, that body of substantial citizens who could not stomach the *World's* sensationalism and thereby missed the progressive leadership which Pulitzer was supplying on the editorial page to a rather limited minority.

Consequently, the *World* always fell short of what it might have achieved, although its ultimate accomplishment was re-

markable just the same. Worse, for a brief period before the
turn of the century, the paper was actually in danger because
of Pulitzer's determination to hold his mass market, no matter
what the cost.

It was the coming of William Randolph Hearst that forced
the *World* into this one really discreditable episode in its history. The New York *Journal* that Hearst started in 1896
showed the city what yellow journalism, a phrase his paper
inspired, could really be. If the *World* had made the old
Herald seemed pale, the new *Journal* outdid Pulitzer's paper
in sensationalism.

Pulitzer fought back. He dropped the price of the morning
World to a penny, and drew every trick he knew out of the bag.
When Hearst began to whip up public sentiment for a war
against Spain, Pulitzer answered with a campaign of white-hot
patriotism that forced his rival to imagine new atrocities, new
issues, and new sensations.

It is still popularly believed that this journalistic conflict of
super-patriotism in the interests of circulation was responsible
for the Spanish-American War; Hearst himself held this exaggerated view. Although the causes of the war were considerably
more complex than a circulation battle between two New York
newspaper publishers, it is nevertheless true that the irresponsible rivalry of these men produced a climate of public opinion
in which it would have been virtually impossible to prevent
war.

The episode was a costly one for both Hearst and Pulitzer.
The cost to Pulitzer was measured in prestige as well as cash,
because the positive virtues of the *World*, as they had been expressed in its crusades and editorials, were lost sight of temporarily in the madness of the war period. The *World*, like
the *Journal*, was banished not only from homes and clubs, but
from public libraries as well.

Godkin condemned both papers with the chill disdain which
dripped from his scalpel pen. "A yellow journal office," he
wrote in the *Evening Post*, "is probably the nearest approach,

in atmosphere, to hell existing in any Christian state, for in gambling houses, brothels, and even in brigands' caves there is a constant exhibition of fear of the police, which is in itself a sort of homage to morality or acknowledgment of its existence."

Financially, the battle of the two titans was exhaustingly expensive. Hearst's bill has been estimated all the way from $500,000 to $8,000,000. Whatever it was, it came out of his own pocket because the *Journal* was not yet a sound financial proposition. Otherwise, the young Californian had nothing to lose in the encounter. The *Journal* had no traditions, no ideals, no superb editorial page to sacrifice. Pulitzer had to put all these attributes on the line, and he also had to draw from his paper's profits. Fortunately, the *World* had, by 1890, not only paid back its purchase price to Jay Gould, but it had created a personal fortune for its owners and made enough to build and equip a $2,500,000 building on Park Row.

There was yet another cost: the further assault on Joseph Pulitzer's precarious health, which already was being held together by sheer will power. For Pulitzer was forced to conduct this toughest fight of his career from the depths of a general physical failure that had forced him, in 1887, to retire from on-the-spot management of the *World*.

At least one of his biographers believes that the breakdown that led to his retirement was precipitated by his fight against another rival editor, Dana of the *Sun*. As the mouthpiece of the city's conservative financial interests, the aging Dana had attacked Pulitzer and the *World* at every turn. Pulitzer referred to his opponent as "Charles Ananias Dana," and Dana in turn called Pulitzer "Judas." Dana pontificated in one editorial: "I have never published a falsehood." Pulitzer retorted sourly: "That's another lie."

In the fury of a campaign over the candidacy of a Tammany man for the District Attorney's office (Dana cynically supported Tammany in this case because Pulitzer was against it), the *Sun* reached its lowest point in name-calling, tossing such epithets at the *World*'s publisher as "renegade Jew," "wandering Jew," and "cringer for nickels in a barroom."

While this shameful campaign roared on to an ultimate Dana victory, Pulitzer scarcely ate or slept. Then came the double shock of defeat and Dana's bigoted invectives, hurled in the closing days. It was soon after that Pulitzer discovered one day he could not see the type on the galley proofs of some editorials. The doctors said his eyesight was seriously damaged, and accurately predicted that blindness would probably result. In time, Pulitzer could see no more than dim outlines of objects near at hand, and then only in late afternoon or early evening.

The doctors also told him that he was suffering from an acute nervous disorder (today it seems probable that Pulitzer's troubles were largely psychosomatic) and they advised him to give up work and worry, take a complete rest, and move to California if possible.

Of course Pulitzer did none of these things. His blindness forced him to stay away from the office, but he maintained a rigid control of his dailies with the aid of a corps of secretaries. These men read to him much of the copy that went into the *World,* and read whatever else in the paper and in other papers, magazines, and books might interest their boss.

He traveled constantly for nearly twenty years, restless, suffering, seeking cures from the world's best doctors. They examined him, saw that his blindness was organic and irreparable, and presumably some of them observed that his "nervous condition" was really severe psychoneurosis, but it is doubtful whether any would have dared suggest the new psychoanalysis as a treatment.

Sick as he was, Pulitzer functioned mentally far better than most people. He edited the *World* from wherever he might be—New York, Bar Harbor, Lakewood, London, Paris, Aix-les-Bains, Wiesbaden, Berlin, Switzerland, the Riviera, or a dozen other places. Sometimes he crossed the ocean and recrossed it without stopping on the other side.

Always, aided by his small army of secretarial assistants, he

edited the *World*. He advised, complained, reprimanded, and
ordered. His criticisms of the paper's reporting and editing
were detailed and most of them were brilliant. Unlike the
younger Bennett's befuddled attempts to edit the *Herald* from
his self-imposed exile, Pulitzer's genius controlled and carried
the *World* to its finest efforts, through the ceaseless flow of
memoranda that issued from him for nearly twenty years.

One of these memoranda read: "Concentrate your brain upon
these objectives: 1st. What is original, distinctive, dramatic,
romantic . . . odd, apt to be talked about, without shocking
good taste or lowering the general tone, good tone and above
all without impairing the confidence of the people in the truth
of the stories or the character of the paper for reliability and
scrupulous cleanness. . . . 4th. Accuracy, accuracy, accuracy.
Also terseness, intelligent, not stupid, condensation. No picture
or illustration unless it is first class, both in ideas and execution."

His instructions to the *World* staff were often studded with
epigrams, some of them now classic, like his admonition that
"Accuracy is to a newspaper what virtue is to a woman."

It must be remembered that the genius which guided and
shaped the *World* through its difficult years and triumphant
years alike, even through the bitter fight with Hearst, came
from a man whose mental and physical condition would have
made a hospital case out of an ordinary individual.

The most prominent symptom of Pulitzer's neurosis was an
extreme sensitivity to noise. At home he lived in a soundproof
room. In hotels abroad he would rent the rooms above, below,
and at both sides of his own suite to insure quiet. Still, inevitably, he would be disturbed to the point of hysteria. The
slightest sound—silverware clinking, someone sipping soup, a
door shutting, a paper rattling—would be enough to set him
off. Only the kind of noise that was not unexpected, and that
he could enjoy, was tolerable. He loved to ride, for example,
and the noise of horses did not prevent him from riding occasionally in Central Park with Arthur Brisbane. The steady

wash of surf on shore he loved, and the gusty whopping of wind did not disturb him.

But let a guest at dinner crack a nut unexpectedly and Pulitzer would suffer a paroxysm of pain, anger, and fright. He would curse violently (an art at which he was a master), shout, shake his fists, stamp his feet, and wind up most often in tears. After these attacks, he would be exhausted and then the physical symptoms would appear in the form of respiratory ailments— colds, coughs, bronchitis, and asthma—and, of course, he had chronic indigestion. As the attacks became more frequent and more severe over the years, his heart naturally began to falter under the strain.

That a man in this condition, blind in the bargain, could run a great newspaper by remote control and display an insatiable curiosity about everything in the world stands as one of the most incredible facts in the history of journalism.

In such crippled state, Pulitzer brought the *World* back from the depths it had reached in the Hearst battle. He made it respectable again, and shaped it as less of a workingman's organ and more a newspaper aimed at those who believed in liberal democratic ideals, whether at home or abroad. It spoke boldly, courageously, even passionately for free speech, personal liberty, and government by constitutionalism. It was against prohibition, a large army and navy, the kind of jingoism it had indulged in during the Spanish-American War, and the movements to annex Hawaii, the Philippines, and the Virgin Islands. As it had always done, it fought hardest against privilege, whether in government or business, and it attacked relentlessly what Pulitzer called "the money power."

Although the *World* generally supported the Democratic Party, it maintained its independence and bolted frequently, notably in 1896, when it opposed Bryan and free silver. It was relentlessly and invariably against the Democratic shenanigans of Tammany Hall. Perhaps most notably it was entirely free of advertising domination, at a time when many otherwise respectable papers could not say the same.

In these later years, the *World* was a profound influence on both the press and the political life of the nation. Grover Cleveland largely owed his first term in the White House to its support. Its success was reflected in the circulation figures. Before Pulitzer's death, the morning edition had reached 300,000, the evening 400,000, and the Sunday edition 600,000.

The earlier split in personality survived in the difference between the morning and evening papers. The morning *World* was the one that upheld Pulitzer's reputation. The evening *World* was a somewhat disreputable sister, playing the old appeal to the masses, and making more money by doing so. While writers of distinction from both sides of the Atlantic, men like H. G. Wells and Frank A. Vanderlip, wrote for the morning paper, the evening edition was busy dissecting, most often anonymously, the lives and loves of the city's more sordid citizens.

Meanwhile, Pulitzer realized, amid the darkness and suffering of his illness, that he could not continue his personal fight against death much longer, and he began to plan for the future of his properties and to implement his plans for the improvement of journalism. As early as 1903 he had announced that he intended to found a school of journalism at Columbia University, and his will provided two million dollars for the purpose. Since its establishment in 1912 more than two thousand graduates, whose names include many of the foremost men and women in the profession, have come from its classrooms.

The other major provision of Pulitzer's will specified that the income from half of the school's second million was to be used for "prizes or scholarships for the encouragement of public service, public morals, American Literature, and the advancement of education." These Pulitzer Prizes have become a trademark in American journalistic life, despite often controversial awards.

When Joseph Pulitzer died in October 29, 1911, as he lay aboard his yacht, anchored in the harbor of Charleston, South Carolina, he had provided what he thought were adequate safeguards for his newspaper properties. The will expressly provided that nothing in it should be "taken to authorize or impower the sale or disposition by the trustees of any of the Press Publishing Company, publisher of the *New York World* newspaper."

Besides this, he reposed a good measure of his hopes in his three sons, Ralph, Herbert, and Joseph. During his last years, he had given them an intensive, often rough, schooling in newspaper management, virtually bullying them into learning the workings of the paper. All of them resented this treatment, particularly Joseph, who was a proud, rebellious young man.

Pulitzer appeared to place most of his confidence in Ralph and Herbert, but it was Joseph who got his closest attention. He sent the young man to the *Post-Dispatch* for a while, then put him to work on the evening *World* as a reporter under Charles E. Chapin, the city editor who, before he murdered his wife and went to Sing Sing, established himself as the toughest man who ever sat at a city desk. It was Chapin of whom the probably apocryphal story is often told that he once greeted a reporter who had been kicked out and beaten up by a reluctant news source with these immortal words: "You go back and tell that so-and-so he can't intimidate *me*."

Chapin is said to have fired young Pulitzer, although the present publisher of the *Post-Dispatch* remembers differently. In any case, when the elder Pulitzer was relieved of his agony at last, it was Ralph and Herbert, not young Joseph, who took over the reins of the *World*.

The man who was its guiding spirit, however, until his death in 1925, was Frank I. Cobb, whom Pulitzer himself had selected as editor. Cobb was a young Detroit newspaperman, a direct, blunt individual whose writing had the elemental, homely, rugged qualities which had distinguished the prose of Cobbett and Greeley. He accustomed the *World*'s readers to his forthright, honest editorials, and he swung the paper steadily to its position as the foremost Democratic voice in the nation.

Under Cobb's direction, the *World* was uncompromisingly

honest, afraid of no one, and came to be known to newspapermen and its readers as the most patriotic and liberal daily the
country had ever known. It fought, in the Pulitzer tradition,
against corruption in government and business, and it was
fiercely independent of party or any other influence.

Its brilliance did not save the *World*. After Cobb's death,
Walter Lippmann succeeded him as editor, but, although he
was splendidly qualified as an analyst and commentator, he was
not the man to edit the *World*. Nor were Ralph and Herbert
Pulitzer the men to manage the *World*'s business side.

The *World* came to an end in 1931, an end that many in the
profession thought unnecessary. The brothers got the Surrogate
Court in New York to set aside the provision of the will which
prohibited sale, and the paper was sold to Roy Howard, repre-
senting the Scripps-Howard interests, for five million dollars,
with a half-million down. Although Mr. Howard expressed the
pious hope that this transaction would mean the rebirth, not
the death of the *World,* the traditions of Pulitzer disappeared
in less than five years. Merged with the *Telegram,* the *World-
Telegram* bore no resemblance to its great predecessor except,
perhaps, in the minds of its new owners.

The Pulitzer idea survived, however, in his namesake Joseph
and the St. Louis *Post-Dispatch,* of which he is presently president and publisher. The *Post-Dispatch* today is one of the best
American newspapers, and certainly the most truly liberal, in
the best sense of that much abused word. As a national newspaper, it has been called the *Manchester Guardian* of America,
and its battles against chicanery and injustice have earned it,
with coincidental justice, many Pulitzer Prizes. It also helped
to keep St. Louis one of the few healthily competitive cities
until as late as 1951, when its worthy rival, the *Star-Post,* threw
in the sponge, leaving the afternoon field to the *Post-Dispatch*
and the morning field to the *Globe-Democrat.*

The giants of nineteenth-century journalism, looking down
today from whatever part of heaven may be reserved for news-

papermen, would be able to see little evidence, or none at all, of the great newspapers they established. All except Joseph Pulitzer, that is, who could see in the *Post-Dispatch* the visible and triumphant survival of the ideals he gave to American journalism nearly a century ago.

7

Last of the Titans:
William Randolph Hearst

WHEN THE PERSONAL JOURNALISM OF THE NINETEENTH CENTURY gave way to the comparatively sober and more responsible newspaper-making we know today, the business lost much of its color. The titans of that flamboyant century—Greeley, Dana, the Bennetts, Pulitzer, and the others—bowed off the stage. As journalism became big business, the big businessmen took their places.

One survived. At the midway point of the twentieth century, William Randolph Hearst (see photograph 4) stood incredibly, ruggedly alone, eighty-eight years old and still the driving force behind a newspaper empire which had endured more than fifty years.

Down the long decades of a fantastic career, Hearst's politics had changed. The publisher who led the extreme right-wing pack of Republicans in full cry after the detractors of General MacArthur in 1951 was the same Hearst who savagely depicted President McKinley, the apotheosis of Republican conservatism, as the leader of a capitalist "plunderbund," which was ruining the honest masses.

Doubtless this did not appear as an inconsistency to Mr. Hearst. In the nineties, Wall Street was the enemy of the people. In the nineteen fifties, the Democrats (and, in fact, all shades of opinion that differed from his own) were the enemy.

The Hearst newspapers, at least according to their own lights, have always been the champion of the masses.

These papers are also unchanged in one other major respect after more than a half-century. They represent the most sensational element in American journalism, as they have during their entire existence. They are at once personal papers, in the old nineteenth-century sense of the phrase; "yellow journals," in only a somewhat diluted sense of the catchword that Hearst's *New York Journal* gave to the language; and sensational organs in such constant matters as typography, layout, and treatment of the news.

Even after the vast Hearst holdings were partially liquidated in 1937, against the day when death and taxes would lay final siege to one of the most remarkable financial fortresses any American ever built, there remained a formidable collection of nineteen newspapers and eleven magazines.

As of 1951, the Hearst newspapers included the *Examiner* and *Call-Bulletin* in San Francisco, the *Examiner* and the *Herald and Express* in Los Angeles, the *Chicago Herald-American*, the *American*, the *Record*, and *Sunday Advertiser* in Boston, the *Journal-American* and the tabloid *Mirror* in New York, the *Albany Times-Union*, the *Sunday American* and *News-Post* in Baltimore, and the *Pittsburgh Sun-Telegraph, Detroit Times, Seattle Post-Intelligencer, Oakland Post-Enquirer, San Antonio Light*, and *Milwaukee Sentinel*.

In the same year, Hearst's magazines included *Good Housekeeping*, in its American and British editions considered by some experts as the second most valuable magazine property; *Cosmopolitan, Harper's Bazaar, Junior Bazaar, Motor, Motor Boating Magazine, American Druggist, Town and Country, House Beautiful*, and *Connoisseur* (with *International Studio*).

The pulsebeat of all these publications lay under the finger of William Randolph Hearst, proprietor of the most amazing journalistic show on earth. From the house in Beverly Hills to which he had retired from the fabulous glories of his enormous "ranch," San Simeon, he kept flowing the endless river of directives to editors and executives, and the policy instructions beginning with the historic words, "Chief says." Hearst's health suffered progressive disintegration for nearly five years before he died in August 1951, but there was little evidence of it in the baskets of editorial matter that Hearst personally wrote, rewrote, and edited—both his own and others' copy. He was actively and indubitably the Chief, as he had been always. Somewhat of an anachronism, perhaps, and as controversial a figure as ever, but still the Chief.

His career can hardly be more than glimpsed in a single chapter; his biographers have confessed themselves abashed at trying to capture it between book covers. But it is possible at least to record the high points of that career and assess partially its effect on American life.

Unlike all the other newspaper titans before him, who had been compelled to pull themselves up from poverty, Hearst was born to wealth, in San Francisco, on April 29, 1863. His father, George Hearst, was a miner who had made a fortune from the vast silver treasures of the West, and later rose to public eminence as a United States Senator. His mother, Phebe Apperson Hearst, a wholly admirable woman who idolized her "Willy," saw to it that the Senator's money, before and after his death, was not stinted when it came to satisfying her son's wants.

From the first it appeared that he wanted to do little more than spend it. At Harvard he was a playboy, often in trouble with the authorities, and contemptuous of his professors, who at that time included some of the greatest figures in American scholarship. To express his contempt for these men, including Josiah Royce and William James, Hearst sent each of them by messenger a handsome chamber-pot, with the professor's likeness on the bottom inside.

For this and other practical jokes the Harvard authorities expelled him, an incident which might have darkened any other boy's life but to Hearst was only a minor affair. His interests were already far from the campus, and they had taken the primary shapes that were to dominate his life. He had gone to Washington in 1885 to see the Presidential inauguration of his father's friend, Grover Cleveland, and thus been introduced to the perennially fascinating world of politics. At the same time, he had become an enthusiastic admirer of Joseph Pulitzer, and the methods by which the *World* was then turning New York upside down.

Only a year before he was thrust out into the world by the Harvard authorities, young Hearst had written optimistically to his father that he was getting on in his studies well enough "to be able to spend considerable time in outside reading and in Journalistic investigation." The letter was written from Washington, where Congress was the subject of his current journalistic investigation. He thought Congress "as stupid as it is possible to conceive of."

It was in this now famous letter that Hearst first broached to his father the idea that he should take over the San Francisco *Examiner,* a shabby, faltering sheet that Senator Hearst had acquired five years before, for political rather than literary reasons. The ambitious son saw in this limping newspaper the avenue to fulfillment of his overpowering desire to emulate Pulitzer.

Hearst's letter to his father described in detail how he would remold the *Examiner* and make it a successful property. More than fifty years later, when the letter was released, Hearst remarked with becoming humility: "At that time my father was the only person in the world who, in my modest opinion, knew more than I did, although I have learned since, to my consternation, that quite a number of other people in this surprising world are gifted with thought reservoirs of a more spectacular order than my own."

There was little of this modesty in the letter, which told the Senator plainly that his son was convinced he could run a newspaper successfully. However, it helped persuade the elder Hearst. The letter was written in 1885, Willy was expelled from Harvard the following year, and in March 1887, he became proprietor of the *Examiner.* Immediately, the result was the paper's spectacular success, as its new owner carried out the promises and plans he had outlined.

In its first year, the *Examiner* demonstrated that the new "New York journalism" which Pulitzer's *World* had inaugurated could be just as successful on the other side of the continent. Soon after Hearst took over, he produced his first major news beat by sending a special chartered train to cover a disaster, the burning of the Hotel Del Monte in Monterey. Taking full advantage of the invention of photo-engraving a few years earlier, in 1884, he began to add picture enterprise to his news methods. Hearst became a camera enthusiast himself, built a darkroom in his Sausalito weekend home, and went on a tour of Europe and Egypt, snapping pictures everywhere.

The *Examiner*'s staff was brilliant because Hearst hired the best men available and he paid whatever was necessary to get them. Money was no object. His managing editor was the extraordinary Sam Chamberlain. Writers like Ambrose Bierce, Arthur McEwen, and Winifred Black were on the staff, and E. L. "Phinny" Thayer contributed the immortal "Casey At The Bat" to the *Examiner*'s columns in that first astonishing year of its existence.

Hearst was also furthering his political interests, perhaps with his young eyes already fixed on the White House. In 1888, he spent $80,000 trying to bring the Democratic National Convention to San Francisco. The attempt was unsuccessful, but the effort scarcely hurt his popularity with the party chiefs.

No one could accuse Hearst of a lack of ambition. What he needed was more money to further it, even though he had his own fortune and the *Examiner* was making money. A few years after his father died in 1891, a windfall, $7,500,000 of it, fell into his lap when his mother sold some mining stock and gave him the proceeds.

It took only a small part of this generous sum, $180,000 to be exact, to satisfy Hearst's desire for a New York newspaper, where he could try out his ideas in competition with the great

Pulitzer himself. But it took literally millions, as he discovered, to buy the circulation he wanted for it.

The vehicle for his experiment was the *Morning Journal,* a financially disabled daily with a short but interesting history. Albert Pulitzer, Joseph's younger brother, had founded it in 1882, sold it for a penny, and filled its columns with scandalous news and even more scandalous advertising. Observing that his brother was doing well with scandal at two cents, Albert raised his price in 1894 and at once lost most of his circulation. Dismayed, he sold the property to John R. McLean, publisher of the *Cincinnati Enquirer,* a scandal sheet in its own right. Mc-Lean put the *Journal*'s price back to a penny, but it was too late and the paper lost so much money that when Hearst offered $180,000 in cash, McLean accepted before the proposition was hardly out of the mouth of Hearst's agent. He even threw in the paper's German-language edition, *Das Morgen Journal.*

The *Journal* appeared, without the prefix "Morning," under its new publisher's direction on November 7, 1895. Its makeup, which mirrored the *World*'s, announced the direction it would take. Drawing upon his vast financial resources, Hearst immediately transformed the decrepit *Journal,* both editorially and mechanically.

On the editorial side, he obtained the best men money could buy, as he had in San Francisco. He robbed the *World* staff of such outstanding fireballs as Arthur Brisbane, Morrill Goddard, Solomon Solis Carvalho, and William H. Merrill. From the *Sun* he took Julian Ralph, acknowledged to be one of the nation's most brilliant reporters. For feature writers he hired such outstanding literary figures as Julian Hawthorne, Bob Davis, and Stephen Crane. He had brought from the *Examiner* some of its best executives and writers, including Sam Chamberlain, Winifred Black, Arthur McEwen, and the noted cartoonist Homer Davenport.

The art department of the *Journal* was full of stars, busy creating immortal comic strips: Dick Outcault and his "Yellow Kid," Rudy and Gus Dirks and the "Katzenjammer Kids,"

Jimmy Swinnerton, and the creators of "Foxy Grandpa,"
"Happy Hooligan," "Alphonse and Gaston," and a dozen
others. In one corner of the art room sat an obscure artist better known for his spectacular drinking bouts—John Barrymore.

In the composing room, George Pancoast, whom Hearst had
brought East from the *Examiner* to be mechanical department
superintendent, developed the first press capable of printing
four to sixteen pages in color, and thus the Sunday comic section was born. In its second year under Hearst, the *Sunday
Journal* also had the distinction of being the first newspaper
to use half-tone photographs printed on newsprint. In that
same year, 1897, Hearst solidified the daily's position by taking
over the decrepit *New York Morning Advertiser,* in order to
get its Associated Press franchise.

The editorial offices of this three-ring circus operated in the
building of the ultraconservative *Tribune,* fronting on Nassau
Street. On the second floor was Hearst's office, a large room
filled with art treasures and splendid period furniture, samples
of the fantastic orgy of buying he had embarked upon. Before
he suddenly stopped in 1937, his collection of European art
objects alone was worth more than forty million dollars.

Into that office one day, clutching cut proofs in his hand,
came a new recruit to the photo-engraving department, a scared
lad named Harry J. Coleman, who was to work through four
decades with Hearst and become one of his top picture executives.

Writing of this encounter years later, Coleman recalled that
he shoved the proofs across Hearst's "elaborately inlaid ebony
desk straight to the hands of the thirty-four-year-old publisher.
I stood aside enthralled . . . when Hearst suddenly spread the
proofs in precise order upon the floor and began a sort of tap
dance around and between them. It was a mild, uncostumed
combination of Carmen Miranda, a rhumba, a Russian dagger
dance and the Notre Dame shift, with lively castanet accom-
paniments produced by his snapping fingers. . . . After I had
observed W. R.'s strange dance, I learned that it was his cus-

tomary method of absorbing pictures and reproductions on newspaper pages. The cadence of it speeded up in tempo with his reactions of disturbance, and slowed down to a strolling rhythm when he approved. Between dances, he scribbled illegible scrawls in longhand on the margins and gave the proofs back to me."

Out of this office came the motive power for the crusades and sensational stories that shocked and stirred the nation for years to come. From the first, the *Journal* was a muckraking sheet, attacking the "criminal corporations" in a manner that would give its followers fatal convulsions today. Hearst hired Ella Reeve "Mother" Bloor, who became a Communist Party heroine in later years, to expose the packing houses, as Upton Sinclair had done in *The Jungle*. Editorially, the *Journal* came out strongly for the eight-hour day, the direct election of United States Senators, woman suffrage, Federal income taxes, labor and municipal ownership.

From this platform it can be discerned that the *Journal* in its long history (and the Hearst newspapers as well) has stood foursquare on both sides of most of the great issues of our time. This was most evident in Hearst's shifting stand on United States foreign policy, a stand that was always violent and highly partisan. The publisher's first crusade in that direction was easily his most noteworthy. Generations of Americans still believe Hearst started the Spanish-American War virtually single-handed, an impression Hearst did his best to create at the time.

It is true, certainly, that the *Journal*'s publisher started beating the propaganda drums against Spain in the first few months after he bought the paper. As early as 1896, he sent the redoubtable Richard Harding Davis to Cuba to report on the growing revolution. His zeal was increased by the actions of Pulitzer, who sensed the tremendous circulation appeal inherent in this issue and launched his *World* into a circulation war-to-the-death with the *Journal*.

Before this time, the two papers had fought on fairly even terms along the sex-and-crime front, although Pulitzer had made the tactical error noted before of lowering the *World*'s price as well as its none-too-high standards. Now, however, the prize was no longer an ordinary news beat but the foreign policy of the United States. The news stories, editorials, pictures, and headlines that Hearst and Pulitzer concocted to sell the war idea made the most incandescent display of unabashed jingoism in the history of American journalism, and the most effective.

The story of the newspaper campaign, often told, is replete with incredible incidents, including Hearst's much quoted telegram to the artist Frederic Remington, who asked to be relieved of his prewar assignment in Cuba: "Please remain. You furnish the pictures and I'll furnish the war." Hearst later denied this story, but the *Journal* undoubtedly did its best to "furnish the war."

By the time the battleship *Maine* blew up in Havana harbor in 1898, and war was declared, the temperature of the *Journal* and the *World* could be measured by their circulations, which were well past the million mark, and the American public was running a war fever that matched them.

Amid the furor, the cold scorn of Godkin dripped from the columns of the *Evening Post,* shortly after the *Maine* episode:

> Nothing so disgraceful as the behavior of two of these newspapers this week has been known in the history of American journalism. Gross misrepresentation of the facts, deliberate invention of tales calculated to excite the public, and wanton recklessness in the construction of headlines which even outdid these inventions, have combined to make the issues of the most widely circulated newspapers firebrands scattered broadcast throughout the country. . . . It is a crying shame that men should work such mischief simply in order to sell more papers.

Hearst spent a half-million dollars covering the war itself. Twenty *Journal* artists, writers, and photographers, led by the publisher himself, were in the forefront of the five hundred newspaper and magazine representatives (more than were needed to cover the entire four years of the Civil War) who deployed into the Cuban hinterlands. A fleet of seagoing vessels carried the Hearst task force, and from its flagship, a chartered tramp steamer, there emerged a special edition of the *Journal,* turned out by the little printing plant it carried in the hold.

In this "comic-opera war," in which those who died were as dead as though it had been fought for far nobler purposes, the newspapermen were in the front lines. Hearst's staff, and he himself, were in numerous engagements. Hearst personally headed a foray from a steam launch to the beach, where he rounded up twenty-six frightened, stranded Spanish sailors and delivered them as prisoners of war.

There was also the famous incident in which the *Journal*'s veteran correspondent, James Creelman, led an assault on a fort at El Caney. Wounded in this successful charge, he was taken to the rear, where his boss suddenly appeared kneeling beside him, wearing a straw hat with a bright ribbon, a revolver at his belt, pencil and notebook clutched at the ready. While the bullets spun around them, Hearst took down Creelman's story carefully, and then, as Creelman remembered it, said: " 'I'm sorry you're hurt, but'—and his face was radiant with enthusiasm—'wasn't it a splendid fight? We must beat every paper in the world!' "

The war effort forced Pulitzer to draw for the first time on his financial reserves; it was then, presumably, that he concluded it would be better policy to withdraw from the epic battle with Hearst. What, after all, could be gained from competing with a man who, besides running up a circulation of 1,600,000, and personally fighting a war he had helped to start, could turn in 1899 to such exactly opposite circulation-getting tactics as publishing, for the first time, Edwin Markham's "The Man With The Hoe."

Thus Pulitzer left Hearst to his own devices, which were quite as remarkable in peace as in war. One of the most significant moves he made was to begin the establishment of his chain. The *Journal* now had a sister, the *Evening Journal.* This became simply the *Journal* after 1901, and the morning *Journal*'s name was changed to the *American* at the same time. To these, along with the San Francisco *Examiner,* he added in

1900 the Chicago *American,* evening, and the *Examiner,* morning. Four years later, in Boston, he founded the evening *American.* These six papers were the nucleus of the chain.

In the political arena, meanwhile, Hearst won as much notoriety for his papers as he had in the Cuban affair. Since 1896 he had attacked President McKinley, as the chief exponent of predatory capitalism, in the most sustained and bitter onslaught that any Chief Executive had endured, perhaps, since Jackson's day. As against McKinley's championing of *laissez-faire* nineteenth-century capitalism, Hearst opposed his "American Internal Policy," which he announced editorially in 1899. Among other things, this policy included such familiar Hearst standbys as public ownership of public franchises, the destruction of "criminal trusts," the popular election of Senators, and development of the public school system.

A year after this pronouncement, Hearst entered politics personally, becoming president of the National Association of Democratic Clubs. McKinley's election to a second term in 1900 was not calculated to soothe the association's new president. The abuse poured out against the Chief Executive in the *Journal* reached a high in February 1901 with the publication of Ambrose Bierce's memorable quatrain, following the assassination of Governor Goebel of Kentucky. Bierce wrote:

> *The bullet that pierced Goebel's breast*
> *Can not be found in all the West;*
> *Good reason, it is speeding here*
> *To stretch McKinley on his bier.*

In April, the *Journal* followed this with an ominous editorial which asserted, in part, that "If bad institutions and bad men can be got rid of only by killing, then the killing must be done."

It was little wonder that when McKinley was assassinated the following September by an anarchist who was said to have a copy of the *Journal* stuffed in his pocket, popular rage turned against Hearst and his papers, and it was widely believed that the publisher had had something to do with the tragedy. The *Journal* was boycotted for a time by libraries, clubs, business and patriotic organizations, and some newsstands, while Hearst was hanged in effigy.

Several "yellow" contemporaries of the Hearst newspapers failed to survive this public revulsion against sensational journalism, but Hearst and his enterprises survived and prospered. The other members of the chain quieted down somewhat, while the *Journal* screamed on triumphantly without changing character noticeably.

In fact, Hearst's survival value was never better illustrated than by the fact that little more than a year after he had swung in effigy from a lamppost, the garroters of his adopted city were helping to elect him to Congress. He was elected from a heavily Democratic district, and with the aid of the Tammany Hall machine, but it was a remarkable demonstration just the same.

Although Hearst had yearned mightily for political honors, he showed a curious indifference to the opportunity presented to him in Washington. He was absent frequently, made few noteworthy speeches, introduced little outstanding legislation, and in time disappeared from the Hill without a trace.

In 1903 he married Millicent Willson, and at the same time published his first magazine, *Motor*. He sought the Democratic nomination for the Presidency in 1904, but the politicians were apparently not warmed by his showing in Congress, and he failed to get it. Apparently the voters of New York were not impressed either, because they defeated his 1905 bid for the mayoralty of New York, although by a very narrow margin.

Hearst made another try for political office in 1906, when he spent between a quarter- and a half-million dollars attempting unsuccessfully to defeat Charles Evans Hughes for the governorship of New York. All the other candidates on his ticket were elected. After this setback, he made only two more attempts at public office. He ran for Mayor again in 1909 but was soundly beaten, and a year later was equally unsuccessful in an attempt to be Lieutenant Governor. At that point he renounced his political ambitions. They had cost him, according to most estimates, nearly two million dollars.

Meanwhile, in the early years of the century, he had acquired *Cosmopolitan,* first of the cheap popular illustrated monthlies, and he continued his fight against the barons of privilege. In 1912, the year of the great contest between Woodrow Wilson, Taft, and Roosevelt, Hearst supported Champ Clark for the Democratic nomination.

With the outbreak of war in Europe in 1914, he entered upon the second extremely controversial portion of his career. Hearst was opposed to the war, particularly against any idea of America's participation. To the Allies in Europe he appeared pro-German, as he did to many Americans. When the struggle began to deepen, England's Prime Minister, Lloyd George, took the drastic action of denying Hearst's wire service, the International News Service, which he had started in 1909, any further use of the nation's mail and cable facilities. The French Government joined in the ban.

Lloyd George, who became a contributor to the Hearst papers after the war, bitterly denounced the Hearst press as pro-German and completely untruthful. In Canada, the reaction was so strong that simple possession of a Hearst newspaper was enough to put a man in prison.

While these curbs were the understandable result of wartime hysteria, it was not so easy to understand Hearst's attitude toward the war itself. He talked like a pacifist as far as American participation was concerned, yet no publisher in history ever waved the flag more ardently in his newspapers.

Typical of this contradictory attitude was his pronouncement on Mexico in 1916, at a time when Pershing was chasing Pancho Villa through the Mexican brush and Wilson was trying vainly to protect American interests in our southern neighbor while not interfering with her internal revolution.

"Our flag should wave over Mexico as the symbol of the rehabilitation of that unhappy country," Hearst wrote in a signed editorial, "and its redemption to 'humanity' and civilization. Our right in Mexico is the right of humanity. . . ."

Hearst owned much property in Mexico, and so it did not

surprise some observers to find him advocating exactly the opposite course six years later.

But while the Hearst papers made threatening gestures toward Japan and Mexico and waved the shamrock for the Irish revolutionists, they continued to talk peace for America and to print anything that appeared to be anti-British.

When America entered the war, Hearst drew in his horns only slightly. As patriotic fervor mounted, the publisher was once more hanged in effigy, and his newspapers were once more banned from many clubs and homes. The *New York Tribune* ran a cartoon in May 1918, depicting the word "Hears-ss-ss-t" coiled snakelike in the American flag.

Wartime passions subsided, however, and the decade of the fabulous twenties, as it opened, found the Hearst properties in good condition, though their owner was still at a low point in the public esteem.

The truth was that Hearst stood at a crossroads in his career. His political life, such as it had been, was over—a fact underlined by Al Smith's refusal to run on the same ticket with him in 1922. He had flirted with the motion picture business, beginning with cliff-hanging serials in New York and winding up with super-productions in Hollywood. These cinematic ventures had cost him about $7,000,000, but gained him the life-long friendship and devotion of his beautiful blonde star, Marion Davies.

Bored with politics and movies, in 1922 Hearst turned in earnest to the occupation that appeared to interest him continuously more than anything else: spending money. The death of his mother in 1919 had added another $18,000,000 to his fortune, but his newspaper and other properties reached their productive peak during the twenties and helped him amass wealth to a net worth of somewhere around $150,000,000—far from being the world's second largest personal fortune, as Fremont Older mistakenly termed it, but certainly the most liquid. Not even Henry Ford could have had as much actual cash in hand as Hearst. He took it with a free hand and spent it just as freely.

No man in American history has ever gone on such an orgy of buying. It was an orgy that reached its climax in the twenties, when he devoted most of his time to it. Enumerating his purchases, one writer noted that they included "newspapers, Egyptian mummies, Elizabethan caudle cups, radio stations, fifteenth-century choir stalls, Gothic hearths, California mountain ranges, Mexican horsehair bridles, hundreds of Madonnas . . . a Spanish abbey . . . New York hotels and apartment houses, thirteenth-century stained glass, periodicals, majolica, Etruscan plates, herds of yaks from Tibet, and Australian emus, moving-picture studios, Crusaders' armor, royal tapestries," and warehouses to hold many of the treasures he bought. Hundreds were never even uncrated.

Besides all this, Hearst bought men—men of talent and ability to manage his newspaper properties and to write for them. The list of writers who decorated the columns of Hearst's papers from time to time would read like pages from a journalistic *Who's Who*. The turnover was high. There were veterans in the top echelons, intensely loyal to the Chief, but in the lower ranks they came and went with unhappy rapidity.

The symbol of Hearst's acquisitiveness, as far as the general public was concerned, was not so much his newspapers as his unbelievable San Simeon, an estate nearly as big as Rhode Island, lying between Los Angeles and San Francisco. Into this 270,000-acre "ranch," as Hearst always called it, he poured nearly forty million dollars, according to some estimates. No other private residence in the world could touch it, with the possible exception of Louis XIV's palace at Versailles. It had four huge buildings, three for guests and one for the owner; carillons; a private zoo; two swimming pools; an armorer; an air field; a private railroad connecting with the outside world; and enough art treasures to fill a museum.

Sitting in the midst of these treasures at dinner, guests would find themselves supplied with paper napkins, a symbol of

Hearst's feeling about this "ranch" on which he used to hunt and camp when he was growing up, before San Simeon was built. The guests were a varied assortment, from Herbert Hoover to Father Coughlin.

When he wearied of the pleasures of San Simeon, Hearst could rough it on his 50,000-acre retreat, Wyntoon, in the shadow of Mt. Shasta, where he created a luxurious Bavarian pleasure dome that far outshone anything in Bavaria.

Politically, he continued to be a puzzle. Here was a publisher who in 1927 published forged Mexican documents intended to show that United States Senators had been bribed, and whose persistent needling of the French in 1930 resulted in his expulsion from that country. Yet in 1931 he urged the adoption of a five-billion-dollar work-relief program to cure the depression, and in 1932, he and his political henchmen secured the nomination of Franklin D. Roosevelt and John Garner.

The Roosevelt honeymoon lasted only a year. By 1933, the Hearst papers were swinging their axes lustily at the NRA, and from that point on, the Roosevelt Administration had no more vocal and undeviating enemy. His hatred for the President led Hearst in 1935 to boost Al Smith, the man who once had scorned him, for the Presidency on a "Jeffersonian Democratic" ticket.

Hearst might have been able to capitalize much more on the conservative reaction to the Roosevelt reform program if he had not, in 1934, for the third time in his history, run afoul of public opinion. On a visit to Germany, he had become publicly enamored of National Socialism, leased his INS service to the German press for an annual $400,000, and begun syndicating articles bylined by Colonel-General Hermann Goering.

Whether it was because of the renewal of public displeasure, the re-election of Roosevelt in 1936, or these factors in combination with numerous others, Hearst suddenly made an about-face in his life in October 1937, though it was not disclosed to the public until the following March.

For the first time in more than a half-century, he stopped buying and began selling. There began a grand shuffling around of his empire, adroitly managed by lawyers, bankers, and Hearst executives interested in putting the immense panoply of Hearst properties in shape against the inevitable day of their owner's death, when taxes might conceivably reduce it to an estate difficult to divide among five sons and to maintain in adequate strength for the future.

First to go was the *New York American,* which had cost its owner $1,000,000 the year before its departure. With a single unimportant exception, it was the first Hearst newspaper property ever to expire. Next on the execution list was the *Rochester Journal.* It was traded in a deal with Frank Gannett that left Hearst alone in Albany among the morning papers. Then the *Omaha Bee-News* disappeared entirely, and the *Washington Times* was leased to his old friend, Cissy Patterson, who had already made a profitable operation of his *Washington Herald.* Universal Service, a wire service for morning papers, lost its identity in a merger with INS.

Then, in 1937, Hearst retired from the active management of his empire, retaining editorial policy and any subsequent profits for himself, and turning over the rest to a regency composed of a long-time Hearst lawyer, his son, William Randolph Hearst, Jr., and various executives of Hearst properties. This cabinet came to be known as the "Young Turks."

The regents completed the work of consolidation. They liquidated warehouses full of art treasures, many of them sold in a memorable exhibition at Gimbel's department store in New York. Such Manhattan real estate as the 41-story Ritz Tower apartment hotel on Park Avenue, once the proud home of Arthur Brisbane, went by the board. Piece by piece, block by block, the trustees disposed of everything that was likely to be unprofitable, and kept only what they considered absolutely sound.

The job took a little less than a decade. By the time the regency came to the end of the ten-year voting powers Hearst had granted them in 1937, the remains of the empire had been in the black for two full years.

Secure in his old age, and looking back on a career that now was stretching incredibly toward the century mark, Hearst removed himself largely from public view. Sometime during the mid-forties he left San Simeon and withdrew to more conservative quarters in Beverly Hills. All five of his sons had become top executives in his enterprises, and these enterprises were in a solvent state. The man who feared death so much, it was said, that he forbade mention of the word in his presence was ostensibly ready to die. Until his last day came, however, there was hardly anyone inside or outside the Hearst organization who was not ready to bet that the Chief would continue unmistakably to function as the Chief. His will passed on control to his sons.

It is impossible to estimate properly Hearst's place in journalistic history in this space or at this moment. But it is entirely safe to say that no more controversial figure ever existed in the business. To some, like Brisbane, he was "the great enlightener"; to others, he was a menace. Some of the same men who called him an anarchist in the muck-raking era lived to bless his name. Others who regarded him as the savior of the workingman learned to curse him as the enemy of the people. Among his employees, past and present, could be found those who swore by him and against him, with equal vehemence.

Whatever his place may be in history eventually, William Randolph Hearst, sitting alone in the twilight of his career, was justifiably certain of one thing. History would never forget him.

8

Raymond, Ochs, and the "New York Times"

PROFESSIONAL ARGUMENTS ABOUT THE MERITS OF THE *NEW YORK Times* eventually come around to one solid, unarguable fact: It is unique. It cannot really be compared with any other newspaper, and this has been true during the entire century of its existence. Serious criticism can be leveled at the *Times,* in both its past and present conduct, but when even the worst of it is admitted, a *Times* man can still point proudly to the great gray fortress on West Forty-third Street and say, "There she stands—the foremost daily in the world." No one will honestly dispute him.

The *Times* is not so much a newspaper as an institution. Some of its executives call it "a paper of record," which fairly well defines its institutional character. The qualities which set the *Times* apart and make it unique are its intention to print "all the news that's fit to print," and its devotion to impartiality. It is sometimes charged that the *Times* sins by errors of omission to satisfy its own peculiar biases, and that occasionally it may be zealously impartial on one side, but these are human flaws which show that institutions, like men, are imperfect.

By and large, *Times* coverage of domestic and foreign news is about as complete as human minds can make it.

Two men have been responsible for making the *Times* an

enduring monument to factual, complete reporting of the news. Henry Raymond, the founder, and Adolph Ochs, who established the modern *Times*, were unlike in many ways as personalities, but in one most important respect they shared identical viewpoints. Both had the same conception of what a newspaper ought to be. Both had the ability to implement their ideal at times when experience and example on every side seemed to demonstrate that their kind of journalism could not succeed.

As dissimilar as the careers of these two men were, the story of their newspaper-making is like a continuous thread that binds together the hundred-year story of the *Times*. Only the gap between Raymond's death in 1869 and Och's acquisition of the paper in 1896 breaks the narrative of accomplishment.

Henry Jarvis Raymond came into New York journalism along a road worn smooth by his contemporaries. His was the story of the aspiring farm boy, but with variations. Born near Lima, in upstate New York, he was the son of a well-to-do farmer who could afford to send him to Genesee Wesleyan Seminary and the University of Vermont, which graduated him with the highest honors, attained at the expense of his health. Teaching was the logical next step for him, but Raymond had already been inoculated with printer's ink. In college he had been a frequent contributor to Horace Greeley's struggling weekly, the *New Yorker,* and consequently he became perhaps the first of the able young men, later to attain distinction, who hit up "Uncle Horace" for a job.

It would have been difficult to imagine two personalities more opposed. Greeley was the zealous, crusading liberal, impatient with what he considered the all too temperate character of the *New Yorker*. Raymond was a nonpartisan man in an ardently partisan era, engaged in the most partisan of all professions outside of politics.

Unfortunately, Raymond also fell in love with politics, thus laying the groundwork for the personal misfortunes which culminated in his untimely death. Greeley's young protégée had a world of natural talent for journalism, and in this field his passion for fair examination of both sides of a question proved to be his best stock in trade. But in politics, his talents consisted of oratory and an ability to analyze complex problems and restate them clearly. His judicial temperament could lead only to political disaster.

At first there appeared to be nothing but success ahead for him. When Greeley founded the *Tribune* in 1841, he made Raymond his chief assistant, and the young man justified his confidence at once by giving the new paper the sound management that Greeley himself was not able to provide. In these early years, Raymond's closest friend was a young Vermonter in the business office named George Jones. While they labored for Greeley, these two men began to plan a paper of their own.

The plan had to be deferred for a time, because neither had enough capital. Jones went up to Albany and entered into the curious banking practices of the time, while Raymond went to work in 1843 for the redoubtable James Watson Webb's *Morning Courier and New-York Enquirer.*

Newspapering became almost a side issue for Raymond, however, as he burrowed deeper into Whig politics, particularly the Free Soil movement being engineered by Thurlow Weed and William H. Seward. The voters sent Raymond to Albany as a State Assemblyman in 1849, re-elected him next year on the strength of a brilliant first-term record, and in 1851 he became Speaker. Meanwhile, he dallied with journalism. Webb, who was violently against the Free Soilers, fired him. Raymond already had another job, as managing editor of *Harper's New Monthly Magazine,* but he spent little time on his editorial chores.

He and Jones still hoped to buy a newspaper. They tried unsuccessfully to obtain the *Albany Evening Journal* from Weed in 1848, but at last, in 1851, they had accumulated enough money to establish the *New York Daily Times,* which appeared for the first time under their joint management on September 18, 1851.

In its opening statement was a sentence which set the tone of the *Times* for a hundred years to come: "We do not mean to write as if we were in a passion,—unless that shall really be the case; and we shall make it a point to get into a passion as rarely as possible."

This was a remarkable declaration at a time when editors were at each other's throats, and when the rising tide of passion over the issue of slavery would shortly engulf all Americans. But it was an exceedingly attractive idea to thoughtful men like Raymond, and to the considerable body of citizens who were repelled alike by the sensationalism of Bennett's *Herald* and the strident righteousness of Greeley's *Tribune*. The *Times* sat serenely on the fence, aloof from the name-calling and unabashed violence of its contemporaries.

No publisher fought the newcomer harder than Raymond's ex-benefactor, Greeley, particularly when the *Times* began to forge ahead and in four years doubled the *Tribune*'s city circulation. Greeley could find some satisfaction in the nation-wide influence of his paper, but in New York State Whig politics, where he hoped to satisfy his inordinate desire for public office, he found his young rival opposing him at every turn.

It was an unfortunate situation on both sides. Raymond had a fatal addiction to the game of politics, and he was good enough at it to get elected but not politician enough to make the most of his opportunities. Greeley had more influence with the voters than most politicians, but he had no talent whatever for the business of politics itself.

In the struggle within the Whig Party between the slave-owning Southerners and the Northern Free Soilers, Raymond won national recognition at the convention of 1852 by his honest, outspoken championship of the Northern wing. When it seemed later that the party might dissolve in dismal failure as the result of its internal pressures, he turned his efforts to holding the Free Soil line in New York State.

The issue of prohibition, rather than slavery, dominated public interest in the state for the moment, and it was over the handling of this political hot potato that Greeley was made the victim of a practical deal which completely alienated him from both the party and Raymond. It was an operation that had important national repercussions.

As Whig boss of the party and of the state convention, Thurlow Weed dictated the choice of candidates. Greeley confidently expected to be given the gubernatorial nomination, but Weed inexplicably ignored him in favor of a relatively unknown upstate politician. Chagrined, Greeley virtually pleaded to be put on the slate for Lieutenant Governor, but the canny Weed concluded that it would be smart politics to balance his upstate man, who was a dry, with a New York City wet. Consequently, he named Raymond for the job, and the ticket was elected.

For Greeley it was a shattering emotional experience. "No other name could have been . . . so bitterly humiliating to me," he wrote later. The direct result was that Greeley came to the Republican national convention of 1860 determined to throw his considerable weight in favor of any candidate who might defeat Weed and his political ally, Seward. Thus, Abraham Lincoln got the support of the nation's most powerful editor, which influenced both his nomination and his election.

This convention marked the end of the Whig Party. Earlier, in 1856, Raymond had attended the birth of the Republican Party, written its first platform, and thrown the influence of his paper behind the new organization, within the rigid limits which the *Times* set itself in supporting anything.

Except for a brief period in 1859, when he covered the Franco-Austrian War in Italy, Raymond devoted most of his pre-Civil War activity to the party he had helped found. As a party politician, he was an incurable temporizer. He tried to get the Presidential nomination for Seward, as a good Weed man would be expected to do, but failing in that, he gave Lincoln the most ardent support during the campaign. In the vital matter of secession, he was for compromise, and in fact, actually opposed abolition until the war began.

The press, in New York and elsewhere, was anything but

unanimous in support of Lincoln. The President could not even rely on the editors of his own party, some of whom attacked him viciously. But he could always depend on Raymond. The *Times* was constant in its support of the administration.

Editorially, Raymond's support of Lincoln was not as effective as the President could have wished, despite its unswerving loyalty. His editorials lacked the fire and conviction of Greeley's, and were not constructed in the we-are-everlastingly-right style of most of his contemporaries, who poured out a barrage of invective against everyone who failed to agree with them.

Raymond's personal part in the war was unprecedented for a publisher. He became a correspondent for his own paper, and distinguished himself as among the best of the small battalion of newspapermen who were constantly at the front, reporting the battles. His accuracy and speed were legendary in the business. Even today Raymond's accounts in the *Times* of the battles of Solferino and Bull Run stand as the best eye-witness reports of these actions.

His remark that he never wrote a sentence without noting that it was only partially true before he got to the end of it was the key to his whole personality as editor, politician, and man. However admirable his passion for fairness and impartiality might be, these were the wrong attributes for the times.

His skill in party strategy, however, made him extremely valuable to Lincoln. At the convention of 1864 in Baltimore, Raymond not only wrote nearly all the platform but was responsible for getting Andrew Johnson on the ticket as vice-president, a move particularly desired by Lincoln. For these services, he was made chairman of the Republican National Committee, and after the President's re-election, Raymond was sent to Washington by the voters as a Representative.

Apparently at the peak of his political career, entering the House with perhaps more prestige than any new Congressman had ever enjoyed, Raymond moved quickly to an unexpected disaster. As administration leader, he was expected to guide Johnson's reconstruction policies to successful enactment against the fierce opposition of Thaddeus Stevens and his friends. Raymond was so confident he could accomplish this that he allowed himself to be completely outmaneuvered by Stevens, who seized control of the reconstruction committee and put his rival in one impossible position after another.

Through it all, Raymond followed his temporizing, middle-of-the-road course, while the violence of the quarrel over reconstruction daily divided party and nation further. Blocked in Congress, Johnson attempted the formation of a third, a Union Party, to gain public support for his policies. Raymond viewed this development with dismay, but Seward and Weed persuaded him to attend the party's first convention in 1866. There the declaration of principles he wrote was not enough to give the wrangling delegates any semblance of cohesion, and the reasoned program he set forth found few supporters among the passionate partisans.

Raymond had to admit failure. Moreover, he lost his job with the Republican National Committee, and Greeley seized the opportunity to berate his enemy in the *Tribune's* columns. With a restraint unknown in those days, Raymond had never used the *Times* to further his own political career, but now he was repaid for his remarkable integrity by the defection of thousands of his readers, who turned to the more positive policies of the *Tribune*.

In state politics, he found himself increasingly out of sympathy with Weed's attempts to hold the party together, and finally bolted it, charging that the Copperheads had taken over. He even came to open disagreement with his friend Johnson.

Raymond's political ruin proved to be a good thing for the *Times*. Freed of his devotion to partisan issues, he imbued his newspaper more than ever with a spirit of real independence, establishing it firmly as an organ of impartial, objective news coverage. Editorially his platform called for tariff reduction,

sound money, and civil service reform—causes the *Times* advocated for years after its founder's death.

That death came prematurely, just as it appeared that Raymond, out of the political woods at last, was ready to guide the
Times to even greater heights. Long years of overwork had
sapped his physical resources, and when an emotional crisis in
his life occurred in 1869, he died suddenly of a cerebral hemorrhage. He was only forty-nine.

Whatever his defects as a politician may have been, they
were forgotten by the men of his own and the opposing parties
when it came time to pay him tribute. Then only the pleasant
charm of his personality was remembered, and the unflinching
integrity which had made him so much respected in his profession. Naturally the highest praise came from Godkin.
Raymond was Godkin's kind of publisher, and the obituary
editorial the Englishman wrote in the *Nation* was a moving
appreciation.

"Nobody has done more, we doubt if anybody has done as
much, for the elevation of the profession," Godkin wrote of
Raymond, and of the *Times* he asserted that it was "nearer the
newspaper of the good time coming than any other in existence."

Most remarkable of all was Greeley's *Tribune* editorial. It
was, as Elmer Davis noted years later, "a flat contradiction of
almost everything Greeley had written about him for twenty-
five years past."

After Raymond's death, the *Times* continued on an even
keel for some time, under the direction of George Jones, who
had managed the business side of the *Times* since he had
helped his friend found it. A quiet and modest man, Jones
realized that he had neither the experience nor the talent to
run the editorial side of the paper, and so he contented himself
with retaining final authority on policy and letting other men
carry it out.

The editors he chose were, in succession, Louis J. Jennings,
John Foord, and Charles R. Miller. Under his direction, the

first two of these executed the brilliant, sustained attack that broke the hold of the notorious Tweed ring on city politics. It was one of the highest points in *Times* history, a brave and skillful piece of work which placed the paper's future at stake, since failure to win the battle would have meant its eclipse.

Jones stuck by his guns in the shadow of catastrophe. He had to fight sharp lawyers, the loss of advertising, and attempts to corrupt both him and his men. At one point, a Tweed henchman offered him a $5,000,000 bribe to quit, but Jones was not only personally incorruptible, he was absolutely determined to break Tweed—and he did it.

The editors who worked for him thought Jones an ideal kind of business-office publisher—a type, incidentally, which he probably represented for the first time in newspaper history. When Miller, as editor, led the *Times* in a bolt from the Republican Party in 1884, Jones agreed with the move, in spite of the losses in advertising and circulation he suffered as a result. In 1888, Jones was personally for Harrison, but made no attempt to dissuade Miller from lining up the *Times* behind Cleveland. Jones boasted (if a man of his reticence could be said to boast) that he had never asked a businessman to advertise in the *Times,* and he had never solicited anyone to subscribe to it.

Jones' extraordinary ability as a manager was never more appreciated than after he died in 1891. The *Times,* considered one of the soundest newspaper properties in the country, faltered and nearly succumbed. In an incredibly short time it lost most of the circulation and advertising so carefully built up over the years. Miller and some of the other executives bought it in 1893, but in three years they saw it drop to a circulation of 9,000, with a deficit accumulating at the rate of a thousand dollars a day. No one in the business thought the *Times* could be saved.

No one, that is, except the thirty-eight-year-old publisher of the *Chattanooga Times,* Adolph S. Ochs (see photograph 5), who had been quietly building a mid-South equivalent of its New York namesake.

Ochs was a Cincinnati boy, the son of accomplished German-Jewish immigrants of good family. His father Julius, who had served with distinction in the Union Army as a captain, had settled in Knoxville after the war. People admired Julius's culture and charm, but they shook their heads about his business ability and no one was surprised when young Adolph was compelled, at eleven, to go to work. His schooling thereafter was intermittent, but his parents tutored him and whatever gaps there might have been in his education were supplied by his place of employment, the *Knoxville Chronicle*, where he began as an office boy.

Through his teens, with occasional interludes in other jobs, Ochs worked at the *Chronicle,* until, at nineteen, he could say that he had performed nearly every business, mechanical, or editorial job a newspaper had to offer. Ochs attributed this part of his education to superstition rather than unusual zeal. The *Chronicle* was a morning newspaper, he recalled, and if he left when his work as printer's devil was over, he had to walk home past a graveyard in the dead of night. If he stayed until the paper went to press, the composing room foreman would walk home with him. While he waited, he had nothing to do but learn the business.

Whatever the motive, this experience enabled him to become a publisher on his own account when he was only a little more than nineteen. He had transferred to Chattanooga and a new job there on a paper which soon folded beneath him. The defunct sheet's rival, the *Chattanooga Times,* appeared ready to follow it into oblivion, so lamentable was the state of journalism in this particular part of Tennessee, but it seemed to Ochs that the *Times* was in need of better management more than anything else.

Taking the long chance that so many young journalists had taken before him, he borrowed $250 and bought a major interest in the tottering property.

Ochs had a profound conviction about what a newspaper should be. "Clean, dignified and trustworthy," he once described it. This was far from being the tone of journalism in general, particularly in such small cities as Chattanooga, but Ochs discovered, as Raymond had in New York, that there was a public for a newspaper which refused to feed on sensation and political passions. Ochs, the *Times,* and Chattanooga all grew up together, and although he lived nearly forty years of his life in New York, the Tennessee city was always his real love.

As the town took on the aspect of a metropolis, considerably aided in its growth by the efforts of its young newspaper proprietor, the Ochs home became the natural center of entertainment for visiting celebrities. The mistress of this home was Effie Miriam, the daughter of a Cincinnati rabbi, Isaac M. Wise, noted leader of Reformed Judaism. Ochs had married her in 1883. Together they welcomed men of prominence visiting the city, and among them Ochs made the friendships which aided him so much later on, when he established his New York paper.

It was a former visitor, a *New York Times* reporter, who sent back word in 1896 that his paper could be bought cheaply. Ochs investigated the situation and worked out a plan which would give him complete control, at the same time setting up a new organization designed to protect the interests of those who had money invested in it and those who might put fresh capital into the paper. He risked $75,000 of his own, most of it borrowed, in the gamble.

To outsiders, the whole venture appeared so hazardous that it was whispered Ochs was actually a "front" for some behind-the-curtains political cabal. Nor did the whispers die easily; Ochs heard them from time to time for two decades, though he made no secret from the beginning that his control of the paper was absolute.

Meanwhile, he worked ceaselessly to rejuvenate the *Times.* He made it in the image of his Chattanooga property, because that was the only way he could conceive of publishing a newspaper. It meant little change for the *Times,* since this was substantially the way Raymond and Jones had meant the paper to be.

Journalistic ethics had changed very little since Raymond's earliest days, so that the *Times,* with its calm, unbiased, nonpartisan treatment of the news, was still a novelty. The professionals were more or less accustomed to this method, as Raymond had exemplified it, but they found it hard to understand Ochs' extension of the idea to advertising policy. No newspaper needed advertising more than the *Times,* yet Ochs turned down ads he thought were morally or financially sour. The other papers fought for advertising of any shade, and the *Herald* was waxing both rich and notorious on its questionable classified advertising for lonesome ladies and adventurous men.

Integrity does not pay off readily, and Ochs had some anxious years with his new property. "I could never have got through my first years on the *Times* if I hadn't been used to being in debt, and to getting out of it," Ochs told a friend years later. There were numerous temptations. Unscrupulous advertisers tried to buy more than space; politicians made him propositions. To these and others Adolph Ochs simply refused to listen, or to compromise.

The advent of Hearst, and the subsequent circulation war with Pulitzer, further endangered the *Times'* precarious position, but paradoxically, it was Hearst who unwittingly drove Ochs to make the decision that saved his paper.

Ochs fought back at Hearst initially by coining the slogan, "All the News That's Fit to Print," which the paper began to carry in 1896. This was intended to inform readers that if they were disgusted by the sex and blood in the *World* and the *Journal* they could turn to the *Times* for relief.

But Ochs realized it would take more than slogans when the heavy financial burden of covering the Spanish-American War was added to his load. This development precipitated a new crisis at the *Times* in October 1898, and some of Ochs' executives argued that since the paper was intended for a quality market, the thing to do was to raise the price from three to five cents.

The publisher had a different idea. He reasoned that even

though "penny press" was the symbol of yellow journalism, it was this same penny that led people to buy the *World* and *Journal*. If they could buy the *Times* for a penny too, he told his board of directors, they might turn from sensationalism. The others thought he had lost his mind. Every expert in and out of his employ told him reducing the price to a penny would stamp the *Times* as just another yellow sheet. Wisely, Ochs followed his instinct and lowered the price.

It was the best inspiration of his life. Circulation jumped threefold within a year, and the *Times* was never in trouble again. It continued to grow as a result of the publisher's ceaseless vigilance, a day-by-day matter of trimming sails to catch every advantageous wind, of plowing back profits, and of constantly seeking means of improvement.

Unlike Raymond, Ochs had no political ambitions, and in fact no entanglements of any sort outside his paper except his work in the Associated Press, which had begun while he was still in Chattanooga. He had exceptionally able help in running the *Times,* particularly after 1904, when Carr Van Anda, generally regarded in the newspaper business as the greatest managing editor of them all, began his long service. Van Anda was an authentic genius who edited the *Times,* as Alva Johnston once wrote, "as if he were its only reader."

It was Ochs, however, who got any blame or criticism that might be directed at the *Times.* Exemplary as the paper might be by comparison, it did not escape attack. Most of this came from liberals and radicals who were irritated by the maddening, undeviating conservatism of the *Times.*

During the first World War, the *Times* annoyed even its conservative readers by suggesting, in September 1918, that the tentative peace proposals offered by the Austrian government should be welcomed and examined. Patriots from far and near denounced Ochs by letter, telephone, and telegraph.

A year earlier the *Times* had brought down the wrath of liberals by commending Columbia University editorially for its stand in the celebrated case of Professor Charles A. Beard, the historian, who had resigned in the controversy over the firing of two faculty members whose views on American participation in the war were considered unpatriotic. A quarter-century later the *Times* was still on the opposite side of the fence from Dr. Beard's isolationist views on American foreign policy, but by that time it was the conservatives who supported Beard and the liberals who backed the *Times*.

Again, the liberals complained that *Times* coverage of the Russian Revolution and succeeding events was far from the truth—a complaint directed also against most of the other newspapers in the country, and the Associated Press as well. In the case of Petrograd, it was said, the AP and the *Times* had announced its demise a half-dozen times, its near capture on three other occasions, its revolt against the Bolsheviks six different times, and had razed it twice by fire. Further, it was charged that the *Times* had been careless with the truth and overzealous in recounting the exploits of some White Russian generals.

The chief complainers in this matter were Lenin and Trotsky, who barred *Times* correspondents from Russia for a while.

Another outcry was raised during the first World War when the *Times* denounced Jane Addams (roughly equivalent to condemning motherhood) for asserting that Allied commanders sometimes ordered liquor or drugs given to troops before an attack.

Nor were the liberals made happy during the twenties by the cavalier treatment the *Times* gave to some of their popular heroes, not to mention its unfriendliness to Senator Robert M. LaFollette, the elder, and its lack of sympathy for labor.

Some segments of the Jewish faith could not forgive Ochs for his opposition to Zionism, and at other times he was accused of bringing a Southern prejudice against Negroes to the operation of his New York paper.

The critics and enemies of the *Times* were fond of asserting that it was the defender of privilege and the status quo because Ochs had made it a successful business property. In twenty-five years he had raised it from near oblivion to an annual net profit of more than two million dollars.

But through it all, Ochs continued to hew to the line he had established for himself, and if the *Times* committed sins in the name of conservatism, they had the virtue of being the honest sins of one man, who was free of connivance or self-seeking. Ochs might be wrong from time to time, but only the bitterly partisan ever doubted his integrity.

By the time Ochs died in 1935, he had built the *Times* on so firm a foundation that only a major catastrophe could have shaken it. It had been recognized for years as an incomparable newspaper. Of all the words written to commemorate Ochs' achievement, none could have been more fitting than the title a *Herald Tribune* man, Gerald W. Johnson, gave to a biography of Ochs written in 1946. "An Honorable Titan," Johnson called him. Few of the other titans could have merited that adjective.

Ochs left the *Times* in good hands—those of his two sons-in-law, Arthur Hays Sulzberger and General Julius Ochs Adler. In 1938, these executives were augmented by the appointment of Charles Merz as editor of the editorial page. Merz, oddly enough, had been one of the *New Republic* men who helped compile a special supplement documenting the charges that the *Times* was falsifying the news from Russia.

The ad-packed and fact-jammed bulk of the *Sunday Times*—legend has it that a *Sunday Times* being delivered to a country subscriber plummeted from its plane and killed an ox in a field below—is the particular province of Lester Markel, a hard-working and hard-driving executive who has devoted much of his extracurricular time and thought in recent years to the setting up of an International Institute of the Press in Zurich for the mutual education of editors in the problems and responsibilities of a free press.

Under the will of Adolph Ochs, the property passes eventually to the three Sulzberger daughters; the husband of daughter Marian is Orvil Dryfoos, assistant to the publisher.

Under its Ochs-inspired management, the *Times* developed year by year, and some observers thought it mellowed a little from the Ochs conservatism. It was said that the *Times* was friendlier to labor, though it could be pointed out that Ochs pioneered in providing newspapermen with decent working conditions at a time when most other publishers had little regard for the welfare of their employees.

The *Times* lightened itself a little, too. It still refused to have anything to do with comic strips, but it introduced more feature material, and levity was occasionally encouraged, although sex was frowned upon. Some critics continued to charge that it defended the status quo and refused to take a four-square stand for humanitarian, progressive causes. Yet the *Times* could reasonably point to its political independence and its defense of decidedly unpopular points of view in matters of foreign and domestic policy.

It is obvious that the *Times* has stood in the same uncomfortable position for a hundred years. The attempt to be fair and objective is no more welcome now, generally speaking, than it was in Raymond's time—in spite of all that is said and written in praise of this ideal. Few people are either fair or objective, and too often the newspaper that seems most fair and objective to a reader is the one that agrees with his point of view.

Questions of viewpoint aside, the preeminence of the *Times* rests today on the fulfillment of Raymond's dream of full and accurate coverage of the news, as it has been carried out by Ochs and his successors. The importance of *Times* coverage can hardly be exaggerated, not only as a matter of record but as a daily flow of information obtainable from no other source. The unexampled foreign correspondence of the *Times* is so thorough and accurate, and draws from so many sources unavailable even to government representatives abroad, that official Washington is said to scan these columns closely to glean news unavailable elsewhere.

The enormous, complex organization on West Forty-third

Street which nightly assembles, edits, and prints this most valuable of newspapers is like a fine mechanism, carefully assembled and polished over the years, animated by an ideal that causes veteran *Times* men to believe honestly that their paper is well beyond mortal comprehension or criticism.

It is, in brief, a monument to that rare quality which for a century has been the basic element of the *Times*—a quality the newspaper business, and the world, have needed more than any other: integrity.

Some Giants
of the Middle West

NEW YORK JOURNALISM DOMINATED THE NATIONAL NEWSPAPER scene from the middle of the nineteenth century to its close. Not that there were no good newspapers nor newspapermen functioning elsewhere in the country, but the New York journals tended to be more national in character and outlook, and the men who owned them were likely to be involved in national politics.

Today there are several outstanding newspapers across the nation which reflect domestic and international rather than purely local viewpoints, while New York has only the *Herald Tribune* and *Times,* leaders though they may be, to remind it of former glories. Nevertheless the tone of journalism west of the Hudson, with few exceptions, has always been predominantly local and insular.

Whether this is a fact to be lamented or not depends pretty much on who is doing the analyzing. A thoughtful man concerned with the fate of the nation and the world, and accustomed to reading newspapers whose editors are trying their best to inform him about what is going on, is likely to view some of the fat, prosperous midwestern dailies with dismay. He finds them devoted almost entirely to local and state affairs, with national news except for two or three top stories relegated to the status of filler material, and foreign news summarized in a single capacious box.

The editors of these papers defend themselves by asserting that people in their towns are concerned with their own affairs, and are interested in what goes on in Washington and abroad only as it affects the immediate circumstances of their lives. The clincher to this argument is the undeniable success of numerous midwestern dailies in small cities. They are smug, provincial papers but they make money.

Sometimes this kind of provincialism is not at all a bad thing, and leads to the creation, ultimately, of a first-class newspaper. One of the best examples of such an evolution is the story of William Rockhill Nelson and his successors, and of the *Kansas City Star,* the great newspaper he founded.

Nelson was an Indianan, born in Fort Wayne in 1841 to parents who had been a part of the westward emigration from New York and New Jersey. In his youth, Nelson was considered a holy terror and it was freely predicted by all hands that he would come to no good end. This state of affairs was a constant affliction to his father, who was a pillar of Fort Wayne and the Episcopal Church.

Although he was a good Episcopalian, Nelson senior was broadminded enough to recognize the disciplinary values of the Catholic faith. He sent his wayward son to Notre Dame, in the hope that the rules and regulations of the Holy Cross Fathers would bring some order into the boy's life.

William's college career lasted just two years, after which the fathers requested him politely not to return. His trouble appeared to be that he had a wild, restless energy which education of itself could not channel. He tried the law for a time, got himself admitted to the bar, and practiced for several years during the Civil War, while his parents effectively kept him out of uniform.

After the war ended, he tried his hand at making one of the quick, speculative fortunes he saw being compiled everywhere.

His plan was to create a cotton-growing empire in the South, but he ended with neither cotton nor money.

Back in Fort Wayne, he turned to the contracting business where he had better luck. Many communities in the midwest were building wooden-block paved roads, and seizing this opportunity, Nelson poured into it his incredible energy to such good effect that he amassed a fortune of $200,000 by the time he was thirty-three—only to see it swept away again by the defection of a partner.

Along with his building, Nelson had taken up politics, and as a Democrat had managed Tilden's state campaign. In the process he learned for the first time what newspapers could do, and stretching out a tentative hand toward this new occupation, he bought a part interest in Fort Wayne's Democratic paper, the *Sentinel*.

That was in 1878. Two years later, Nelson was a confirmed newspaper publisher. He had found his real interest in life. Having found it, he looked about for a bigger field of operation and chose Kansas City, where he founded the *Kansas City Evening Star* on September 18, 1880.

The *Star* had some national political preoccupations, editorially. It announced itself as "independent but never neutral," and proved it by backing such liberal candidates, regardless of party, as Grover Cleveland and Theodore Roosevelt, when Nelson happened to think they were the best men available. This lack of a "party line" was the best proof possible to the *Star*'s readers who might have been initially skeptical when the paper declared it had no fixed policy.

But it was not primarily on its political independence that the *Star* rose to eminence. Its success was the result of Nelson's ideal of a newspaper's function. He expressed it in two words: community service. In its news columns, the *Star* was intensely local, a family newspaper for Kansas City families. Where the New York giants had relied for fame upon the thunder and influence of their editorial pages, Nelson believed that the most valuable men on a newspaper were the reporters.

There was plenty of service to be rendered in Kansas City. Since before the Civil War, it had been a town notorious for wild, swirling tides of corruption, lawlessness, and violence. It was a sprawling, reckless city, at the mercy of unprincipled men. William Rockhill Nelson, as it was so truly said later, "pulled Kansas City out of the mud."

If the Kefauver Committee could have whisked itself back in time to the eighties or nineties, it would have found things not very much changed in Kansas City. The basic elements of municipal corruption (not materially changed anywhere in the country during the past half-century) were present in the same forms: fraudulent elections, gambling and vice of every description, all of it existing because of the benevolent and well-paid protection of those in public office. As in Chicago, Philadelphia, New York, and other cities, public transportation was a public scandal, and Kansas City also suffered from civic unsightliness. The place still looked like an unkempt frontier town.

Against these evils Nelson crusaded fearlessly, relentlessly in the *Star*. He intended to make his paper the primary instrument of civic reform, a paper every citizen of goodwill could respect, read, and follow. The campaign was exceedingly difficult, but one by one the *Star* accomplished its aims. Political corruption, if not ended, was brought within bounds, and a program of rehabilitation gave Kansas City the luxuriant parks, broad streets, and impressive boulevards it enjoys today.

In the process, Nelson made good on his promise that the *Star* would be read in every home in Kansas City. This was almost literally true in 1901, when the paper, together with the morning *Times,* which it had acquired that year, was offering thirteen editions a week (morning, afternoon, and Sunday) to subscribers for the unprecedented figure of ten cents.

At that price, and considering the character of the paper, which was a quality job in every respect, few citizens could refuse to subscribe. Ten cents, however, covered only a small part of Nelson's publishing expenses. The remainder, plus profits, had to come from advertisers.

Few papers have ever so completely dominated their advertisers. Because the *Star* and the *Times* saturated the circulation zone, including a weekly issue that went to farmers for only twenty-five cents a year, an advertiser simply could not do without these media. He might object to the rates, and a good many did, or he might boycott the papers and try other methods, as some rebels tried to do. In the end he came back begging for space.

As the years went by, Nelson became a familiar and much respected figure in Kansas City. He shunned politics and every other outside enterprise to devote his time to the *Star,* for which he did little actual writing but exercised firm control over every line of copy that went into the paper. A formidable man to look at, with his huge frame, bulldog face, and immense dignity, he was nevertheless a warm and friendly personality whose friends were innumerable. Those close to him called him "the Colonel," a mark of affectionate respect rather than military rank.

Before he died in 1915, he saw Kansas City become the place he had dreamed of, the focus of the whole Missouri Valley, a metropolis surrounded by comfortable suburbs whose snug residences were the result of Nelson's unremitting crusade to encourage home-building and suburban developments.

As for the *Star,* it passed on to greater glory in other hands. In our own time, having absorbed its competition, it stands alone in Kansas City, and is nearly as much a one-man paper under the direction of Roy Roberts, the noted editor who has kept it in the front rank of dailies. Roberts' corpulent, bespectacled figure has been a familiar one for years, not only in newspaper councils but in those of the Republican Party. Although nominally an independent paper, the *Star* is considered the authentic voice of central midwestern Republicanism, and it is a voice that is listened to with respect in national political circles of both parties. At home, Roberts has continued Nelson's unremitting attacks on local corruption, and the *Star* has several times distinguished itself in this fight.

During the last twenty-five years, the *Star* has been a training ground for some of the best writers in the country. A list of *Star* alumni would include a fair percentage of the top foreign correspondents, many of the leading magazine editors and writers, outstanding newspaper and press association editors and writers, and more than a smattering of novelists, short-story writers, playwrights, and radio and television news commentators. Probably no other newspaper in the country can boast so many talented ex-employees.

Many *Star* men have gone to the Associated Press, which may be a reflection of the close relationship between the agency and the paper's two great editors. Nelson was a director of the AP, and it was almost his only outside interest; Roberts has long been active in AP affairs, in various capacities.

The story of the AP itself revolves around the careers of two other midwestern editors, who advanced Nelson's ideal of community service by creating one of Chicago's finest papers, and then brought the same high conception of responsibility to organizing and directing the greatest of news-gathering associations. These men were Victor Fremont Lawson and Melville Stone.

Lawson was born in Chicago in 1850, the son of Norwegian parents. His father built up a real estate fortune, as so many others did in the boom that carried Chicago onward and upward from Civil War times until the end of the century, but he lost most of it in the Fire of 1871. Before he died in 1873, his son had enjoyed the advantages of a good education at Phillips Academy, although his health was none too good and soon compelled him to forsake books for an outdoor life.

Returning to Chicago after his father's death, young Lawson took up what remained of his inheritance. This included a part interest in a daily called the *Skandinaven,* a Norwegian paper which Iver Lawson and some associates had founded. Victor was not a complete stranger to newspapers. While he was still in public school, he had worked in the circulation department of the *Chicago Evening Journal,* and he had observed the remarkable influence of his father's paper on the thought patterns of the Scandinavian population clustered in the midwestern states.

Lawson was, in fact, an expert observer of people and events. He watched with more than ordinary interest in 1876 the founding of a new Chicago paper, the *Daily News,* in the same building that housed the *Skandinaven.* The editor of this aspiring but shaky property, first penny paper in the West, was a young man he had known in grammar school, Melville Stone.

Stone came from Hudson, Illinois, where he was one of six sons of a Methodist circuit-rider who made tools for sawmills on the side. He was born in 1848, the year the AP also had its birth, and there was never any doubt about the boy's choice of career. At ten he could set type, and while he was still in his teens he became a reporter for the Chicago *Republican.* He was only twenty when he was assigned to cover the convention that nominated General Grant for the Presidency.

For reasons never wholly explained, Stone interrupted his promising newspaper career to buy a part interest in an iron foundry, and later tried to establish a theater ticket agency. Both enterprises were wiped out in the same fire which demolished Iver Lawson's real estate fortune. After that Stone went back to newspapering.

With two partners, he launched the *Daily News* on a shoestring, publishing an experimental edition on Christmas Day of 1875 and beginning regular publication the following month. For six more months the paper staggered along, losing ground every day, until it faced extinction. At this point Lawson stepped in and offered to buy it. The partners were only too glad to get rid of their penny white elephant.

Lawson had the perception to see what was wrong with the new publication. Stone's partners were not primarily newspapermen, and Stone himself had no interest in the management side of the business. His talents were strictly editorial.

Lawson, on the other hand, had extraordinary abilities as a
newspaper manager, and he was certain that with a man like
Stone in the editor's office and his own strong hand at the helm,
the *Daily News* could be a real force for the betterment of
Chicago's civic life.

Like Nelson, Lawson felt a strong sense of duty to his city,
Chicago's moral and political climate was simply Kansas City's
on a larger scale. There were many who yearned to reform it,
but they were outnumbered by those who were satisfied to
enjoy it.

Lawson had definite ideas about what a newspaper should
be, and he enunciated these in the columns of his new property.
The *Daily News,* he wrote, would be:

CANDID—That its utterances shall at all times be the exact truth. It is
independent but never indifferent;

COMPREHENSIVE—That it shall contain all the news;

CONCISE—The *Daily News* is very carefully edited, to the end that the
valuable time of its patrons shall not be wasted in reading of mere trifles;

CLEAN—That its columns shall never be tainted by vulgarity or obscenity;

CHEAP—That its price shall be put within the reach of all.

On this platform, and sparked by Lawson's management, the
Daily News in a few years became a successful paper, one of
the country's best. It obtained an Associated Press franchise in
1878 by taking over the *Evening Post,* and in 1881 it appeared
with a morning edition. This offshoot became the *Record,*
later the *Record-Herald* until it suspended publication in 1914,
a demise which occurred largely because Lawson did not want
to be connected with any paper published on Sunday.

During his seven years of editorship, Stone demonstrated
that he was the best executive Lawson could have obtained to
direct the editorial operation of the paper. People liked his
frank, engaging personality, and they respected his constructive
approach to problems. Professionally, he had the true newspaperman's profound, absorbing interest in everything that
went on in the world.

Ill health overcame Stone in 1888. He was compelled to leave the *News,* and for two years traveled through Europe in a leisurely manner, recouping his strength. Back in Chicago, he thought it best to avoid the strain and excitement of newspaper life, and for the second time in his career turned to other fields. He became president of the Globe National Bank, and interested himself in Chicago civic affairs, serving as treasurer of the Chicago Drainage Canal, and as president of both the Citizens' Association and the Civil Service Reform League.

Meanwhile, Lawson had become involved in the major fight of his career, a contest that eventually drew Stone back into the newspaper business.

The epic battle had its origin in the character of the times. The last decade of the nineteenth century was marked by vast financial manipulations, uncontrolled by regulatory laws. Great fortunes were made and thousands of small investors ruined in the clashes between financial titans. The outstanding phenomenon of the times, from an economic standpoint, was the remarkable growth of corporate trusts. Lawson, with his sharp talent for observation, was keenly aware of how these trusts had taken over commodities of every description, from whisky to kindling wood, barbed wire to ice. As a newspaper proprietor, he saw at first hand how financial news coming on the wire from New York could be specially phrased, or even delayed for a time, so that financiers in the inner circle could make fortunes.

It was a state of affairs that troubled Lawson, particularly because he saw that predatory monopoly had begun to stretch out its hands toward the flow of news.

The key to that danger lay in the disjoined arrangement under which the Associated Press was operating in 1890. In the beginning, there had been two organizations: the Western Associated Press and the New York Associated Press. After years of intermittent warfare, these two had merged their interests in 1882, under a plan by which they were operated under the direction of a Joint Executive Committee, consisting of three New York men and two from the West.

By 1890 the Western publishers were full of misgivings about this arrangement, and they were also disturbed about the rapidly growing strength of their rival, the United Press— not to be confused with the UP of today. Then, as now, however, the difference between these two associations was that the AP had been organized on a cooperative basis, its elected members sharing the cost of gathering and distributing the news, while the UP was a commercial organization that would sell its news on a fee basis to anyone.

At the 1890 meeting of the Western AP, the members aired their suspicions freely. They suspected that the shadowy New York financial management of the UP was somehow in collusion with at least a part of the AP's joint committee—a suspicion confirmed by the fact that the UP appeared to be getting news from the AP report, and the further circumstance that when the UP was unreliable in its report, the AP was likely to be wrong on the same stories.

As a result, the Westerners appointed a three-man committee to investigate, with Lawson as its head. As he began his months of careful examination, Lawson realized that there was plenty of fire beneath the smoke when numerous attempts were made within the AP to discredit and even abolish his committee. He began to believe that the corruption went right to the top.

At a special meeting in Detroit in 1891, Lawson was able to tell his fellow members the whole shocking story of betrayal. The nation's newsgathering facilities, he reported to his astounded audience, were in the hands of a trust which was controlled by three men. One was the director of the United Press, Walter Phillips; another was William Laffan, New York *Sun* business manager; and the third was the financier, John Walsh. The three constituted the UP's principal ownership, and they controlled the AP's news as well by virtue of a secret agreement with certain members of the AP's Joint Executive Committee, who had been induced to join the plot through private gifts of valuable stock.

When the Westerners heard the names of the AP men involved, they could hardly believe it. There was Dana himself, the *Sun*'s distinguished editor and chairman of the Joint Committee; the eminently respectable Whitelaw Reid, the New York AP's representative on the committee; two prominent Western publishers, W. H. Haldeman and Richard Smith, both Western AP committee representatives; and William Henry Smith, the combined AP's general manager.

This cabal was providing the UP with most of the AP's coverage without charge, which, of course, meant that the UP's operating cost was at a ridiculous minimum and the corresponding profits were divided among the plotters as dividends. There were other sordid details, chief among them the document which led to exposure of the whole ring—oddly enough, a formal contract executed in 1888 to legalize what had become so large that the partners no longer trusted each other.

The Western AP acted swiftly. It accepted the report of Lawson and his committee, with all its recommendations, and made Lawson chairman of a new Executive Committee. Among other things, this meant the dissolution of the East-West partnership in the AP. The New York AP could not be expected to survive.

There loomed now a hard struggle to wrest control of the news from the conspiring Easterners. Far from contrite, Laffan, Dana, Phillips, Walsh, and the others were determined to wreck the Western AP too, and make their monopoly of newsgathering secure. Dana was brazen enough to proclaim publicly in the editorial columns of the *Sun*:

Those journals of The Associated Press that are distressed by reason of the superior and more accurate news that is regularly supplied by the United Press are hereby informed that there is no necessity for their remaining in such a state of unhappiness.

The United Press is prepared to furnish the news, foreign and domestic, to any newspaper that is ready and willing to pay a reasonable rate for the same; and that without discrimination on account of race, complexion or previous condition of servitude.

Thus the battle lines were clearly drawn. Either the Western AP's members had to resolve their own differences and work together as a strong, united front to put control of the news in the hands of the individual members who cooperated to gather it, or else the trust that controlled the UP would control all the news, and they would sell it for profit alone, which meant that commercial interests would always come before the integrity of the report.

It was a lengthy, involved struggle. The Western AP first reorganized itself as the Associated Press of Illinois, setting up as a complete nonprofit cooperative. In 1892, the New York AP gave up entirely, the UP getting what remained of it, which meant virtual control of all foreign and Eastern news.

At this critical juncture, Lawson called on his old friend Melville Stone to step in as general manager and help save the AP. Years later, writing of the motives that impelled him to accept, Stone declared:

> I had a secret longing to return to the printer's craft. And much more controlling than any personal interest was the question of public duty. . . .
> . . . The people, for their information—indeed, for the information upon which they based the very conduct of their daily activities—were dependent upon the news of the world as furnished by the newspapers. And this business of news gathering and purveying had fallen into private and mercenary hands. Its control by three men was quite as menacing as that of the governmental autocrats of ages agone.
> A national co-operative news-gathering organization, owned by the newspapers and by them alone, selling no news, making no profits, paying no dividends, simply the agent and servant of the newspapers, was the thing. Those participating should be . . . all equally zealous that in the business of news gathering for their supply there should be strict accuracy, impartiality, and integrity. This was the dream we dreamed. . . .

Installed as general manager, Stone immediately went to London and concluded a ten-year contract with Reuter's Telegram Company, the British newsgathering agency, for exclusive American rights to its European report. This agreement also included the use of the French agency, Havas, and of Berlin's

CTC (Continental-Telegraphen-Compagnie), operating in Germany, middle and southern Europe.

The next development was an all-out fight between the UP and the AP for domestic clients—or members, in the AP's case. The UP was initially successful in this new struggle. It had the advantage of capital to draw upon, whereas the AP was both short of reserves and hard hit by the financial panic of 1893. However, at an emergency meeting late that year, Lawson, Stone, and James E. Scripps, the colorful, fighting editor of the *Detroit Tribune,* rallied the apprehensive members and generated so much enthusiasm that voluntary contributions created a subscription fund of more than a half-million dollars.

With that kind of backing, Lawson, Stone, and Charles Diehl, long an active figure in the AP, went on a bold invasion of the Eastern stronghold to get as many papers as possible away from the UP and into the AP fold. Their success was spectacular. Ranging from New York up and down the seaboard, they captured John Cockerill's *New York Advertiser,* Horace White's *Post,* Pulitzer's *World,* the *Staats-Zeitung,* the *Brooklyn Eagle,* and two smaller New York papers; the *Syracuse Herald* upstate; the *Worcester Spy, New Haven Union, Boston Herald,* and other New England papers; Frank Noyes' *Washington Star;* most of the Philadelphia papers; the *Baltimore Sun* and *American;* and at last, early in 1894, the four Chicago papers which had been the UP's chief midwestern stronghold.

The UP fought back with every weapon, honest or dishonest, at its command. In 1895, Stone found out that it was pilfering AP dispatches, and he trapped the robbers by one of the oldest tricks in journalism. In a story about a provincial revolt in India, Stone inserted a sentence referring to the leader of the rebellion as Siht El Otspueht. Then the story was sent out to member papers and immediately popped up also in the papers of UP clients, who discovered too late that the native chief's name spelled backwards asserted: "The UP stole this."

The end was not far off. As soon as Adolph Ochs bought the *New York Times* in 1896, he announced that it would join the

AP as soon as its UP contract ran out. By March of the following year, only Dana's *Sun* and Hearst's *Journal* remained as UP clients in New York.

Soon after, Dana filed a petition of bankruptcy for the UP. The fight had cost the AP $1,000,000, over and above its normal operating expenses, but the victory was well worth it. The papers which still refused to join the AP banded together as the Publishers' Press, and in time merged with the Scripps-McRae service to form the United Press Associations we know today— still a rival of the AP, but under a far different kind of management.

The AP suffered one more nearly disastrous setback in 1898, when the *Chicago Inter-Ocean* sued the agency and the Illinois Supreme Court ruled that its reports had to be furnished to any newspaper which applied for them. Consequently, in 1900, the AP dissolved in Illinois and reorganized in New York as a nonprofit corporation under the laws of that state. The principle was not challenged again until 1943, when the government instituted an antitrust suit against the AP following a denial of membership the previous year to Marshall Field, publisher of the newly founded *Chicago Sun*. Colonel Robert McCormick, the *Chicago Tribune*'s publisher, led the fight against the government, but on an appeal, the Supreme Court decided against the AP.

As for Stone and Lawson, they lived out the rest of their careers with increasing distinction. Stone served as general manager and secretary of the AP until he was succeeded by Frederick R. Martin on his retirement in 1921. Stone set the conservative, accurate tone of the AP report and established the association's excellent foreign bureaus, which have continued under the management of Kent Cooper since 1925. Stone had a highly confidential whirl at high-level diplomacy when, in 1905, he succeeded in preventing the breakdown of negotiations between Russia and Japan, ending in the peace that concluded the war of 1904-05. Following his death in

1929, in New York, Stone was buried in the National Cathedral at Washington, D.C.

Lawson, too, maintained a lifelong interest in the AP, as president from 1894 to 1900, and as a director from 1894 until he died in 1925. But after the fight with the UP had ended, and he recovered a measure of the health he had lost in the exhausting battle, he turned his attention to building up the *Daily News*.

After the Spanish-American War, which had shown him the difficulty of getting unbiased reports from abroad, written for American readers, he began to establish the string of correspondents in Europe and Asia that resulted in the magnificent foreign service of the *Daily News,* unrivaled outside of the *New York Times.* Widely copied by other papers, it was an organization that distinguished the *Daily News* long after Lawson's death, attaining further honor under Colonel Frank Knox's management.

At home, Lawson continued his zeal for reform. Nationally he was the moving force behind the bill passed in 1910 which established the system of postal savings banks. In Chicago, he put the *Daily News* in the forefront of every movement aimed at civic betterment, meanwhile fighting back at the interests that had for years been profitably tied to City Hall by political and financial bonds.

Lawson practiced personally what he preached in his paper. He gave freely of time and money to such things as free lectures in public schools, better government, the founding of hospitals, support of religious and charitable organizations, and symphony orchestras. In these ventures, he was aided by his wife, a humanitarian in her own right.

Victor Lawson was a quiet, religious man, a prototype of the good citizen, modest and humane. Like his friend Ochs, he lived to see the newspaper he owned and the Associated Press he helped found criticized for their shortcomings, both real and imaginary. But he had the satisfaction of knowing that the *Daily News* was a prime constructive force in his home town, which was his idea of a newspaper's mission, as it had been Nelson's. He enjoyed the knowledge, too, that in the creation of the Associated Press he had achieved a historic victory for the principles of freedom and accuracy in the gathering and dissemination of news.

No newspaperman could have asked for more.

10

Two Southern Gentlemen

As the deepest emotional experience in the life of the American people, the Civil War left behind it not only the human wreckage and economic problems which are always the heritage of armed conflict, but a vast, unprecedented moral and intellectual vacuum.

No Southerner living in 1866 doubted that the South would rise again, but the proud spirit that had sustained the Confederacy along the hard road from Fort Sumter to Appomattox now lacked direction and meaning. Its military leaders were no longer of value, and its political leaders could not show them the way. There was misery, bitterness, crushed pride, and a feeling of stunned acceptance everywhere in the South, but in few quarters could be found anyone who had an answer to the big question: What next?

Normally the press would have provided a platform for those who had answers, and the heat of public debate would have led to the formation of public policy. The Southern press, however, was not well equipped to lead. There had been numerous papers founded in the States below Mason and Dixon's line, but, with rare exceptions, they had spoken for their own towns rather than the region. There had been a few able editors among these early newspapermen, but none of a stature to match the giants of the North.

The war was a sharp dividing line in this respect, as it had been in so many others, and the South began slowly to develop a press of its own. It was a young postwar publisher who proclaimed the real answer to "What next?" after the Southern states had spent two decades trying to bind up their wounds.

Henry W. Grady understood the people of his region well. He knew that it was not political guidance they needed, since that would have to come now from their representatives in Washington. What they wanted desperately was someone who could crystallize the new forces that were moving in the South and put them into words—words capable of fashioning a program the people could follow with hope and honor.

Grady was uniquely qualified to answer that need. First of all, he had the family heritage so important in the South. His father had emigrated to Georgia from North Carolina in 1846, but his mother was a native of Athens, the quiet little university town where Henry was born in 1850. Ann Elizabeth Gartrell, his mother, was related to most of the prominent families of Athens, in that intricate interweaving of cousins and aunts which is the perennial conversational delight of Southern ladies.

Henry grew up in the traditions of Athens, Georgia, and the South. As a boy, he watched his father ride off to war as captain of the Highland Guards. Letters trickled back from him, reporting with quiet pride that he had been made a colonel, noting tersely that he expected to come to grips with the Yankees on the green battlefields of Virginia. Then came the news that bound so many Confederate families together with ties that endured far beyond the end of the war. Colonel William Grady had been killed at Petersburg.

Life went on in Athens. Young Henry, who was a model boy from all accounts, stayed in his home town and did what was expected of him. He went through the local schools, then walked in another direction from the family mansion for four more years until he was graduated from the University of Georgia. Classmates and townspeople thought him a lovable, talented young man. He was so superior at speaking and writing they did not take very seriously his disdain for the exact sciences.

In his freshman year he joined the Methodist Church and fell in love with an admirable girl named Julia King. They were engaged and she joined the church with him.

After graduation he departed from Athens for the first time, but only to go as far as the University of Virginia, where he studied law for three years and then came home to Georgia, though not to Athens. His first job out of college was one any senior with newspaper ambitions might have envied. He was hired as editor of the *Rome Courier*. The only previous newspaper experience he had known, if it could be called experience, was the contribution of intermittent pieces to the *Atlanta Constitution* during his student days.

It must be remembered that Grady was not a struggling young unknown, as most of the Northern editors had been at the beginning. He came of a good family with ramified connections, in comfortable financial circumstances; he had the advantages of an excellent education; and finally, he was a youth of high ideals, unlimited good spirits and absolute self-confidence.

Only with these facts in mind can his brief career in Rome be understood. His employer, the *Courier*'s publisher, instructed him to leave local politics alone. Grady insisted on denouncing the corruption he had immediately discovered. When his boss demurred, Grady went out and bought the town's other two papers and merged them. Next day he was hard at work bringing down his editorial wrath on politics and his former employer.

In other places, perhaps, this would have led to Grady's quick rise to fame as a fearless, successful publisher. In Rome, it was considered an outrage against the proper order of affairs, and the new paper disappeared.

Grady went home to Athens, married his Julia in 1871, and next year set out for Atlanta to try publishing all over again, in company with two partners who were as idealistic as he was.

They established the *Atlanta Herald,* a paper distinguished more for its youthful high spirits than anything else. It too disappeared, taking with it the last of Grady's inheritance from his father.

Not at all discouraged, and convinced that he was destined for a life of high purpose, Grady marked time for a while, writing occasionally for the *Constitution* and the *Augusta Chronicle.* He could have been editor of the *Wilmington Star,* but Grady believed the world held better things for him, and instead he traveled up to New York and began to look for work.

The *Herald* gave him an opportunity to try a piece, and it turned out so well that he was made special Atlanta correspondent for the paper, as part of the elaborate system of news coverage which the elder Bennett had established. This job was the ideal combination as far as Grady was concerned. He was in his native Georgia, he was resident in its most active city, and he was doing the only kind of work that ever interested him.

Grady's successes and failures up to that point could be accounted for by his personality, which was nine-tenths an eager boyishness. He had never really outgrown his college days. If it was a weakness in the sense that it had caused his business failures, it was a decided asset in making opportunities for himself. People high and low warmed to him, wanted to do things for him, were captivated by his ingenuous charm.

Consequently, when he met Cyrus W. Field in 1879, it is hardly surprising that Grady was able to charm him out of a $20,000 loan, with which he bought a quarter-interest in the *Atlanta Constitution.*

It was a turning point in his life. Aware of the opportunity he now possessed, all of Grady's best qualities came to the forefront. He remained boyish, sentimental, and pious in his personal life, but in the *Constitution* he brought into play his uncanny news sense, his analytical powers, and his ability to speak directly to the popular mind in whatever he wrote.

As he wrote, there emerged from his editorials and other

contributions the first voice of hope the crushed Confederacy had heard since the war's end. Answering the great question, "What next?" he replied in effect, "Plenty!"

Diversify your crops, he told his fellow Southerners; examine the resources of your own locality and try to develop them. We *must* bring manufacturing to the South, he insisted, until most of his readers could not help but believe him. The Negro has a new status whether we like it or not, he declared boldly; somehow the whole problem must be adjusted.

Grady's voice was soon heard everywhere. The pebble he dropped in the *Constitution* spread ripples across the dark, nearly stagnant waters of the postwar South until they washed northward even to the shores of Yankee New York. There his words were repeated and republished in Northern newspapers. They were welcomed almost as much there as in his native region, because people were weary of wartime animosities, which had persisted so long afterward through the bitter days of Reconstruction. To be told by a Southerner that it was possible to forget the past and look toward a constructive future was extremely heartening.

It was a significant landmark in postwar history when the New England Club of New York City asked Grady to deliver a speech to them in December 1886. He accepted, and what he told the New Englanders that night ranks as one of the finest speeches in the annals of American oratory. It was a short speech, titled "The New South," but it was delivered with fire and flourishes in a style outdated today, and its passionate sincerity reached far beyond the platform. Generations later high school and college orators were still declaiming it.

In this speech Grady summed up what he had been saying in the *Constitution* about the social and industrial regeneration he visioned for the South. His success immediately broadened his audience, for he was at once in demand everywhere in the country.

In fact, it was his zeal to spread the gospel of regeneration which brought about his untimely death. Speaking on "The

Race Problem in the South" at Boston in 1889, he contracted pneumonia in the damp, chilly New England December, managed to make the long journey back to Atlanta, and died only two days before Christmas. The whole country mourned his passing.

The renascence of the South which he began was, of course, not an overnight accomplishment. Nor must it be supposed that one man, however able, could eradicate the emotional scars of the war and give new life to a whole stricken region. Only time could heal the wounds, and the new life was a matter of generations. The industrial, progressive South that is rising so rapidly today, however, is based solidly on the principles Grady enunciated.

These principles are the best memorial to Grady's memory, since even his famous speech, like the ringing, sonorous editorials he wrote, belongs to the sentimental oratory of another age. His newspaper survived his death handsomely in the hands of his two brilliant colleagues, Clark Howell and Joel Chandler Harris, who is better remembered for his immortal Uncle Remus tales. Both Grady's name and his journalistic principles are perpetuated in the University of Georgia school of journalism named for him.

During Grady's lifetime, and for three decades afterward, one other voice spoke for the South editorially. Henry Watterson was the only other great Southern editor of his time, and because he outlived Grady, came to be considered before he died as the bridge between the old Confederacy and the new South.

As editor of the *Louisville Courier-Journal*, Watterson might have been handicapped in his role of Southern spokesman by the fact that Kentucky is a border state, not considered by some diehards as part of the real South. Today the *Courier-Journal* office is only four blocks south of the Mason-Dixon Line.

The location was no handicap chiefly because of Watterson's overpowering personality. He did not attain recognition so much by reason of what he said, as Grady did, but because of the immense authority with which he said it, and because, after Grady's death, no one remained in the South to challenge him. When he spoke, therefore, most Northern editors and a good share of those below the Line accepted his opinions as representative of the region. Moreover, during Reconstruction days his position in a border state that had stood with the Confederacy enabled him to act as a kind of editorial mediator between North and South.

Watterson was born on the fringes of the South, in Washington, D.C., ten years before Grady's birth. His father was a Tennessee Congressman, and so Henry grew up in two homes, the national capital and the ancestral homes of his mother and father in Tennessee.

Aside from the fact that he was sick much of the time, Watterson's childhood was altogether remarkable. At first his parents thought he might become a concert pianist, so marked was his talent, but his left hand was weak and he lost the sight of his right eye, so eventually he had to give up the piano. At twelve he had accompanied his nine-year-old friend, Adelina Patti, who later became one of the world's great singers.

It was not music that made him such a privileged youngster, but the opportunity he enjoyed to meet great men and to watch at first hand the march of history. That kind of schooling, supplemented by insatiable reading, more than made up for what he lacked in formal education, which consisted of a short session in Philadelphia's Protestant Episcopal Academy.

Watterson's playground was, as often as not, the House of Representatives. There his father let him play at being a page boy. One day he saw John Quincy Adams slump in his seat, and the business of the House came to a shocked standstill while the old statesman was borne away from the chamber to his death. Once his father took him to the Hermitage and there Jackson dandled him on his knee. In Watterson's lengthy lifetime he knew all the Presidents from Jackson to Harding, and also such Presidents-to-be as Coolidge, Hoover, and Franklin Roosevelt.

He grew up breathing the atmosphere of politics, and even after his father turned to a career as newspaper editor and the family was back in Tennessee, he had the example of the elder Watterson before him. Like his father, young Henry was a Union man by conviction and a Democrat by tradition. His Northern sympathies were reinforced in 1853 when he became a reporter for the *Washington* (D.C.) *Daily States,* after a short term of reporting for the *New York Times,* and was assigned to cover the inauguration of Lincoln. Watterson came to have a profound admiration for the President, and years later was still writing tributes to him.

When the war began, Watterson was convinced that Southern resistance would be short-lived, and turning down a lieutenant-colonelcy in the Union Army, he went home to Tennessee with the idea that he would stay there and write until the argument blew over.

At home he found that it was impossible to hold aloof from the conflict. As he put it in his autobiography, "The boys were all gone to the front, and the girls were . . . all crazy." Watterson had little, if any, enthusiasm for the Southern cause, but the social pressures were too much for him and he joined the Confederate Army.

"Marse Henry's" relations with the Army were highly informal during the four years he served it, but it provided the springboard to his later career. He began on General Leonidas Polk's staff, but sickness overtook him and apparently it was decided by the higher echelons, though it has never been made clear, that Watterson would be more useful employing his editorial talents as a propagandist.

Still in uniform, he went to work for a Nashville newspaper which was busy turning out Southern propaganda. The fall of the city compelled him to return briefly to real military service, but it was not long before he was made editor of the official Tennessee newspaper in Chattanooga. Watterson called it the *Rebel* and made it over into a house organ for the Confederate Army.

For the first time Watterson had a paper all to himself, with an opportunity to show what he could do. What he did was to make the paper outstanding through his writing, in which he displayed for the first time the impact and richness of expression that made him one of the country's best editors later on. While he was editing the *Rebel*, too, he met Walter N. Haldeman, publisher of the *Louisville Courier*, who was to become his partner.

Their partnership was several years away, however. Watterson had to give up the *Rebel* in the face of advancing Union armies nearing Atlanta, and once more he spent a period as staff officer to various generals, including Johnston and Hood. The Confederate government then picked him for a dangerous secret mission—to try to reach Liverpool, England, and unload some cotton shipments for desperately needed cash. Unable to get out of the country, he was compelled to return to the South, where he again became an editor, in Montgomery, Alabama.

After the war, he moved up to Cincinnati, went to work for the *Evening Times*, and assumed editorial control of it when the editor died suddenly. Watterson didn't stay long in his $75-a-week chair. He was on the move, to Nashville this time, where he operated a newspaper for a short time, got married, went on a London honeymoon, and returned to work for the *Nashville Republican Banner*.

It was while he marked time on this paper that his fortunes took a final turn. Two offers came from Louisville: one from his friend Haldeman to edit the *Courier*, and another from the aging editor of the *Journal* to help him run the property. Watterson wrote to Haldeman and proposed the obvious, a merger, but when Haldeman refused, Watterson accepted the *Journal's* offer.

There was a six-month-long, rather polite skirmish between the two papers before the inevitable merger occurred, on November 8, 1868, and Watterson began his long career as editor of the *Courier-Journal*.

At once he assumed the role that Henry W. Grady, then only eighteen, would soon make his own. The difference was that Watterson dealt in much more specfic terms than Grady, demonstrating his background in politics. He too wanted to regenerate the South and mend the breach between the broken parts of the nation, but whereas Grady argued for broad principles in the fields of social and economic action, Watterson advocated a specific political deal in which the South would guarantee civil and legal rights for its Negroes in return for certain rights and privileges lost to the North by the war.

Such prominent national figures as Greeley and Carl Schurz backed his proposition, but of course it was fought by powerful segments of opinion on both sides of the Line. At the Liberal-Republican nominating convention of 1872, held in Cincinnati, these three combined with Samuel Bowles; Murat Halstead, editor of the prominent *Cincinnati Commercial;* Whitelaw Reid and Horace White to back Greeley's run for the Presidency. Joseph Pulitzer attended this convention as a delegate from Missouri.

Although Greeley was defeated, Watterson believed that the campaign had helped to bring North and South closer together because Liberal-Republican ideas had been spread far and wide. Two years later, Watterson had found a hero to replace Greeley —actually not so much a replacement, because Marse Henry admired Greeley intermittently, but he considered Samuel J. Tilden as "the ideal statesman," the only man in public life he had seen who could come near Lincoln.

For two years Watterson built up Tilden toward the famous disputed election of 1876. To deal with matters at first hand, he went to Washington in the summer of 1876 and sat in the House of Representatives in a chair left temporarily vacant by the death of a Louisville Representative. He was there part of the next winter, while a special Electoral Commission ultimately decided the contested election for Rutherford Hayes. During these proceedings, Watterson sent back inflammatory dispatches to the *Courier-Journal,* but they were largely the product of intense feeling and anticipated disappointment.

The defeat of his hero left a mark on Watterson's political soul that lasted the remainder of his life. He could never again be depended upon to follow anybody's party line. The Democrats could not command his loyalty, as they had in the past, and whoever happened to be in the White House could be sure that sometime during his occupancy he would incur the displeasure, if not the open antagonism, of the Colonel.

His running quarrel with Cleveland attained a point of violence in 1892, when it appeared that the President would run for a third term. Watterson told the Kentucky Democratic Convention in words that forecast dire predictions made nearly a half-century later: "I will not vote for his nomination, if his be the only name presented, because I firmly believe that his nomination will mean the marching through a slaughter house to an open grave and I refuse to be a party to such folly."

Watterson described Theodore Roosevelt as a man who was "as sweet a gentleman as ever scuttled a ship or cut a throat." He abused "The Man on Horseback," as he called Teddy, at the risk of circulation and public disfavor, in the face of the President's overwhelming popularity with the voters. By this time, Watterson had become so noted an editor that his editorials were carried as news on the wires, and consequently his feud with Roosevelt attracted nation-wide attention. One of his pronouncements is reminiscent of another attack on another Roosevelt, made by a prominent editor in our own times. Watterson asserted that Teddy was a paranoiac who wanted to be a dictator, and he urged the Roosevelt family to put their psychopathic relative away.

Woodrow Wilson fared little better. Watterson supported him through the war, but criticized him severely before it began, and afterward split sharply with him on the League of Nations issue. While the war went on, Watterson was a vociferous patriot. As early as 1914, he declaimed: "To hell with the Hohenzollerns and the Hapsburgs!" and repeated this sentiment at appropriate intervals until 1918. When the United States declared war in 1917, his editorials on the subject won him a Pulitzer prize.

In 1918, he sold his interests in the paper, became editor emeritus, retired to Florida, where he had spent an increasing amount of time, wrote his two-volume autobiography, "Marse Henry" (the affectionate name by which he had been known for years), and died in Jacksonville in December 1921.

With his passing, it seemed to many people that a part of the South itself had died. To Southerners he was a figurehead, a symbol, an institution. Villard wrote accurately of him that "whenever he appeared on a Southern platform men and women beheld the 'Lost Cause'. . . ." Yet he was not a professional Southerner. When he wanted to, he advocated ideas deeply offensive to many of his old Confederate supporters. That was why Booker T. Washington could say of him: "If there is anywhere a man who has broader or more liberal ideas concerning the Negro, or any undeveloped, I have not met him."

Somehow, though, Watterson never emerged as a fighting liberal, a great editor cut along the lines of Bowles, Godkin, and White. He was a personality, not a hewer to the line, and like so many colorful public figures, he struck off where his fancies dictated. The Whites and the Godkins and the Greeleys were not his true friends, however logical it appears that they should have been. Perversely, he preferred Dana.

His greatest accomplishment was beyond doubt the substantial work he did to bridge the postwar gap between North and South. The hundreds of thousands of words he poured out in his editorials were not only the natural verbosity of his time but the expression of a man who had much to say.

Watterson's style, bombastic yet effective, could not be mistaken by anyone, though the editor often signed his initials to editorials to make certain they were recognized. Long after other editorial writers had yielded to the changing times and shortened their writings to a more modern length, Watterson continued to turn out editorials which ran all the way from two to nine columns, sometimes spreading luxuriously across three pages.

His physical personality was equally unmistakable. He was a commanding figure. His one good blue eye, which he used far beyond what should have been its powers, fixed visitors from beneath eyebrows that presaged John L. Lewis. He had an abundant mustache and a goatee, in the style Northerners still associate with Kentucky Colonels. His voice was a high but powerful staccato, at full cry capable of being heard for a considerable distance.

Around him grew a network of legends. Cartoon and tall tale pictured him as the typical Colonel with a mint julep in his hand, lounging picturesquely amid magnolias and white columns. Actually he disliked the "Colonel" sobriquet, preferred champagne, still wine, and beer in that order, and worked harder than anyone else on the paper. It was true he had a fine Southern mansion, Mansfield, with spacious verandahs and green lawns, where he presided in patriarchal splendor with his wife and children.

At the office, Marse Henry was a one-man show. He commanded an enormous respect and devotion from his staff, though he was figuratively peering over their shoulders while they worked. Tom Wallace, a veteran *Courier-Journal* man, recalled that when he was made "amusements editor," Marse Henry summoned him and remarked: "As amusements editor you will have to associate with me somewhat intimately. It will not hurt your intellect, but it may destroy your morals."

He hated errors in his papers in direct proportion to his devotion to draw poker, one of his most satisfying recreations. He was a conversationalist as exuberant and lengthy as his editorials, and he knew how to prepare lobster Newburg expertly. Marse Henry resented the story that he was a hard drinker. That was about the only legend that irritated him. He insisted that most of the Watterson stories were apocryphal, but he often told the tales himself with chuckling amusement.

As he neared the end, Watterson felt himself further and further removed from the stream of national life, and he began to take a dim view of newspapers generally. He thought they were not what they used to be, seeming not to understand that the world was in the same predicament. But he regarded the state of newspapering and the nation, where prohibition and equal suffrage had come about despite his disapproval, with characteristic wry humor. Once Wallace visited him at Mansfield, where he lay in bed surrounded by books, and told him that the editorial page was under serious discussion at the office.

"I do not see the slightest reason for anxiety," Marse Henry told him. "I read all of the editorials every day. I don't see anything in the paper that shouldn't be said, or anything that, without the slightest loss, might not be left unsaid."

In his autobiography, he excoriated the modern newspaper with these words: "Neither its individuality, nor its self-exploitation, scarcely its grandiose pretension, remains. . . . There continues to be printed in large type an amount of shallow stuff that would not be missed if it were omitted altogether. But, except as a bulletin of yesterday's doings, limited, the daily newspaper counts for little, the single advantage of the editor—in case there is an editor—that is, one clothed with supervising authority who 'edits'—being that he reaches the public with his lucubrations first, the sanctity that once hedged the editorial 'we' long since departed."

Watterson died in the gloomy belief that civilization might well not last much more than seventy years longer, an idea that seems more reasonable today than it did at the start of the twenties. But at least the recrudescence of the South to which he and Grady contributed so much was a result that must certainly have pleased him.

Country Editors

WATCHING THE CLASH, BY DAY AND NIGHT, OF JOURNALISM'S BIG city giants, it is easy to overlook the men who have walked the nation's Main Streets, gathering the news of their neighbors and friends for publication in newspapers whose sphere of influence usually stops near the county line.

Some of these editors have refused to be overlooked. Their names and papers have been known and recognized everywhere in America, and occasionally abroad. Others have labored obscurely all their lives and died poor, but with the consolation of knowing they served their communities. Whatever their status, the country editors have been major factors in community life since Americans started living together, and in some respects have performed a more useful function than their big city brothers.

Probably the first country editor of any consequence in America was Joseph Dennie, who set a pattern for rural journalism which was followed for generations after his death. An only child, Boston-born in 1768, Dennie's childhood was spent both in Boston and in Lexington, where his parents took him when the British were at the gates of New England's capital in 1775.

There he read everything in his father's library that he could lay hands on, a preoccupation which did nothing to fit him for the commercial career his family had planned. Two years of business life amply demonstrated his unfitness for it, and he was sent to Harvard, where he balked at the discipline and dry lectures. He never got over his resentment toward the university.

Dennie at first chose the law for a vocation, though with no great enthusiasm. He was admitted to the bar, but the extent of his practice did not give him much encouragement. Turning for the first time to writing, he embarked on a series of essays in which he attempted to combine the virtues of Addison and Goldsmith. Titled the "Farrago," these were printed, for the most part, in various New Hampshire papers, and were reprinted in a short-lived Boston weekly that Dennie founded in 1795, called the *Tablet*.

When the *Tablet* expired after thirteen numbers, Dennie returned to New Hampshire, where he had served his apprenticeship as law clerk, and came to rest in the village of Walpole. He appeared to attract men like himself—that is, "wags, wits and literati," Federalists all, who liked to meet and argue literature and politics, in the manner of the more famed Hartford Wits. Out of meetings with such men, Dennie was inspired to begin a new essay series, which he called the "Lay Preacher."

These essays appeared first in the local paper, the *Farmer's Weekly Museum*, which had been started by Isaiah Thomas. They were witty, critical, and elegant, like Dennie himself, and as Frank Luther Mott remarks so truly of them, were "probably the best periodical essays ever produced in America."

The effect they made can be judged better when one remembers that in this period of America's growth, weekly newspapers sprouted like grass after rain as journeymen traveled from one town to another, setting up papers where none had existed before. Most of these sheets were highly imitative of city papers, put together largely with items clipped from their metropolitan cousins, and highly neglectful of the only commodity they really had to sell—local news.

Dennie's "Lay Preacher" essays were so excellent that other

papers, both daily and weekly, reprinted them and the author found himself famous. Knowing a good thing when they saw it, the publishers of the *Farmer's Museum* made him editor in 1796. Dennie got his friends to write for the paper, made it a Federalist organ, and in less than two years had produced a newspaper that was read nearly everywhere in the settled parts of America.

Joseph T. Buckingham was printer's devil at the *Museum* in those days, and years later in his book, *Specimens of Newspaper Literature,* which remains a standard source book today, described how Dennie appeared to him when he saw the editor in a Walpole tavern, where he had been preparing copy for the printer. Buckingham wrote:

> In person he was below rather than above the middling height, and was of slender frame. He was particularly attentive to his dress, which, when he appeared on the street, on a pleasant day, approached the highest notch of the fashion. I remember him . . . dressed in a pea-green coat, white vest, nankin small-clothes, white silk stockings, and shoes or pumps fastened with silver buckles which covered at least half the foot from the instep to the toe. His small-clothes were tied at the knees, with ribband of the same color, in double bows, the ends reaching down to the ankles. He had just come from the barber's shop. His hair, in front, was well loaded with pomatum, frizzled and powdered; the ear-locks had undergone the same process; behind, his natural hair was augmented by the addition of a large queue (called vulgarly the false tail) which, enrolled in some yards of black ribband, reached half way down his back. Thus accommodated, the Lay Preacher stands before my mind's eye as lifelike and sprightly as if it were but yesterday that I saw the reality.

Oddly, the fame of Dennie and the *Farmer's Museum* did not make the paper successful financially. It tottered along for some time through successive failures, while the editor worked for less pay, until Dennie became convinced that Walpole was too small for his talents. Repairing to Philadelphia, he worked for a while on Fenno's *Gazette of the United States,* until in 1801 he founded a weekly magazine, the *Port Folio,* devoted to literature and politics. This publication became the country's leading literary publication until the founding of the *North American Review* in 1815. Its long list of distinguished contributors included the publisher, whose "Lay Preacher" essays continued to appear.

Unfortunately, Dennie was never able to get many of his essays published, though the forty that were printed at Walpole in 1796 were in 1803 "the most popular work on the American continent," according to an English traveler. Another selection appeared in 1817.

Dennie died in 1812 in an undeserved obscurity. Besides the lasting worth of his essays, he wrote the first noteworthy page in the history of American country journalism.

For a long time there were no other such pages. Until the Civil War, country papers were distinguished by their variety more than anything else. They were four-page sheets, on the average, though some were larger, and devoted themselves mostly to politics. People looked to their editors for political enlightenment as they did to their preachers for spiritual truths. The country editor's office was often a forum where the questions of the day were debated violently.

After the war, with the expansion of the nation toward the Pacific, country journalism attained hitherto unimagined numerical proportions because papers in the new, sparsely settled countries were nearly all weeklies. Two papers could, and usually did, exist in villages no larger than a thousand in population. They were small by modern standards, averaging four pages with six to nine columns per page, but they managed to print some local news and advertising along with the usual miscellaneous space-filling items and the inevitable political comment.

While the war went on, these papers got welcome help through a device that has become a thriving business today—the furnishing of "patent insides," or papers with the inside already made up by some other paper or agency, and pages one and four left blank for the country editor's use. The practice began with the *Baraboo* (Wisconsin) *Republic,* which utilized ready-made contents from the *Wisconsin State Journal* in Madison. More than a thousand papers were getting patent insides from various competing syndicates by 1872.

Between 1870 and 1890, the number of village weeklies tripled to more than 12,000, most of them in towns under 10,000, but some in villages no larger than 300 people. In those days an aspiring editor needed very little capital to put himself in business. Press, type, and an imposing stone were the chief requirements, plus credit, patience, and initiative. It was harder to keep them going after they were started, since publishers as well as printers were a migratory lot who tried another town when one failed them. One midwestern editor founded twenty-six papers in his peregrinating career.

Yet in spite of these transitory characteristics, the country press in general was in a thriving condition, with a good many papers of solid, substantial, and generally independent character. Circulation could run as high as 3,000, at a subscription rate varying from a common two dollars in the seventies to half of that figure in the next decade.

This rising tide of weekly journalism reached a peak about 1914, when there were 14,500 listed. By that time weeklies had assumed a general pattern much like that of today, with the emphasis on community events. In the period of their growth, while city dailies had increasingly fed readers larger doses of crime and scandal, national politics and international affairs, the country editors had correspondingly learned that the life of the community and the rural area around it was the source of their own life. The rise of rural free delivery also strengthened circulation, although at the same time it brought big city papers into competition.

The emphasis on local news meant, too, that the editors were more than ever prominent in local affairs, particularly politics, and consequently the country press tended to be more partisan while the city press was becoming less personal.

In this prosperous time for country journalism, when its character had solidified, it was natural that for the first time since Joseph Dennie there would be men whose voices could be heard outside their own restricted territories.

One of the first of these was Edgar Watson Howe, who, as plain Ed Howe, "The Sage of Potato Hill," published the *Atchison* (Kansas) *Globe* for thirty-six years and was known to millions of his fellow Americans.

Howe and most of the other brilliant figures in country journalism operated dailies rather than weeklies, but the towns were small and the character of the papers represented the best in the newspapering that exists in rural America.

Howe was born in 1854, the descendant of an English-Pennsylvania Dutch family and the son of a stern Methodist circuit-rider who brought up Ed in a rigid, puritanical manner, deep in the hills of northern Missouri. The elder Howe was the kind of preacher who went on for a half-dozen hours at a time, and whipped his son if the boy fell asleep in his front-pew seat.

Ed was only fourteen when he got a shock far worse than any that were the result of his father's discipline. Preacher Howe abruptly ran away with a lady member of his flock, leaving his wife and several children to look after themselves. This event, coupled with other traumatic occurrences in Howe's young life, left him with a permanent hatred of religion and women.

His father had done Ed some good, however, by permitting him to learn typesetting in the print shop he ran on the side in Bethany, Missouri, and after the elopement, Ed was able to start his working life at once by becoming a tramp printer. One summer he spent in Salt Lake City, working for Brigham Young.

His real career began shortly after his twenty-first birthday, when he settled in Atchison, Kansas, population 12,000, and with a stake of $200 and the help of his brother Jim, began publishing the *Atchison Globe*. The brothers gathered the news, wrote it up, set the type and did the printing, as so many other shoestring country-paper editors operated in that period. The difference between these others and the *Globe* was solely Ed Howe. His style—he did most of the writing—was so sparkling and the paper was so well edited that within a month the *Globe* was in the black, and in a few years the two competing newspapers in town folded up.

As soon as he had beaten his competition, Howe did something so extraordinary that it has probably never been duplicated in American journalism. He began a relentless attack on religion and the churches—this in a small town in the heart of God-fearing Kansas! The reaction at first was incredulity, then the counterattack began.

Other papers sprang up to combat the *Globe,* but somehow they failed to last long. Advertisers boycotted the paper and subscribers canceled subscriptions, but Howe refused to retreat. Instead he roamed the streets of Atchison and the country roads around it, getting all kinds of news from all kinds of people. As his son, Gene Howe, has written with pardonable pride, "He was the greatest reporter in America; he was so regarded by many leading newspapermen. The *Globe* vibrated with his sparkle and humor, and it became the most quoted daily in the United States. Opposition could not stand against it; Atchison people simply could not resist reading his paper."

Gene Howe pictured his father in a *Saturday Evening Post* article as "the most wretchedly unhappy man I ever knew," and the facts bear him out. A born crusader, fighting against institutions as firmly fixed in human life as anything could possibly be, he alternated between exuberant fits of his crusading zeal and moods of deepest depression when he saw that he had failed to accomplish what was plainly impossible. "It's me and not my ideas," he would say. "I haven't been able to make people understand; I must make everything so plain, so simple that they will see the truth." He was depressed 80 per cent of the time, his son estimates.

His views on religion and women seem incredible in retrospect. He believed it when he wrote: "To me, the most wonderful thing in civilization is religion. That people should have advanced so marvelously in everything else, as they have done, and carried along with them a doctrine they know to be untrue, is a fact I have marveled at all my life. Never have I known a sincere religious man or woman."

He believed it, too, when he told his readers that men and women were natural enemies, that civilization was threatened because women had become spoiled and extravagant, and he urged an actual revolt of the nation's men against their women. He thought a girl ought to have only one engagement and one marriage, and he was shocked whenever one of his friends married a widow. He thought a woman should be her husband's chattel, with no rights and no privileges. Once he wrote that if a husband ever sank to the point of helping his wife on with her coat, he ought to leave her because he was henpecked.

In spite of these extreme views, Ed came to be accepted by Atchison in time. People ignored what he wrote about religion and women, or else they were amused by his more excessive blasts. Much of their tolerance may have been due to the fact that Ed Howe had put Atchison on the map. His *Globe* was quoted by newspapers everywhere, particularly the witty, sarcastic quips known as "paragraphs," for which he was best known. One issue of the *Boston Globe* carried fifty-eight paragraphs clipped from its Kansas namesake. As America's most famous small-town editor, he was given dinners and awards and generally lionized. In fact, Howe dominated his community so thoroughly that it was known far and wide as "Ed Howe's town."

Besides his *Globe* writings, he produced in 1882 a first-rate novel which still stands up well today, *The Story of a Country Town,* and his autobiography, *Plain People,* published in 1929, remains as one of the best of its kind.

At fifty-seven Howe retired from the *Globe,* turned it over to his son Gene, and amused himself in his retirement by editing a little magazine called *Ed Howe's Monthly,* in which he made a continuing frontal attack on everything in American life that displeased him. That included politicians, have-nots, and liberals. Howe was an extreme conservative whose god was business. But the indignation and venom he put into the monthly attracted few customers, and eventually he gave it up. He died in 1937, at the age of eighty-four, consistent to the last in every one of his views.

Ironically, it is not these views which have earned him a place in journalistic history. His brilliant editorship, his novel, his autobiography—all these are remembered, but even more the pungent little paragraphs that still glow with sardonic wit. Here are a few samples:

"Families with babies, and families without babies, are so sorry for each other."

"Don't be ashamed if you can't play the piano; be proud of it."

"If you want to get a man very angry, get someone to pray for him."

"Women like to attend weddings, to hear the big, sweet, juicy promises the bridegrooms make."

"I once wondered how the banks made their money, but when I procured a loan I found out."

"Nearly every unsuccessful man we ever met was a good billiard player."

"When a woman is on her last legs, she starts a boarding-house; a man starts a fire-insurance agency."

"Some people never have anything except ideals."

"A man has his clothes made to fit him; a woman makes herself fit her clothes."

"A woman is as old as she looks before breakfast."

"What people say behind your back is your standing in the community in which you live."

"The difference between a good woman and a bad one is that a bad woman raises hell with a good many men, while a good woman raises hell with only one."

That was Ed Howe.

In another part of Kansas lived another Kansas editor, equally famous, who was Howe's antithesis. William Allen White was as brilliantly and uncompromisingly blunt about his beliefs as Howe, but he was blunt on the side of humanity and ideals, while the Sage of Potato Hill was iconoclastic about the people he really loved. Consequently, White lived to see himself a much admired American—not in spite of his faults, but because of his virtues.

White was born on a Thursday morning in February 1868, in the town of Emporia, Kansas. For the work that he was going to do he could have had no better training than working on the *Kansas City Star,* under William Rockhill Nelson, because the kind of community service philosophy that Nelson was practicing in Kansas City was the idea that White brought back to his native Emporia in 1895, when he bought the town's five-year-old *Gazette* for $5,000 and began a career with it that lasted until his death.

White was a born editorial writer. He spoke the language of the people, not only Kansans but those in small cities and towns everywhere in the country. Intellectual writers on city papers might sneer at his folksy approach and language, but it was White's words that were remembered and repeated.

The year after he took over the *Gazette* he leaped to national prominence with a single editorial, "What's The Matter With Kansas?" Answering his question, in part, White declared:

We all know; yet here we are at it again. We have an old mossback Jacksonian who snorts and howls because there is a bathtub in the state-house; we are running that old jay for governor. We have another shabby, wild-eyed, rattle-brained fanatic who has said openly in a dozen speeches that "the rights of the user are paramount to the rights of the owner"; we are running him for chief justice, so that capital will come tumbling over itself to get into the State. We have raked the old ash-heap of failure in the State and found an old human hoopskirt who has failed as a business man, who has failed as an editor, who has failed as a preacher, and we are going to run him for Congress-at-large. He will help the looks of the Kansas delegation in Washington. Then we have discovered a kid without a law practice and decided to run him for attorney-general. Then for fear some hint that the state had become respectable might percolate through the civilized portions of the nation, we have decided to send three or four harpies out lecturing, telling the people that Kansas is raising hell and letting the corn go to weeds.

This editorial was aimed at the Populist ticket and was used as ammunition by most of the country's Republican newspapers. In later years, when White's political beliefs had become much less partisan, he remarked that the editorial represented "conservatism in its full and perfect flower."

Nevertheless, Kansas and the nation recognized a new and potent voice when it heard one. No wonder that a large and appreciative audience waited to see what the *Gazette*'s editorial page had to say when it so frequently got such gems as this on January 28, 1901, titled, "Carrie Nation and Things":

Carrie Nation is wrong—dead wrong. Many people who are right are wrong. John Brown was. So was Christ, for that matter. Probably if the *Gazette* had been published in Jerusalem 2,000 years ago, it would have stood by the social order and the dignity of the law, and would have cautioned people to keep away from the mob that followed Christ over the country, listening to his spurious doctrine. Probably the *Gazette* would have referred to the Sermon on the Mount as "incendiary talk" delivered to the "ragtag and bobtail yesterday out on Mount Tabor." The *Gazette* also probably would have referred to his charlatan tricks in serving free lunch, and would have advised the people "to keep their heads and not be led into foolishness by an unknown fellow who goes about the country imitating the fakirs of India and stirring up dissension with the established church". . . .

Now, as to Mrs. Nation! She is crazy as a bedbug. There is no doubt about that. And she won't stop the sale of beer by her foolish crusade. Also by appealing to anarchy she discredits the very law which she would have the jointist respect. She has, by her unwomanly conduct, forfeited every claim she may have had to respect as a woman, and she deserves richly everything she has got—and more, too.

But still that is merely her personal side of it. There is also this side: she is giving a great big horse-type object lesson which tells the people in simple, homely words of one syllable that a man who sells whiskey illegally, or a man who encourages him, has no moral right which a white man is bound to respect. It's just as well to keep that lesson in view—even if it takes a crazy woman to carry the banner.

White rapidly drew away politically from his early conservatism, and by 1912 he was a Progressive Party national committeeman in Theodore Roosevelt's unsuccessful third party attempt. As the years went on, he was as faithful to the Republicans as he was to Emporia, but it was the kind of faithfulness that left him free to criticize, and even to sit on the fence if he desired.

He worked for years, quietly and behind the scenes with other Republicans, to get Herbert Hoover into the White House and thereafter supported him editorially when he could conscientiously do so, but as a liberal Republican, he forthrightly expressed disillusionment with his man.

When Julian Street wired him at Hoover's Rapidan Camp in 1931, urging White to "beg" Hoover to make a strong speech at the American Legion convention in Detroit, White replied, "We talked over the speech. He has no dramatic sense and could not do the thing as you and I would like to have seen it done and as the occasion cried for it. He is a grand administrator but has no sense of public relations. He can press a button and call a man in and hire him or fire him wisely, but he can't hold a joint debate with him, and that is the trouble. He is all right. I am very fond of him. But he is not for this hour. . . ."

Always White spoke out boldly, no matter whom he might offend. When the Ku Klux Klan began to be a power in Kansas in the early twenties, he noted that an organizer had come to Emporia, and a week later declared editorially: "The Ku Klux Klan is said to be reorganizing in Emporia. It is an organization of cowards. Not a man in it has the courage of his convictions. It is an organization of traitors to American institutions. Not a man in it has faith enough in American courts, laws and officials, to trust them to maintain law and order. . . . It is a menace to peace and decent neighborly living and if we find out who is the Imperial Wizard in Emporia, we shall guy the life out of him. He is a joke, you may be sure. But a poor joke at that."

When the Klan showed its strength by electing an Emporia mayor and got both major party nominations for state governor, White announced he would enter as an independent because he wanted to "offer Kansans afraid of the Klan and ashamed of that disgrace, a candidate who shares their fear and shame."

The Klan candidate won, but White knew that Kluxism was a transitory affair in Kansas, and when Hiram Evans, the Imperial Wizard, proclaimed a speaking tour of the state in the spring of 1926, White predicted: "He will find what was once a thriving and profitable hate factory and bigotorium now laughed into a busted community; where the cock-eyed hedragon wails for its first-born, and the nightshirts of a once salubrious pageantry sag into the spring breezes and bag at the wabbly knees.

"The Kluxers in Kansas are as dejected and sad as a last year's bird's nest, afflicted with general debility, dizziness on going upstairs, and general aversion to female society."

White did not always couch his barbs in such exotic terminology. He could be as effective with a straight, deadly clarity of language that cut through even the pretenses of 1926 and the Great Bull Market in America.

"What a sordid decade is passing!" he wrote then. "It will be known in American history fifty years hence as the time of terrible reaction. . . . It will not be the story of a weak man like Harding nor a silent and unemotional man like Coolidge. They are mere outer manifestations of the inner spiritual traits of the people. The spirit of our democracy has turned away from the things of the spirit, got its share of the patrimony ruthlessly and gone out and lived riotously and ended feeding among the swine."

He did not hesitate to attack such sacred institutions as the D. A. R., when the organization blacklisted him in 1928 along with others it considered as liberals and pacifists. White charged in an editorial that "The D. A. R. has yanked the Klan out of the cow pasture and set it down in the breakfast room of respectability, removing its hood and putting on a transformation. Mrs. Brosseau [D. A. R. president] is a lovely lady with many beautiful qualities of heart and mind, but, in her enthusiasm, she has allowed several lengths of Ku Klux nightie to show under her red, white and blue."

White fought the New Deal, but always fairly, and not too consistently. Stopping in Emporia during the campaign of 1936, President Roosevelt remarked that he appreciated "Bill White's support for three and a half years out of every four."

Down to the end of his life, which came on January 29, 1944, White continued to battle for what he believed was honest and right. He even criticized his fellow publishers in terms which would have been profoundly resented if they had come from anyone else.

In 1939, he wrote that "the most serious danger that menaces the freedom of the American press is the obvious anxiety of rich publishers about the freedom of the press. . . . The publisher is not bought like a chattel. Indeed he often is able to buy those who are suspected of buying him. But he takes the color of his social environment. . . . The average publisher is pretty generally against organized labor. He is too often found opposing the government control of public utilities. He instinctively fears any regulation of the stock exchange. The right to strike seems to the rich publisher and his Chamber of Commerce friends to be sheer anarchy. It is inevitable that the managing editor and editorial writers who want to hold their jobs take their professional views and get their professional slant from their boss, the man who signs the payroll check. . . . It often happens, alas too often, that a newspaper publisher, reflecting this unconscious class arrogance of the consciously rich, thinks he is printing news when he is doctoring it innocently enough. He thinks he is purveying the truth when much that he offers seems poison to hundreds of thousands of his readers who don't move in his social and economic stratosphere."

When the question of American participation in the second World War divided the country in 1940 and 1941, and most of the Republican right wing took an isolationist stand on the question, White became chairman of the influential Committee to Defend America by Aiding the Allies, denounced alike by Bundists and Communists. He did this in spite of the fact (as his son, William L. White, points out in editing his father's autobiography) that he personally did not believe that America should enter the war, nor that aiding the Allies should give the Axis a reasonable excuse for warring against us.

Probably the most memorable piece Bill White ever produced had nothing to do with politics. It was the obituary he wrote one May morning in 1921, three days after his sixteen-year-old daughter Mary died suddenly after a fall from her horse. The town was moved by it first, then the whole nation as it was picked up and reprinted in newspapers everywhere, read on the radio, used in women's magazines, reprinted in anthologies, and within a year included in four textbooks. For twenty years thereafter, and longer, it appeared again and again in anthologies and school readers. White himself believed it would survive longer than any of his other writings.

A portion of "Mary White" deserves reprinting here because it represents the real soul of small-town journalism, the feeling for life and death an editor has when he deals personally day after day with the readers who are almost literally on his doorstep. This is something no city newspaper can reproduce. It is something that country editors get into their writings time and again, though very seldom with such sweet simplicity as White put into words about his daughter that were torn from his heart. The obit ended:

Her funeral yesterday at the Congregational Church was as she would have wished it; no singing, no flowers save the big bunch of red roses from her Brother Bill's Harvard classmen—Heavens, how proud that would have made her!—and the red roses from the *Gazette* force—in vases at her head and feet. A short prayer, Paul's beautiful essay on "Love" from the Thirteenth Chapter of First Corinthians, some remarks about her democratic spirit by her friend, John H. J. Rice, pastor and police judge, which she would have deprecated if she could, a prayer sent down for her by her friend, Carl Nau, and opening the service the slow, poignant movement from Beethoven's Moonlight Sonata, which she loved, and closing the service, a cutting from the joyously melancholy first movement of Tschaikowski's Pathetic Symphony, which she liked to hear in certain moods on the phonograph; then the Lord's Prayer by her friends in the High School.

That was all.

For her pallbearers only her friends were chosen: her Latin teacher, W. L. Holtz; her High School principal, Rice Brown; her doctor, Frank Foncannon; her friend, W. W. Finney; her pal at the *Gazette* office, Walter Hughes; and her brother Bill. It would have made her smile to know that her friend Charley O'Brien, the traffic cop, had been transferred from Sixth and Commercial to the corner near the church to direct her friends who came to bid her goodbye.

A rift in the clouds in a gray day threw a shaft of sunlight upon her coffin as her nervous energetic little body sank to its last sleep. But the soul of her, the flowing, gorgeous, fervent soul of her, surely was flaming in eager joy upon some other dawn.

Country journalism boasts almost no editors today like Ed Howe and William Allen White. There are a few weekly editors of exceptional ability, men like Henry Beetle Hough and his *Vineyard Gazette,* and John Gould and his paper in Lisbon Falls, Maine, who catch the quiet rhythm of the way their readers live. Most of the other publishers, however, are too busy fighting cost figures, trying to pacify advertisers, treading softly so as not to offend anyone, tailoring ideas to local prejudices, and imitating the big city papers, which day by day encroach on their circulation zones.

It may be that changing times and changing economies have caught the country press in a hopeless dilemma, but it is hard to believe that the day will ever come, though it well might, when an editor of talent is not able to hold an honest, intelligent mirror before the face of a small community. If it ever comes, something irreplaceable will have passed from American journalism.

12

Editors of the Pioneer West

WHOEVER FIRST CALLED THE WEST "WILD AND WOOLLY" MAY NOT have been thinking of cowboys and Indians at all, but of the western editors who made journalism free-swinging and flamboyant in the style to which the plains and mountains had accustomed them.

Certainly there is nothing elsewhere in the history of the American press to compare with the life and times of Frederick Gilmer Bonfils and of Harry Heye Tammen, the formidable partners who made the *Denver Post* the noisiest, if not the greatest, medicine show in the entire newspaper carnival. Their exploits have been fully recorded by Gene Fowler in his classic *Timber Line*. In these pages it is possible to provide only a fragrant sniff of the brew that Bonfils and Tammen concocted in the heady altitudes of Denver at the turn of the century.

Bonfils came of a thoroughly unexciting and respectable family. He was born near Troy, Missouri, in 1860 to a probate judge and a sweet Virginia lady who populated the West with seven other children. Bonfils' grandfather was a modern languages professor in the universities of Alabama and Transylvania, a Corsican *émigré* who married a Boston girl seven times removed from John Alden.

There was nothing in Bonfils' early career to indicate his future, except that he had a short temper and appeared restless.

He went to public school in Troy, got an appointment to West
Point, left without graduating, worked briefly in a New York
bank, married a girl from suburban Peekskill, and took her out
to Canon City, Colorado, where he had secured a job as drill-
master and mathematics instructor in a military school. After a
short time he went back to Troy, sold insurance for his father,
and served as a clerk in the Missouri legislature.

About that time he discovered, or at least partly discovered,
his enormous talent for promotion by getting into the real
estate business, where he sold portions of sovereign Texas to
willing emigrants from Missouri and Kansas. That led directly
to the great real estate boom when Oklahoma Territory was
opened in 1889. While this frantic scramble lasted, Bonfils
acquired what he needed to move on to larger operations:
money.

Now at last he cut loose from his conventional past and
emerged into the atmosphere of quick profits and high-calibre
spellbinding. Fortified with his real estate profits and a file of
convenient aliases, he descended on Kansas City and set up an
enterprise he called the Little Louisiana Lottery. He looked the
part of proprietor. He was dark, trim and handsome, with a
black mustache—a veritable Clark Gable of a man who had the
clothes, the manner and the confidence of a Mississippi River
gambler.

Such a man could scarcely hope to escape public notice, but
Bonfils unfortunately fell under the outraged scrutiny of William Rockhill Nelson, who saw in him a threat to that civic
virtue which the *Star* was celebrating with every issue. The
Star pointed an accusing finger at Bonfils, and continued to
point until the authorities were compelled to look in his direction. After a feeble gesture toward jailing him, they took him
instead to the city line. It was hardly possible to confine Bonfils; he could only be eliminated, if peace and sanity were
desired.

At this juncture, in the year 1895, the exiled entrepreneur of
the Little Louisiana Lottery encountered Harry Tammen, in

what could only be described as a historic meeting. Harry, it seemed, had taken a shorter route to the outer limits of respectability. Born in Baltimore in 1856, the son of a German druggist who had somehow emigrated as an attaché of the Netherlands consulate, Tammen was tossed into the world at the tender age of eight, upon the death of his father. He had enjoyed only the briefest schooling at Knapp's Academy; consequently, he began his career as pin boy in a bowling alley.

In time, however, Tammen worked up to being a bartender, an occupation at which he excelled. Like Bonfils, he was in character for the part he played—chubby, goodnatured, and an old hand at exchanging confidences. Thus equipped, he came out to Denver in 1880, where he presided before the long mirror in the Windsor Hotel. On the side he engaged in various speculative ventures, including *The Great Divide,* a piece of promotional literature disguised as a newspaper, and a curio shop in which unwary tourists were sold mementoes of the West's glorious past. On a good day, the shop could sell the scalp of a single famous Indian chief seven or eight times. The other items on display were of similar authenticity.

Talking a tourist into a scalp was only idle practice for Harry Tammen. He unleashed his full persuasive powers on the day he talked Bonfils into investing $12,500 of his good Kansas City money in the *Denver Evening Post,* which had been established three years before and was struggling for its life. The partners took over on October 28, 1895, dropped the "Evening" from the title, and began newspaper publishing's strangest career.

To the profession of journalism, Bonfils and Tammen brought profound ignorance and an accurate knowledge of human nature. They knew that Denver was a wide-open town, in which murder could be gotten away with literally and figuratively. They had two policies: to proclaim loudly and often that everything they did was for the public good, and to attack public officials or any other goat available with mile-high headlines, red ink, shocking captions, or whatever device came readily to hand.

The *Post* cuddled up to its readers. It was "Your Big Brother," the trusting Denverites were informed—"The Paper With A Heart And Soul"—and its crusades, which began at once, were customarily captioned, "So The People May Know."

It was only natural that Bonfils' first crusade under that righteous caption should be against lotteries, a subject on which he was a qualified authority. But he had learned more in Kansas City than how to make a dishonest dollar. He had observed the operation of the *Star* and saw how it had established itself solidly by concentrating on local news and the welfare of the city. He intended to operate, consequently, on the principle that "a dog fight in a Denver street is more important than a war in Europe."

The two men were ideal partners. Tammen was the promoter, the man who thought up the outrageous stunts which kept the *Post* constantly under the public's nose. Bonfils was the shrewd gambler whose hands were never far from the money drawer, which he kept shut tightly for thirteen years while profits were rolled back into the till so that the *Post* would be in a solid position. Meanwhile, its initial circulation of 4,000 had climbed to 27,000 in three years, then to 83,000 by 1907, a figure which its three competitors could not equal in combination, let alone singly.

At that point Bonfils considered the partnership a sure thing and took steps accordingly. He began by paying himself and Tammen salaries of $1,000 a week. The *Post* was moved to one of the best locations in town, and there the partners indulged their passion for red, which had been expressed before only in the familiar screaming red-inked banner headlines on the front page. The walls of their new office were painted a flashing red. They called this sanctum "the Red Room"; Denverites called it "The Bucket of Blood."

Out of the Bucket flowed a steady stream of the most sensational journalism Denver or any other American city had seen, not excluding New York. No one was safe from the *Post,* neither the just nor the unjust. Libel suits fell like gentle rain on the partners, but nothing deterred them. When legal action failed, the outraged victims sometimes came to the office and fought a few rounds with one or the other of the proprietors.

Once the paper's beautiful sob sister, Polly Pry, whose real name was Leonel Campbell, turned up a story about a man accused of murdering and eating his partner on a gold-hunting expedition. That was a story the *Post* could warm up to in its own special way. Later, a lawyer retained by the partners to get a parole for the desert cannibal charged into the Red Room and fired a volley at the partners with his side-arms. Fortunately the counselor's aim was abominable, and pretty Polly Pry rode in heroically to the rescue. Bonfils and Tammen escaped with minor wounds.

On another occasion the *Post* embroiled itself in a violent struggle between the operators of Denver's street railway and the employees of the company. The *Post,* in spite of its bleeding red headlines in behalf of the people, was on the management's side in this strike, and a mob of strike sympathizers, who sensed an inconsistency in the paper's attitude, swarmed into the *Post* plant and took it carefully apart.

For all the cynicism of its proprietors, however, the *Post* was in reality on the people's side more often than not, which saved from utter mockery the pious motto adorning the paper's new home: "Oh, Justice, when expelled from other habitations, make this thy dwelling place." To justify that invitation, the *Post* fought for reforms in the use of child labor, in the management of prisons, and in the conduct of public officials. One winter Bonfils became a coal dealer when the *Post* decided that the cost of coal was too high. He leased some mines and trucked fuel around town to his readers, at a much lower price than the local dealers were charging. The *Post,* said Bonfils, would keep its subscribers warm and happy.

The other positive aspect of the proprietorship was the Chamber of Commerce touch Bonfils gave to the *Post,* rising from his own love for the outdoors. If he believed in anything, Bonfils was sure that God had meant Colorado when He said

Eden. The ex-gambler had no love for the green table and the smoke-filled room in these later years. He was forever selling the extraordinary virtues of Rocky Mountain fishing, golfing, and hunting, and he considered the climate provided for these activities as made in heaven. If a cloudburst started rock slides, caused flash floods, and raised general havoc in the mountains, Bonfils was likely to remark calmly that the rain was good for the farmers, who raised the finest crops east or west of anywhere.

Against such tendencies toward reform and healthy living, readers had to balance the hate and fear that the *Post* unquestionably inspired by its unpredictable crusades and attacks. Then, too, there were the crazy things it did that came under the head of promotion, or simply outbursts of personality.

These were sometimes not too far out of the ordinary—treasure hunts, the planting of an Eve in the Estes Park Garden of Eden, penny-tossing contests among Denver children for coins tossed from the *Post*'s balcony, and various junkets dreamed up by the resourceful Tammen.

The partners occasionally went in for larger affairs, however. Once, as a magnificent and utterly useless gesture, Bonfils journeyed all the way to Africa merely to greet his friend Theodore Roosevelt, when the gleaming glasses and bristle of mustache poked out of the jungle at the end of Teddy's celebrated wild-animal hunt.

Tammen had an affinity for animals, too. He liked elephants. To satisfy this passion, he started a circus and operated it as a pastime. It was really no more than a dog-and-pony show at first, but it prospered. He named it for his noted sports editor, Otto Floto, and eventually it became the Sells-Floto circus, a name still dear to older Americans. The circus was in trouble for years, what with escaped animals, a long legal wrangle with the Ringling Brothers, and another over the use of the four Sells brothers' pictures. Tammen loved every minute of it, and Bonfils put his hand in with crusading editorials against the "circus trust."

A legal affair of a different sort brought the partners into national prominence in 1924, when Senators investigating the Teapot Dome scandal extracted enough information from Bonfils to satisfy themselves that the *Post*'s attacks on Harry F. Sinclair, chief figure in the scandal, were inspired by a man who had filed suit against him. The suit had been settled and the *Post*'s attacks stopped simultaneously with Sinclair's payoff of a million dollars.

It was not the first time they had been in this kind of trouble. In 1914, the Interstate Commerce Commission had happened upon an item recording $60,000 paid to the *Post* by the Rock Island Railroad for a purpose quaintly listed as "editorial advertising."

In the oil scandal, the Committee on Ethics of the American Society of Newspaper Publishers recommended that Bonfils be expelled from the organization. He escaped on a technicality, and three years later resigned of his own volition.

While this affair was developing, Tammen died in 1924 and Bonfils was left to carry on alone in his greatest battle, one of the hardest fought circulation contests in American newspaper history.

Bonfils had already experienced a near disaster in this field. When he opened the cash box for the first time in 1908, he took out enough extra money to buy the *Kansas City Post,* which the partners published until 1922. It was never a successful proposition, however, because the methods that were so profitable in high, wide and handsome Denver were greeted with considerable horror in Nelson's town. The paper cost them $250,000 and they sold it for a million and a quarter dollars to the *Kansas City Journal,* a nice profit in any city. The venture, however, had cut into the *Post*'s profits.

The *Post* could afford it. By the twenties it was making more than a million dollars a year, and its circulation was 150,000 daily and twice that on Sunday. This strong position gave Bonfils an edge when, in 1926, he was compelled to fight for his life against the *Rocky Mountain News*. This paper had not been a serious competitor since John C. Shaffer, publisher of the *Chicago Evening Post* and some Indiana papers, had bought three properties and merged them to make the *News*. But in 1926 he sold it to the Scripps-Howard League and the war was on.

Bustling, energetic Roy Howard had no intention of permitting Bonfils to intimidate him as he had Shaffer. If the *Post* wanted to put on a three-ring circus, he could do it too. Thus for two hectic years Denver's citizens witnessed a fantastic and extravagant episode.

Bonfils started a morning edition to compete with the *News*, and Howard replied with an afternoon edition to meet the *Post* on its own grounds, consequently the two were prepared for twenty-four-hour battle. Then they pulled out every circulation stunt in the newspaper bag of tricks. Perhaps the most spectacular was the classified ad contest, in which the papers offered as much as five gallons of free gas to every customer who inserted a want ad in the Sunday paper. That proposition, while it lasted, made every Sunday a Roman holiday in Denver as the citizenry went joy-riding on tankfuls of free gas and the newsboys staggered under the weight of Sunday editions which often ran more than a hundred pages, mostly want ads.

Of course this kind of war was ruinously expensive to everyone concerned, and both managements were glad when Bonfils and Howard were brought together by the Denver Chamber of Commerce and agreed to call it off. The extra editions were dropped. No one missed them.

Bonfils' stormy career did not end with this truce. He was in trouble—or rather, he was making it—right up to the last. In 1932, when he was seventy-two years old, he sued the *News* for $200,000 libel for publishing an address by Walter Walker, publisher of the *Grand Junction Sentinel,* who had told a political convention, referring to Bonfils: "The day will come when some persecuted man will treat that rattlesnake as a rattlesnake should be treated, and there will be general rejoicing. . . . Bonfils is a public enemy and has left the trail of a slimy serpent across Colorado for thirty years."

The *News* had no recourse except to prove the truth of the publication. Its lawyers drew up a bill of forty-one counts which reviewed Bonfils' career in a manner that would have been difficult for the old man to answer if the case had ever come to trial. But he was spared this indignity. He fought it off as long as he could, consenting at first to have a deposition taken, then abruptly changing his mind and refusing to answer any more questions at the deposition hearing, for which he paid a $25 contempt of court fine.

In the midst of the turmoil, Bonfils was taken to the hospital and operated on for an ear abscess. Less than a week later he was dead of toxic encephalitis and pneumonia. On his deathbed he was baptized in the Roman Catholic faith, presumably at the wish of his wife, who was a member of the Church. He left an estate valued at more than eight million dollars; Tammen's had been appraised at two million. Both men left much of their fortunes to good works of various kinds.

Thus ended a fabulous journalistic tale, but one that would have been considered only a slight exaggeration of the normal climate in San Francisco, that bohemian, cosmopolitan, bold and brave city of the Golden Gate, where Hearst and his *Examiner* were in the forefront of a shifting pack of fighting newspapers, all at each other's throats.

To tell the lusty, exciting story of San Francisco newspapering would require far more than the space of this volume, but it may be possible to let one man stand for the spirit it represented. Few would argue that any better man could represent it than Fremont Older.

He was a Wisconsin boy, born on a farm near Appleton in 1856, the descendant of a stouthearted Londoner who had fought in the French and Indian War. His father and mother were ardent abolitionists, and otherwise were God-fearing, pioneer farmers. Emory, the father, went off to fight with the Union Army when the Civil War began, and died a dreary death in a Confederate prison in 1864, leaving his pretty, black-haired wife to support herself and their two sons. She did so at first by selling books, particularly a biography of the farmers' national hero, Horace Greeley. Reading this book that was so popular with his mother's customers, young Fremont first acquired the determination, amounting almost to fanaticism to be a newspaperman like Greeley.

No other editor considered in these pages endured so much to reach his goal. No one who has read Evelyn Wells' moving biography of Older can forget the picture drawn in the early chapters of the tall, awkward youth trudging from job to job, from temporary home to another shelter, driven by a desperate inner fire toward something he could not define, suffering almost incredible hardships.

His mother, still in her early thirties and an attractive woman, had remarried and moved to California with her new husband. Consequently Fremont was left first with his stern, ultra-religious aunt, and later with other relatives whom he stayed with briefly before he moved on.

Older had only a country schooling, with the addition of a few months in Ripon College. Following the example of Greeley, he learned to set type at a very early age, and it was this trade that he always fell back upon after he made brief excursions into farming, working as a cabin boy on a river boat, and laboring in a carriage shop. He worked for one little paper after another in Wisconsin and neighboring territory, sometimes for only a few weeks, sometimes longer. Always he would be driven onward to something else, for reasons he could not even give himself.

When he was seventeen, his mother sent him enough money to come West, and he landed eagerly in San Francisco, certain at last that he had found a home. But it was as difficult to find the place he sought there as it had been in Wisconsin. He began as a printer on the *San Francisco Morning Call* in 1873, and for the next ten years he drifted from paper to paper in the West, good enough at his job to be a foreman, but finding no opportunity to do editorial work.

Many different composing rooms saw this tall, spare young

man with the burning fire in his deep eyes. He went from Virginia City, Nevada, to Reno, to Oakland, to Santa Barbara, and Bodie and Redwood City.

At the last stop, on the *Times and Gazette,* he got his chance to go out and get the news, besides setting type, and showed the publisher such burgeoning talent that he was made business manager, then editor.

Probably any other young man would have stayed in Redwood City and made the most of it. But San Francisco drew Older back to its steep streets and gay cafes, its drifting fogs and its indefinable spirit that made it for so many people the one place in the world to live. He went back there in 1884 and never left it again except for temporary absences.

By this time he had established himself as a writer and editor, and he was beginning to get a reputation as a man who knew how to build circulations. That was a real attribute in a town as fiercely competitive as San Francisco, where newspapers bloomed like saloons.

After a few years on several of these papers, Older was sitting at the city desk of the *Morning Call* in 1895 when R. A. Crothers hired him to be managing editor of the *Bulletin,* a rapidly fading property in which Crothers had just purchased a half-interest. It was a job that for the first time crystallized the desire that had been blazing inside Older for so many years. Now his tremendous energy and talent were directed toward one object: success. He intended to be ruthless about it. As he wrote in his autobiography, he didn't care that his sensational stories and headlines "might make people suffer, might wound or utterly ruin someone."

Such driving force was bound to produce results. In Older's case it increased *Bulletin* circulation within a year from a faltering 9,000 to a profitable figure which thereafter climbed steadily until it reached 100,000 before his editorship ended. It took a little longer to increase advertising proportionately and put the paper completely in the black, since it had been losing $3,000 a month.

Like most of the great editors, Older was a crusader. At first he did not crusade for moral reasons, or because of any deeply felt convictions, but only to get circulation for the *Bulletin* and help his personal fortunes.

The first mouthful he bit off was enough to choke an ordinary man. For years the Southern Pacific Railroad had dominated California politics by the primitive process of widespread and quite shameless bribery, including legislators, municipal officials, and a good many of the state's newspapers. The *Bulletin* itself was down on the railroad's free list at $125 a month. It was this gigantic network of corruption that Fremont Older declared his intention to break up.

His first move was to get his friend James D. Phelan to run for mayor of San Francisco, and with the help of the *Bulletin,* elected him. Fremont intended to set up a "reform government" that would be an entering wedge to the railroad's political machine; he had no particular interest in reform for its own sake. Phelan, however, was utterly honest in his campaign promises, and once he was in office, he set about to fulfill them. He gave the city one of the best and most progressive administrations it had ever known, and after Older had watched his man labor devotedly and unselfishly for the public welfare, he began to absorb some of the same spirit. He acquired, as he wrote later, his "first social sense."

The central fight of Phelan's administration was to obtain a new city charter. This, in turn, involved the state of corruption in the city's public utilities, which were returning regular subsidies to the *Bulletin* as well as to other papers. The *Bulletin's* publisher was naturally reluctant to close off so easy a source of income, and Older found himself opposing his boss.

There began a lengthy, involved, and frequently violent battle. Abraham Ruef, boss of city politics, contrived to get a machine man, Eugene E. Schmitz, elected mayor in 1901. This return to the old corrupt state of affairs impelled Older to declare that he would expose Ruef, Schmitz, and all their works, no matter what it took to do it.

Older had to fight not only the machine but sometimes his own editor. It was not simply a war of words, either, because the stakes were large for Ruef, and Older's will was indomitable. Once Older was kidnapped by a gunman who got buck fever before he could kill the editor. Older, in turn, kidnapped a Chinese confederate of Ruef's who, he thought, could give him the information he needed. In the end, it was Older who won. Ruef went to jail on an extortion conviction in 1908. During the trial, the prosecuting attorney was shot dead in the courtroom, and Hiram W. Johnson first came into the public eye as the man who succeeded him.

No sooner had Ruef been safely tucked away than Older began to have second thoughts about what was wrong with society. It was not the individual, like Ruef, he decided, but the system itself. Thereupon he began a crusade to get Ruef out of jail only six months after the boss had been incarcerated, a move that brought him little sympathy from the public.

Older was so engrossed in the subject of penal reform that he did not care whether people thought he was crazy, or had "suddenly gone soft," as one critic put it. He arranged the release of a San Quentin convict, ran his story, "My Life In Prison," in the *Bulletin,* where it attracted national attention, and then used the man to help him organize a bureau at the paper devoted to helping ex-convicts get a new start. The bureau aided hundreds of men within a few years.

He also came out strongly against capital punishment, and as his assault on the social system widened, he crusaded for the rights of labor unions and labor leaders, including some extreme left-wingers of the day. He was, of course, roundly condemned for these crusades, but Crothers, the publisher, still allowed him his platform and he used it in nearly every edition.

Then came the *cause célèbre,* the fight that not even Crothers would back. In some circles, the guilt or innocence of Thomas J. Mooney and Warren K. Billings is still argued vehemently today, as to whether they were responsible for the bombing of a Preparedness Day parade in San Francisco on July 22, 1916.

Considering the patriotic fervor of the time, the reaction of citizens both there and in the rest of the nation can well be imagined when Older asserted, as did most labor groups and left-wingers of every description, that the two men had been framed and that their conviction was an injustice. This was bad enough, but when he printed letters in the *Bulletin* the following year appearing to prove that there had been perjury in the trial, the outraged cries of the paper's advertisers reached the ears of the publisher, who ordered Older to drop the argument. Older naturally refused to do it, and he was invited to resign.

Of all the publishers in town who might have taken up the fight for him, the least likely, looked at from today's viewpoint, would have been William Randolph Hearst. In those days, however, it was logically Hearst, the friend of the masses, the enemy of the Southern Pacific, who stretched out a welcoming hand to Older, made him editor of the *Call*, and told him to "bring the Mooney case with me," as Older recalled later.

By one of those odd freaks of journalism, Hearst merged the *Bulletin* with the *Call* eleven years later, and Older found himself in command of the paper he had been asked to quit, as president and editor of the *Call-Bulletin*. He held these posts until his death.

As a Hearst editor, Older went right on crusading. Not the least of his crusades was for his boss, whom he much admired and defended at every opportunity. In turn, Hearst gave him a free rein, although the publisher had been on the opposite side of a good many of Older's *Bulletin* campaigns.

The years on the *Call-Bulletin* were the happiest of his life, he said later. As he grew old, he lost both his zeal for crusading and his faith in it. The social system, he concluded, could not be reformed that way, and the most you could say for crusading was that it would do what he had said originally it was intended to do—build circulation. In these later days, he settled down to enjoy his own writing and the company of his second wife, Cora, whom he had married in 1893. He helped her write an authorized biography of Hearst. The rest of the time he spent reading fiction and writing occasional editorials for the paper.

Older died suddenly of a heart attack in 1935, collapsing over the steering wheel of his car after he had spent a pleasant afternoon writing an editorial on Montaigne's essay on death. His grave, on the beautiful Santa Clara County ranch, Woodhills, which he loved so dearly, was marked by stones brought to it by friends from all over the world.

With Older's passing, the last of the old newspapering days on the Coast slipped into memory. Long before that time Western journalism had sobered down and begun to develop the respectable papers it possesses today. But it still has a special flavor, indigenous to the soil in which it flourishes.

When the historian adds up Bonfils and Tammen, the rambunctious early days of Hearst and his *Examiner,* the flamboyant eras of the *Chronicle*'s early career, and the fire-and-brimstone story of Fremont Older, not to mention dozens of other lesser papers and personalities, it can be readily understood that to students of journalism the old West was wilder than Hopalong Cassidy ever knew.

13

Cyrus Curtis and His Editors

ONE OF THE PARADOXES OF JOURNALISTIC HISTORY, THOUGH IT IS not particularly puzzling, concerns the publishing career of Cyrus H. K. (for Hermann Kotzschmar) Curtis (see photograph 6), a Portland, Maine, newsboy who became America's foremost magazine publisher and its most dismal failure as a newspaper owner.

Here was a man whose magazine properties surpassed all others in circulation and advertising, and continue to be among the leaders nearly twenty years after his death. The genius that created them in time earned Curtis a gross annual personal income estimated at ten million dollars a year. Yet when he applied his talents to the newspaper field, he failed in the most complete and spectacular manner.

Another aspect of the paradox is that this man, who created the most successful magazine editorial formulas ever seen in America up to the mid-twenties, was not an editor himself and knew it. The magazines which today comprise the Curtis Publishing Company—the *Saturday Evening Post, Ladies' Home Journal* and *Country Gentleman* (*Holiday* was founded after Curtis's death)—were the products of other brains.

The key to the paradox is that these brains were personally selected by Curtis, who had an uncanny ability to choose the men best able to carry out the publishing ideas he originated.

Curtis's enormous success can be attributed to these facts: He planned magazines which would appeal to the American middle class, whose tastes and ideas he understood better than his publisher contemporaries; then he got men with a particular genius for editing whatever magazine he had in mind; and finally, he let his editors edit with a minimum amount of interference.

It is obvious that Curtis's chances for success with this formula depended on the soundness of his ideas, his understanding of the people who were to be on the receiving end of them, and his judgment in picking editors. In all three respects, he was seldom wrong.

As a journalistic businessman, Cyrus Curtis exerted a pronounced, if indirect, influence on the reading habits of millions of Americans, and he revolutionized the magazine business. How he did these things is a story considerably more fascinating than the man himself, who in spite of his many fine personal qualities, was anything but an exciting individual.

His rise followed conventional lines up to a point. The start of his career was in the best American tradition, beginning at thirteen in his native Portland when he bought a $2.50 press and turned out on it a paper called *Young America*. He might have gone on directly from this project, puny and juvenile though it was, if his family's home had not burned down in the disastrous Portland fire of 1866. The family lost everything and Cyrus had to leave high school after his freshman year to get a job.

Curtis considered the misfortune a temporary setback. He worked briefly as errand boy in a Portland drygoods store, then went down to Boston to be a salesman in a similar establishment. After this came short successive terms in the advertising departments of three Boston newspapers. The whole preliminary episode took only four years out of his life. By 1872, twenty-two years after his birth date, he was in the business that made him a fortune.

His first magazine, discounting the youthful Portland venture, was a weekly, the *People's Ledger,* which he started almost entirely on hope. Like all Curtis publications, it was based on an original idea, in this case the offering of a story complete in each issue—a staple item in magazines today. To avoid expenses, since at first he had no money to meet them, Curtis obtained his stories from the convenient reservoir of the public domain. Some of them were thirty years old, but people read them anyway.

For six years he made a fair living with the magazine, until rising printing costs prompted him to move to Philadelphia, where he thought he could publish more cheaply. Curtis's active business mind told him he was on the brink of big things, but his instinct told him that the *People's Ledger* was not the proper vehicle to ride to success.

After two years of Philadelphia publication, he sold his property and went to work as advertising manager of a weekly edition published by the *Philadelphia Press,* while he planned his next move.

In a year he was ready, and in 1879 launched the *Tribune and Farmer*—price, fifty cents a year. The Curtis idea embodied in this new publication was a supplement for women, and exhibiting another of his talents for the first time, he chose as editor his wife of four years, Louisa Knapp Curtis. The idea grew much faster than the *Tribune and Farmer* itself, and in 1883 Curtis turned over his interest in that publication to his partner.

The supplement, which he called the *Ladies' Home Journal,* had gathered in 25,000 subscribers in its first year of publication. Curtis went to work to increase this list, using promotion methods which are common today but represented something new in the magazine business in the nineties. The subscription price was still fifty cents a year, but the publisher put on a group campaign—that is, four subscriptions for a dollar if they came in together. The offer doubled circulation in six months. Curtis followed it with an advertising campaign and once more doubled his list in the same period. By mid-1885, *Journal* circulation was 200,000.

Curtis now had something substantial to offer his advertisers, and he could turn his attention to the magazine's contents. Without any disparagement of his wife's efforts as editor, he realized that he needed a strong editorial personality at the helm. Everyone supposed that the new editor would be a woman, but Curtis displayed once more his amazing insight into magazine publishing problems and chose a man.

He could hardly have picked a more unusual man for the job. Edward William Bok had been born in the Netherlands, of a prominent Dutch family, and had emigrated with his parents to New York in 1870. After an impoverished boyhood in Brooklyn, divided between public school and various odd jobs, including reporting children's parties for the *Brooklyn Daily Eagle,* he had left school at thirteen to be a Western Union office boy.

The story of Bok's rise is best told in his famed autobiography, *The Americanization of Edward Bok,* a classic of its kind. Here it is enough to note that he became an editor in his early teens by preparing hundred-word biographies for the backs of portrait souvenir cards of famous Americans; wrote theater news for the *Eagle;* published theater programs; edited a church organ for Henry Ward Beecher; speculated in Wall Street at eighteen with the help of Jay Gould; worked as a stenographer for two publishing houses; turned his church paper into a magazine; started a highly successful syndicate which specialized in women's features; and became advertising manager of *Scribner's Magazine.*

All this in a little less than two decades after he had arrived in America, a poor immigrant boy who spoke no English. Curtis had observed the later years of this remarkable progress, and in 1889 offered him the editorship of his *Journal.* Against the advice of his friends, Bok took it.

Curtis's plans for his magazine were both editorial and promotional. Editorially he charged Bok with getting noted writers for the *Journal*'s pages. He intended to put an advertising promotion behind these names. Next he doubled the *Journal*'s page size, and in spite of expert advice, also doubled his subscription price.

These devices boosted circulation to one million copies in 1893, a fantastic figure for those days. Curtis lived to see the total pass two million, though the magazine suffered a few lean years after Bok's retirement. In our own time, it exceeds four million, with an advertising linage far ahead of any other magazine.

Curtis continued to be the business mainspring behind the *Journal*'s spectacular rise, but it was Bok who became synonymous with the *Journal*, adding as much to his own fame as the publication's. The Dutchman was an authentic genius, with the exaggerated faults and virtues which appear to be primary components of such ability. A good many people considered him "difficult," meaning that they found his monumental ego hard to take. Bok often appeared to believe quite sincerely that the world revolved around him. He regarded opposition almost as a personal affront. It was said of him, too that he did not particularly care for women, *per se*.

Whether this was true or not, he had remarkable insight into the feminine mind, seeming to know by instinct what would interest women in a magazine. He was a humanitarian of the first order, the benefactor of innumerable educational and cultural institutions (he left two million dollars to charity in his will, not counting what he spent in his lifetime), and he worked hard for the cause of world peace through his famous Peace Award and by other means. He wrote more than a dozen books.

Plainly, Curtis had picked the right man to edit the *Journal*. It was Bok who brought Howells, Twain, Bret Harte, Kipling, and others into the *Journal*'s fiction pages, and through his acquaintance with most of the public figures of his time, he was also able to get articles by Cleveland, Harrison, Theodore Roosevelt, Taft, Wilson—in fact, he could get nearly anyone he desired.

Knowing that women like causes, he made the *Journal* a fearless crusader for various kinds of reform, not all of them popular. This was a revolutionary step in more ways than one. Bok assumed that women would think about such things, while other editors proceeded on the assumption that all a woman asked of a magazine was undisturbing entertainment. He also departed from the anonymity that characterized most magazines, whose editors believed that they should be as impersonal as possible. Bok injected some of the personal journalism of the time into the *Journal*—not, perhaps, because he thought of it as a circulation booster, but simply because it would have been impossible for him to have kept his own overwhelming personality out of the magazine.

Some of Bok's crusades were safe enough. He came out strongly for woman's suffrage, which was exemplary for a woman's magazine. He favored the kind of civic rehabilitation that William Rockhill Nelson preached in Kansas City, and Victor Lawson advocated for Chicago. He also called for the elimination of billboards, the improvement of Pullman cars, the banning of Fourth of July fireworks, and the outlawing of public drinking cups.

These were unexceptionable crusades, but it was a different matter when he called on the public to fight power company monopoly of Niagara Falls, and when he announced in 1892 that the *Journal* would no longer accept patent medicine advertisements. The legal war that resulted from this move ended in passage of the Food and Drugs Act of 1906.

Bok also dared public opinion by discussing venereal disease in the *Journal*, a move that shocked the magazine business almost as much as it did his readers. He took the momentary loss of subscriptions, confident that the women who read the *Journal* would ultimately back him up. They did, and since then the *Journal* has discussed the facts of life more freely with its readers than any other magazine in the field. Bok showed that taboos could be broken, if the breaking were put on a high enough plane.

He lost only two of his major campaigns. As an ardent patriot, he tried to wean American women away from Paris

fashions to native designs. They politely ignored him. Again
he besought them to give up aigrettes, fashioned from nesting
herons who were being ruthlessly slaughtered for the purpose.
Once more the ladies would have none of it. Bok had the last
word anyway by successful pressure for state and national conservation laws to protect the herons.

For thirty years Bok edited the *Journal,* giving it the full
benefit of his extraordinary personality, and he allied himself
with Curtis in another way by marrying his daughter, Mary
Louise. But he had determined to retire on his thirtieth anniversary, which came in September 1919. The last issue he
edited carried a million dollars worth of advertising, and circulated more than two million copies; it was the most successful magazine in America, aside from its sister publication, the
Post.

Thereafter he devoted himself to writing his Pulitzer prize
winning autobiography, to his philanthropies and his numerous
other interests, which ranged from writing poetry to fishing and
gardening. Bok died in 1930, at sixty-seven, leaving two sons
and much else to perpetuate his name.

Bok was one of the two great editors who wrote the name of
Curtis larger than any other in the magazine business. George
Horace Lorimer, editor of the *Saturday Evening Post,* was the
other. The two men were essentially unlike in temperament,
and there was little love lost between them. Indeed, a silent
feud developed which lasted as long as both worked for Curtis,
though outwardly they observed the social amenities and be-
haved in public like other proper Philadelphians.

Lorimer was a genius in his own way. Not as many-sided as
Bok, he was much more of a magazine man, and perhaps the
one man above all others Curtis could have chosen to be editor
of his *Post.*

It could have been nothing less than sheer instinct which led
Curtis to acquire the *Post* in the first place. When he bought it
for $1,000 in 1897, it was, as Irvin Cobb put it, "an elderly

and indisposed magazine." Its paid advertising in one issue totaled $290.

Cyrus Curtis saw in this decrepit property an opportunity to do for American men what the *Journal* was already doing for the country's women. He was also wise enough to see that it should be a weekly. In this field the competition included *Frank Leslie's Magazine* and *Collier's,* both of which cost ten cents and dealt mostly with current events; *Puck* and *Judge,* both humor magazines; and the *Youth's Companion,* for young people. A good many of the leading newspapers published weekly supplements, a few of them as good as the magazines.

All American magazines had suffered a general decline since the Civil War. The English pattern of magazine-making, which *Harper's* had clung to stubbornly, was reflected in the monthly magazines which led the field. They published such genteel literary articles as "Boston At The Century's End," "The Modern Group of Scandinavian Painters," "Australasian Extensions of Democracy," and "Life Among The Nomadic Lapps." Fiction was in the genre of the worst British novels.

The *Post* was no better when Lorimer became editor. It had sixteen pages and no pictures, very little advertising, and much material that was simply clipped from English newspapers and magazines.

Out of this situation Curtis proposed to create a magazine that would sell for five cents, meeting the newspapers on their own financial ground. He intended, however, to leave the news to them and build a weekly periodical of a quality that a newspaper could not approach. He foresaw that the dailies would quickly occupy a field by themselves, if they had not done so already, and that the magazine market was ripe for something new and noncompetitive. The experts warned him that there was no potential audience for a national weekly, and that the five-cent price was economic suicide. Besides, they said, the weekly as a periodical form was on its way out.

Curtis was unconvinced. He had the idea and the magazine; now he needed a man to develop both, as Bok had done with

the *Journal.* In Lorimer he found the man who made the *Post*
what Will Rogers called "America's greatest nickelodeon." He
came to the editor's chair on St. Patrick's Day, 1899. When he
left it nearly thirty-nine years later, on the last day of 1936, the
Post had been for three decades one of the most successful and
significant magazines in the history of American letters.

Lorimer became the articulate voice of millions, the purveyor
of entertainment, advice, and political sentiment to a considerable body of Americans—yet he was almost unknown to the
Post's readers. Of the more than three million people who
bought the magazine at the peak of its circulation, only a few
knew its editor as more than a name on the masthead. Lorimer
remained an anonymous figure until the final issue of the *Post*
under his editorship, when for the first time he signed an
editorial. Nevertheless he was the man whom nine Presidents
of the United States recognized as the potent spokesman for a
sizable bloc of voters, and upon whom thousands of writers,
both famous and unknown, looked as a god to whose Olympus
every creator of prose aspired.

From his early youth until he died in 1937, less than a year
after his retirement, Lorimer was a leader. Before he was thirty
he had achieved business success in the packing industry; and
he had been so excellent a reporter for the Boston papers
that he would surely have risen to the top in the newspaper
business. After he came to the *Post,* he wrote three best-selling
books, two of which are still selling after more than forty years.
In fact Lorimer would have been successful at any occupation,
but editing the *Saturday Evening Post* was the job that fitted
him best.

Lorimer was born in Louisville, Kentucky, in 1867, the son
of a noted Baptist evangelist who was one of the most powerful
evangelical ministers this country has ever known. When
George Claude Lorimer died, the scholarly *Boston Transcript*
termed him "an important American." It was in Boston and
Chicago that he performed his most notable labors for the
church.

Because the Reverend Lorimer was called from one pastorate to another, young George had separate boyhoods in Louisville, Albany, and Boston—but mostly Boston, where he got his grammar school education at the Dwight School. Then the family moved to Chicago, and Lorimer went to Mosely High School. Whatever time he could spare after classes he devoted to hunting prairie chickens.

"In those days," he recalled, "I could take my gun after school and within thirty minutes' ride of the Chicago City Hall find jacksnipe, wild duck, prairie chicken and golden plover." To get the money for shells he made a deal with his mother—a dollar for every one of Plutarch's *Lives* on which he could report in detail.

Later George entered Yale in the class of 1888, along with such promising students as Irving Fisher and Alonzo Stagg. Shortly before he was to return for his sophomore year, he met P. D. Armour on the street one day. Armour was one of his father's richest parishioners, and the young man greeted the eminent packer respectfully. When he asked George Horace what he was doing these days and the young man told him he was at Yale, Armour snorted. "Give up that nonsense," the familiar story quotes him, "and come to work for me. I'll make you a millionaire."

That idea appealed to Dr. Lorimer's son, who even then had a good understanding of Armour's philosophy. He asked his father what he should do, and the elder Lorimer remarked sensibly that he would have to decide that for himself. The decision was not difficult. The thought of making some money on his own appealed strongly to him. He took the job, which turned out to be a menial one at the mailing desk.

Lorimer came early and stayed late. He loved business. It never occurred to him for a moment that he was underpaid and overworked, because there was nothing in the world he would rather have been doing at that moment. After two years, he became assistant manager of the canning department, and as a minor executive, he had an opportunity to meet and talk with a good many of Armour's friends, the pioneer merchants and railroad men who were creating the American business empire, and he met the empire builders from abroad, such men as Sir Thomas Lipton. Always he asked questions about their careers, and instinctively he performed as an editor would, mentally translating the meaning of their lives into understandable terms.

These meetings were the sources of inspiration for the biographies and autobiographies which so enthralled *Post* readers.

After five years of work for Armour, Lorimer married the dazzling redheaded daughter of a Chicago jurist, and soon after was made head of the canning department. He might have gone on indefinitely if ambition had not driven him to take a flyer in the wholesale grocery business, a venture which ended disastrously.

It was then that he turned to the business of writing. After a few diversions, he wound up on the *Boston Post,* where he worked on the night side at eighteen dollars a week. Refused a two-dollar raise, he switched to the *Herald,* where one memorable day he read a routine story on the telegraph desk which announced that Cyrus H. K. Curtis had bought the name and goodwill it possessed of the *Saturday Evening Post*—net paid circulation, 10,473. Mr. Curtis, the story said, hoped to find an outstanding editor who could make the publication successful.

Within an hour, Lorimer had wired Curtis, asking for a job. Curtis wired back that he would be in Boston the following week and would be glad to see him at the Hotel Touraine. There, on a divan in the lobby, the two men talked one morning for about ten minutes, after which they shook hands and parted. Curtis had hired Lorimer as the first—and last—literary editor of the *Post.*

When he got to Philadelphia, he discovered that Curtis was permitting William George Jordan to go on editing the magazine while he searched for a better man. Early in 1899, Curtis grew impatient, fired Jordan, and went to Europe to look for a successor, leaving Lorimer temporarily in charge as managing editor. Curtis's search was unsuccessful, and as Lorimer explained later: "When Mr. Curtis returned to Philadelphia, he liked the way things were going so well that he made me editor in chief of the periodical."

He had improved the *Post,* during his few weeks of trial, so noticeably that Curtis had felt justified in giving him the direction of it, but the magazine was still far from successful as a business venture. It lost a staggering amount every week.

Lorimer's program of reconversion included buying vigorous fiction by well-known writers; attuning the *Post*'s articles to American life, particularly politics; making the editorial page the heart of the *Post;* and increasing the magazine's advertising revenue.

By dint of working day and night his first year in the job, Lorimer began to accomplish these objectives, though sometimes he virtually wrote an issue himself. For a few anxious months his job was at stake, and only Curtis's faith saved it for him. At the first stockholders' meeting held after the publisher's return from abroad, Bok was for getting rid of the *Post.* He was afraid the magazine's continuing losses would hurt his *Journal* in time, and if it succeeded, Lorimer would be a potentially serious rival in the company.

Bok was supported by the company treasurer, who came to Curtis one day in a cold sweat of anxiety to point out that the *Post* was $750,000 in the red.

"Well," said Curtis, unperturbed, "Mr. Lorimer's got $250,-000 to go before he touches a million. I like round numbers."

Such faith was justified eventually. At somewhere near the million mark in debits, Lorimer's magic began to work. The *Post* made back its losses at an astounding rate as circulation and advertising shot up together. It was never in trouble again.

As the *Post* began the new century, it was in safe waters and Lorimer was solidly at its helm. Curtis made only one attempt to interfere. He protested against one of the short stories that Lorimer had unearthed.

"My wife doesn't think it's a very good piece to be in the *Post*," he remarked.

"I'm not editing the *Saturday Evening Post* for your wife," Lorimer told him bluntly.

Curtis turned away and said nothing. He wasn't angry. He knew when he had the man he wanted, and it was his policy to give an editor full control without interference. In Lorimer's case, he raised his editor's salary to $250 a week, which was his way of saying, "Go ahead."

Lorimer knew exactly what he wanted to make of the *Post*. It was to be a magazine without class, clique, or sectional editing, but intended for every adult in America's seventy-five million population. He meant to edit it for the whole United States.

There was but one dish missing in the basic *Post* menu that Lorimer planned to serve his readers, and that was business fiction. He could not interest any writer in the business story. In vain he pointed out that "the struggle for existence is the loaf, love or sex is the frosting on the cake," and that every business day was full of comedy, tragedy, farce, romance—all the ingredients of successful fiction. Business was a dominating factor in the lives of Americans, but the nation's writers ignored it.

There was one man specially qualified to write on the subject and that was Lorimer himself. He knew it, and that was why in the summer of 1901 he began writing, nights and weekends, the *Letters From A Self-Made Merchant to His Son,* a perennial classic which survives today in a dozen languages. Reader response to the series was tremendous. There were five thousand letters before the end of 1901. The *Letters* and two sequels, published in book form, were instantaneous best-sellers the world over, shot the *Post*'s circulation up to new high figures, and produced a flood of articles and stories on business themes.

Lorimer stayed one jump ahead of other editors in these first competitive years by virtue of a practice which had brought him more writers than any other. That practice was his rule to return a decision on any manuscript within seventy-two hours, and to pay immediately upon acceptance.

It had taken a few months for the effect of that policy to make itself felt; then came a tide of manuscripts. Until then it had been virtually impossible for an American writer to earn his living by writing. Aside from a few eminent novelists, and men like Mark Twain, no writer depended on his art for his bread; he had independent means or a job.

In the nineties it was not at all uncommon for a writer to wait months before he knew whether his manuscript had been accepted or rejected. If it was accepted, he had to wait for his money until the piece was published, which might be a few months or a few years. One magazine even told its contributors: "Sending of printed proof sheets is no guarantee of acceptance."

Lorimer was the first editor to pay on acceptance, and young writers flocked to the *Post*. Even the established writers came along after them, because the *Post* paid adequate prices and it cost them no more than a week's time to learn whether a story they had written was acceptable to the editor. These reforms, plus the *Post*'s increasingly good prices and Lorimer's genius for selecting talent, brought new writers to the magazine in droves, and in 1908 its circulation shot past the million mark.

By that time it had taken on, in rough form, the distinctive character it would retain for the next quarter-century. And it had become more than the nation's leading magazine: It was an American institution.

People not familiar with the inner workings of the organization sometimes assumed that Curtis, as publisher, was responsible for its phenomenal success. He always disabused them. "I take down some of the profits," he often said, "but the *Post* really belongs to Lorimer. I would no more think of telling him how to run it, what to print and what not to print, than I would think of telling Commodore Bennett how to run the *New York Herald*. Lorimer is the *Post*, and the *Post* is Lorimer."

Fragments of the dream life of the very rich frequently

pervaded the *Post*'s pages, because Lorimer understood that this was the pleasant vision of millions of middle-class Americans, who yearned first for the good things they saw in the *Post*'s advertising pages, and second for the lucky break that would project them into a world of yachts, beautiful women, and champagne. Meanwhile they stuck perforce to their meat and potatoes and beer, to that vast complex of American business life which was guaranteed to make the dream a reality—if and if. That was the life most of Lorimer's writers depicted in fiction, mixed generously with the romance that made reality unbearable.

At the heart of the *Post* was the editorial page, and at the core of the page were Lorimer's own editorials. For years these columns were a sounding board for the continuing crusades of the Boss, as he was known to those who worked and wrote for him. There he argued in his crisp, incisive prose for "the extension of our national parks, the protection of wild game, the conservation of our national resources." There he demanded "drastic reforms in the administration of justice." There he fought against the cancellation of war debts, and for the ever tighter restriction of immigration. There he preached the fundamental isolationism of Washington's Farewell Address. And there, finally, in the last four years of his tenure, he fought the New Deal, and lived to see his page become the rallying point for a majority of *Post* readers, who had grown up with the magazine and with Lorimer—grown up as much as he had and no more.

Branching out from both sides of the editorial page was the solid structure of the *Post*'s substance, fiction and articles. The articles were divided roughly into political and nonpolitical, and probably the most effective belonged in the former category, where they existed as potent extensions of the editorial page. Even the nonpolitical articles had purpose and direction in most instances; there were few with no other purpose than to entertain.

The influence of *Post* articles was remarkable. Sometimes

it was difficult to tell where interpreting America left off and telling America began. As Ed Howe once put it: "I often think a thing is not really published in the United States until it appears in the *Saturday Evening Post.*"

The genius that made the *Post* was perhaps best expressed by the veteran Chicago newspaperman, Harper Leech, who wrote after Lorimer's death in his *Chicago Daily News* column: "Somebody said of Bruce Barton in the age of Coolidge that he had the wave length of the American people. Maybe Coolidge said it, and he should have known about that wave length, because he had it himself for several years. But the late George Horace Lorimer had it for the first third of the twentieth century, and then some. And because of that the files of the *Saturday Evening Post* are a mirror of the American mind from 1900 to date. Lorimer's passing has evoked the usual success story that appears after a man who has done a big creative job moves on. But the way it strikes me is that Lorimer couldn't have helped being a great editor. He knew the folks."

That was the essence of it. America and the *Post* were Lorimer's twin passions, when all was said and done—crossing and recrossing the continent, studying the sky for signs of rain, inquiring about the crops and talking to hundreds of people; putting out the nation's number one magazine with inexhaustible energy and enthusiasm. These things were his life.

Lorimer's *Post* and Bok's *Journal* were the successes of Curtis's life. The *Country Gentleman,* which he acquired in 1911, was eventually successful too, but it took six years of time, careful nursing by Lorimer, who put it out with his left hand for awhile, and two million dollars of company money.

With such successes in mind, Curtis's disastrous attempt to build up a comparable newspaper chain is superficially difficult to understand. When he acquired the *Philadelphia Public Ledger,* he was determined to spend whatever was necessary to make it the best newspaper in the country, "the *Manchester Guardian* of America," as he advertised it. He added an evening edition to this most respectable and conservative of Philadelphia papers, gave it a superb foreign service rivaling the *Chicago Daily News* and *New York Times,* and celebrities from William Howard Taft down wrote for it.

By 1926 the morning and evening *Ledger* had climbed to a combined total of 315,575, and the Sunday edition had reached 437,024. Yet the *Morning Ledger* expired not long after, in spite of Curtis's efforts to save it by buying and merging two other Philadelphia papers with it.

Curtis had an even worse experience in New York, where he bought the *New York Evening Post,* and spent more than ten million dollars trying to make it pay, even to the extreme of turning the historic paper into a tabloid. Eventually he had to sell it for a figure said to be well under $300,000.

His last newspaper effort came in 1930, when he bought the *Philadelphia Inquirer.* Unlike the other purchases, this property was a going concern, well worth the eighteen million he invested in it. But three years after Curtis died in 1933, the former owners bought back their paper, which appeared to be going the same way as Curtis's other investments. The *Evening Ledger* was bought by the *Evening Bulletin* in 1942, and the *Sunday Ledger* merged with the *Inquirer* in 1934. Fortunately for Curtis's peace of mind, the final collapse of his newspaper dreams was postponed until after his death.

Most critics have concluded that his failure in the newspaper business came about because he did not find the right man to manage his properties, as he had with his magazines. No Lorimers or Boks appeared, and the men who did manage the newspapers lacked sufficient editorial vision and managerial ability. This failure was deplorable because of the ruin and near-ruin it inflicted on old and respected newspapers which deserved to live and thrive, but it was a small patch on the large fabric of Curtis's immense success. A middle-class man himself always, in spite of his wealth, he understood the amorphous mass of middle-class America, and his magazines reflected the lives of these citizens.

Aside from the debt owed to him by schools, colleges, and

hospitals everywhere in the country who benefited by his exceedingly generous philanthropies, American journalism is also indebted to this quiet, modest, retiring man, who hated publicity and loved yachts and music. For Cyrus Curtis, whether he intended it or not, provided in his magazines a rich and varied record of what a majority of Americans thought about, dreamed of, aspired to, enjoyed and disliked in the first decades of this century.

Medill, McCormick,
and the "Chicago Tribune"

JOSEPH MEDILL WALKED INTO THE *CHICAGO TRIBUNE* OFFICE FOR
the first time on a spring morning in 1855. He was then a
beardless young man of thirty-two, with a square Irish face distinguished for its firm, straight mouth and jutting, stubborn
chin. His thick dark hair grew low over his ears, with discreetly
short sideburns. The black string tie he wore between the
wings of his collar, the frock coat and the congress boots, were
distinctive parts of his habitual dress.

Medill devoted forty-four years of intense effort to making
the *Tribune* a success. For the first eight years he was managing editor, or general manager, as the position was called at the
time. He was editor-in-chief from November 1863 to August
1866, except for brief periods as Washington correspondent.
Then he spent a short time in public life, serving first in the
Illinois Constitutional Convention of 1869, later on the Civil
Service Commission, and as mayor of Chicago. But he devoted
himself again to his paper in 1874, when he took complete editorial and financial control and retained both until he died.

The concrete result of his labors was a sound newspaper
property. That was the most substantial part of the legacy he
left to the family members who came after him. His more
intangible assets—the characteristics which enabled him to
found the dynasty—he passed on through his two daughters,

who married into the Patterson and McCormick families and united the three lines.

Robert Rutherford McCormick (see photograph 8), present editor of the Chicago *Tribune,* and his cousins, the late Eleanor "Cissy" Patterson and the late Captain Joseph Patterson, were the children born to the Medill daughters, and it was these three who built the empire which became so controversial a part of American life in our time. Their interlocking ownership of great newspapers—the *Tribune,* Captain Patterson's *Daily News* and Cissy's *Washington Times-Herald*—and numerous subsidiary interests established them as publishing entrepreneurs rivaled perhaps only by William Randolph Hearst.

Today, with two of the triumvirate gone, Colonel McCormick stands alone. The Washington and New York newspapers are operated now by subordinates, but the Colonel is their ultimate directing head and thus their policies and practices continue without significant interruption.

Because these papers represent a consistent, unanimous, and more than ordinarily vigorous extreme-right-wing voice in American politics, they are often thought of as simply a political phenomenon bred of these troubled years. But their viewpoint is rooted deeply in family history, particularly in the life of Joseph Medill, who was the embodiment of the *Tribune* in his day as Colonel McCormick is now. Medill's journalistic philosophy is reflected in his grandchildren's newspapers, and the powerful financial empire they have built was made possible by the trust he left for them.

Medill was a fighting leader in the era of personal journalism, when that kind of newspapering was consistent with a lusty, growing, brawling America. He was a midwestern James Gordon Bennett, and his paper was often more uninhibited than Bennett's *Herald.* It tried lawsuits in its news columns, used everything short of gutter language in assailing its enemies, and stopped at nothing when it advocated a cause. This description substantially fits McCormick's properties, modified only by the restraints which the libel laws impose.

Colonel McCormick's approach to the problems of his time is strikingly similar to that of Medill's, and the problems themselves are not essentially dissimilar. Both proclaimed their journalistic ideals in the most lofty terms. Medill, on the subject of a newspaper's duty, declared it should be "the organ of no man, however high, no clique or ring, however influential, no faction, however fanatical or demonstrative, and in all things to follow the line of common sense." The Colonel has often expressed nearly identical sentiments. "News should be printed in strict accordance with its value as news," he once remarked in a speech.

Their attitudes toward organized labor are almost exactly alike, although Medill blamed liquor for the workingman's downfall. In personality, Medill was intensely egoistic and his self-esteem led him into eccentricities as odd as some of those displayed by the present generation of his family. For example, he had a penchant for oddities and curiosities. He was in the habit of clipping miscellaneous items which happened to attract his attention and sending them to the composing room marked "Must, JM." McCormick preserves this custom in ideas sent to the city desk and elsewhere in the *Tribune* organization— memos which do not require a "must" but only "RRMc."

Medill did not let his educational lacks restrain him from taking a bold position on scientific matters. At one time or another he rode a half-dozen scientific or pseudo-scientific hobbies, such as simplified spelling, the sunspot theory, and the blue-glass theory. The *Tribune* flew in the face of outraged public opinion for years with such spellings as "infinit," "favorit," "telegrafed" and similar fancies. Some of these have disappeared, but other phonetic simplifications appear in the paper today.

The *Tribune*'s editor attributed all natural phenomena to sunspots until one day he heard of the existence of microbes and immediately adopted this as the new explanation. Soon after, an unfortunate reporter, writing according to *Tribune* policy, asserted that the plague in Egypt was caused by sunspots.

Medill went through the copy, crossed out the word "sunspots" wherever it occurred and substituted "microbes."

By a curious chance, Medill was actually a British citizen by nativity. His father, an Ulsterite who married an Episcopalian girl, settled on a farm near St. John in New Brunswick, Canada, when the family emigrated from Ireland. They thought they were settling in America, but this strip of border was in dispute and Canada got it eventually, instead of Maine. However, they emigrated to Stark County, Ohio, when Joe was nine, and there the boy grew up for the next twelve years on his father's farm.

He got his education by reading whatever books he could borrow. He read history, especially Gibbon and Hume, and he devoured travel and biography. Like Lincoln, he would walk miles for a book. On Saturdays he trudged nine miles to Canton for instruction in Latin, logic, and natural philosophy from a clergyman. In his spare time he went about his home neighborhood getting subscribers for Greeley's weekly *Tribune*.

At twenty-one he began to study law in Canton, was admitted to the bar, and practiced for three years in New Philadelphia. He spent a good part of his time in the town newspaper office, where lawyers, teachers, and everyone interested in politics gathered. When he wasn't arguing the questions of the day, Joe Medill learned to set type and operate a hand press. He even wrote an editorial now and then.

That turned him for good to the newspaper business. He bought the *Coshocton Whig*, in northwestern Ohio, operated it successfully for two years, then moved up to Cleveland and established a Whig morning paper called the *Daily Forest City*. He shared Raymond's conviction that the Whig party's day was over and that salvation lay with the Free Soilers, consequently, he consolidated his paper with a Free Soil journal edited by a South Carolina abolitionist. They named the new paper the *Cleveland Leader* and dedicated it to the job of uniting the antislavery elements. Medill thereafter campaigned ardently for the formation of the Republican Party and was one of the moving spirits in its founding.

Preoccupied though he was with politics, Medill found time to marry one of the girls he had taught during a brief occupancy of the master's chair in a district school. She was Katharine Patrick, a New Philadelphia girl. They were married on September 2, 1852, and they had three children, all girls. One of the girls, Elinor, later married Robert W. Patterson, Jr., of a hardy Scotch Presbyterian family, much involved with the church. Another daughter, Katharine, married Robert Sanderson McCormick, descendant of a well-to-do slaveholding family from the Valley of Virginia, whose line included the inventor of the reaper, Cyrus Hall McCormick. Thus the McCormick-Patterson generation we know today was established: Colonel McCormick was one of Katharine's two sons, and Captain Patterson and Cissy were Elinor's children.

As for Medill, he was aware that his own marriage was the extra push he needed to enter the journalistic big time. Matrimony and ambition combined to make him seek greater fortune in the West, and at the suggestion of Greeley, he went to Chicago in the spring of 1855. Greeley told Medill that it would be a good idea to start a penny paper in Chicago, and arranged a meeting there for Medill with another friend of his, Charles H. Ray, of Galena, Illinois, then the state's metropolis. Dr. Ray had been editor of the *Galena Jeffersonian*.

Medill and Ray arrived in a Chicago of 85,000 population that pulsed with restlessness, expanding activity. They carried letters to each other from Greeley and met in the parlor of the Tremont House, where they were introduced by the proprietor. Their personalities were ideal for a journalistic partnership. Medill was a business and editorial genius; Ray was an ardent reformer. The result of their meeting was a historic decision. They decided not to start a new paper, but to buy into the up-and-coming *Chicago Tribune*. Medill bought a third interest; Dr. Ray took a fourth.

With that purchase an era in midwest publishing history

began. The *Tribune* was already eight years old, but its real career began when Joseph Medill entered the office. From that moment, the *Tribune* transcended the simple role of newspaper. It became a state of mind and has remained so to this day.

One of the first men to walk into the office and take out a subscription was a rising young Illinois politician, Abe Lincoln. "I didn't like the paper before you boys took hold of it," Abe told them. "It was too much of a Know-Nothing sheet."

There was no doubt about the *Tribune*'s politics from Medill's advent, and no question of its influence. By his use of the paper as a political weapon, Medill unquestionably helped shape the course of American history. In 1859, his paper was surpassed in power only by the New York *Tribune,* and it completely dominated its own part of the country. This power was a prime factor in the election of 1860. The *Tribune* helped to push the doubtful Western states into the Lincoln camp, and Medill himself, in collaboration with Dr. Ray and the Illinois politicos, was one of the chief backstage movers who got Lincoln nominated in the convention.

To do it, Medill had to oppose Greeley, the man indirectly responsible for his position. But he had no hesitation in taking a bold and arrogant stand, which foreshadowed the *Tribune*'s present-day isolationism. As one historian has written, "He looked upon the Republican party as the product, in part, at least, of his own efforts." Consequently, he could proclaim editorially: "If we are to have the cooperation of the party elsewhere, well; if not, Illinois is sovereign, and her sons can walk alone!"

Again, he wrote, "Chicago is the pet Republican city of the Union, the point from which radiate opinions which more or less influence six states." To this the neighboring *Cleveland Plain Dealer* replied sharply: "The principal productions of Chicago are corner lots, statistics and wind."

Nevertheless, Medill's boast had more truth than wind in it. From 1861 to 1865, Medill and his *Tribune* preached the

Union and emancipation with an increasingly powerful voice. The paper fought against wildcat money; it urged the development of railroads; and it grew with Chicago.

As Lincoln's real character emerged in office, Medill appeared more and more, along with some of the other men who had put the President in power, as an opportunist who was far from sharing Lincoln's vision and ideals. Medill spoke in letters of Abe's "very weak and foolish traits of character," and in one letter to his brother William, who was killed at Gettysburg, he displayed his own character in a most revealing fashion. He wrote in part:

> The insults received from England [meaning British help to the Confederacy] must be wiped out, and the only reparation she can give us is to vacate North America. Peacibly [sic] if she will—forcibly if we must. And as to France, she has taken a mean and cowardly advantage of this nation to crush poor Mexico, which will not be allowed. We shall permit no nation to abuse Mexico but ourselves. We claim the right to turn her up on Uncle Sam's knee and spank her bottom for not behaving herself as in 1846, but will permit no one else to touch her. . . . In future wars black and yellow men will be freely used to fight. We will not be so careful about spilling the blood of niggers. England holds India with Sepoy troops who hate her. How easy for us to hold the South with black troops who love the North and are devotedly loyal. Old Abe says, "Bring on your niggers. I want 200,000 of them to save my white boys as soon as I can get them." Our people are learning sense. The war has pounded new ideas into their heads and old prejudices out. It is a great teacher, and great progress is never made by a people except through war. The tree of Liberty must be watered by the blood of patriots at least once in every three generations.

Again and again, Medill solidified the foundations of Middle West insularity in his battles with the eastern papers and their publishers, particularly Bennett's *Herald,* which he called the "Satanic." Bennett retorted editorially that the *Tribune* was "the sewer into which goes everything too dirty for its New York namesake to print."

Medill emerged from the war richer and more of a "realist" than ever. The conflict had affected his paper advantageously, as it had newspapers everywhere. The greatest effect, of course, was on circulation. From only 18,000 in 1861, *Tribune* circulation rose to 40,000 in 1864, and the paper began to make real money for the first time.

Disaster appeared always to be Medill's friend. When the great fire wiped out Chicago in 1871, the *Tribune* emerged with what was probably its most famous editorial, titled "Cheer Up," which declared "Chicago shall rise again!" It helped inspire the city's magnificent comeback, and Medill swept easily to victory as mayor in October 1872, running on a "Fire-proof" ticket. Two years later, however, he was back on the job, with his son-in-law, Robert W. Patterson, as managing editor.

Under Medill's direct control, which he now assumed for the first time, having increased his interest to a majority, the paper became more conservatively Republican than ever. Its circulation—hanging around the 40,000 mark in the seventies but doubling in the eighties—was still small by comparison with the other Chicago papers, but the paper was prosperous. Advertising revenue continued to increase. The editorial page maintained its Civil War prestige. In general, it was one of the country's best newspapers, from the purely professional standpoint.

During this period, Medill distinguished himself chiefly by his bitter opposition to labor. In the railroad strike of 1877, the *Tribune* referred to the strikers as "the scum and filth of the city," and declared that, "Capitalists would offer any sum to see the leaders . . . strung up to a telegraph pole." The paper headlined a riot between strikers and police as "RED WAR," and an "Assembly of the Communists." In an editorial of 1884, the *Tribune* asserted, almost unbelievably, that "the simplest plan" to deal with strikers, "when one is not a member of the Humane Society, is to put arsenic in the supplies of food furnished the unemployed or the tramp. This produces death in a short time and is a warning to other tramps to keep out of the neighborhood."

Whenever he could do it profitably, Medill stood on the side of civic virtue. While the nation's cities fought to get the World's Fair in 1893, Medill was one of those who made certain that Chicago's ten-million-dollar bid got the plum. He was an original stockholder and a director of the Exposition. At the *Tribune* office he supervised the paper's coverage, which was the best in the city. A special bureau in the fair's administration building was the center for a staff which wired its news direct to the *Tribune,* where it was handled by a special copy desk.

As time went on, Medill let active control of the *Tribune* fall more and more into the hands of his managing editor, Patterson. Less interested in politics than in newspapering for its own sake, Patterson gave the paper a more temperate tone and made it a little more flexible. It was no longer Medill's personal organ.

However, the gradual transfer of power only modified and did not change the *Tribune's* basic principles. It was still vituperative in behalf of big business. It still opposed union labor, government regulation of business, and any politician who dared to criticize it. In local politics its stand was determined by the views of the rich and influential Commercial Club, and by whatever a public official had to say about the paper's ninety-nine-year lease of the Chicago school board's land on which its plant stood.

Medill died in 1899, only three months before the *Tribune* achieved one of the most noteworthy news beats in its history— first to reach the whole world, even the President of the United States, with the news of Dewey's victory at Manila. This would certainly have delighted the old man who had passed away on his ranch near San Antonio, according to legend, with the classic newspaperman's query on his lips, "What's the news?"

Two days after Medill's death, the *Tribune's* managing editor, James Keeley, got a letter from him, mailed before his death. It was a packet of clippings intended for the paper and marked in the editor's decisive handwriting, "Must, JM." It was a last tribute to Joseph Medill that the clippings went into the *Tribune* without question—not as a mark of respect for the dead, but simply because "Must, JM" meant what it said.

There followed an interval of a dozen or so years in which the *Tribune* was nominally in the hands of its family owners, represented by Patterson and Medill McCormick, JM's grandson, but was actually directed by Keeley, one of journalism's unjustly neglected figures. Keeley was for three years in absolute editorial control of the paper, the only time it was ever guided by an outsider. During his regime, the *Tribune* became more of a *news*paper than it had ever been before or has been since, and chalked up several of the outstanding news beats in its history; though Patterson got the credit for them from the *Tribune*'s own historians.

Keeley was an English foundling who grew up on the London streets. He came to America at sixteen and served his apprenticeship on the *Kansas City Journal*. At twenty-one he moved to the *Tribune,* and in an incredibly short time the rookie reporter was the best man in the shop.

He was not quite twenty-eight when he became the *Tribune*'s city editor in 1895. He had been in this country only twelve years. His theory of news, which he expressed later, was: "News is a commodity and for sale like any other commodity." The trait which made Keeley such an outstanding salesman of that commodity was his utter devotion to the news itself. That devotion sometimes made him seem more like a one-purpose machine than a human being, as it has so many other city-room executives, but he made the paper's heart beat with an untiring, efficient steadiness equal to his own.

As an editor Keeley had the instinctive quality of being able to see all sides of a story at once and then to extract every drop of news from it. He was not a writer, like Medill, nor a professional thinker, like Greeley, but he knew preeminently what news was and how to sell it.

He brought a prodigious energy to his job. Before Keeley's day—and after it—city editors on morning papers left the office at 6 P.M., leaving the job of getting the paper to press in the hands of the night city editor. Keeley stayed at the office until midnight in his city editor days. Even as managing editor he stayed most nights until the first edition was running, about midnight, and then lingered on to lay the groundwork for the next day's labors.

One of the first jobs Keeley did on the *Tribune* was to unify the paper's staff and give it needed morale. He did it by letting the executives under him know that they could depend on him to protect them and back them up under attack, and at the same time he expected them to protect their subordinates. Working newspapermen responded eagerly to that kind of leadership from the top. New men hired by Keeley came on the staff, including such memorable figures as James O'Donnell Bennett, Edgar Sisson, Harvey Woodruff, Ring Lardner, John T. McCutcheon, and Walter Eckersall. Among all these talents, Keeley played no favorites. He gave praise rarely, and then in the form of short congratulatory messages rather than verbally.

The staff produced equally memorable crusades and stories, including Keeley's personal battle to stop the slaughter of people from Fourth of July fireworks; the coverage of the Iroquois Theatre fire in 1903; the famous story of Paul Stensland, the bank president who disappeared in 1906 with hundreds of thousands in embezzled cash, whom Keeley himself finally tracked down in Africa; and exposure of the bribery and corruption that elected William Lorimer to the United States Senate.

In all this, Keeley was trying to give *Tribune* readers his ideal of "personal service," which he once expressed in this way:

The big development of the modern newspaper will be along lines of personal service. The newspaper that not only informs and instructs its readers but is of service is the one that commands attention, gets circulation, and also holds its readers after it gets them. . . . It must enter into the everyday life of its readers and, like the parish priest, be guide, counselor and friend. . . . There should be no partisanship in politics, no prejudice in religion, no hostility to organized labor, no antagonism to wealth *per se,* no color of opinion; in fact, opinion should be barred from the report of every happening, every meeting, every public discussion, everything that goes to make up the daily grist of news. I say it should be; I admit that it is not. . . . But the man in charge of a newspaper must be impersonal as a judge and his every act must meet the acid test of duty to the people as a whole.

At the zenith of Keeley's career on the *Tribune,* disaster overtook him. He left the paper in 1914 to take over management of the *Chicago Record-Herald.* "Did he jump or was he pushed?" his biographer asked. The evidence indicates that he was pushed. Apparently he became aware that he was disliked in high places, particularly by Robert Rutherford McCormick and Joseph Patterson, who had come into the business in 1910 and were rising fast in it. It was clear that they were going to be its dominant figures. They were chiefs of the tribe; Keeley was a hired hand. Facing the inevitable, he took the first good opportunity that came his way, before the royal cousins could act.

As though to prove this theory themselves, the paper's new management permitted a brief obituary on an inside page when Keeley died. The other Chicago papers carried it on page one.

With Keeley's departure in 1914, McCormick and Patterson stepped into complete control of a thoroughly sound property. The paper had the prestige built up and bequeathed by Medill; it had the personal service connection with its readership established by Keeley; and it had a demonstrated political power.

The *Tribune* was ready to build, and it had acquired the kind of builders it needed for financial success. Patterson began to originate the famed comic strips and other features which so increased *Tribune* circulation. McCormick applied the business pressure to put the paper in the big-money class; Keeley had been no businessman.

In eight years the cousins succeeded in doubling *Tribune* circulation. From 1914 to 1921, daily figures went from 261,278 to 499,725, and Sunday circulation from 406,556 to 827,028. In the same period, advertising jumped in columns from 43,503 to 76,703.

Behind these figures lay the instant success of such Patterson-inspired comics as "Andy Gump," "Moon Mullins," and

"Little Orphan Annie." Patterson also originated the idea of printing a daily directory of motion picture theaters and their attractions. In line with this he conceived the plan of printing newspaper versions of serial thrillers showing concurrently in the local picture houses. Prizes were offered for the best solutions to the mysteries.

On the business side, McCormick leased the Canadian forest lands and built the Quebec and Ontario paper mills which enabled the *Tribune* to save a paper manufacturer's profit and compete more successfully with Hearst, who got paper for five dollars a ton less than the standard price.

This kind of smart business ended Keeley's and Hearst's dream of Chicago newspaper dominance. Keeley had become publisher of the *Herald,* a merger of the *Record-Herald* and the *Inter-Ocean.* The *Herald* was backed by big Chicago names—Samuel Insull, Julius Rosenwald, Ogden Armour, and others—but by 1918 it had been beaten into submission by the aggressive McCormick-Patterson combination. It merged with Hearst's *Examiner* to become the *Herald-Examiner.* Twenty-one years later the *Tribune* ousted that rival, too, and thus occupied the morning field alone until Marshall Field's *Sun* rose to challenge it.

The cousins appeared to be an unbeatable team in 1918, but disintegrating influences were already at work in the partnership; these were brought to a climax by the World War. The difficulty lay in an essential difference of personality between the two men. Patterson, born into a rich family, educated at Groton and Yale, had always been in rebellion against his environment. His zeal for reform movements had led him into the Socialist camp, where he embarrassed his cousin and his family by denouncing most of the things they stood for.

McCormick, on the other hand, also a rich-boy product of Groton and Yale, embarked from New Haven in 1903 as a six-foot-four, awkwardly stiff young man who was alone much of the time and felt that the world belonged to him because he was a McCormick. His favorite sports were riding, polo and hunting to hounds. After a brief period as lawyer, alderman, and president of a sewage disposal project, he came to the *Tribune* in 1910 well equipped to assume a management position.

The cousins started out as very different people, and for a time the gulf between them was wide, as Patterson's early left-wing leanings led him into the New Deal camp which McCormick spent a large share of the *Tribune*'s space in denouncing. But the coming of the second World War ended the ideological schism, and the cousins were thenceforth united in isolationism and hating Roosevelt, though Patterson's *Daily News* continued, in its own eyes at least, to be the voice of the proletariat.

As the years went on, too, Patterson's personality showed itself as more like his Chicago cousin's in many respects. Like McCormick, he presented a dictatorial, stubborn, ruthless and unstable side to the world—a personality characteristic of Cyrus McCormick, Joseph Medill, and other strong men of the dynasty. Patterson, also in common with these men, had a charming side to his personality which few besides his intimates ever saw.

The Colonel has eccentricities which have been widely publicized, but Captain Patterson had some of his own, less well known, like his aggravated claustrophobia and his spells of hero worship for such unlikely people as lion tamers and female stage and screen stars. His restlessness was expressed, as is his cousin's, in a love of flying. He had McCormick's unpredictability of mood, and his deep suspicion of things alien, some of his compulsion to withdraw from the world at times, and some of his flatness of emotion.

These similarities were not pronounced, however, until the later years. At first the two seemed to be going in exactly opposite directions. Both cousins became *Tribune* correspondents at the start of the first World War. Patterson, with his proletarian leanings, refused to accept the special privileges to which his position entitled him. McCormick not only accepted the privileges, he enlarged upon them. Patterson was at Vera Cruz in 1914 to cover the trouble there, and later went on to Belgium as an observer of the German invasion. McCormick went abroad in 1915, bound for the Eastern Front. In London he had lunch with Prime Minister Asquith and paid a visit to Churchill, then First Lord of the Admiralty. When he had completed a round of social calls in London, he moved on to Paris and then to Russia. Correct in white tie and tails, he interviewed the Czar. Later, smitten with an idea, he hired a movie cameraman and together they made the first war newsreels ever filmed, which were shipped back to Chicago and shown there with great acclaim. When he returned home, McCormick also wrote a book about his adventures.

The cousins were agreed on German efficiency, mistrust of England, and most of all on the necessity for American isolation from "Europe's war." Nonetheless, they were vociferous editorially in advocating invasion of Mexico in 1916, and entered into the affair themselves.

Patterson turned down a commission and enlisted as a buck private in a National Guard artillery unit. McCormick entered as a cavalry major. The authorities tried to make the younger cousin a general, on the basis of his family connections, but he would have no part of it.

While Patterson sweated it out in the artillery, McCormick leased a hacienda and received high-ranking officers. The cousins met by accident one day in a San Antonio hotel, and McCormick was forced to introduce Private Patterson to General Funston as they ascended in an elevator. The general and the private shook hands without embarrassment on either side, to McCormick's amazement.

After the Mexican affair, the cousins were united on only one thing: their intense opposition to American involvement in the war in Europe. The *Tribune* shouted against American participation in much the same words it used a quarter-century later when war came again. It was not until six months before United States entry that the paper yielded to the inevitable. Changing tone abruptly, the *Tribune* became superpatriotic and the cousins again plunged personally into battle, and again each made the plunge in his own fashion.

Patterson worked his way up from the ranks to a second lieutenant's commission, which he held when he was shipped to France. He saw service in five major engagements, was gassed and wounded, and eventually became a captain. McCormick joined Pershing's staff and went to Paris as a member of it. Later, he went to the front with an artillery unit, but by the end of the war, he was in an executive post as commandant at Fort Sheridan, Illinois.

It was in France, on a night in 1918, that the cousins met and conceived the *New York Daily News*. Captain Patterson was called from his battery to meet McCormick, newly a colonel, at the French village of Mareuil-en-Dole. The conversation began in a farmhouse near the Ourcq River, but the noise of operational movement in this field headquarters drove them to climb out a rear window and sit on a manure pile in the back yard, where it was quieter. There they drank scotch and watched the distant flashing of an artillery barrage.

Patterson was full of an interview he had had a short time before with Lord Northcliffe, during a London furlough. Northcliffe had told him the story of his *London Daily Mirror,* and how this tabloid had climbed to an 800,000 circulation at that time. Northcliffe added, Patterson told his cousin, that he believed New York was ripe for a similar tabloid. The story impressed McCormick.

The conversation must also have turned to postwar prospects for the *Tribune,* particularly the taxes which the government would be able to assess on *Tribune* profits. This was a sore point with McCormick, the businessman, and perhaps he saw in Patterson's tabloid aspirations a way to siphon off potential taxable income into a venture which might also turn out eventually to be profitable. Then, too, there was the undeniable advantage, which cropped out indirectly as the conversation went on, that the cousins would be separated and Patterson would take complete control of the New York paper if it were successful. The diverse characters of the two men made them incompatible, if nothing worse, and the separation was welcome.

All in all, the idea pleased both. They shook hands on the agreement and parted. On June 26, 1919, the *Tribune* launched its tabloid pictorial morning newspaper, the *New York Daily News.* Patterson divided his time between New York and Chicago for about five years, but when the new tabloid showed symptoms of becoming an unprecedented success, he moved to New York permanently, and as the decade of the twenties moved toward its disastrous climax, Colonel McCormick stood alone at the helm of the *Chicago Tribune.* Once more it was a one-man newspaper.

The quarter-century from 1920 to 1945 covers the establishment of Colonel McCormick's world. Millions of words have been written about that world—denouncing, defending, explaining, rationalizing—but no final word can be written unless the Colonel chooses to set down his memoirs.

When McCormick reestablished the Medill pattern of personal journalism in the *Tribune* immediately after the first World War, it was successful for nearly a decade because it suited the times. In the same period the *Tribune* and the *Daily News* were also immensely successful in a business way because of the unquestioned executive ability of both McCormick and Patterson. Liberal opponents of these men are prone to forget that the cousins were extremely able businessmen and that the newspaper business is indebted to them for numerous mechanical and editorial developments.

Tribune business history since 1920 is a record of continuous success, but *Tribune* political and editorial history in the same period is the story of steadily declining influence. The same thing can be said for the *New York Daily News,* except that the *News* never had any considerable editorial influence to lose.

McCormick did not come to national attention until President Roosevelt inspired a large section of the American press to a continued, bitter assault on the government which does it no credit. The Colonel was the leader in this movement. He turned the *Tribune* into a bitter, personal organ of a kind not seen in this country since the days of the nineteenth-century publisher-politicians. It surpassed Medill's best efforts.

This hatred carried over into America's participation in the second World War, which the *Tribune* opposed as it had in the first war. Sometimes it was difficult to tell whether the *Tribune* was fighting the common enemy or the Administration's conduct of the war. Today the *Tribune* and its publisher represent the foremost newspaper voice of the Republican Party's extreme right wing.

The greatest damage done to the *Tribune* by this long crusade has been its editorial treatment of the news, in an era when the business as a whole was endeavoring, painfully and with considerable difficulty, to come closer to the ideal of objective news in the news columns and editorial opinion on the editorial page.

In other respects, the *Tribune* is an admirable newspaper. Mechanically it is far above most others, and editorially it is exceptionally well written and edited. Its city coverage leads the Chicago field, and it has long had an outstanding sports department and a superlatively good Sunday book section. Its readership extends through Illinois, Iowa, Wisconsin, Indiana, parts of Ohio, and the western coast of Michigan, and it is often accepted by its rural subscribers as an authority second only to the Bible.

It is perhaps unfortunate that these and other good qualities which make the *Tribune* a leader in the business are overshadowed and sometimes forgotten by the Colonel's extreme political views and the *Tribune*'s painful arrogance in proclaiming itself as the fountainhead of righteousness. The *Tribune* is the foremost exponent of the school which contends that anyone who disagrees with its ideas is either a dupe or a dope.

Although it has come to advocate many of the same policies, the *Daily News* has had a somewhat different history and is not usually regarded in quite the same light. As America's largest newspaper, it got off to a shaky and unpromising start. In the beginning, it was a joke in the trade. Other publishers and editors called it "the servant girl's Bible." Newspapermen on regular-sized dailies looked upon the *News* coldly and worked on it only as a last resort. Then, almost overnight, the situation changed. In a year the *News* jumped from eighteenth to eighth place among New York's English-language dailies; in two years it was in second place, behind the *Evening Journal;* within five years it was first. Circulation jumped from a low point of 26,636 in August 1919 to pass the million mark in December 1925. The *Sunday News,* launched on May 1, 1921, achieved fourth place among its competitors during its first full year of existence and averaged 308,318 copies for 1922. Two years later it was in second place, just behind Hearst's *New York American.* Two years after that it overtook the *American* with 1,234,189, thus establishing a new Sunday circulation record in the United States.

When the *News* was four years old and a booming success, Hearst belatedly entered his own tabloid competition, the *Daily Mirror,* but although it survived, the *Mirror* was never more than a dim reflection of the *News.*

In his historic effort to out-*News* the *News,* Bernarr Macfadden then proved conclusively with the *Evening Graphic* that there is a point beyond which tabloidism becomes paranoia. The *Graphic* went insane and was committed to the history books within a few years. After these attempts, the *News* was alone in its field.

From its low point in 1919, the *News* climbed steadily for reasons which have never been adequately explained. The theories range from the idea that a popular limerick contest turned the tide, to Patterson's own theory that New Yorkers had discovered the paper's convenient size. Probably it was the simple meshing of supply and demand. The *News* had what the postwar public wanted. One writer summarized it accurately in 1938: "By turns sobby, dirty, bloody and glamorous, the *News* covered each in the manner that would most effectively appeal to the more elementary emotions of a truck-driver, and to the truck-driver in everyone."

After the crash of 1929, the *News* astutely changed editorial pace. "We're off on the wrong foot," Patterson announced. "The people's major interest is no longer in the playboy, Broadway and divorces, but in how they're going to eat, and from this time forward we'll pay attention to the struggle for existence that's just beginning. . . ."

A major result of this decision was the paper's passionate support of the Roosevelt Administration for nearly eight years. Its new policy was consonant with the New Deal's program of social reform, and the *News* was as vociferous an advocate of the program as McCormick's *Tribune* was its unwavering enemy. It took the issue of isolationism to make the *Tribune* and the *News* a political as well as a financial axis. There is not the slightest evidence, however, that Patterson's attacks on Roosevelt had any more practical political effect than his support, and his isolationist views actually had a contrary effect on New York voters in 1944.

Captain Patterson was a proud man, six feet tall, with gray, bristling hair, a square face heavily seamed, lips straight and thin, eyes deepset, hands large and thick. He walked with a heavy, decisive step. In sharp contrast to the Colonel's sartorial elegance, the Captain was often dressed in a way that would shame his reporters, and at his best, he was no more than baggily orthodox. With all his faults and virtues, he was a dominant personality, perhaps a genius, and these facts had to be recognized even by his enemies. When he died in 1946, it was plain that the *Daily News* might carry on satisfactorily in other hands, but Patterson himself was irreplaceable.

This was even more true of Patterson's redheaded sister, Eleanor Medill "Cissy" Patterson, late publisher of the *Washington Times-Herald*. Stanley Walker once termed her "an everlasting problem child," a kinder way of saying that she was a rich woman who always had her own way about virtually everything. Her newspaper was highly successful under her personal management. She published it in the spirit of the *Tribune* and *Daily News*, with the addition of an incandescent feminine temperament.

Cissy started off to be a creature of society, as her mother wanted her to be, but after her first stormy marriage to a Polish count, she drifted gradually toward a career in journalism. She got into the newspaper business through the back door, by virtue of her friendship with Hearst. They were old friends, and Hearst had every reason to trust his judgment when, in 1930, Cissy talked him into letting her be editor of his *Washington Herald*. He paid her a ten-thousand-dollar annual salary, moreover, a figure which was scarcely reflected by the *Herald*'s fluttery circulation.

It was one of Hearst's better speculations, because Cissy promptly brought personal journalism to Washington in the old familiar family manner. In the national capital, where intrigue has always been the major industry, Cissy's personal approach was just what the doctor ordered. As the paper went along under her direction, Cissy supplemented the diet with features, an element previously inclined to undernourishment in Washington newspapers. The combination nearly doubled the *Herald*'s 60,000 circulation from 1930 to 1936. By that time, Cissy was in the saddle and already had the publisher complex.

She differed in some respects with Hearst's policies, and in 1937 she leased the *Herald* so that she could express her own views. Later in the same year she leased the evening *Times*, published from the same plant, and in 1939 bought the properties to publish them as the *Washington Times-Herald*, in morning, evening, and Sunday editions.

These papers compete against the conservative *Star*, afternoons and Sundays; the afternoon Scripps-Howard tabloid *News*, which has never been a financial success but is often first with the news; and the liberal, superbly written and edited *Post*, one of the country's best newspapers.

The *Times-Herald* has never approached its competitors in the primary matter of news coverage. Like the other family properties, it is edited with a fine disregard for objective report-ing. Nor is it the equal of the other Washington papers in news presentation, but when the figures are added up, the *Times-Herald* outsells its competitors. After Cissy's death in 1948, the paper was for a time in the hands of its executives, then it was directed by another woman, the Colonel's young niece, "Baizie" Miller. She left the paper in 1951 after a disagreement with McCormick, who now is its remote control director.

Cissy's departure left Alicia Patterson, the Captain's daugh-ter, as the only female representative of the clan in the newspaper business, aside from Mrs. Miller. Her amazingly successful Long Island newspaper, *Newsday*, started in 1940 with 11,000 copies printed daily. After six lean years, it started climbing to its present circulation of about 130,000. Situated in Nassau County, on Long Island, in the midst of one of the fastest growing sections of the country, its prospects are excel-lent, and Alicia, an able, imaginative woman, has made her paper the lively kind of organ that shows every sign of growing up with the country.

It could well be that "Miss Patterson" (or Mrs. Harry F. Guggenheim, to give her the married name she does not use at the office) will prove to be the best-balanced and eventually the most successful member, everything considered, of a dynasty that has been one of the most powerful journalistic voices of the last hundred years.

The Heritage of Whitelaw Reid

WITHIN THE RANKS OF THE TWENTIETH-CENTURY REPUBLICAN party press, the Old Guard nationalism of the *Chicago Tribune* under Colonel McCormick met its most effective foil in the independent internationalism of the *New York Herald Tribune* under the Reid family.

The parent *New York Tribune*'s identification with the creation of the modern Republican Party, with Horace Greeley and the cause of abolition, made it the logical custodian of Republican party principles. To this birthright, by the time the *Tribune* combined with the *Herald,* had been added the heritage of Whitelaw Reid.

In early spring of 1924, at a time when the trend toward consolidation of newspaper properties was gaining momentum, Frank A. Munsey dined with the dowager Mrs. Whitelaw Reid and her son and daughter-in-law, Ogden Mills Reid and Helen Rogers Reid.

Munsey, who had been investing millions of dollars, buying, combining, and scrapping newspapers ever since 1901, owned the *New York Herald* and wanted the Reids to sell him their *New York Tribune,* then the city's only other Republican morning newspaper, so that he could make the two papers one.

This the Reids would not think of; to them the *Tribune* was an honored trust. Just the previous year they had moved the paper uptown into a fine new plant, the first to refine the "gravity-feed" system of production, whereby copy was kept moving steadily from the editorial rooms on the upper floors, down through the composing and stereotyping rooms, to the press and mail rooms on the bottom level.

Before the evening ended, the Reids had turned the tables and persuaded Munsey to sell them the *Herald,* along with its Paris edition, for $5,000,000.

By this time few traces remained in either the *Tribune* or the *Herald* of Greeley's "mental eccentricity" or of Bennett's "moral eccentricity," extremities of character that had kept the papers so far apart in the heyday of personal journalism. The inspiration of Greeley's editorial influence and Bennett's news enterprise, however, had been kept alive. Now they were united.

The merger marked the end of Munsey's dreams of empire. At one time he had hoped to build a great newspaper chain, using the straight business approach that had enriched his grocery stores and had multiplied "forty dollars to forty millions in forty years." But newspapers are more than mere merchandise, a fact that Munsey never seemed to comprehend.

When Munsey died, two years after the *Herald Tribune* deal, his role in history was searingly epitomized by William Allen White, the Kansas sage, on the editorial page of the *Emporia Gazette*:

> Frank A. Munsey contributed to the journalism of his day the talent of a meatpacker, the morals of a money-changer and the manners of an undertaker. He and his kind have about succeeded in transforming a once-noble profession into an eight per cent security. May he rest in trust!

To the *Herald Tribune,* which was to remain in the hands of a single family longer than any of its competitors, the Reids brought a different conception of journalism.

Long before, Whitelaw Reid had already been committed to independent Republicanism and to rigid tenets of good taste when Greeley called him to the *Tribune* three years after the end of the Civil War.

Reid had been born on a thriving farm near Xenia, Ohio, in 1837—the year that the murder of Elijah Lovejoy, abolitionist editor in neighboring Illinois, helped to galvanize antislavery sentiment. Early in his career Reid dedicated himself to abolition, to support of Abraham Lincoln and, therefore, to the new Republican Party that had been born out of the emancipation movement.

As editor of the *Xenia News,* Reid wrote:

The *News,* it is scarcely necessary to say, will maintain those Republican principles which are destined finally to become the political creed of the nation. . . . But while thus distinctly expressing my adherence to Republican principles, I wish to be clearly understood as adhering to the PRINCIPLES, and to the party only so long and so far as it remains true to those principles. Parties are mutable and liable to corruption and perversion; principles are enduring. I have no intention of enrolling myself among the number of those party slaves who fear to believe save as the party may direct, and blindly follow their leaders, no matter whither their course may tend.

Reid's sense of morality and manners was even more deeply ingrained than his political faith.

A letter written to his brother Gavin from Miami University in Ohio when Reid was a student there reflects the Scotch Covenanter character of his upbringing. Outlining the rugged daily schedule he had set for himself, he mentioned his morning walks and added:

It is, however, contrary to the strict law of the college, and I always try to be back before anybody else is up. The law is that we must be in our rooms from 7 in the evening till Chapel next morning. It is, however, only intended to prevent the students from being on the streets late at night, and I do not know that they would make any objection to walking in the morning. I met Prof. Stoddard one morning anyhow and he spoke to me very politely.

Reid was, as he proudly told his brother, "getting in Greek a grade of 99 and 100, all the time" and "about the same, I believe, in the other studies."

Odd that Reid in his twenties, tall and slender, with a neat black moustache, well groomed, educated, polished, and accustomed to comfort, should have caught the fancy of gnarled and homespun old Horace Greeley, who could remember poverty and who often scoffed at the futility of smearing effete college men with printers' ink.

Only the hot political temper of the times penetrated Reid's reserve so that, in his hatred of Stephen Douglas, he could stoop to condemn Lincoln's opponent "to the very bottom of the gutter of humiliation, where he will rot and stink and stink and rot forever."

Partisan sympathy brought Greeley and Reid together during the Presidential campaign of 1864. Greeley knew by then of the high reputation Reid had gained as a war correspondent and as a writer from Washington for the *Cincinnati Gazette,* under the pen name of Agate. Reid's graphic first-hand account of the bloody battle of Shiloh had been the talk of newspaperdom.

A year or so later Greeley wrote:

FRIEND REID: Supposing you should have a good chance to come to this city on the *Tribune,* would you do so? And how much would you think a fair compensation? . . . I write this apropos to nothing in particular, but with a view to possibilities. You will answer as tardily and cloudily as you please—or even not at all.

Later Greeley told Reid that before long he intended to retire as active editor of the *Tribune,* and toward the end of 1867 he wrote:

I hope you will authorize me to buy one or two *Tribune* shares for you. I believe it will pay, even in 1868 and thereafter. And I believe you are mistaken as to my withdrawing from active direction of the *Tribune* in 1869. I guess I shall be able to do it. At all events I hope to try.

The next letter said:

I will be in Cincinnati during the Winter. Will you be there when I am? If the mountain will not come to Mohamet, etc.

In the spring of 1868 Reid finally joined the *Tribune* as chief editorial writer. The next year, when Greeley had trouble with his managing editor, the following notice appeared on the *Tribune* bulletin board:

The office of Managing Editor is abolished, and Mr. Whitelaw Reid will see that Mr. Greeley's orders are obeyed, and give instructions at any time in his absence to subordinates.

Greeley was often absent from the office, on lecture tours and political visits to Albany and Washington. With quiet authority and grave courtesy, Reid enforced Greeley's wishes as well as his own strictures against bad grammar, slang, and poor taste. When he lectured on journalism at New York University the *Times* dubbed him "The Professor."

Almost as if to complement his dignified reticence, Reid brought John Hay, one of Lincoln's secretaries, to the *Tribune* as editorial writer. Hay, an outspoken and debonair poet and diplomat-in-the-making, had been a warm friend of Reid's in the Washington days. Although they thought alike on many things, the contrast in personalities was striking. Reid once found this note on his desk:

Farewell, I hear a voice you cannot see. It is at Newburgh. I will meet you at the Century tomorrow at a ghastly hour, very drunk. For tonight the G.M.O. (Great Moral Organ) will worry along without

JH

By now Greeley was deep in the campaign to end the corruption of the Grant administration, and in 1872 he sent Reid to Cincinnati to watch over his chief's candidacy at the Liberal Republican convention. This convention was so heavily guided by famous editors—Sam Bowles of Springfield, Massachusetts, Horace White of Chicago, Murat Halstead of Cincinnati, and Henry Watterson of Louisville—that somebody said it resembled an annual meeting of the Associated Press.

After Greeley's nomination, Reid, now a stockholder, took full charge of the *Tribune,* writing to Greeley:

With your permission, I shall endeavor to keep the *Tribune* out of all newspaper controversies. This is the uniform policy of the *London Times* and it seems to me that there is no better occasion for us to introduce it here. For myself I mean to make no reply to the dirty attacks of the *Times* upon me, or to the malignant onslaughts of the *Post* upon our position. If we are grossly misrepresented it is always possible to make a brief, impersonal statement setting the matter right without naming the newspaper or provoking controversy. I feel sure that this is an indispensable feature of our policy for the campaign, and hope that in this judgment I may have your approval.

Already Reid was setting the *Tribune* on the path toward the more impersonal journalism to come.

Greeley, on going back to his office after his defeat in the election of 1872, was greeted by an editorial in his own paper finding "Crumbs of Comfort" in the fact that "blatherskites and political beggars" and "red-nosed politicians" would no longer be welcome at the *Tribune* since the editor had lost "any credit with the appointing powers." Resenting the slur against himself and his friends, Greeley scribbled a repudiation of the editorial but Reid refused to print it.

When Greeley died within the month, Charles A. Dana relentlessly revealed the story in the *Sun* and concluded that "the blow which seems finally to have overthrown his reason was struck by his assistant in the conduct of the *Tribune*, Mr. Whitelaw Reid."

Greeley had given Reid good reason to regard himself as heir apparent to the paper. In the interregnum after Greeley's death, an internal political and financial plot developed over control of the *Tribune*, but Reid managed to collect a syndicate that bought up a majority of the stock and assured him absolute authority.

Reid's critics, branding the *Tribune* the organ of predatory wealth, made the most of the fact that some of the syndicate's money came from Jay Gould, sharp railroad speculator whose scheme to corner gold in 1869 had caused the Black Friday panic.

The *Tribune* signaled its rebirth under Reid by leaving its old rookery and moving into the "tall tower" on City Hall Park, which was long to remain a downtown landmark; at the time only the Trinity Church steeple stood higher against the sky.

The next step was to restore the *Tribune* to its rightful place as the voice, as well as the conscience, of Republicanism. Reid's abhorrence of the depths to which Grant's administration had dragged the party organization kept him out of its councils until four years after Greeley's death. In 1874 Reid promoted Samuel Tilden, the Democratic candidate for governor of New York, but the famous contested Presidential election of 1876 found Reid and the *Tribune* back in line, supporting Rutherford B. Hayes for the Presidency against Tilden.

The following year Reid directed publication in the *Tribune* of a number of enigmatic messages in cipher that had been dispatched by Democratic leaders during the campaign. Ingeniously decoded by *Tribune* staff members in subsequent issues, these messages involved the Democratic party in a plot to coerce the Southern vote. The *Tribune*'s exposé stands as a masterpiece of newspaper enterprise.

In this period, the *Tribune*'s labor troubles led to a milestone in the mechanics of newspaper production. Greeley had been the first president of Typographical Union No. 6, but his sympathies had been with cooperative effort, not with strikes as a labor weapon. In the hard times of the seventies, Reid established an open shop when the typesetters refused to accept retrenchments. Strikes and boycotts followed. During the great railway strike of 1877, the *Tribune* declared that "authority ought not to rest until it has swept down every resisting mob with grapeshot" and that labor violence must be subdued "though it cost a thousand bloody corpses." Reid had come to regard both trade unions and combinations of capital as "public enemies."

Midway in the seventeen-year-long strife with the printers, Reid heard that a young inventor named Ottmar Mergenthaler was successfully experimenting with a machine more efficient than the fastest hand compositors or any known typesetting device. In 1885 he formed a syndicate with a number of other publishers to finance further experiments. The next year the new machine was set up and demonstrated in the *Tribune* plant. Reid started the mechanism, christening it the "Linotype" and Mergenthaler set the first line.

Within a year the Linotype had saved the paper $80,000, and in less than two years about sixty machines were in use in the composing rooms of syndicate members. Most of the type that appears in the newspapers of today is produced by type-casting machines that work on principles similar to those introduced by Mergenthaler.

In his own office on the eighth floor of the *Tribune* tower, before a cozy log fire, fingering fascinating new gadgets like pushbuttons and pneumatic tubes, Reid pondered the *Tribune*'s destined role in journalism.

"In making a newspaper," he wrote, "the heaviest item of expense used to be the white paper. Now it is the news. By and by, let us hope it will be the brains."

Reid brought brains to the *Tribune*. Besides John Hay, Charles Reade, Bret Harte, Walt Whitman, John R. G. Hazzard, Henry Krehbiel, William Winter, Julius Chambers, George W. Smalley, and others contributed to the intellectual distinction and literary quality of its pages. Following a precedent set by Greeley in the elevation of Margaret Fuller at a time when literary criticism was almost exclusively man's domain, Reid gave full play to the work of Ellen Mackey Hutchinson, who later married Royal Cortissoz, longtime art critic for the *Tribune* and biographer of Whitelaw Reid, and to the Indian lore of Helen Hunt Jackson, who wrote *Ramona*.

The high degree of feminine recognition and participation eventually became one of the most distinctive features of the paper.

Before Hearst and Pulitzer plunged New York into an orgy of yellow journalism, Reid had written:

There is not an editor in New York who does not know the fortune that awaits the man who is willing to make a daily paper as disreputable and vile as a hundred and fifty thousand readers would be willing to buy.

Reid permitted the *Tribune* to make some minor concessions to the sensationalism of the day but the paper managed to retain its essential "highbrow" conservative character and sur-

PHOTOGRAPH 1

James Gordon Bennett, Sr.

PHOTOGRAPH 2

Horace Greeley

PHOTOGRAPH 3

Joseph Pulitzer

Acme Photo

Acme Ph[o]

PHOTOGRAPH 4

William Randolph Hearst

PHOTOGRAPH 5

Adolph S. Ochs

Acme Photo

Acme Photo

OTOGRAPH 6. *Left to right: Cyrus Curtis, Governor Theodore Roosevelt, and Edwin Hop-*
son

PHOTOGRAPH 7

Whitelaw Reid II

Newsweek *Photo by Ed Wer*

Acme Pho

PHOTOGRAPH 8. *Left to right: Joseph Patterson, Mrs. Chauncey McCormick, Colonel and M* *Robert R. McCormick, and Chauncey McCormick*

PHOTOGRAPH 9. *Heywood Broun*   PHOTOGRAPH 10. *Frank E. Gannett*

PHOTOGRAPH 11. *John Cowles and Gardner Cowles, Jr.*

PHOTOGRAPH 12
Erwin D. Canham

The Christian Science Monitor

PHOTOGRAPH 13
Palmer Hoyt

Photo by Albert Moldvay, The Denver Post

PHOTOGRAPH 14. *Mark Ethridge and Barry Bingham*

PHOTOGRAPH 15

Marshall Field, III

Halsman

PHOTOGRAPH 16

Henry Robinson Luce

Life *Photo by Leonard McCombe*

PHOTOGRAPH 17

Drew Pearson

vive the competition, partly because Reid's growing fortune had been otherwise augmented—by his Linotype interests and by marriage.

Reid for many years had enjoyed fatherhood vicariously through the adoption of the orphaned daughters of his brother Gavin, but John Hay and other friends had begun to chide him for his continued bachelorhood. In 1881, at the age of forty-four, Reid married Elisabeth Mills, only daughter of Darius Ogden Mills, wealthy Californian. They honeymooned in Europe, leaving John Hay in charge of the paper. News from home of the assassination of President Garfield broke into their idyll; Garfield was an old personal friend as well as Reid's political triumph, for by now Reid had become a President-maker.

More and more Reid turned from editorial duties to active participation in politics and diplomacy, until in the end they became his fulltime occupation.

In 1889, when Reid was appointed minister to France by President Harrison, he again left Hay in the editorial chair. On his return to the United States, Reid became Vice-Presidential candidate on the unsuccessful Harrison ticket.

During the campaign the *Tribune* ran an editorial reminiscent of Reid's attitude toward the Greeley candidacy:

> On this point it becomes the *Tribune* to speak briefly and simply. The distinction was not sought, and cannot induce a more zealous and loyal support of the Republican ticket by the *Tribune* than it would have given to any candidate whom the convention could have chosen. The nomination of Mr. Reid does, however, impose upon this journal special obligation to courtesy and fairness and patriotism which it will endeavor so to discharge as to deserve the approbation of friends and the respect of opponents.

In 1897 Reid became special ambassador to England at Queen Victoria's jubilee, and in 1898 he joined the American peace commission in negotiations with Spain. He attended the coronation of Edward VII, again as special ambassador, and in 1905 President Theodore Roosevelt appointed him Ambassador to Great Britain, or, as the *Tribune*'s style-book always insisted, to the Court of St. James's.

John Hay, meanwhile, had become Secretary of State and it was his pleasure to write Reid that the countersigning of Reid's commission was "the crowning act of a friendship and close association for forty years."

Rumors began to spread, similar to rumors the family was to hear and deny again in years to come, of offers to buy the *Tribune*. Discrediting them, Reid explained in a letter to the President that, so far from thinking of selling, he was only waiting for his son, Ogden, to be graduated from law school at Yale to take over the paper.

Upon graduation, Ogden Reid practised law briefly before he became a cub reporter on the *Tribune*. On an early assignment he impressed Lord Northcliffe so favorably that the British journalist wrote a letter of praise to the elder Reid. Ogden Reid moved on up the line to serve as copyreader, city editor, and night editor.

Through eight years, both in New York and on visits abroad with his parents, Ogden Reid saw a great deal of Helen Rogers, petite, softspoken and efficient Barnard College graduate whom Mrs. Whitelaw Reid had hired as social secretary, to supervise the name-studded guest lists on Mrs. Reid's lavish entertainment schedule.

In 1911 the populace of Racine, Wisconsin, had occasion to gape in awe when Whitelaw Reid, looking every bit the statesman with his white-crowned high brow and his white vandyke, arrived in his private car with Mrs. Reid to attend the wedding of his son and Miss Rogers at the home of her brother.

Ogden Reid became managing editor of the *Tribune* in March. Later that year, while the young Reids were preparing to join his parents in London for the holidays, word came that the Ambassador had been stricken with a severe attack of asthma. Whitelaw Reid died on December 15, 1912.

Mrs. Whitelaw Reid inherited controlling interest in the *Tribune*, but she stayed abroad and her matriarchal influence on the paper was felt only indirectly, mostly in cases where staff members had an exaggerated idea of her sense of propriety. She gave her son a free hand over the staff.

Only slightly younger than his father had been when he took over the *Tribune* at the age of thirty-five, Ogden Reid was quite unlike him in appearance and temperament. Convivial and democratic, somewhat nervous in manner, he was often more at ease in the neighboring cafe where newspapermen congregated than he was in the councils of the mighty.

During the first six years of their married life, Helen Rogers Reid concentrated on rearing their first two children, Whitelaw and Elisabeth; on turning the family estate at Ophir Hall up the Hudson into a paying farm; and on the woman's suffrage movement. In 1918, with her cause well won and with her children beginning to grow up, Mrs. Reid joined the advertising staff of the *Tribune* at her husband's request.

Almost at once things began to hum. In her first year she doubled the paper's advertising linage by going herself directly to clients and persistently assailing them with facts and figures, and by stimulating the salesmen with pep talks, bonuses, prizes, and achievement charts.

After the move to the new plant and the purchase of the *Herald* in the twenties—with time out for the birth of a second son, Ogden Rogers Reid, in 1925—Mrs. Reid's firm purposefulness expressed itself in most of the *Herald Tribune*'s activities. She came to occupy a position of power and prestige in journalism almost unique among her sex.

In 1930, with Mrs. William Brown Meloney, editor of the paper's Sunday magazine, *This Week,* in charge, she instituted the annual Current Events Forum, bringing women's club leaders to the Waldorf-Astoria ballroom in New York to hear about the problems of the world. Keyed to the needs of the moment, catholic in topic, and nonpartisan in approach, the Forum drew speakers of high caliber, willing and even eager to appear on its platform. Mrs. Reid, always tastefully attired, presided with simple dignity, whether presenting Hollywood stars, best-selling authors, or Supreme Court justices.

Through these years Ogden Reid remained selflessly in the background, but no strategic decisions were made without his full approval and he was capable of stubborn resistance. Mrs. Reid felt that President Hoover's "noble experiment," the Prohibition Amendment, should be given a chance but she did not attempt to impose a dry policy on the paper over her husband's opposition. Those on the staff who knew him best saw in him much of the firmness of his mother and his wife, if less of the arrow-like speed and relentless drive.

When Mrs. Whitelaw Reid died in the south of France in 1931, the Ogden Reids inherited half of a fortune that the depression had whittled down from an estimated $20,000,000; the other half went to Ogden's sister, Jean, wife of Sir John Ward. The return of Mrs. Reid to America for burial was duly chronicled on the front page of the *Herald Tribune,* but the careless reader might not have been fully aware that she was deceased, for, in keeping with the *Tribune*'s taboos, nowhere in the story did the word "body" appear.

Beginners on the staff, it later developed, had been instructed by sub-executives not to use that distasteful word, nor the word "blood." These orders often led to strange elisions and circumlocutions: "a stained coat was found at the scene"; "a sanguinary battle." The words "rape," "pregnant," and "syphilis" had not yet found their way into most family newspapers, but on the *Tribune* self-appointed interpreters of the proprietor's imagined likes and dislikes even frowned upon the word "sexual" —until an overzealous copyreader changed the name of the Congress for Sexual Hygiene to the Congress for Social Hygiene.

One evening when Ogden Reid accepted the invitation of *Herald Tribune* copyreaders to attend a departmental get-together, he was asked about the embarrassing taboos, with a plea for their relaxation. Reid declared that he had never known of their existence and ordered them abandoned forthwith. Copyreaders ceased to worry so much about what they had been warned might upset the elder Mrs. Reid at her breakfast table, but the *Herald Tribune* continued, in its tradition of good taste, to use objectionable language sparingly.

City editor Stanley Walker, some years before he deserted New York for his native Texas, inspired a carefully chosen, and not too well paid, staff with his own sharp style. Sitting at the head of the rewrite battery, Robert Peck, his verbiage close-cropped as his hair, could turn the telephone directory into a saga or a chuckle. Alva Johnston was as adept at unmasking a deceased pastor's hypocrisy in a manner not to offend the most devoted member of the congregation as he was at clarifying the mysteries of a scientific symposium. John O'Reilly made snakes and monkeys more engaging than humans, without requiring them to talk. W. O. McGeehan's sports prose was as hearty and uninhibited as the belch that rumbled over his desk. Walter Lippmann brought from the defunct *World* his reasoned liberalism to glow across the page from Mark Sullivan's measured conservatism.

In those years, too, the *Herald Tribune* realized the ambition expressed way back in Xenia by Whitelaw Reid to make his paper a model in appearance. In 1918 the *Tribune* had been the first newspaper to set headlines in the faster-reading upper-and-lower-case Bodoni type, and in 1931 the *Herald Tribune* won the first Francis Wayland Ayer cup for typographical excellence—an honor that came to it repeatedly thereafter.

While the *Herald Tribune* developed, its European stepchild died and was reborn. After the Reids took over the *Paris Herald* from Munsey, that "incredible newspaper" continued to provide a haven for wandering reporters and copyreaders. Although it never sank to the depths of its venal French contemporaries, it was not always a worthy newspaper; it shocked Mrs. Reid as well as more disinterested readers in 1932 by editorial approval of Mussolini—a stand possibly influenced by its desire to retain valuable Italian government travel advertising. It functioned chiefly as a clearing house for continental news for its infinitely superior New York parent, as a harbinger of society gossip about boat-train arrivals and Riviera tourists, as an advertising medium for German and British steamship lines, and as a refuge for footloose journalists.

The *Herald* was called "a newspaperman's alcoholic dream," with fires set in the wastebaskets for amusement; Sparrow Robertson hailing everybody as "my old pal" and continuing to send his copy from Harry's New York Bar even after the paper ceased publication; staff writers turning in letters from the Old Philadelphia Lady to give an edge to the paper's Mailbag on dull days, stirring up controversies over the relative merits of American and French breakfasts; itinerant reporters inventing stories of islands appearing and disappearing in midocean.

The *Herald* fell before the Nazis in 1940 and its editor, Laurence Hills, stayed behind, dying in Paris during the occupation. In 1946, after the liberation, the paper was revived as the European edition of the *New York Herald Tribune* under Geoffrey Parsons Jr., son of the highly regarded chief editorial writer on the home paper. Economy eliminated Parsons' post in 1950 but by then the reincarnated *Herald* had assumed a more responsible and reputable, if less legendary, role than its predecessor.

On the parent paper in New York, signs of the rise of a new generation and of new postwar policies and practices began to appear.

The elder of the two Reid sons, Whitelaw (see photograph 7), since graduating from Yale in 1936 and studying the printing trade at Rochester and at the Mergenthaler plant in Brooklyn, had gone to work, first in the mechanical department, next on the business side, then on the city staff of the family's paper, and finally, before the war call came, in London during the blitz as a correspondent.

In the war he served as a lieutenant junior grade in the ferry division of the U.S. Naval Reserve. In June 1945 he piloted a four-engine Privateer across the Pacific. While stationed at Iwo Island, he made flights to the shores of Japan and his squadron cooperated with the Fleet in the final actions against the Japanese.

Young Whitelaw returned to the *Herald Tribune* in February 1946, as editorial assistant to his father. In March he became chairman of the New York Herald Tribune Forum for High Schools, and in April he assumed the presidency of the Tribune Fresh Air Fund, a seventy-five-year old service activity of the paper for the city's underprivileged children.

Ogden Mills Reid died on January 3, 1947 at the age of sixty-four, and ten days later, Whitelaw Reid, in his mid-thirties, his crew-cut hair and springy walk giving him a boyish look, was named editor and vice-president, with his mother serving as president of the company.

One disaffected staff member, Stanley Woodward, scrappy sports editor who had been supplanted by Robert Cooke, hailed the change derisively as the triumph of Yale's Class of '36 over the paper's destinies. Cooke happened to be a classmate of young Whitelaw, as did John Crosby, winner of many awards and much praise for his mordant pioneering column on radio and television.

If Woodward's misgivings were true, they were at least consistent with the paper's traditions. The elder Whitelaw Reid had gone to a college whose sons liked to call it "The Yale of the West" and had strongly impressed upon his contemporaries his high estimate of the value of college training for journalism.

Among the new features promoted by the second Whitelaw was a page for Young Moderns. Soon after the page had been launched under the direction of Dorothy Brandon, Whitelaw married Mrs. Brandon's daughter, Joan.

"Whitey" Reid's younger brother, "Brownie"—Ogden Rogers Reid—became a reporter on the paper after serving in the Army as a paratrooper. One of his early assignments was a revelation of the workings of the Communist underground.

With the ingress of the younger generation, the *Herald Tribune* took on a lighter tone and sought, with sharper editing for easier reading, to broaden its appeal without sacrificing its reputation for intellectual and cultural awareness. More comics appeared; the paper acquired, and later lost, the spicy chatter of the Broadway impresario, Billy Rose, but compensated by presenting in print the colorful radio-television personalities of Tex McCrary and Jinx Falkenburg.

In a sense the *Herald Tribune* deserved the cognomen once given to Dana's *Sun* and later to Pulitzer's *World* of "the newspaperman's newspaper." Its warm personality stood out from the cold institutionalism of so much of the nation's press.

Copy boys like Homer Bigart and Joseph Herzberg rose to positions of honor, the former as war correspondent and Pulitzer prize winner, the latter as city editor. Keen correspondents like Bert Andrews in Washington, another Pulitzer prize winner, gave the news columns substance and conviction. Women writers like Margaret Parton and Marguerite Higgins upheld the paper's distaff tradition and proved by their yeoman work in Korea, India, and elsewhere that incisive reporting of war and world affairs was no longer exclusively man's realm.

The Reids also established fellowships to permit deserving correspondents of other papers to go abroad for a year of study.

The *Herald Tribune* found the going rough in its role as the voice of responsible Republicanism. It had been relatively easy in the twenties and early thirties when the Republicans had been in power and when the family was represented in government by Ogden Livingston Mills, nephew of Mrs. Whitelaw Reid, who was first Assistant Secretary of the Treasury and then, briefly, Secretary.

The long years as "loyal opposition" during the Roosevelt and Truman administrations found the *Tribune* straining to revitalize the party and to serve as its conscience. In the summer of 1951, a *Saturday Review of Literature Poll* of 332 Tokyo, Washington, and United Nations correspondents found the *Herald Tribune,* next to the *New York Times* and along with the *Christian Science Monitor,* the fairest of the nation's press in its coverage of the politically charged controversy over

President Truman's removal of General MacArthur from the Far Eastern command.

As long and often as it was possible, the *Herald Tribune* tried to get the party as a whole to accept the liberal, internationalist philosophy of Wendell Willkie. Joseph Barnes, its foreign editor, went around the world with Willkie and the "One World" idea that Willkie fostered was largely a product of that trip.

Editorially the *Herald Tribune* indulged in much soul-searching and semanticism, concluding reluctantly in 1948 that "there is no liberal view, no really self-consistent and logical body of principle and policy." Young Whitelaw Reid was committed, with the quiet strength of his father, to the "independence" of the paper's Republicanism.

For its pains it was rewarded by denunciation from two opposite and equally unwelcome sources. Andrei Vishinsky, Russian delegate to the United Nations, lumped it with the Hearst press as an anti-Soviet warmonger, and Hearst's Westbrook Pegler published a series of columns purporting to show that the *Herald Tribune,* "formerly known to the profession and laity as a pillar of the Republican Party, the British Empire and the Church of England," although presuming to political respectability, was little more than an uptown edition of the Communist *Daily Worker.*

Mrs. Reid could well afford to ignore such intemperate evaluations, but she did not ignore more immediately damaging rumors that gained momentum after the *New York Sun* folded in 1950.

While the publishers of the nation were holding their annual convention in New York, Mrs. Reid filed a complaint with the Attorney General of New York State against rumors that the *Herald Tribune* was likely to follow the setting *Sun.* She declared:

I have never had nor do I have any intention of selling or attempting to sell the *New York Herald Tribune.* No one has ever been authorized to engage in any discussions on behalf of the paper looking to its sale, much less to offer it for sale.

The *New York Herald Tribune* is operating on a profitable basis as it has continuously for many years. Its daily circulation is at a postwar high. Its advertising exceeds that of 1949. It is against this background that seemingly organized rumors so preposterous as to include the possibility of mergers with other newspapers or even loans from other newspapers have been circulated.

Thus emphatically Helen Rogers Reid rededicated the *New York Herald Tribune,* firmly established as one of the world's truly great newspapers, to the trust of a noble heritage.

E. W. Scripps

THE HISTORY OF AMERICAN JOURNALISM THROBS WITH RICH tradition, heart-warming legend, and lofty purpose. Sometimes the glories of the past have been kept glowing; sometimes allowed to languish; sometimes fanned into new life; sometimes dissipated, traduced, and transmuted.

The spirit of Scripps is one of the richest legacies of the lot. Today the *Detroit News* and the Booth Newspapers in Michigan; the Scripps League of Newspapers in the Northwest; the John P. Scripps papers on the Pacific Coast, and, most importantly, the Scripps-Howard cross-country chain, with its allied interests, the United Press and three feature syndicates, all stem from the same family source. The towering genius in the journalistic clan that sparked these widespread enterprises was Edward Wyllis Scripps.

It took Lincoln Steffens, greatest of the turn-of-the-century muck-rakers, whose own mind ranged far and deep, to comprehend the full measure of the man. When Steffens learned that Jo Davidson had been commissioned to sculpture a bust of E. W. Scripps, he wrote:

> You must do a great thing with Scripps. He is a great man and an individual. There is no other like him: energy, vision, courage, wisdom. He thinks his own thoughts absolutely. He sees straight. He sees the line he is on and his thinking sticks to that. I regard Scripps as one of the two or three great men of my day.

He is on to himself and the world, plays the game and despises it. He is sincere and not cynical. Really he should be done, but as a full-length standing figure so as to show the power of the man, the strength he took care to keep from being refined; he avoided other rich men, so as to escape from being one; he knew the danger his riches carried for himself, for his papers and for his seeing.

Rough, almost ruthless force, but restrained by clear, even shrewd insight; an executive capable of fierce action, restrained by the observation that a doer must not do too many things himself, but use his will to make others do them. And he did that all right. Read some of his letters to editors, the young fellows he was driving so hard and letting alone.

The grandfather of E. W. Scripps had been a publisher and bookbinder in London and one of his cousins was an early editor of the *Chicago Tribune*. Born in Illinois in 1854, the youngest of thirteen children of James Moggs Scripps, Ed was an awkward, red-headed farm boy, with a conspicuous cast in his left eye, inherited from his mother's side of the family.

He was often called "the laziest boy in Schuyler county," but the term displeased him and he denied it. In his "disquisitions," a series of analytical statements about his life and philosophy dictated for the understanding and guidance of his children, he used many pages to explain the "laziest boy" background. The course of his days as a boy on the Rushville farm was prophetic of the shrewd long-distance executive he was to become.

Thinking back, he could recall no days or even hours of idleness. He seldom joined his brothers or schoolmates on the playgrounds. He was a poor milker but an excellent field hand who could cover more ground plowing or hoeing than the hired man covered. He liked to work in the field and he liked to compare his work with that of the others. Accidentally he discovered that if several boys or men were working together, row by row, each trying to do as well as or better than his neighbor, talking and arguing with one another, they accomplished more.

His father fell ill when Ed was fourteen, and Ed, whose older brothers had already left home, had to run the farm. With his father's consent he hired boys from town to work with him; he paid them twenty-five cents a day as compared with the dollar-a-day wage for farm laborers. He spaced off the field with equal numbers of rows and then the boys began to race. Soon, because he was so experienced, they voted Ed out to act as referee. Ed followed the boys over the ground a bit, sat watching them from the fence rail, then got out his book and read in a shady fence corner.

"My mother used to say after I had grown to manhood," he wrote in his disquisitions, "that a not infrequent post of mine was on a fence rail. She said that Eddie always seemed to be sitting on the fence watching the other fellows work. She added that it looked to her as though I was running my business in the same way I had run the farm."

Then, as later, he wrote in "Some Outlandish Rules for Making Money," his idea was: "Never do anything that you can get someone else to do for you. The more things that someone else does for you the more time and energy you have to do those things which no one else can do for you."

Ed's half-sister, Ellen Browning Scripps, eighteen years older, was probably the greatest early influence in shaping his character. The only member of the family interested in formal education, Ellen had gone to Knox College at Galesburg, Illinois, graduating when Ed was four. The task of teaching Ed, as well as nursing him through a sickly childhood, fell to her. She read Shakespeare to him when he was eight, read him Scott and Tennyson and Longfellow. Schoolbooks were never so important to him as the books at home, and, with the exception of Ellen, he held all schoolteachers in contempt.

When he was thirteen, Ed by chance got a two-hour lesson in compact, condensed news coverage from his older brother James, home on a vacation. The conversation began over the "Peter Parley Tales," old stories condensed from books and written in simple popular language, which Ed sat in the attic reading. James told Ed he wanted to put this same idea into newspaper form—a small daily, with large type, containing in condensed simple form all the news and features other bigger papers contained.

James applied the idea when, after an apprenticeship in Chicago and Detroit, he founded the *Detroit News* in 1873.

Ed's awe of his older brother wore off as he grew older and Ed often disagreed with him. As adults they never got along. Once when Ed was visiting Detroit, James looked out a hotel window at striking teamsters and police fighting in the street below and remarked, "If I were mayor of this city, we'd teach those teamsters a lesson."

Ed responded: "My sympathies are all with the men. No, I'll have no interest in your paper here."

A year or so later, however, when he was eighteen, Ed did leave the farm and go to work on the *News.* Ellen and another brother, George, had already joined James there.

Cleveland was the birthplace of what eventually became the Scripps-Howard chain. In 1878, the year after a great railroad strike had helped crystallize Ed's interest in organized labor, Ed borrowed $10,000 from his sister and brothers and went to Cleveland to start the *Penny Press.* Applying the lessons in tightly edited journalism that he had learned from James, Ed set out to dramatize his paper's independence of the "interests" and any of the pressures of power or privilege.

One day, under the editorship of Robert F. Paine, the *Press* in a routine news item recorded the fact that E. W. Scripps had been fined $10 for driving his horses recklessly "while intoxicated." For a full minute after Scripps saw the item, Paine recalled later, "his eye was on mine, with all of the benevolence of a gar-pike glaring at a nice, fat minnow. Then the stern features relaxed, and into his eyes came that smile which those who knew him will never forget."

Paine's salary was raised and for years afterward he remained at Scripps's side as editorial lieutenant.

From Detroit Ellen sent lively features in short, snappy paragraphs. Published first in the *Detroit News,* this "Miscellany" of Ellen's served as the inspiration for the eventual creation of the Newspaper Enterprise Association for the distribution of syndicated features. Ellen herself soon moved on from Detroit to Cleveland to work with Ed.

As soon as the *Cleveland Press* began to make a profit, Ed persuaded his brothers to buy the *St. Louis Chronicle* but, like some of his other ventures, it met hard going.

"I was up against a better man," Scripps said frankly. "Joseph Pulitzer, who ran the *Post-Dispatch,* beat me at my own game."

That same year, James E. Scripps put $10,000 into the *Penny Paper* in Cincinnati, and, in 1882, while E.W. was traveling in Europe, sent Milton McRae from Detroit as advertising manager. On E.W.'s return the next summer, he bought the majority stock in the Cincinnati paper, changed its name to the *Post,* and led a fiery crusade against political corruption.

The *Post*'s pious tone would seem inconsistent with the personality of its publisher were the complexities of his character not considered. Scripps did not live by copybook maxims; he set his own standards. Although he believed in and tried to practice the Ten Commandments and the Golden Rule, he was not a religious man. His behavior in his early years was as unconventional as were the thoughts on every imaginable subject which he put down in later years in his disquisitions, taken in 1951 from the old black steel box, in which they had been kept until his grandchildren should be grown, and edited by the husband of one of his granddaughters, Charles R. McCabe, in a revealing self-portrait, *Damned Old Crank.*

One day in Cincinnati, over the protests of McRae, who had become business manager of the *Post,* Scripps had reporters from the rival papers summoned to his office to meet a woman who had called on him there.

"She used to live with me as my mistress in Detroit," E.W. explained. "She was paid for what she did and we parted on good terms. She has come here today threatening to revive that story and asking for money. I don't pay blackmail. You are at liberty to print the facts. So far as I am concerned the incident is closed."

The papers handled the story with moderation.

While the *Post* was fighting Cincinnati's political bosses, Scripps paid little attention to its balance sheet because, he said, "I felt that I would rather lose the *Post* as a business than possess it as a fat, greasy prosperous prostitute."

After Scripps settled in Cincinnati, he found a boarding house about sixteen miles out in Mills Creek Valley. At a church festival near there he met Nackie Benson Holtsinger, eighteen-year-old daughter of the pastor at nearby Westchester. Tired of affairs and the "temporary monogamy" of mistresses, E.W. had determined to become a good husband and father and was coldbloodedly looking for a wife. When he met "Miss Nackie," his calculating pursuit became a desperate, headlong romance. They were married four months later and moved into his home in Westchester.

Scripps felt fulfilled as his children were born, six in sixteen years. He was startled to find that fatherhood put an end to his complete egoism. "Each newcomer," he wrote, "brought a renewal or extension of what I might call 'non-egoism.'"

Now there was a purpose and a timelessness to his newspaper business.

In 1887 E.W. took charge of the newspapers while James went abroad for gallstone treatments. When James returned two years later, the business had been revolutionized, new presses bought, and the little Detroit paper expanded into a big business with a staff of men trained and disciplined by E.W. E.W., in fact, had set out to show how good he was, hoping his brothers, James and George, would make him actual head of the whole concern. Instead James, on his return, frightened and suspicious of the enlarged operation, fired E.W. not only as president of the Detroit News Association, but as president of the Scripps Publishing Company that operated the *Cleveland Press*.

E.W. was enraged. He knew he had taken great liberties,

investing large sums in presses and in staff, shaping executives and writers in his ways of doing and thinking. But he felt that his tremendous effort and daring in establishing a successful pattern—even though it was not one James would have followed—should be rewarded rather than repudiated. He feared that what he accomplished might not survive without him. It did, the *Detroit News* particularly waxing prosperous because of his brother's business ability.

E.W. was also angry at his brother George, who, during James's absence, had agreed in writing to turn over control of the *Cleveland Press* to E.W. and who now, although he argued with James about it, was unable to carry out his bargain. Nevertheless E.W. made friends with George, whose weakness and dependence on him was great, because he felt George would suffer from a break with him. He broke completely with James, for whom he had "not an ounce of sympathy."

E.W. had left the affairs of the *Cincinnati Post* largely to Milton McRae, under whose cautious hand it had lost much of its influence in labor circles. Although McRae's conservatism and humorlessness irked Scripps, McRae was a shrewd businessman and he basked in the publicity and personal attention that Scripps shunned.

In 1889 Scripps and McRae formed a partnership that gave Scripps two-thirds of the profits and McRae one-third and permitted Scripps "to go where he pleased, live where he pleased and do as he pleased," free of all business details. Scripps remained a vague figure so far as the general public was concerned, while McRae held the spotlight with his help in founding the American Newspaper Publishers Association, leadership in the Boy Scout movement, many speeches and other public activities.

"Let the other fellow have all the glory," a Scripps disquisition said. "Let him occupy the place in the limelight. For me I only care to have the power."

So it was that in 1890 at the age of thirty-six, E.W. decided to retire from active administration of his papers. He examined his affairs and saw that he would have a good basic annual income. As McCabe put it in his introductory note to *Damned Old Crank*: "A combination of misanthropy, raw nerves and family exacerbations drove him as far away from his kind as was possible without loss of nationality."

E.W. chose for his home a great windswept mesa, some 2,100 acres, about sixteen miles from San Diego, in the farthest southwest corner of the United States. Here he not only could get away from people; he could also get away from colds of which he had been fearful all his life. With his wife and three children he moved to Miramar Ranch in 1891. Three more children were born there. One of them, Edward Wyllis Scripps Jr., died when he was only seven, causing a grief so deep to E.W. that he never got over it.

At Miramar, Scripps built a Spanish-style house surrounding a patio with fountains in its center. He planted thousands of trees, mostly eucalyptus, orchards of lemons, oranges, and grapefruit, and collected every variety of cactus he could find.

It was typical that Scripps planted his citrus orchard at Miramar because people told him that he could not raise citrus fruit in that locality, and he wanted to prove that he could. So he had holes blasted out of the hardpan with dynamite, soil hauled in from the valley, planted his trees, watered them, and fertilized them at exorbitant costs until he got one crop, then abandoned the project.

He built a great network of roads, for practical purposes and for access to the natural beauty of canyons or pine forests. He loved roadbuilding because of the obstacles that had to be overcome. His roads stimulated the city and county to follow his example, and E.W. became a road commissioner, the only public office he ever held.

From Miramar, in spite of his announced retirement, he set up a long-range management of his enterprises and expanded his chain. The promising young men he found as editors and business managers of his new papers were each entitled to purchase 10 per cent of the stock, if and when the paper began making reliable profits, and at the incorporating price, which usually was the actual amount of money invested in the property up to that time. Usually they did not have the money to pay for their stock, so the central office of the concern loaned it to them at 6 per cent interest.

These papers were typically rowdy, rambunctious little sheets, published on a shoestring in shabby quarters. Scripps was sad to see that as they grew prosperous they became conventional—perhaps cautious—and less concerned with the problems of working-class readers. He tried to stop this trend but, in most cases, succeeded only in modifying it or slowing it up.

Scripps editors came to Miramar to sit at the Old Man's feet, sometimes for weeks at a time, listening and absorbing his individualistic philosophy. Old Man Scripps, now boasting a bushy red beard and covering his balding head with a skullcap, dressed casually and distinctively, his trousers tucked into the tops of high boots, usually of white kid. He held court with his men in feudal splendor, scrutinized, advised, and admonished them and sent them on their way to work out their own problems.

Although he emphasized each paper's autonomy, E.W. did his utmost to train his editors to feel and think as he did. Each new editor went through a rugged period—often a month—as the Old Man's guest at Miramar. Every morning he listened to the Old Man talk. He returned to his paper inspired and stimulated and whether or not his own stamina or the circumstances surrounding his paper enabled him to carry out E.W.'s principles, he never forgot what the Old Man said.

E.W. wrote:

Although I have been personally responsible for the founding or purchase of not less than forty newspapers, I doubt if I have directly given a total of five hundred orders to all the men employed on these papers. *My life's work has mainly consisted in selecting a few score of men,* studying each, and then offering them opportunities and inspiring them, by my talks and letters, each to develop what was best in him to the highest extent.

Some of the principles he enunciated to them, as stated in his disquisitions, were:

The people of the United States should be taught that there should be a revolution in the country, a lawful revolution, a revolution of laws, and they should be taught how best to obtain this revolution. . . .

Organized labor is an effort in this direction. Organized labor is not socialistic. . . . There is more room for individualism in labor unionism than in any form of democracy yet invented. . . .

. . . I have sought to teach the common people the value, even the necessity, of combination. Although I fully recognize the many evils inherent in trade unionism, I have advocated its extension, the perfection of its discipline, and its comprehending political activity. . . .

In a municipal contest between the great majority of the citizens—the working class—and the capitalistic element, I would aid my partisans even did I know that their success would give the city poor government and that the success of their opponents would give the city good government. . . .

In fact . . . I have only one principle and that is represented by an effort to make it harder for the rich to grow richer and easier for the poor to keep from growing poorer.

He talked much of the "moral principle of protest" directed against

The governmental system that had to be wrong because it was old.

Undemocratic government carried on under the false name of democracy.

Too great usurpation of power on the part of the rich and the intellectual that is used to oppress the less fortunate. . . .

The inequality of opportunity. . . .

Outworn theology and superstition. . . .

All authority that was not based upon the immediate and voluntary present desire and wish of those who submitted to the same. . . .

All sort of legislatures whose members obtained position by corrupt practice, by chicanery, by false pretenses. . . .

Of the Scripps papers, the founder said:

We can hold together, having supporting us the army of our followers, so long as we fight hard and fight and win our battles for them; so long as we fight against privilege and success, by degree transferring some of the privileges from the few to the many.*

Scripps summed it all up in "A Letter to a Young Editor,"

* From *Damned Old Crank*, edited by Charles R. McCabe, with permission of the publishers, Harper & Brothers.

written to Paul Edwards, then starting out with the Houston paper in Texas:

I would advise you to begin your course as editor of this paper with one object and only one object in view, and that is to serve that class of people and only that class of people from whom you cannot even hope to derive any other income than the one cent a day they pay for your paper. Be honest and fearless with them, always without regard to the goodwill or the ill will of the so-called business community. . . .

Be diplomatic, but don't be too damned diplomatic. Most men fear to speak the truth, the bald, bold truth, to any man or community because they fear that the men or the community is not prepared to endure such frankness. I think this is a mistake. It is rare indeed when the circumstances are such that a conscientious man can lose anything by fearless, frank speech and writing.

While he thus aligned himself on the side of the poor and the underprivileged, E. W. Scripps lived at Miramar like a lord, shouting at the servants across the court of his great house. When his wife went horseback riding, he insisted that the groom remain the proper number of paces in the rear. He repeatedly said that he would make any sacrifice—his fortune, perhaps even his life—for what he called the common people but he'd be damned if he would live with them.

"The loneliness of my life is great," he wrote. "I am hated by the rich for being a renegade and I am hated by the poor for being rich. I am not wise enough or learned enough to be an acceptable member in the highbrow club. I have learned too many things to make me a comfortable companion of the man in the field, on the street and in the shop."

Given to overstatement, Scripps said he drank the equivalent of four quarts of whisky and smoked some forty Havana cigars a day, and that although for twenty-five years he was continuously under the influence of alcohol, he was seldom drunk or "even unpleasantly stimulated." Even discounting his own estimates somewhat, he must have been, as he said, an "outrageous toper," yet many people never knew he drank at all. When, in his forty-sixth year he realized that he was almost blind and his body weak and flabby, he saw that he must quit drinking or

die soon. The question in his doctors' minds was whether he
had the will power to stop. E.W. thought he had because fifteen years earlier he had painfully broken the morphine habit,
acquired after an excruciatingly painful eye condition. Now,
rather than continue to drink and live in blindness and weakness, he got a doctor to go everywhere with him and he stopped
both drinking and smoking.

The achievement that E. W. Scripps himself was to regard as
his life's greatest service to the people of the country still lay
ahead of him.

Leaders in the reorganization of the Associated Press let it
be known that the Scripps papers might be left out in the cold
unless they joined up at once without reservation. E.W., his
brother George, who had now parted with James and cast his
lot with E.W., and McRae, were infuriated. George, according to E.W., "had a very pugnacious disposition so long as he
had someone to lead him in a fight." McRae, however, was
panic-stricken and begged his partners to enter the AP before
it was too late. E.W., who had paved the way for what was to
happen, sent McRae with their application, not as clients but
as first-class voting members. The application was rejected
with ridicule and contempt and McRae came out fighting mad,
ready to help launch a new press association. E.W. was prepared, with telegrams and prospectus, ready—on instant of application—to serve all clients with an evening news report.

His Scripps-McRae Association for news distribution was
combined with two other agencies in 1907 to form the new
United Press. The move cost the Scripps papers several hundred thousand dollars more than they would have paid to be
members of the AP. E.W. said that the United Press would
have to be big, that it would be either a flat failure or a property worth many millions. Few newspapermen, except those in
the Scripps employ, felt that this venture had any chance for
success.

E.W.'s aim was to make sure that every man who wanted to
found a newspaper could get the wire service he needed.

Against monopolies, he was convinced that, were it not for the UP, the controlling stockholders of the AP and Hearst would combine into a trust. He felt that the competition of the UP, founded to "disseminate news that is of value to the public and that is against the interests of the plutocrat band," would make it impossible for the AP to suppress the truth or to spread falsehood.

"Perhaps my greatest reason . . . ," Scripps said, "was that I knew that at least 90 per cent of my fellows in American journalism were capitalistic and conservative. I knew at the time at least that unless I came into the field with a new service, it would be impossible for the people of the United States to get correct news through the medium of the AP."

Meanwhile George Scripps had died, leaving a large part of his fortune to E.W., including his share in the *Detroit News*. James contested the will but finally agreed to a settlement out of court that gave him the Detroit paper and E.W. the rest of the Scripps press properties. Divorced from the chain, the *Detroit News* continued a long and prosperous career on its own, under James E. Scripps and his descendants. A son-in-law of James Scripps, George Booth, fared forth from the *News* and bought the *Grand Rapids Press,* from which he developed— with two brothers—Michigan's chain of eight Booth papers.

After getting the United Press under way, E. W. Scripps announced his active retirement from the Scripps-McRae concern in 1908, saying, "I like to play dead and watch the property I've built."

He also watched the world and talked with the men who came to him at Miramar—scientists, artists, politicians, statesmen. He plumbed their minds and dictated away on his disquisitions.

When the *Los Angeles Times* plant was dynamited in a union fight, Scripps wrote a defense of labor's right to use any weapon in its arsenal, because the employers "have every other weapon: jobs to give or withhold, capital to spend or not, the bar and the bench, the press to state our case and suppress theirs, the government and the legislature, the police and the militia."

When Lincoln Steffens and Clarence Darrow, the noted liberal lawyer who had come to California to defend the accused dynamiters, visited Scripps at Miramar, Scripps talked to them about his newspapers and complained that the young men he hired were too easily corrupted.

"I get me bright young men from the classes that read my papers," he said. "I give them the editorship and the management, with a part interest in the property, and, in a year or so, as the profits begin to come in, they become conservative and I have to boot them back to their class."

Shortly after his supposed retirement Scripps commissioned Negley Cochran, one of his editors who became his biographer, to experiment with an adless, tabloid paper. Scripps, for his own reasons, did not reveal himself as publisher. In his instructions to Cochran, he wrote:

FIRST: The paper shall receive no income except from the sale of newspapers.

SECOND: It shall always be the organ, the mouthpiece and the friend of the wage-earners who get small wages, and of that class who are not working for wages but still maintain themselves by daily labor of the humblest sort. Our paper is to be the poor man's advocate whether the poor man be right or wrong.

Later he told Cochran:

Our one great business is to get an audience. Whatever else it is our paper must be excessively interesting, not to the good wise men and the pure in spirit, but to the great mass of sordid, squalid humanity. Humanity is vulgar; so we must be vulgar. It is coarse; so we must not be refined. It is passionate; therefore the blood that runs in our veins and in our newspapers must be warm.

The *Day Book* began publication in Chicago in 1911. The expense of publication was arbitrarily limited from the start to $2,500 a month, which included everything but paper. News was boiled to the bone. When the *Day Book* first went on the stands in the Loop district, the other newspapers had it thrown off by order of the Chief of Police, Cochran reported, but an influential alderman had it restored. A staff that included Carl Sandburg, the poet, got out the midget daily for six years.

After the United States entered the first World War in 1917, Scripps came out of retirement and summoned Cochran to Washington as his editorial adviser. Cochran reluctantly suspended the *Day Book,* convinced that the experiment had proved the practicability of making an adless newspaper pay.

Meanwhile Scripps had been grooming his sons to carry on after him. He kept them from college lest they acquire a sense of superiority by buying themselves knowledge and training that the "common people" couldn't afford.

Jim, the eldest son, was first trained to accept responsibility for management of the ranch at Miramar and then given the business management of the Scripps-McRae papers. He had been named chairman of the Scripps-McRae board in 1908 on his father's retirement and had taken over control of the Coast group of papers.

John, the second son, received similar tutoring on the ranch, and then was put in charge of the editorial side of the papers. He married McRae's eldest daughter and died in 1914 at the age of twenty-six, before he could assume the full role planned for him in the Scripps domain.

Robert Paine Scripps, the youngest son, had announced at twelve that he wanted to be a poet. His father required him to read history three hours a day and submit to examination on what he read. Before he was seventeen, Bob went to work on a Scripps paper in Philadelphia, first as a circulation canvasser, later as a reporter. From there he went to Europe to study municipal government and then to the central office in San Diego. Starting out on his own, he tried to get on a paper in Bakersfield, California, but when subscription soliciting was all that was offered, he turned to work in the oil fields. Then he went north to the California seacoast town of Eureka, got work reporting marine arrivals and clearances for a dollar a day. His first front-page spread came when he rushed forty miles with the sheriff to a battle between lumberjacks and circus roustabouts, in which three were killed. From Eureka he accompanied the novelist Jack London to Honolulu. Australia was the next stop, where he worked on papers and studied political, social, and business conditions, reporting regularly to E.W.

When Bob came home, his father put him to work setting down his impressions in a book for his father's eyes alone and building up his health under a physical instructor. In March 1917 he married Margaret Culbertson of Pasadena and in May of that year, when his father went to Washington, Bob went with him.

The wartime crisis which brought E. W. Scripps out of retirement also resolved the future careers of his two remaining sons.

Resenting his father's reappearance in the field, Jim lined up the Coast group of papers under his direction in editorial opposition to the pro-Administration policy of the other Scripps papers. E.W. called Jim to Washington and won his consent to the appointment of Bob as editor-in-chief of all the Scripps-McRae papers.

In the midst of a wartime conference, E. W. Scripps suffered a paralytic stroke and the doctor ordered him to Florida for eight months. Bob Scripps, barely twenty-one, took up the job where his father left off.

Jim Scripps was so much like his uncle James that it was inevitable that E.W. would break with his elder son just as he had with his brother. E.W. wrote:

When I want to figure out what Jim will do under certain circumstances I figure out what James would do under the same circumstances—and then I know what Jim will do. He has something of James and George in him but very little of me. I will have a hell of a time with Bob; he will have to have his fling, but I think you will find that when he settles down he is more like me than either Jim or John.

At present Jim has no great respect for, nor desire for the possession of, large property. At present he regards money as valuable only for the use it can be put to and for the purchase of petty comforts of life for himself and family.

He has not discovered by his own experience and feeling that there is little joy in possessing, and that there is only great delight in the full exercise of his faculties in accomplishing things. He probably never will interest himself much in any such occupations as I have had, or in anything else but business—that is to say, upon the acquirement of larger and larger fortune.

James has, I believe, only contempt for the altruist. I am quite sure that he regards me as something very nearly like a hypocrite in my professions on moral subjects.

In 1920 E.W. and Jim quarreled irrevocably. Jim had acquired control of five of the coast papers, and after Jim died the following year at the age of thirty-four, these papers continued to publish separately, first as the Scripps-Canfield, later as the Scripps League, under Jim's widow and then his sons. In June 1951, when the Scripps League acquired the *Kalispel Daily Inter-Lake* in Montana, its other remaining enterprises included papers in The Dalles, Oregon; Provo and Logan, Utah; Pocatello and Coeur d'Alene, Idaho; and two radio stations, all with headquarters in Seattle. (Another offshoot from the main line appeared in 1934 when John P. Scripps, grandson of both E. W. Scripps and Milton McRae, established a small group of newspapers in Southern California.)

E. W. Scripps devoted his last years to scientific and philanthropic projects and to relaxation on his ranch and on his yachts. In 1920 he had established Science Service for the purpose of translating the technical language of scientific writers into what he called "plain United States." In outlining its purpose, Scripps wrote:

All of the best writing by men of exceptional ability on all such subjects appears only in scientific publications and books which are absolutely unknown to the public and rarely indeed studied by the journalists of this country who have the ability to, and actually do, mold public opinion. Every thorough scientific man who is in the habit of reading daily newspapers is constantly reminded that there is a vast quantity of misinformation being constantly spread abroad by our newspapers.

The first aim of this institution should be just the reverse of what is called propaganda. Its objects should never be to furnish arguments or facts for the purpose of producing partisans for any particular cause. Its sole object should be to present facts in readable and interesting form—facts upon which the reader could and probably would base his opinion on a subject of politics or sociology or concerning his duty with regard to himself and his fellows.

Dr. Edward Slosson, the first director of Science Service, was succeeded in 1933 by Watson Davis.

Early in the 1920's, Scripps endowed the Foundation for Research in Population Problems at Miami University in Ohio and, with his sister Ellen, established and financed the Scripps Institute of Biological Research at La Jolla, which was ultimately turned over to the University of California under the name of the Scripps Institute of Oceanography. Ellen had followed her brother to San Diego and engaged in widespread philanthropies there until her death in 1932.

From his retirement, E. W. Scripps wrote to his son, Bob, in 1924:

> It is my opinion that the value of the properties over which you exercise control might well increase manyfold if your chief aim were merely to cause increase in wealth.
>
> However, I repeat now what I told you when I first launched you in your career: That I would prefer that you should succeed in being in all things a gentleman, according to the real meaning of the word, than that you should vastly increase the money value of my estate. Being a gentleman, you cannot fail to devote your whole mind and energy to the service of the plain people who constitute the vast majority of the people of the United States. . . . You are, and can be, continually, entirely free from any temptation to cater to any class of your fellow citizens for profit. You have not nor should you at any time ever have any ambition to secure political and social eminence.

In that year the chain was supporting Robert LaFollette, the Progressive candidate for President; fighting the Ku Klux Klan; and advocating recognition of Soviet Russia.

When Carl Magee was persecuted, slugged, and driven out of business in Albuquerque, New Mexico, in his press fight to smash the Fall ring, which cast a shadow over the Harding administration, Bob Scripps purchased his paper and restored Magee to the editorship.

On March 12, 1926, E. W. Scripps entertained, as he rarely did, on his yacht moored in Monrovia Bay, off Liberia. He had withdrawn finally to the sea, living like a potentate on a series of yachts, subject to nobody's concern or wishes except those of the people who worked for him and were paid for their efforts. After the guests went ashore that hot spring night, E.W. complained of feeling ill, remarked that possibly he had smoked too much, and within an hour was dead of apoplexy, at the age of seventy-two. He died, as he wished to die, proudly and alone, and was buried, as he had ordered, at sea.

E.W.'s will left to Robert Paine Scripps, the only surviving son, controlling interest in papers in fifteen states, the United Press Associations, the Newspaper Enterprise Association, Acme Newsphotos, United Features Syndicate, newspaper mechanical and supply properties. With Robert Scripps at the editorial helm, business management had been entrusted to Roy W. Howard, successor to James Scripps. McRae had retired in 1914, and in 1922 the Scripps-McRae organization had officially changed to Scripps-Howard. After the Old Man's death, emphasis shifted sharply from Scripps to Howard.

To an extraordinary degree E. W. Scripps left his heirs free to make what they would of the papers he built; the trust instruments gave great power and discretion to the trustees.

17

From Scripps to Howard

BACK IN THE DAYS WHEN E. W. SCRIPPS WAS COURTING NACKIE Holtsinger in the Ohio countryside near Cincinnati, a tollgate stretched across the road at Gano between his boarding house and Nackie's home. In his impatience to see her, Ed usually jumped his horse over the gate or the hedge alongside or turned off into the field. He paid little heed to the Scottish family of Wilsons who lived in the cottage there, even though daughter Elizabeth had been Nackie's schoolmate.

Some years later, Scripps learned that Roy Howard, by then a reporter on the Scripps *Cincinnati Post,* was the son of Elizabeth, the tollgate keeper's daughter, and of William Howard, her Irish railroad-brakeman husband. This information, with its sentimental association, aroused in Scripps an interest in the young reporter that, in Scripps' own view, opened opportunities for Howard and greatly influenced his whole career.

Born at the tollhouse on the Dayton turnpike on January 1, 1883, Roy Wilson Howard was an only child of two years when Scripps rode by. Five years later the Howards moved from Gano to Indianapolis where Roy started out on his career in the accepted role of newsboy, carrying two routes, one of them turning him out of bed at three in the morning.

Roy went to Manual Training High School in Indianapolis, worked at lunchtime in the school cafeteria, and ushered eve-

nings at the opera house. Soon he began to write high school
items for the *Indianapolis News* at space rates.

Graduation ended his formal education, leaving him with a
lifelong indifference to "book learning" and a preference for
doing and acting by hunch and by instinct. He went to work
for the *News* as a cub at eight dollars a week, continuing to
carry papers as well.

The morning that his father died of tuberculosis, Roy showed
up at his typewriter as usual and went home only after the city
editor had found him there in tears.

Soon Howard followed Ray Long, his friend on the *News*
who eventually became a famous Hearst magazine editor, over
to the *Star* as sports editor. Then Howard moved on from
Indianapolis to St. Louis as assistant telegraph editor on the
Post-Dispatch under O.K. Bovard, the hard-driving editor
whose zeal and pride of craft helped preserve the Pulitzer
pattern.

Pulitzer's other paper, the *New York World,* was then—as it
remained for the rest of its life—the bright magnet that drew
so many ambitious young newspapermen from the hinterland.
Howard, on a summer vacation, went to the gold-domed *World*
tower on Park Row to look for a job but didn't get past the
office boy.

With Pulitzer's *World* closed to him, Howard left the *Post-
Dispatch* and accepted the offer of Ray Long, who had moved
into the managing editorship of the *Cincinnati Post,* of a job
as news editor there for less money but a chance to work for
Scripps. Scripps was still almost an unknown outside the newspaper world and Pulitzer was already famed; in the eyes of
Bovard and his colleagues such a shift was folly, but Roy
Howard knew his own mind and luck was with him. It was
then that Nackie Scripps received a letter from her mother reminding her who Roy Howard was.

Not long afterward Howard got his wish to go to New York,
as correspondent for the Scripps-McRae News Service. When
this agency was merged with the Publishers Press and the

Pacific Coast Scripps News in 1907 to form the new United
Press Associations, Howard became vice-president and general
news manager.

All this time Howard's path had not directly crossed that of
Scripps. When they finally did meet at Miramar, Scripps found
him

> . . . a striking individual, very small in stature, a large speaking coun-
> tenance and eyes that appeared to be windows for a rather unusual intel-
> lect. His manner was forceful, and the reverse from modest. Gall was
> written all over his face. It was in every tone and every word he voiced.
> There was ambition, self-respect and forcefulness oozing out of every pore
> of his body. . . . However, so completely and exuberantly frank was
> he that it was impossible for me to feel any resentment on account of his
> cheek.

As Howard recalled the interview, Scripps pushed his glasses
up on his forehead, slowly looked Howard up and down, and
said, "My God, another little one!"

Howard knew that the thing that Scripps hated was a man
who would knuckle under to him, and he replied, "Yes, but
maybe a good one this time."

That was in February 1908. Two months later, upon the
death of the UP's first president, John Vandercook, the directors of the UP appointed Howard to the vacancy on a temporary
basis. Having other candidates in mind himself, Scripps was
surprised when he found himself being urged to let Howard
have the job permanently.

"Certainly at this critical point in his career," Scripps observed, "he owed everything to the fact that he was the tollgate
keeper's grandson. My fancy was tickled with the idea."

However, as Scripps took pains to point out, Howard, the
upstart, made good. As general manager and president of the
United Press, which was rapidly expanding into an important
newsgathering and distribution agency, Howard hobnobbed
with the world's great, with premiers, foreign secretaries, generals, and leaders in every field. He became a particular admirer and intimate of Lord Northcliffe, a giant of the British
press.

At first, Howard's mother kept house for him and traveled with him, until, in 1909, Howard married Margaret Rohe, a New York magazine and newspaper writer, who took up her place at his side on his travels as well as rearing their two children, Jane and Jack.

In 1918 occurred the incident of the "false armistice" that Howard and the United Press were called upon to explain again and again for years to come. Four days before the actual signing of the armistice which ended hostilities between Germany and the Allies, a cable filed to the United Press by Howard touched off premature celebrations of victory and peace all over America.

According to Howard's account of how it happened, he learned of the reported armistice on his arrival in Brest on the morning of November 7. He spent the day accompanied by an American staff officer visiting the various American and French army and naval bases seeking confirmation. At four o'clock in the afternoon he made a second call on Admiral Henry B. Wilson, commander of the United States Naval Forces in France, who told him that he had just officially notified the American Fleet in European waters of the time and place of the signing of the armistice. The Admiral held several copies of his supposedly official dispatch, and upon request handed one copy to Howard and detailed his aide to accompany Howard to the cable office to expedite the message through censorship. The New York office of the United Press put the news on its wires immediately after receiving the cable. The Associated Press promptly reported that no such word had reached either Washington or Paris officially.

Less than two hours after Howard's message had been sent, Admiral Wilson dispatched his aide to inform Howard that the report was unconfirmed and might be premature. Howard immediately filed a correction but, as he learned later, the correction was held up by the naval censorship in New York on orders from Washington until ten o'clock the following morning. By then, of course, the damage had been done.

After investigation, Howard accepted the explanation that the false report that he had relayed had been instigated by a German agent who had tapped a private wire into a Paris Embassy in a desperate effort to stop the war before the Germans suffered further.

However much the whole unhappy business may have let down hopeful millions, it brought Howard's name to the world's attention and egged him onward.

In making Howard first business director of the Scripps-McRae interests and then Jim Scripps' successor as chairman of the board in 1920, E. W. Scripps was paving the way for his even bigger plans, as was evidenced when the name of the organization was changed to Scripps-Howard in 1922.

Meanwhile the immediate direction of the UP, which had been the instrument of Howard's rise, passed into other hands. Scripps had considered the founding of the UP his greatest service; Howard had done his part in stimulating and guiding its dynamic growth. As was to be the case with E.W.'s newspapers, the UP had lost its early militant motivation—"against the interest of the plutocrat band"—although it could still be counted on for a less conventional handling of the news than the conservative AP.

Karl Bickel, able, brilliant, on the intellectual side, was the UP's president when E. W. Scripps died, but under his tutelage, Hugh Baillie was already balancing his reportorial experience with learning business management. Baillie became UP president in 1935. Broad-shouldered and square-jawed, with crew-cut hair and athletic stride, Baillie, not too patient with "think stuff" and more for the blood-and-guts story he could still write so well himself, proved to be a vigorous executive. Under him the UP continued to expand the world market. Like Roy Howard, Baillie kept his hand in as a reporter, traveled widely, and interviewed world leaders.

Howard, meanwhile, concentrated upon the newspaper chain and particularly upon getting it a foothold in New York, a city that Scripps always shunned and Howard always fancied.

Within less than a year after the Old Man's death, Roy Howard gained his metropolitan outlet by buying the *New York Telegram* from William T. Dewart, Frank A. Munsey's executor. Howard imported some of the chain's brightest talent from Cleveland and other Scripps-Howard centers to breathe life into the spineless old sheet, but for complete acceptance it needed the prestige of a local name and reputation.

Howard's eyes were still on the *World* and at a chance shipboard meeting between Howard and Ralph Pulitzer in 1929, Pulitzer agreed that if he ever sold his papers he would talk with Howard first. Thus newspaper history found Howard and the Pulitzers, in February 1931, persuading the Surrogate in New York to let them break old Joseph Pulitzer's will, which had enjoined the sons to "preserve, perfect, and perpetuate" the Pulitzer papers. Caught off guard, the *World*'s staff made a frantic and futile eleventh-hour effort to raise enough money to buy and keep alive the beloved "newspaperman's newspaper" on which they were so proud to work. But the *Morning World* was abandoned, the *Evening World* incorporated into the *World-Telegram,* and Howard's New York venture had its base.

The national depression in which the *World* died had moved the Scripps-Howard papers to criticism of President Hoover, whose election they had favored in 1928. They called for a sweeping redistribution of wealth and aid to the unemployed. A series by Robert Scripps inveighing against the "idiocy" of capitalist accumulation was accompanied by editorial comment that "free men will not starve in the midst of wealth." The papers broke with Hoover on the issue of prohibition repeal.

Howard, savoring politics, worked to get Newton D. Baker, Scripps-Howard general counsel, nominated on the Democratic ticket, but that failing, the chain's editors voted at their customary policy conference in French Lick, Indiana, to support the party's nominee, Franklin D. Roosevelt, since the Democratic platform opposed prohibition.

Within a year after Hoover's defeat by Franklin D. Roosevelt, the Scripps-Howard papers were acclaiming the "New

Deal revolution," flaying "government by money changers," and warning against the "Bourbon diehards" who would attempt to "stigmatize" Roosevelt's program as "socialistic." The Scripps-Howard editors, again in 1936, voted to support Roosevelt against Landon.

The *World-Telegram*'s first great crusade, the New York mayorality election of 1933, routed Tammany and swept the Fusion candidate, Fiorello H. LaGuardia into office, for which the alumni association of the rival *New York Post* four years later gave Howard a gold medal.

It was becoming increasingly apparent, however, that Howard's sympathies and aspirations did not coincide with those of the chain's founder, although he continued to regard himself as a liberal. As New Deal legislation regulating big business hit home to him and his friends, Howard became restive and irritated. In 1935 he wrote to Roosevelt that large-scale industry was harnessed by taxation, which it considered "revengeful," and suggested "a breathing spell and a recess from further experimentation until the country can recover from its losses." The Scripps-Howard papers followed up the letter by attacks on "silly public works," on the Works Project Administration, on the Wagner wages-and-hours act, and other Administration measures.

In 1937 Howard lost the services of his old friend Lowell Mellett, editor of the Scripps-Howard *Washington News,* who saw the New Deal as the expression of the old Scripps progressivism. In the early twenties Mellett had written a series of articles denouncing "government by courts," and the papers had urged limitation of the power of the Supreme Court. Now, however, the Scripps-Howard papers, along with most of the rest of the nation's press, vigorously opposed Roosevelt's plan to reorganize the Court, and Mellett quit the *News* rather than go along with the attacks upon Roosevelt's "court-packing scheme." Other old Scripps men who felt that Roosevelt was closer to the spirit of Scripps than was Howard—men like Max Stern, Robert Horton, Herbert Little, George West—also left the organization. Some of them, along with Mellett, went into the developing government information service.

In Howard's view the Supreme Court move "signalized the New Deal's abandonment of its original liberalism in favor of modified state socialism, government by bureaucracy and a bastardized brood of political 'isms'."

Though deep in politics and business, Howard all the while relished the role of "ordinary reporter." He had been the first American newspaperman to interview Japan's Emperor Hirohito, and he followed this up by an unprecedented interview with Russia's Stalin, which he got on a hunch wire sent from Paris. After three hours and a half with Stalin, which he found easy, Howard turned to the interpreter and said: "Tell Mr. Stalin today is Sunday but I hope I didn't keep him from church."

Stalin replied, laughing, "Well, you did, but I'll forgive you."

Howard's dapper and dandified figure, the loud checks of his shirts, the bold stripes of his double-breasted suits, the matching bow ties and handkerchiefs of gaudy hue, made him conspicuous wherever he went and he went everywhere.

At his home and in his red-lacquered office in the Park Avenue skyscraper headquarters of the Scripps-Howard empire, Howard further indulged his taste for the spectacular, surrounding himself with his favorite Oriental antiques. The office rug was made to order in China, the waste basket fashioned from an ornately decorated rice barrel, the Chinese sofa adorned with embroidered cushions; a hand-carved screen stood at one side and scrolls hung on the walls; even the lavatory was all black and gold.

Roy Howard was as unlike E. W. Scripps, in appearance and in attitude, as Bob Scripps was like his father. Bob, just over six feet tall, had a commanding presence but was quiet and sensitive, allowing executives wide latitude and keeping in the background at Miramar or at his home in Connecticut except for visits to New York to confer with Howard. Forrest Davis's biographical sketch, written for the *Saturday Evening Post* in

1937, described Scripps as "king with final power of yea and veto," Howard as "prime minister, ruling boldly, conspicuously, restlessly, but only with Scripps's consent."

Less and less was heard of Scripps, who had retreated to Miramar. In 1938, stricken with a hemorrhage, he died as his father had, on his yacht at sea, in Magdalena Bay, off Lower California, at the age of forty-two.

The Scripps trust agreement provided that Howard, William W. Hawkins, United Press veteran and vice-chairman of the Scripps-Howard board, and George B. ("Deac") Parker, editor-in-chief of the chain, would succeed Robert Scripps as trustees, each to be succeeded in turn by the sons of Robert Scripps as they reached the age of twenty-five.

None of the founder's grandchildren was yet old enough to take over, and so, in 1938, Roy Howard became the sole ruler of the empire that he had dominated for some time. But he was always careful to point out that neither he nor any other single individual controlled the editorial policies of Scripps-Howard. Those policies, he insisted, were a composite of the opinions of its general editorial board, appointed under the trusteeship.

It was no longer an expanding empire numerically, several of its papers having been abandoned in the thirties, including the one-time hard-hitting crusaders like the papers in Akron and Toledo. Economics had forced papers everywhere by then to contract and concentrate.

This was also the period of another journalistic phenomenon —the burgeoning of a new type of opinionated columnist. Columnists—or colyumists, as they had been called—before the thirties were largely collectors of bits of verse and humor or light essayists. Expression of opinion was still nominally limited to its proper place on the editorial page. Then, nurtured by the public's depression-bred perplexity about economics and social problems, a spate of special columns began to be widely syndicated, signed by experts—self-styled and otherwise—who expounded, interpreted, and admonished.

The Scripps-Howard papers and allied agencies circulated

their full share of the pronouncements of the exponents of the new personal journalism. The dramatic story of two of those columnists, of their relation to one another and to Roy Howard, throws considerable light upon both the transmutations of Scripps-Howard policies and upon the conflicts and concerns of the turbulent thirties.

Heywood Cox Broun (see photograph 9), big of body and of heart, had been a sports writer, dramatic critic, and humorous stylist for the old *World* until his easy-going nature was stirred to indignant protest against what he saw as the rank injustice of the Sacco-Vanzetti case in Boston. There, he felt, an innocent shoemaker and fish peddler were being railroaded to execution for a payroll robbery merely because they were philosophical anarchists and convenient scapegoats. He hammered so hard on the case in his *World* column that Ralph Pulitzer asked him to desist and when Broun refused, Pulitzer fired him.

Roy Howard promptly got Broun to go over to the *Telegram* on his own terms as to freedom of expression and salary, appending to his *Telegram* column the words: "Ideas and opinions expressed in this column are those of one of America's most interesting writers, and are presented without regard to their agreement or disagreement with the editorial attitude of this paper."

Howard added: "In the liberalism which is their cardinal creed, Scripps-Howard strives for the toleration which it seems to us is too frequently lacking."

Howard and Broun went jovially around together and those who saw the cocky little publisher and the great shambling columnist who looked "like an unmade bed," remarked, "Here comes Roy Howard and his tame bear."

Broun was happy working for Howard. He spearheaded a "Give a Job" campaign during the depression, staged a Broadway benefit show, ran for Congress on the Socialist ticket, and Howard did not hold him back.

Broun was on hand at the *Telegram* to greet his old colleagues when some of them came over with Howard's purchase of the *World*. "I'm sorry to see the *World* papers die," Broun said. "Nobody's any more sorry than I am. It's just as well Roy Howard got them, if you [the staff] couldn't. In the last few years I've felt that the *Telegram* was often more courageous and liberal than even the *World* papers. I feel that the *World* died because it lost courage."

The death of the *World,* throwing newspapermen jobless into the streets without warning at the height of the unemployment crisis, spurred Broun's interest in organizing newspapermen for protection of their security. When the publishers' code of the NRA excluded reporters as "professionals" from its minimum-wage benefits, Broun launched the American Newspaper Guild. As the struggle with the publishers began, Broun announced at a newspaper code hearing: "I may add that if a news-writing guild cannot obtain those things which seem to us fair, then news-writing unions will."

Howard called a meeting of *World-Telegram* employees and warned them that Broun never finished anything he undertook. This time Howard was wrong. Broun was in the movement heart and soul; he saw the Guild as part of history. He was elected as the Guild's first national president and held the post until his death six years later.

Meanwhile Howard brought a neighbor columnist to live across the page from Broun on the *World-Telegram* and to be syndicated along with Broun to the Scripps-Howard and other papers.

Westbrook Pegler, son of a Hearst newspaperman in Chicago who had grown up in the old rough-and-tumble "Front Page" tradition, wrote so sharply and provocatively on the sports page that Howard hired him away from the *Chicago Tribune* to do a general interest column and gave him the same freedom he had given Broun.

Pegler, confessedly ill at ease as a think-writer, had a sulky, angry, iconoclastic style. He used a kind of shock technique. One of his early columns, dealing with the lynching of two kidnapper-killers in San Jose, California, defended such mob violence as a protest against the effectiveness of slow and venal law enforcement. Howard appealed to Pegler to modify the column but finally let it be printed as written. Naturally it provoked a flood of criticism from outraged readers.

The clashing viewpoints and divergent moods of Broun's "It Seems to Me" and Pegler's "Fair Enough," across the page from one another, made exciting reading. Broun, sharp with some capitalists, with enemies of the New Deal and of the Guild, was humanitarian and warm in spirit. Pegler, foe of any form of totalitarianism, was misanthropic and bitter. Charles Fisher wrote of Pegler in his "clinical study," *The Columnists*: "He has very adroitly avoided the danger of taking an honorable stand in defense of anything except Walt Disney's Snow White."

Broun was committed to unionism in general, was for the working man—as Old Man Scripps would have said—"right or wrong." To Pegler, unions were almost always wrong. Willie Bioff, West Coast representative of the International Alliance of Theater Employees, and George Scalise, of the Building Service Employees, were both effectively "Peglerized" by masterful reporting and sent off to jail; Pegler won a Pulitzer prize for the job. Pegler's columns left the impression, however, that most of America's 12,000,000 trade union members were the victims of similar racketeers.

Pegler resigned from the Newspaper Guild when it abandoned the craft unionism of the American Federation of Labor in 1937 and affiliated with the Committee for Industrial Organization, bringing into its membership stenographers and other nonunionized employees of newspaper plants as well as editorial workers.

As the Guild fight grew, Howard asked both Pegler and Broun to keep the Guild out of their columns. They tried, but when they slipped, Broun's column was slashed; Pegler's stood. Pegler began to call Broun such names as the "fat mahatma," "Old Bleeding-Heart Broun," and the "one-man slum." Broun diagnosed him as "the square Peg in a round hole."

No longer at home with Scripps-Howard, Broun sought outlet for his philosophy in the liberal national weeklies and in a newspaper that he started with a number of friends, *The Connecticut Nutmeg.* In the *Nutmeg* Broun wrote a piece in which he said that "Square Peg's" tragedy was that he was not the man he pretended to be.

His native sympathies are deep and wide. When he is aroused by some ancient wrong he can be more eloquent than any newspaperman I know. . . . And yet upon all too frequent occasions he writes as if he has taken over the role of light heavyweight champion of the underdog and game warden for the preserves of the overprivileged. Sometime somebody should take the hide off Peg because the stuff inside is so much better than the varnished surface which blinks in the sunlight of popular approval.

Broun blamed it on the hard-boiled, querulous, and materialistic fiction that Pegler had created to hide a nature that was actually shy, sensitive, and sentimental. Noting that Pegler could go to a flood and come back with nothing more than one of those columns about the income-tax pains of men with yachts, Broun suspected that Pegler "must have been bitten by an income tax."

Pegler, in turn, accused Broun of insincerity in hiring "a fink and a scab" on his *Nutmeg,* and then, on December 9, 1939, harking back to a column written fifteen months earlier in which Broun had refused to attack the Stalin government "which he regarded as the greatest effort ever made for human betterment," Pegler said of Broun: "I have seen recent superficial expressions of disappointment in Moscow but never an outright recantation, and even if I saw one I would have to treat it as I treat changes of front by Stalin, Hitler and Browder."

Broun and Howard, too, had reached the breaking point. Earlier, in a "letter to a famous publisher," printed in the *New Republic,* Broun had written:

Do you honestly think the great American public is all steamed up about your income tax? Take off your false whiskers. There's nothing

immoral or unethical in your espousing the conservative cause all along
the line, but doesn't that pretense of progressivism sometimes cleave in
your gullet?

All your arguments are based upon the premise that you're a great
success. You've scrapped some great papers and what have you to show
for them? What's left is an eight-column cut of the Quints asking permission to go to the bathroom.

(Broun referred to the Dionne Quintuplets of Canada who
were under contract to the Scripps-Howard Newspaper Enterprise Association for exclusive photographs.)

When Broun's contract expired it was not renewed and
Broun transferred to the *New York Post.* Broun's first column
in the *Post,* and the last one he ever wrote, was a call to President Roosevelt to accept the nomination for a third term. On
December 15, 1939, Broun died of pneumonia, and having
been converted to Catholicism in the last year of his life, was
buried after a funeral service that packed St. Patrick's Cathedral with his followers and his friends.

When time came to renew Pegler's contract in 1944, Howard
asked Pegler to agree to certain stipulations. Although Howard shared Pegler's point of view, the criticism of the columnist that impressed him most as a publisher was that Pegler
had become "the stuck whistle of American journalism." Howard, reminding Pegler that it was felicity in sports writing
and the light touch that won him his first popularity, wanted
to specify in the contract that Pegler would confine his attacks
on the Roosevelts and labor racketeers to three days a week.
Pegler replied that he could not "be funny a la carte" and, ten
days before the old contract expired, he reported to Howard
that he had signed up with Hearst's King Features Syndicate
where he could write as he pleased six days a week (it was
abundantly clear by now that what pleased Pegler also pleased
Hearst).

In a public statement Howard said: "The impact of Mr.
Pegler's writing upon the opinion content of any newspaper is
very great—so great in fact that the editorial voice of Scripps-

Howard could only continue audible by resort to a stridency which we do not care to employ."

During the period of the Broun-Pegler dispute, Rollin Kirby, liberal Pulitzer prize-winning cartoonist, who had been inherited with the *World,* also departed from the *World-Telegram* in disillusionment.

Explaining the departure of men like Millett and Kirby, Howard said:

> On a large metropolitan paper, the executive and operational demands make it impossible for the editor to write all the editorials expressing the paper's views and policies. It is the practice to select men from the more seasoned members of the staff who have grown up in the concern, are thoroughly familiar with the newspaper's policies, are in harmony with them, and are agreeable to the task of interpreting them through the paper's editorial columns. These men are not drafted for this task. In voluntarily accepting their jobs they do so with a full understanding that their efforts are in effect an extension of the editor's thinking and of his efforts. . . . It is their function to voice policy, not create it.

When, a few years after Broun died and Pegler departed, a longtime reader threatened to cancel his subscription unless the paper got rid of its "two pro-Communist writers, Mrs. Eleanor Roosevelt and Mr. Thomas L. Stokes," Howard took occasion to restate his policy of editorial independence.

Admitting that he was no more in tune with those two columnists than was the reader, he denied that either was pro-Communist. Dissociating himself from their political philosophy, he paid tribute to Stokes's honesty, patriotism, and integrity, and to the sincerity of Mrs. Roosevelt's humanitarianism, adding:

> Editorship of an independent newspaper properly administered involves no rights or privileges of intellectual dictatorship. Rather an editorship is a trusteeship to be administered in the public interest. The freedoms guaranteed the American press by the Constitution were not for the personal aggrandizement of any editor. They were designed to insure to the readers the fullest possible access to the truth and the greatest possible divergency of viewpoint.

There was no question that the opinions of Stokes and Mrs. Roosevelt, although in many respects close to those often voiced by E. W. Scripps, struck a discordant note in their current surroundings. In 1940, Howard had wooed Wendell Willkie for the Presidency and after the Republican convention the nominee joined Howard on his yacht moored at Philadelphia. In the next two elections the Scripps-Howard press was all out for the election of Thomas E. Dewey and in full cry against the "socialism" of the New Deal and the Fair Deal.

At the end of 1946, Robert Paine Scripps Jr., two years past the stated age of twenty-five but delayed in assuming his responsibility by war service, replaced Hawkins (who meanwhile had married the widow of the senior Robert Scripps) as trustee of the Scripps-Howard institution. Born in Washington, D.C., young Bob Scripps was educated at home until he attended Webb School at Claremont, California. Then he took some agricultural courses at the University of California at Davis. He worked for a short time in the business office of the trust before entering the Army, where he rose from private to sergeant, finally commanding a regimental reconnaissance platoon for the 161st infantry in the Philippines. After the war he became a farmer, raising alfalfa, sheep, and cotton on a substantial property that he co-owned with his uncle in Fort Stockton, Texas. Bob Scripps, a shrewd businessman, conscientiously attended to his duties as a trustee even when it interfered with his farming, but made no secret of the fact that he was completely disinterested in newspapering, either on the editorial or business side.

A month later, the second son, Charles Edward Scripps, reached twenty-five and Deac Parker stepped down. Chairman of the trust and now titular head of Scripps-Howard, Charles had attended Webb, and William and Mary and Pomona Colleges. He worked briefly on the editorial side of the *Cleveland Press* under Louis Seltzer, one of the chain's editors cast most closely in the Scripps mold, and then served in the Coast Guard. Charles displayed more interest, however, in the mechanics of publication than he did in ideas or politics.

In 1949, the year that Deac Parker died, Charles Scripps became chairman of the trust and titular head of Scripps-Howard. Walker Stone succeeded Parker as head of the Washington bureau, which was, in practice, the fountainhead from which the concern's national and international policies emanated, but no successor was named to Parker's more important post as editor-in-chief, to which he had been appointed by Robert Paine Scripps. Old Man Scripps had always warned against the concentration of editorial and business control in the hands of one man.

In January of the following year, the *New York World-Telegram,* bellwether of the flock that now included nineteen newspapers published under the slogan, "Give the people light and they will find the way," bought the sinking *New York Sun* from Thomas Dewart, son of the man from whom Howard had acquired the *Telegram.* The big, bulky *World-Telegram and Sun* that resulted took pride in the fact that it now united under one roof three great traditions of American journalism, combining the ideals of Pulitzer, Scripps, and Dana, but the caustic *New Yorker* gibed that these three great names were now buried in one grave.

Of the deal, the rival and aggressively liberal *New York Post* said:

> Thus, in death, New York's intransigent organ of conservative Republicanism is mated with the daily that once drew its inspiration from the fighting liberal tradition of the old *World.* Yet the union is not entirely incongruous. The latterday editorial pages of the *Sun* and *World-Telegram* have been wedded in most causes. Together they hated Roosevelt and together they embraced all the great Old Guard causes. It might be said that the *World-Telegram's* hardening conservatism destroyed the *Sun's* last reason for existence.

Within six months after the merger, the *World Telegram and Sun* was forced to suspend publication for two summer months by a Newspaper Guild strike over contract negotiations, but came back fatter and stronger than ever.

Local autonomy still allows wide variation among the other member papers—in Cleveland, Cincinnati, and Columbus, Ohio; in Houston, Fort Worth, and El Paso, Texas; in Covington, Kentucky; Evansville, Indiana; in San Francisco, Washington, Indianapolis, Knoxville, Memphis, Birmingham, and Denver—and many of them continue vigorous crusades against municipal corruption along the old Scripps lines.

But, Charles McCabe noted in his introduction to *Damned Old Crank*:

> Since the death of the founder there has been a growing tendency on the part of his legatees to hand over control of the words they sell to "those bright boys from off the streets." Today an aggressive management makes policy along lines that would have horrified the founder—"their money does their thinking, too. . . ." This policy is ratified by a supine and largely indifferent ownership. Such third generation capitulation to the boys who carry the hod is not unknown in other trust-ridden American business enterprises. It is very nearly customary when receipts run over ten million dollars annually. Its appearance in the Scripps organization has led some employees to the wry observation that the founder ought to be called "Whirling Ed." *

Samuel H. Scripps was slated to succeed Roy Howard as trustee on his twenty-fifth birthday, October 30, 1952, thus restoring the family to full nominal control of the properties. His interests were in the arts, and if he should decide not to take up his option, as seemed likely to some, the succession would fall—either at once or two years later—to the fourth and last son, E. W. Scripps II, a student at the University of Nevada who occasionally worked for the *Reno Daily,* a personable youth with a reporter's approach to life, who would reach twenty-five on November 26, 1954.

Of the two granddaughters of E. W. Scripps, the younger—Nackey Scripps Gallowhur, wife of a New York chemical company executive—had turned more toward horses and painting than toward newspapers, and the other—Margaret Scripps McCabe, wife of the editor of her grandfather's disquisitions—was a good newspaperwoman before her marriage but by now fully occupied with her family. She was as deeply concerned as her husband over the turn the papers have taken.

Would the return of the Scripps family to full control of their properties swing the papers back toward the courageous

* With permission of the publishers, Harper & Brothers.

championship of the common man that gave them their original character? Only time could tell.

As for Howard himself, at sixty-nine he was still strongly in the saddle, and his son, Jack, was firmly established as general editorial manager of Scripps-Howard. E. W. Scripps' original estimate probably still held true:

> . . . Howard's self-respect and self-confidence, right from the start, were so great as to make it impossible for them to increase. Doubtless to himself his present situation in life, his successes and his prosperity, all seem perfectly natural, and no more and no less than he expected, if he ever wasted his time in forecasting. Of which, I have very much doubt.

Out of Ohio: Knight and Cox

At a time when other newspaper chains of the nation were standing still or losing ground—numerically, at least—balding, sharp-eyed John Shively Knight of Akron, Ohio, and his newspapers were on the move.

When Knight acquired the *Chicago Daily News* in October 1944 he already owned the *Akron Beacon-Journal,* which his flamboyant father had owned before him, the *Miami Herald* in Florida, and the *Detroit Free Press,* both of which he had bought.

Knight shared the Miami field with James M. Cox, fellow Ohioan, who also operated the Dayton and Springfield papers in the home state and, eventually, the combined papers of Atlanta, Georgia.

Knight was admittedly on the lookout for more papers to run, but said that he had never set out to be a Hearst or a Howard, avoided orthodox chain practices, and bestowed a large degree of autonomy upon his individual dailies. Strategic location of his enterprises enabled him to operate in, and commute among, key centers of industry and labor: Akron, the rubber capital; Detroit, the automotive capital; Miami, air transport and winter mecca and link with Latin America; Chicago, railroad and industrial hub of the Middle West.

The forceful character that these cities came to know elicited adjectives like *go-getting, two-fisted, hard-boiled, tough-minded,* and gave John Knight a distinctive place in the familiar father-to-son, businessman-editor pattern of American newspaper publishing.

In Akron, where it all started, a plaque at the entrance to the *Beacon-Journal* building proclaims the credo established years ago by John Knight's father, Charles Landon Knight:

> We are ourselves Free—Free as the Constitution we enjoy—Free to truth, good manners and good sense. We shall be for whatever measure is best adapted to defending the rights and liberties of the people and advancing useful knowledge. We shall labor at all times to inspire the people with a just and proper sense of their condition, to point out to them their true interest and rouse them to pursue it.

C. L. Knight had been a cowhand, a schoolteacher, and a freelance writer before he went from Pennsylvania to Akron in 1900 to become advertising manager of the *Beacon-Journal* (founded in 1839 by Hiram Bowen). His son, John Knight, had been born six years earlier, on October 26, 1894, in Bluefield, West Virginia. In 1906 C. L. Knight began buying out the *Beacon-Journal* and acquired full control in 1915. By that time, John, who had attended Central High School in Akron and Tome School in Maryland, had enrolled at Cornell University in New York state.

When the United States declared war in 1917, young Knight left Cornell and enlisted in a motor transport corps that was soon at the front lines working with the 1st and 26th Divisions. Later Knight won an infantry commission at Langres and was transferred to the 29th Division. A month or so before the Armistice he went into the air service. Knight recalls that it was in the Army that he learned to get along with taxi drivers and other Americans of a kind with whom his lot had not been thrown before.

When Knight got out of the Army he had, by his own account, "a little money from shooting craps," and he went on to California. He wasn't at that time too sure that he wanted to go into newspaper work for he found the West most alluring.

Meanwhile, back home, his father—C.L.—had been busy writing the peppery editorials that made him loved and feared.

"To me the world is the gaudiest old thing that a humorous God ever made out of nothing and tossed into space as the happy hunting grounds of Homo Sapiens," he once told his readers.

However, at another time, he had this to say about the world's inhabitants:

> However great a failure man is and however terrible conditions his everlasting greed and selfishness have brought upon this world, we cannot send him back to the cave again. He is not lovely, but he is here. We cannot knock him on the head and be done with him as he probably deserves. . . . Once more we must begin to wash the mud off the brute, to bind up his wounds, to commence again the old task of regeneration.

C.L.'s editorials, all written in pencil, went to the linotype machine of Adam Brubeck, the only printer in the shop who could make out the old man's miserable scrawl. The editorial might be a dry-era attack on "God damned probeesh," a phrase he had picked up from his wine-loving gardener, or it might be about "Saint Woodrow" Wilson or "Wonder Boy" Hoover, "the Great Engineer." C.L. had opposed the first World War so bitterly that he was publicly accused of pro-Germanism. With trenchant pencil he fought the Ku Klux Klan and the political bosses, even though he ran a political machine of his own.

Georgia-born, C. L. Knight had been a Southern Democrat until he became a Bull Mooser in 1912. In 1920 he ran for Congress as a Republican and defeated Ohio's tree-surgeon politician, Martin L. Davey. "Tired of answering bells," he returned to Akron from Washington with a profound distaste for Congress. In 1922 he ran for the Republican nomination for Governor of Ohio but was defeated by the big-city bosses and the dry forces.

Eventually disillusioned with politics, he asked in his editorial column: "Why should the public go to the polls when there is nothing to vote for except a jackass and another bond issue?"

It was a mistake for his father to go into politics in the first place, John Knight felt. "He was too impetuous," the son once said. "His defeat was a personal tragedy. C.L. was politically ambitious, but, with his newspaper background, he could never do the orthodox thing. He was a foe of all hypocrisy. He hated what we would call today stuffed shirts and he loved to puncture them. When the rubber barons came around to tell him what they wanted put into the paper, he would tell them' that their subscriptions were worth no more than any others. Nobody could tell him anything."

With amusement Knight recalled the puckish way his father used to get together people of diverse backgrounds and points of view at the weekly barbecues and corn roasts he gave for the staff and guests during the summer at his Hudson farm, twelve miles from town. A local rector might find himself sharing steaks, beer, and ideas with Harry Daugherty of Harding era notoriety or Clarence Darrow of Tennessee "monkey-trial" fame.

Twice a week C.L. gathered together his cronies—the post-master, the druggist, a merchant, a county commissioner—who liked to drink and play poker with him. Other evenings, when there were doings in town, he would appear dramatically in a scarlet-lined opera cloak.

C. L. Knight's opinion of the journalism of his day was not high. "Where once, as in the old days of Dana, we had the jour-nalistic gem casket," he wrote, "we now have the garbage cart of flotsam and jetsam which neither amuses nor instructs an un-derstanding mind."

Yet he had enough faith in it as a career to induce his son to come back from California, despite the young man's reluctance, and join him on the *Beacon-Journal*. C.L. put Jack to work reading exchanges for a year, and then let him try his hand at sports writing, which the youth chose to do under the name of Walker.

"I was ashamed of the stuff," Jack Knight later admitted. "I didn't write well enough. I just kept my mouth shut and even when I got the title of managing editor in 1925, which was really a misnomer, I worked along with the old hands. I wrote a few editorials, and my father, to encourage me, told me some of them were good."

The *Beacon-Journal*'s files reveal an anonymous staffman's estimate of John Knight in his managing editor days. The article, after discussing Knight's urbanity, his presence in the composing room wearing his vest even on the hottest evenings, his "aggressiveness balanced by a sense of fair play," added:

> In the office he is as democratic as it is possible for a competent managing editor to be and outside he is an ideal companion. The writer does not know whether he is naturally democratic, but from what he has heard is rather certain that he was not always so. A man can't take an active part in a newspaper editorial department without becoming that way, though, and so Knight has added this to his other good qualities.

To counter the impression that he was cold and aloof, Knight called the staff together and explained that he was not the back-slapping type. His driving energy overcame his father's scoffing opposition to new-fangled notions—the purchase of syndicated entertainment features, printing late afternoon editions on gaudy green paper, building a new plant for the *Beacon-Journal*. But when the elder Knight returned from a vacation in Florida and saw his new offices, all done up in Oriental draperies and fine furnishings that he had no hand in choosing, he retired in disgust to his comfortable old-shoe quarters and sent his editorial copy from there to the shop by boy.

C. L. Knight died in 1933 at a time when the *Beacon-Journal* was struggling against the depression. After the banks ran out of cash, John Knight, who had taken over the paper, paid his help in scrip. They traded the scrip with local merchants and he thus staved off staff retrenchments.

Editorially Jack Knight moved forward cautiously. Although he had on his staff Ed Harter, a man who could duplicate the Old Man's style, Knight did not make use of his talent to carry on the *Beacon-Journal*'s flashy editorial tradition. For a while the paper took on an impersonal tone.

Then, in 1936, a dramatic gesture called national attention to the *Beacon-Journal*. At that time 15,000 workers struck in Akron's biggest rubber factory, Goodyear. Former Mayor C. Nelson Sparks, at one time a close friend of Jack Knight, had organized a "Law and Order League" and was exhorting non-strikers to march on the factory and throw the gates open by force.

The *Beacon-Journal* came out with a stinging frontpage editorial calling Spark's activities "deliberately provocative and inflammatory" and declaring that "we need no vigilantes here." The rival Scripps-Howard paper was so impressed that it replated its own front page to pay tribute to the *Beacon-Journal*'s wisdom.

At about the same time, perhaps with a backward glance toward the personal journalism of his father, John Knight began to inject his own views directly into the pages of his paper by means of an initialed feature, "The Editor's Notebook."

Looking ahead, Knight began to seek openings outside his home state. Since 1927 the Knights had owned the *Massillon Independent* and for a few years they had owned the *Springfield Sun,* both in Ohio.

In October 1937 John Knight elicited the services of Smith Davis, Cleveland newspaper broker. (The story of Smith Davis is beyond the province of this book, but his behind-the-scenes negotiations played an extraordinary part in the interchange of press properties all over the country and made him rich and powerful.) Through Davis, Knight bought the *Miami Herald* from Colonel Frank B. Shutts for $2,000,000.

The deal brought Knight within the battle area of Moses L. Annenberg of Philadelphia, owner of the *Miami Tribune,* who had figured in Chicago's violent circulation wars. In December Knight traded the profitable little Massillon paper for the *Tribune,* which he promptly suspended.

The only opposition left in Miami was the *News,* owned by James M. Cox, who was even more widely known in party politics than he was in publishing. The Knights' path had first crossed that of Cox early in the century when C. L. Knight sold the *Sun* in Springfield to Cox, who added it to his Dayton, Canton, and Springfield papers, comprising the News League of Ohio.

James Middleton Cox had worked on a farm, in a printer's office and taught country school before beginning his newspaper life as a reporter on the *Cincinnati Enquirer.* Cox's *Canton News,* which he bought in 1923 and sold in 1930, attracted national attention when political gangsters made its editor, Don R. Mellett, a martyr to crusading journalism by shooting him dead in the dooryard of his home on July 16, 1926. (Don Mellett came from the same Indiana family that produced Scripps-Howard's rebellious Lowell Mellett.)

Cox spread out from Ohio and moved first into Miami and then into Atlanta, where he bought the *Journal* in 1939, all the while remaining active in Democratic politics, first as Congressman from Ohio, then as Governor for three terms, as nominee for the Presidency in 1920, and as delegate to the World Monetary and Economic Conference in London in 1933.

James Middleton Cox Jr. graduated from Yale in 1923, moved along after his father on the same course, established Radio Station WHIO in Dayton, and stood in the line of succession like the younger Knight and the many other American heirs who have given continuity to family prestige in the press. In Miami, Cox's vice-president and general manager on the *News* when Knight came to town was D. J. Mahoney, a leader of one of the city's Democratic factions.

Young Knight had expected a fight there for news, business, and circulation. Instead of entering the field boisterously, as his father might have done, Knight moved conservatively and "tried to take the paper out of politics." It was not a knockdown fight.

Editorial policy in Miami was left largely in the hands of

John D. Pennekamp, associate editor, who was later joined by energetic Lee Hills, hired from the *Cleveland Press* as managing editor. Published in predominantly Democratic territory, the *Herald* was operated under Knight as an independent newspaper. John Knight's brother, James L. Knight, became business manager of the paper and later general manager.

After he had gained a firm footing in Florida, John Knight absorbed his only hometown opposition, the Scripps-Howard *Times-Press,* making Akron, with its 300,000 population, the largest one-newspaper community in the country.

The role of monopoly publisher at first proved "distressing" to Knight, more difficult than competition, in that "you don't shoot so fast and throw things around so vigorously."

Two years later, again through the auspices of Smith Davis, the broker, Knight bought the *Detroit Free Press,* Michigan's biggest morning newspaper, which had come upon hard times, from eighty-one-year-old Edward D. Stair. Knight paid $100,000 down on the $3,000,000 price, which was paid off in full three years later. Within ten years, the *Free Press,* which in its hundred-year history had brought fame to such staff members as the editor-columnist Malcolm Bingay and the folksy poet Edgar A. Guest, had increased its circulation from 293,000 to 436,000. The Detroit field remained about evenly divided among the *Free Press,* the *News,* owned by the W. E. Scripps interests, and the *Times,* a Hearst paper.

Characteristically, Knight moved with care in Detroit. His first step, after touring the city's boulevards and byways, was to invite a number of union leaders to lunch with him. Detroit, like Akron, was a hot spot of labor strife; inevitably Knight found himself and his newspapers involved. They became the target of organized labor as the result of the widely publicized "Guadalcanal story," which the *Akron Beacon-Journal* printed in January 1943. The story charged that sick, hungry Marines had been forced to unload a ship at Guadalcanal on a Sunday because National Maritime Union members had refused to work on the Sabbath on the ground that this was against the union rules. The story was distributed by the Associated Press, played up all over the country, and editorially discussed. Later Admiral William F. Halsey, Jr., commander of the American forces in the Solomons, denied the charges emphatically. The union filed a libel suit for $1,000,000 damages against the *Beacon-Journal,* but a Cleveland Federal district court eventually dismissed the suit on technical and jurisdictional grounds.

In direct labor relations with his own employes, Knight granted that he harbored no love for the American Newspaper Guild, but added that he had always negotiated in good faith. In other internal affairs of the newspaper business and profession, as in his attitude toward the Guild, Knight went along in general with the family of American newspaper publishers, but often with more candor and originality than some of his fellows.

He said that he became disgusted with men who went to editorial conventions and orated about freedom of the press when at home they didn't use what they had. "They are usually frightened, timid rabbits," he added, "when real questions of freedom of the press arise."

As president of the American Society of Newspaper Editors in 1944 he set in motion the campaign against world-wide barriers to the free flow of information.

In October 1944, after complicated financial transactions, Knight bought the *Chicago Daily News,* which had been on the market since the death six months earlier of its owner, Frank Knox, then Secretary of the Navy. Knight's bid was reported to be no higher than some others submitted, but the executors of the estate were convinced that he would "preserve and strengthen the character of the paper."

In Chicago's evening field, Knight came up against Hearst's *Herald-American* and the *Times,* liberal tabloid. It was not until the *Sun* later absorbed the *Times* that he entered direct competition with Marshall Field III. He showed at the start that he did not desire to antagonize the giant of Chicago journalism, Colonel Robert R. McCormick's morning *Tribune.* Almost at once Knight dropped from the *News* a series of cartoons that had ridiculed "Colonel McCosmic," the self-styled military expert. "I fight my own fights but have no desire to inherit the quarrels of others," Knight once declared.

Knight also subordinated the foreign coverage that had made the *News* famous to the sprightly local coverage sparked by Basil L. (Stuffy) Walters, editorial genius whom Knight had brought to Detroit the previous spring from the Cowles papers in Minneapolis. Walters, highly touted as an editorial and promotion expert and stunt man, introduced many innovations to the *News*.

Together with the *St. Louis Post-Dispatch,* the *News* exposed the Republican machine's attempts to influence the press of some fifty small Illinois towns by putting editors of newspapers on the payroll of the state government. It campaigned for a clean-up of crime conditions on Chicago's notorious Skid Row and had staff members who had joined Alcoholics Anonymous write the moving inside story of that organization's work.

At the end of five years, the *News* had paid off most of its $12,500,000 mortgage, had passed the *Herald-Examiner* in advertising, and was challenging both the latter and the all-day *Sun-Times* in circulation.

Chicago became the center of Knight's editorial and publishing activities, but he kept the family home on Portage Path, in Akron's green West Hill section—no longer the most fashionable part of town but still far enough from the rubber factories to escape their pungent odors. The vine-covered, gray brick house, set among spreading maples, with a swimming pool in the back, was the boyhood home of John Knight's three sons: John S. Knight Jr., a paratrooper who was killed in Germany during the second World War; Charles Landon Knight II, who became a reporter in Port Huron, Michigan, after graduation from Ohio State University and later joined the *Detroit Free Press;* and Frank, the youngest, who attended Culver Military Academy. Their mother was Katherine McLain of Massillon before she married Knight in 1921. She died in 1929 after a tragic illness and Knight never returned to the house where they had lived together. In 1932 Knight married Mrs. Beryl Zoller Comstock of Chicago, the former wife of a wealthy rubber manufacturer.

Near the Knight home, along what was once the western boundary of the United States, stood the Portage Country Club, one of the many clubs in various cities to which Knight belonged. It was here that some of his associates, whom he had ribbed as "economic royalists," ribbed him in turn as a "traitor to his class." It was here also that he hired a club professional to teach him golf, promising to pay double if his score was brought down into the seventies within a given time. It was and he did, subsequently winning title after title on the local links.

It was just after Knight had driven off the eighth tee at the Indian Creek Club in Miami Beach with a foursome of friends in May 1945, Jack Alexander related in the *Saturday Evening Post,* when a messenger came over from the clubhouse with the news that Knight's eldest son had been killed in action.

The other players wanted to abandon the game, but at Knight's request the foursome played on. The game was completed in grim silence. Knight's score on the par-3 eighth hole was a five, but after that he tightened up and finished the round just a few strokes off his usual game. "I felt," he explained afterward, "that I just had to keep going. It's just the way I do things." For a month or two thereafter he was unable to go near any of his newspapers.

Alexander noted that this reserved and aloof man, who had never thoroughly broken out of his shell, was in his professional life more of an adapter than a pioneer, operating largely as a salvager and a renovater of established journals.

Quoting the opinion of friends that the only interest that could conceivably deflect Knight from newspapering was diplomacy, Alexander recalled the service that Knight had given during the second World War as liaison man of the United States Office of Censorship with the Ministry of Information in London.

His task was to smooth out some difficulties that had arisen between the two agencies, and during his mission, which turned out amicably, he came to like and admire the English. On returning to this country, Knight, who was always a dapper dresser, took to lounging around in a silk dressing gown and an Ascot tie. From his talk about the English, his friends gathered that nothing would please him more than to be appointed Ambassador to the Court of St. James's. When asked about this, Knight smiles and says, "Nobody would think of giving me a diplomatic job. I'm too outspoken." *

When asked what kept him on the go, in golf or in journalism, John Knight was likely to answer with disarming frankness. His motivation was, he thought, pride. Of course he liked money and the things it could buy but he had enough for his personal needs. Because of his father's dominating character and vivid reputation, townspeople had said that young Jack was a rich man's son who would never amount to anything. When C. L. Knight died, the son heard that a rival editor had predicted that the *Beacon-Journal* would fail. Knight resolved then that he would show them.

A friend of Knight's father also played a prominent part in Knight's financial success. John Henry Barry had been brought to Akron from Pennsylvania by C.L. when Jack was a youngster in high school. Barry, who chose the rhumba for relaxation even in his late sixties, was intensely loyal to his old colleague's son and took a paternal attitude toward him.

Soon after Knight took over the *Detroit Free Press* a full-page advertisement in the paper publicized the sale of salacious and irreverent books. Knight repudiated the ad and demanded the resignation of the man responsible. Barry, unwilling to defend the ad itself, upheld the man who solicited it. He walked into Knight's office, arms folded, and told the publisher in Dutch-uncle terms that nobody could be fired in his domain.

Knight editors are told to "Investigate Everything." They frown on so-called off-the-record conferences and dig for their own information.

Since 1945 three of the newspapers, the *Detroit Free Press,*

* Reprinted by permission of the author.

the *Chicago Daily News,* and the *Miami Herald,* have won the Pulitzer public service award. In 1950 alone the *Chicago Daily News* won more than twenty different awards—from Sigma Delta Chi, the University of Missouri, Inland Press Association, the Chicago Newspaper Guild, and other professional newspaper groups. In November 1951 Knight signalized the national recognition Lee Hills had won for the Miami paper by promoting Hills to executive editorship of the *Free Press* as well as the *Herald,* with headquarters in Detroit.

One of the outstanding achievements in Chicago was the success of the Saturday Triple Streak edition, which stressed week-end reading. The Saturday paper sells for ten cents and the circulation loss over the previous period when it sold for five cents was negligible. This was a bold move at a time when most publishers were content to let the Saturday paper find its own level, usually a low one.

The makeup of the papers varies according to localities. In Miami, for instance, the *Herald* is typed conservatively because newspaper reading in Miami is apt to be more leisurely than in a city like Detroit where worker and executive alike are on the job early.

"The problems of one city can be quite different from the publishing and editing tasks of another," Knight says. "That is why our papers do not look alike, or follow the usual chain practices of using 'sacred cow' stuff from the home office. Actually we don't have any 'home office.' The newspapers are individually tailored for the communities they serve. Only 'The Editor's Notebook' is 'inflicted' upon them."

The "Notebook," which Knight writes weekly for his newspapers, besides elucidating his political philosophy, reveals some of his "irks," which include torn-up streets, Martinis with too much vermouth, double features at the movies, politicians who can't make a speech but don't know it, Columnist Westbrook Pegler on his off-days, mosquitoes, and cold ham picnics.

Knight came to staff meetings and editorial conferences equipped with a checklist, marking off item by item as he disposed of it. An efficient, methodical, staunch citizen, he had acquired, in place of his father's passion, a studious talent for orderly organization. He remembered that his father always thought he was too conservative and tried to get him into poker games for higher stakes.

Even though he might not shoot for all or nothing, he gambled for high stakes and won. If he lacked his father's flash and flair for phrasemaking, with his "Notebook" and public activities he had restored a modicum of the personal journalism that the elder Knight so eloquently typified.

C. L. Knight, who said once that perhaps he had given more advice and taken less than any man living, once warned editorially:

> . . . It is our duty to still hold high our ideals of public service or else get out of the newspaper business. Better it is that you should set fire to your plant, leave town by the light of it and take to raising speckled peas on a windy hillside with a bob-tailed bull, than to remain a human cash-register editor.

And when the *New York Sun* gave up the ghost in 1950, the younger Knight commented, "More than anything else the setting of the *Sun* is a graphic illustration of what can happen to any newspaper when it lives with a cash register in the place where its editorial heart belongs." Which led *Fortune* to observe: "Well, in the city rooms of the *Detroit Free Press, Chicago Daily News,* and *Miami Herald,* Jack Knight is not exactly regarded as the kind of sport who lights his cigars with dollar bills; but as a capable editor, as well as a good business-man [his *Daily News* made a modest $1 million last year in Colonel McCormick's back yard] he had a right to make the good point he did."

If newspapering as represented by Jack Knight lacked some of the flavor his father's generation gave it, it had gained in substance and it was moving along with history. The stories of the old timers often made better telling, partly perhaps because there is less reticence in revealing the foibles and the fancies of the departed than there is in embarrassing the living.

But also the press itself as an institution, and therefore its practitioners, have changed. The economics of newspapers, requiring editors to be exceptionally astute businessmen if they are to survive at all, inevitably makes most of their products more impersonal and less colorful. Social pressures, just as inevitably, require them to curb extravagant individualism.

Few romanticizers about the good old days would really welcome a return to the swashbuckling and free-wheeling atmosphere of name-calling, duel-fighting, and news-faking. The editor no longer carries a gun or keeps one handy in his desk drawer against the day when irate citizens, singly or in menacing groups, storm the sanctum. The mail today is more likely to bring an invitation to address the Chamber of Commerce than an offer for a ride out of town on a rail.

Thus, few such rowdy and iconoclastic legends as surround the names of the older generation of journalists have grown up about the contemporary generation. In the company of the modern businessman editor-publisher, John Shively Knight and James M. Cox of Ohio (except for the latter's fling in politics) are no more exceptions than are the Cowles brothers from Iowa.

19

The Cowles Brothers

ON FINISHING HARVARD IN THEIR TWENTIES, JOHN COWLES AND his brother Gardner (see photograph 11) began looking for fields to conquer. As they entered their fifties, with an inherited headstart, they could claim among their achievements ownership of all the newspapers in two large cities, of two successful national magazines, a prosperous news feature syndicate, experimentation in various new media, ownership of three radio stations, valuable service to the government, and other personal honors.

Their father, Gardner Cowles Sr., spent his childhood and youth in the nineteenth century in the Oskaloosa home of his Methodist-minister father, on a pay-as-you-go basis with a one-dollar-a-week budget for necessities—a home typical of the sober thrift that characterized the period of Iowa's greatest industrial and farm expansion.

"At an early age I knew that I would never have money given to me; that I would never be helped to get jobs and that it was up to me alone if I succeeded in business," the elder Cowles once said.

He served a varied job-apprenticeship while working his way through school and college, pasting strips of paper over button cards in a department store, folding papers for the *Muscatine Journal,* selling maps from door to door. He was twenty-one when he took his first steady job, as city school superintendent in Algona, for $80 a month. In 1884 he married Florence Call, one of his Algona teachers.

Gardner Cowles later became a partner in the weekly Algona paper, the *Republican,* and, at the same time, began making loans on Kossuth County land. Through land deals he gathered enough capital to invest in banking in a dozen northern Iowa towns; through bidding on star route mail contracts he added to his income and gained a knowledge of the state's geography that helped him later in mapping circulation routes for his papers.

The year 1903 was a milestone in the Cowles saga. In January the last of six Cowles children—three boys and three girls— was born. They named him Gardner Jr., but his father thought he looked like an Irishman and dubbed him Mike. In November of that year Gardner Cowles Sr. plunged overnight from banking into newspapering.

His old friend and neighbor, Harvey Ingham, who had moved to Des Moines the year before to become editor of the *Register and Leader,* had wired that the paper, in which he owned one-sixth stock, was about to be sold out from under him. Cowles supplied the $300,000 to buy the paper and then— finding its debts bigger and its circulation smaller than represented—he turned the editorial control over to Ingham and set about to build up its circulation from a low 16,000 by studying maps, memorizing timetables, and perfecting fast delivery. Within eight months the paper was making money. Five years later, he bought the evening *Tribune* from Charles D. Hellen. In 1924 Cowles acquired the Scripps-Howard *News* and in 1927 the *Capital.* All were consolidated into two papers, the morning *Register* and the afternoon *Tribune.*

Staff members soon learned not to use the word *monopoly* in the Cowles presence. He tried at once to remove whatever stigma attached to the word. He established a Bureau of Accuracy and Fair Play to stand watch on the paper; he pitted the editorial staffs of morning and evening papers against each

other to preserve the stimulus and appearance of competition—
a practice that is often followed, at least superficially, in one-
paper towns.

In 1934 Hellen, the former owner of the *Tribune,* returned
from temporary retirement in California, and attempted to
break the monopoly by establishing a new paper, the *Des
Moines Herald.* He set up a press in the basement of a five-story
building, hired reporters, printers, advertising men, pressmen.
The help—many of them former Cowles employees who had
been fired, had quit because of disagreements or had lost out in
the shuffle of shifting ownerships—sat around, playing cards to
pass the time, waiting for the day of the grand opening. It
never came. The venture vanished and nothing more was heard
of it.

While his papers were growing, Cowles was expanding his
other interests. He became director or trustee in a number of
Iowa banks, colleges, and hospitals. He served on a Public
Lands Commission in 1931, and was called by President Hoover
to a directorship in the Reconstruction Finance Corporation in
1932. The President later bestowed upon his friend and fellow
Iowan a typical token of his esteem—a steelhead trout he had
caught. A chance remark made by Herbert Hoover became a
standing joke between the Cowles brothers. "One of those
Cowles boys is mighty smart," Hoover said.

Neither John nor Mike nor their third brother, Russell, an
artist who took no interest in journalism, ever knew which one
he meant.

Gardner Cowles Sr. had many philanthropies. He and his
wife created the Gardner Cowles Foundation which already has
given about $2,000,000 to Iowa colleges for libraries and science
laboratories and which built a Negro community center in Des
Moines called Willkie House.

Gardner Cowles and his slogans hovered always over the
Register and Tribune building even after advancing age kept
him at home. "Gardner Cowles Month," an annual tribute
within the paper, was regularly launched by a big dinner at

which a representative of each department renewed his pledge to the founder—the editorial staff promising to abide by its concept of unbiased political news, the circulation staff to aim for a higher figure.

Once, while vacationing in Arizona, the Old Man delivered his speech in reply by telephone; oldtimers knew it by heart.

"We must have more circulation to get more advertising to make a better paper to get more circulation to get more advertising. . . ." and so on, like a scratched phonograph record.

And Kipling's: "It ain't the individual nor the Army as a whole, but the everlastin' teamwork of every bloomin' soul."

And: "Things don't just happen. Somebody makes them happen."

And, finally, a warning that things weren't going so well and everybody had better watch the expenses. Circulation and economy were his bywords.

The *Register and Tribune* claimed to be one of the first city newspapers in the country to make circulation pay a fair share of production costs. By 1942 a stockholders' meeting report revealed that the gross revenue from circulation on the papers was $3,500,000, more than half the total revenue from circulation and advertising together.

Years before other dailies were concerned with paper shortages, the late Harry Watts, then business manager, had thought of ways of trimming margins and cutting column rules to save $100,000 a year on newsprint.

With a little more warmth and a little less caution than his father, but with like energy and conscientiousness, Gardner Jr. continued the business policies that made the papers pay.

Mike, like John, went to Phillips Exeter Academy and Harvard. At Harvard his classmates found him a quiet and good, but not spectacular, student. He belonged to the exclusive Delphic Club and edited the *Crimson*.

Afterward he passed through a spell of wanting to be a gentleman rider but gave it up after he almost broke his neck trying.

His first marriage ended in divorce, and the Cowles papers printed the story of it, with pictures, on the front page.

Mike served successively as reporter, city editor, news editor, associate managing editor, and executive editor—with his father still in the saddle—all the time injecting new life into the papers. Mike's chief interest was always in news and pictures, while John and the Old Man concentrated on circulation and advertising.

In the early twenties George Gallup was an obscure instructor at the University of Iowa. The Cowleses had been instrumental in bringing him to Drake University to teach journalism. In 1925 they asked Gallup to conduct a survey of newspaper readers to find out what interested them most. Dr. Gallup reported that people preferred pictures to type and that they liked best to look at related pictures. The Cowleses substituted sequence pictures for isolated shots in their rotogravure section and this, along with exceptional sports coverage, increased the Sunday circulation 50 per cent.

Dr. Gallup went on from the Cowles assignment to develop his own opinion polls and to become head of the noted American Institute of Public Opinion.

Mike Cowles bought his first airplane in 1928 and instituted the technique of rushing news and pictures from all over Iowa and the Middle West to Des Moines by air. At least two planes, one an autogyro, and sometimes three, were used to bring in the Saturday shots on which a staff of fifty worked. Mike was not a devil-may-care fellow but he did have enthusiasms that must have worried his careful father. When somebody remarked that this Saturday sports coverage was an expensive business, Mike replied, "Yes, but we get a hell of a lot of fun out of it."

Mike put the family into the radio business, first with a small station at Fort Dodge, Iowa, then another in Yanktown, South Dakota, and two in Des Moines, until the Federal Communications Commission ruled that no newspaper could own more than one radio station within its circulation area.

Not everybody in Iowa liked what the Cowleses were doing for the journalism of the state. Aside from political differences, editors of many of the state's smaller papers—most of whom were to the right of the Cowleses—resented the intrusion into their fields; a daily newspaper association was formed to combat the ability of the Cowleses to bring in papers faster and sell them cheaper. Little advertisers, whose rates were raised along with those of big advertisers, complained that they had to pay for circulation outside the city that brought them slight return.

Some of the newspapermen who "remembered when," shed a nostalgic tear for the good old days of competition in Des Moines. They felt that what the papers had gained in technique and decorum they had lost in vitality and courage.

They remembered the *Tribune* under Billy Hale, the editor who sensationalized and personalized the paper to meet the last-ditch fight of the *Capital* and the *News*. Reporters faked stories and headlines were full of blood and thunder.

Once in response to a mysterious call, the police found a girl's clothing and diary on the river bank. Broad coincidence brought Hale's reporter to the scene simultaneously, in time to get the diary for daily serialization. The river was dragged for days but no girl's body ever turned up.

Again, Paul Prugh, news editor, set the stage in an abandoned house for a gambling den mystery; he scattered playing cards about, revolvers, knives, and letters and some blood he got from a slaughter house. Then he fired a few shots one midnight to attract the police. The story made copy for a long time.

Hale braved libel, sponsored weird contests, threw shears and pastepots at the men who fought with and loved him. He died in 1927 just two weeks before his boss achieved a monopoly in Des Moines.

Firmly established in Des Moines, the Cowles boys moved on to Minneapolis—while the *Register and Tribune* forged ahead until, at the century's half-way point, its daily circulation of 367,000 was larger than the 196,000 population of Des Moines, and the Sunday edition was speeded by truck over 50,000 miles of Iowa roads to seven out of every ten families in the state.

In 1935 the Cowles brothers paid $1,000,000 for the poor but progressive and respected *Minneapolis Evening Star,* which had been one of the nation's rare experiments in cooperative ownership. It remained under the management of its former publisher, John Thompson, for two years, but in 1938 John Cowles left Des Moines and became a citizen of Minneapolis, where he and Mrs. Cowles reared their family of two sons and two daughters.

In August 1939 the *Star* Company bought the *Minneapolis Journal,* daily and Sunday, and merged it with the *Star.* In the spring of 1941, with war impending, the Cowles brothers took over the *Tribune* newspapers and consolidated the Sunday *Star-Journal* (which had already passed the Sunday *Tribune* in circulation) with the Sunday *Tribune.* Both John Cowles and the former owner of the *Tribune* had come to the conclusion that Minneapolis was only large enough to support one Sunday paper. Cowles continued the *Tribune's* afternoon edition, called the *Times,* and made repeated efforts to sell it, approaching thirty or forty publishers and soliciting the aid of newspaper brokers. In the end, the *Times* was offered for sale for simply the appraised value of its plant, but still no purchaser appeared. Ultimately, since the *Times* had been losing large amounts of money and since its circulation was steadily declining, despite efforts to expand it, Cowles was forced to suspend the paper.

In the purchase of the *Tribune* properties the Cowles brothers acquired the 1,000-acre Glendolough Farm in northwest Minnesota, where thousands of ducks and pheasants are hatched and released each year to improve Minnesota hunting.

From almost the moment of his arrival in Minneapolis, John Cowles plunged, if such a word can be used to describe the calculating shrewdness of most of the moves the Cowles brothers made, into Minnesota's community and political life.

Reader interest studies at the University of Minnesota School of Journalism, which had received a generous Cowles grant, showed that editorial-reading increased markedly in Minneapolis after the papers changed ownership. Comparison with the National Continuing Study in Readership conducted by the Bureau of Advertising revealed Minnesota to be well above average in this respect.

Gideon Seymour, elder brother of Forrest Seymour, who had risen to editorship in Des Moines under the tutelage of high-principled W. W. Waymack, contributed intelligence and spirit and catholicity to the editorial page, which he developed into a forum for the expression of widely varying points of view. One of the strongest drawing cards in the Cowles Minneapolis deck was the folksy column of Cedric Adams, and, through it and the paper's clever promotion and advertising campaign, Adams became a widely known radio personality. The unorthodox theories and practices of Basil L. Walters enlivened the news columns and developed the special talents of the staff.

After Walters left Minneapolis for the Knight papers, Gideon Seymour added many of Walters' duties to his own. Carroll Binder was brought from the *Chicago Daily News* to become chief of the editorial page. Later, Binder, as American delegate to the United Nations Freedom of Information conferences, moved on to the world scene as a vigorous leader in the fight to prevent passage of international regulations that might curb the press more than they would promote the freedom that they ostensibly aimed to protect.

Like those in Des Moines, the Minneapolis papers were usually identified as "liberal Republican" and John Cowles himself characterized his policies as "intelligently conservative." His papers for the most part promoted men in public life who held broad internationalist views, thus clashing with the isolationist *Chicago Tribune,* which penetrated the fringes of the Cowles circulation areas.

They took an active part in promoting the political career of Wendell Willkie. After Willkie was defeated in the Presidential election of 1940, John Cowles went on a trip to England with him, and later Mike Cowles, along with Joseph Barnes of the *New York Herald Tribune* and the Office of War Information, accompanied Willkie on his globe-circling junket that produced the best-selling booklet, *One World*.

Both brothers played loyal-opposition roles in the wartime government. John Cowles served with the Lend-Lease Administration in Washington and, on the basis of his experience there, often spoke in public on the significance of aid to foreign countries and world amity.

Elmer Davis, director of the Office of War Information and often the target of ill-considered attacks charging that his Democratic allegiance gave the war agency a pro-Roosevelt bias, enlisted Mike Cowles as domestic director partly to give the organization political balance in the eyes of the public.

It was during Mike Cowles's period of service that a number of top-flight writers led by Harry Pringle resigned from the OWI, largely in protest against what they regarded as the emergence of the advertising-agency psychology and the attempt to sell the war to the public by means of slogans. The issues were confused and the blame for the blow-up did not rest squarely upon Mike Cowles, but he left the OWI soon afterward and returned to his own domain, in which his major concern by now was the magazine *Look*.

The origins and development of *Look* paralleled the local expansion of the Cowles papers in Des Moines and Minneapolis. As far back as 1925 John and Gardner Cowles had been impressed by proof of the public appetite for pictures, which had been displayed in one of the first polls conducted for them by George Gallup.

In 1926 a scrawny, red-haired kid from Belmont, South Dakota, forced by lack of funds to quit his studies at Drake University, showed up in the *Des Moines Register* office. He said his name was Vernon Pope and offered to work for nothing for a while to prove his worth. City Editor Paul Prugh put him on and later got him $10 a week. When explosive Editor Billy Hale returned from vacation to find a new face and a new item on the budget, he fired Pope. Later, while Hale was away ill, Pope was rehired. Hale never came back and Pope stayed. His colleagues said that he turned in more copy than anybody on the staff and they attributed much of the papers' early success with pictures to his resourceful and imaginative mind.

Pope and the Cowles brothers experimented first in widespread distribution of their narratives-in-pictures by syndication to twenty-six large newspapers. After considerable further experimentation with pictures in the Des Moines Sunday paper and the syndicate, they began, in 1933, active plans for a "picture-language" magazine. The nucleus of *Look*'s original organization was a handful of people selected from the *Des Moines Register and Tribune*. Months before the actual publication date these seven people laid out picture-stories, reworking the dummy many times.

Look sold phenomenally from its first issue. Nobody knows how much of the initial sales can be attributed to a fluke. Walter Winchell broadcast the fact that if the cover of the first issue, carrying an innocent picture of Greta Garbo, were folded in a certain way an obscenely startling effect could be achieved. Three days later the issue sold out. Gardner Cowles, no prude, but sensitive to public censure, ordered the American News Company to pick up and destroy all unsold copies throughout the country. That issue, which became a collector's item, sold 705,574 copies and every issue thereafter passed the million mark.

Within its first year, on November 9, 1937, *Look* reached a circulation of 2,000,000. It outgrew the space allotted to it by its parent organization, the *Des Moines Register and Tribune*, and had to be removed to a floor with more room. By its fourth year, the entire *Look* organization, except the mail and subscription department, was moved across country to New York. The eastern office had existed there for some time, and most of *Look*'s editorial contacts originated there.

Look's early emphasis on snakes, sex, accidents, and gore sold magazines but raised eyebrows. The *New Republic* called it a "morgue and dime museum on paper" and could think of no reason why *Look* "should not go to a circulation of 10,000,000—if the supply of corpses holds out and the people don't get tired of looking at them."

Mike Cowles was moved to retort in defense:

> *Look* has been criticized as sensationally thrilling. My only reply is that life itself is thrilling, and the more thrilling nature of *Look* gives it an intense reading which makes it all the more influential with its readers.

As *Look* became more certain of success under the dynamic editorship of Vernon Pope, it published effective picture editorials on child labor, civil liberties, slums, tuberculosis, the Ku Klux Klan.

The once-critical *New Republic* noted:

> *Look* . . . is the journalistic marvel of the age . . . it has made the best pictorial study of civil liberties in the United States we have seen anywhere . . . we salute *Look* for its courage in showing the seamy side of American life as well as for the skill with which it has done the job.

Mike Cowles once said that in its infancy *Look* made every possible mistake. It was often sued for libel. Its character changed with the years. A publicity release in 1944 said:

> *Look*'s early practice of exposé has long since disappeared in favor of a distinctly constructive policy. The editors are convinced that most readers catch the spirit of the magazine they see regularly. That is why *Look* omits material that cannot be presented in any form save that of depression or attack. It has consistently maintained a positive point of view through the crisis days of the war in the belief that a family picture magazine on the home front has a definite morale job.

The disappearance of lusty liberalism from its pages coincided with the departure of Vernon Pope and the appointment of Harlan Logan as editor, after a dispute over policies and practices. Logan, an athlete and a Rhodes scholar, went to *Look* from *Scribner's* in 1940. For many years he had taught at New York University and served as a "magazine analyst." The schoolmaster approach he took to *Look* showed up in the contents. No publishing venture was ever carried on with more theories, tests, tryouts, polls, plotting, charting, graphing, memoranda, and conferences. If it gave the offices the atmosphere of the schoolroom, it resulted in a finished product.

As side issues *Look* published a number of picture books, on such varied topics as Air Power, How to be Attractive, and Woodrow Wilson, and produced movie shorts for newsreel theaters, built upon features that had appeared in the magazine.

After a flurry of postwar experimentation with all sorts of publishing ideas, the Cowles brothers in 1950 added to their magazine budget a pocket weekly called *Quick*.

Ten years earlier Mike Cowles had said:

The most notable publication successes of the last decade have all been publications which condensed their content more than their predecessors: (1) The *Reader's Digest* substantially abbreviated, and, in the public opinion, improved, long-winded magazine articles; (2) *Time* magazine condensed the long-winded newspapers; (3) the *New York Daily News* further abbreviated the news and added many pictures.

Quick seemed to be the ultimate in abbreviation and condensation; it reduced paper and print near to the vanishing point. Its tiny, almost vest-pocket-size pages were packed tight with news briefs, photographs, and sketches, and it caught on at once.

Less successful was another Cowles venture which barely lasted out the year, and cost the Cowleses more than a million dollars. It was the luxury magazine *Flair*, pet project of Mike Cowles' third wife, who had been Fleur Fenton, an advertising agency executive. More novel in appearance than in content, it attracted considerable attention and some ridicule because of the oddities in format: a peekhole cutout in the front cover, pages that unfolded accordion-like from the inside, inserted sheets of odd shapes and sizes. Much of the subject matter was tied in closely with advertising or barely concealed commercial promotion. The artwork was ambitious and the entire undertaking obviously costly. *Flair* gallantly saluted its critics by publishing in its final issue a number of cartoons that had poked fun at its tricks and pretensions during the year.

Obviously the Cowleses had been concentrating in recent

years on expanding their national magazine and their radio interests—with stations in Des Moines; Yankton, South Dakota; and Boston—and seemed content to confine their newspaper activities to their two monopoly cities of Des Moines and Minnesota, despite earlier predictions that with Hearst settling into old age and Scripps-Howard in its prime, the Cowles brothers were the nation's up-and-coming chain publishers.

After the death of Gardner Cowles Sr. in 1946, Mike Cowles became president of the Des Moines papers, but he left them in competent hands and established his headquarters in New York. With John Cowles concentrating on Minneapolis, the brothers insisted that they were not, and had no desire to be, chain publishers in the commonly accepted sense. In all truth, their newspapers had few aspects of centralized control and operation. (There is no family connection with the W. H. Cowles papers of Spokane, Washington.)

In Minneapolis, as in Des Moines, the papers' readers were by no means confined to their cities of publication or even to the immediate areas. The *Star* and *Tribune* were home-delivered to more than 1,000 cities in Minnesota and western Wisconsin. Therefore the Cowles brothers were able to say that they were up against local competition in many communities if not in the home cities.

Across the Mississippi River from Minneapolis in St. Paul another expanding publishing family had achieved another big-city monopoly. Herman Ridder, a German immigrant who had developed the *New York Staats-Zeitung*, had bequeathed that paper on his death in 1915 to his three sons, Bernard H. and the twins, Joseph and Victor. Beginning with the *New York Journal of Commerce*, famous old paper that they bought in 1927 and merged with the *Commercial Advertiser*, the Ridders added half a dozen English-language papers to the *Staats-Zeitung*. These included dailies in the Dakotas, in Duluth, and, most importantly, the *St. Paul Press* and *Dispatch*.

The Twin Cities, however, are such separate entities that the Ridders and the Cowleses did not directly compete. The one-publisher situation in both cities, a situation that existed in eleven out of every twelve American communities, gave ammunition to critics like Morris Ernst, in his book, *The First Freedom,* to the Luce-Hutchins Commission on Freedom of the Press, and to various academic studies of the trend toward monopoly in the press.

While many other publishers shrugged off these expressions of alarm that democracy would thus be deprived of the diversity of fact and opinion needed for its full functioning, John Cowles accepted the challenge and spoke out often to make a case for monopoly. Monopoly, he insisted, could be a boon as well as a curse. In the first place, Cowles pointed out, actual monopoly of news did not exist, because news magazines, radio, and television offered real competition in one-publisher cities. In the second place, the elimination of papers on the financial borderline was bound to continue because of rising newspaper costs and there was no use crying about it.

Accepting a distinguished service award for the *Star* and *Tribune* from the University of Missouri School of Journalism in 1951, Cowles declared that the best newspapers in America, except in the competitive cities of New York, Washington, and St. Louis, were those that did not have a newspaper competing with them. Not having to win over readers from a rival, he added, they were "better able to resist the constant pressure to oversensationalize the news and the pressure of immediacy, which makes for incomplete, shoddy and premature reporting."

Cowles admitted that newspapers, whether competitive or not, had a responsibility to restrain themselves from whipping the public into a frenzy with cartoons, news stories, and editorials that were "so violent as to be almost psychopathic." He used for illustration the "emotional orgy" that some papers were currently stimulating over General MacArthur, who had just been relieved of his Far Eastern command by President Truman.

"If a monopoly newspaper is really bad," Cowles concluded, "then it won't last as a monopoly. New competition by abler and more socially moral newspapermen will eventually displace and supersede it."

Monopoly, naturally, does not function alike in every city where it exists. Not far from Minneapolis, in Madison, Wisconsin, for instance, it took a strange turn. When the assets of the two newspapers there were combined in a single business operation, the papers continued to go their separate ways editorially. Rival staffers on different floors barely recognized one another, and William T. Evjue, rambunctious editor of the evening *Capital-Times,* lashed out in the spirit of the old LaFollette Progressivism against the conservative Republican stands taken by the morning *Wisconsin State Journal* under co-owner Don Anderson.

Readers in other cities who could count on only one publisher for their supply of local and world daily information and opinion in print had different stories to tell.

Frank Gannett
and the Newer Chains

HIGH ON THE GROWING LIST OF ONE-MAN NEWSPAPER COMMUNI-
ties in the country stands Rochester, New York, third largest
city of the most populous and wealthy state in the union. Headquarters of the group of dailies owned by Frank Ernest Gannett
(see photograph 10), Rochester is but one of a dozen communities in which his papers operate without opposition.

Outside those areas, particularly in the 1940's, Gannett became better known for his national pressure politics than for
his regional publishing activities. After a fruitless campaign
for the Republican Presidential nomination, he continued to
direct the Committee for Constitutional Government, which
from 1937 on sent out millions of pieces of propaganda, principally directed against government interference with free enterprise.

After passing his seventieth birthday in 1946, Gannett spent
less time in Rochester than he had in the past and more in
Florida, but his personal interest in his properties did not flag.
By his brisk movement he might have been set down as a man
of fewer years. His gray hair slicked back, he dressed jauntily,
but in conservative blues, browns, or grays. The Phi Beta
Kappa key adorning his vest was not won at Cornell where
Gannett went to college but was awarded to him later by the

Hobart chapter of the scholastic fraternity to honor his publishing achievements and educational connections.

Gannett husbanded his health with the same care that he piled up his pennies and made his minutes count. He took vitamin pills as conscientiously as he collected metal clips from letters that came to his desk. He learned golf with the same application that he studied spelling. Gannett's sobriety, his concentration on work to the exclusion of casual play, helped to limit his circle of close personal friends.

Even when Gannett wintered in Florida he kept up a round of conferences, meetings, speeches, and correspondence with the home office. The Gannetts fittingly entertained such guests as Jacques Cartier of Paris, the Hapsburg princes, Felix and Otto, Lord Beaverbrook and Anthony Eden at their rambling home on Sandringham Road outside Rochester, a copy of an English country-house that Gannett bought in depression times at low cost.

Some years ago, impatient at being slowed down on his way home in his car, he campaigned in his papers for, and got, synchronization of the traffic lights on Monroe Avenue.

When he wanted to go fishing for bass on the Canadian shore of Lake Ontario—muskelonge trolling, a favorite sport in those waters, was too slow for him—he sent his schooner Widgeon II on ahead and flew across the lake to board it on the other side.

Gannett's first plane, with his own pilot to fly him and Gannett executives about the country, was turned over to the government during the second World War and replaced when the war was over. On one flying trip to Europe he visited the rulers of a dozen countries in about as many days.

Even on foot, he moved rapidly, with short quick steps; he rarely strolled—until, on doctor's orders after a cerebral accident in 1948, he was forced to slow down. Busy all his life, Gannett always seemed in a hurry to go places.

In the late 1930's Gannett acquired the site of his birthplace, Gannett Hill, in the picturesque Finger Lakes country of west-central New York state. Possession of Gannett Hill symbolized for him final triumph over poverty-ridden beginnings. Gannett's newspapers flourished in the very areas where his father's farms and hotels had failed.

The father, Charles, was of English-American stock, and at the close of the Civil War, in which he served as a private, he married Maria Brooks, whose ancestors were Scottish and Dutch. Charles Gannett and three brothers went to the hill that bears their name in 1870 and set up farms in the wilderness. Charles built a hilltop house, and there Frank was born on September 15, 1876.

In an authorized biography, Samuel T. Williamson wrote:

> The boy weighed twelve pounds, and Maria Gannett nearly died. When the ordeal was over, relatives comforted her and admired the baby. The usual things were said. Someone had to remark, "This boy might be President some day." Whether she believed that observation or not, it made an impression upon Maria Gannett, lying in childbed. She never forgot it, and it strengthened her in her determination that her children must make something of themselves—that, to use an expression her son heard her frequently use, they might "be somebody." The most helpless of all, of course, at that time was newly born Frank Gannett, and possibly without her knowing it, that son became Maria Gannett's favorite child. Of all her children, six in all, she had suffered most in bearing him. "Some people," Frank Gannett explains, "are fondest of those they do the most for."

Handicapped by ill health as an aftermath of his Civil War service, Charles Gannett found the going too hard, and in 1877 sold his place for a few dollars and became a tenant farmer a few miles away at Blood's Depot, now known as Atlanta, New York.

Frank started to school there and, according to Williamson, his mother continued, with the aid of the works of Benjamin Franklin, "to inspire Frank to make himself useful, to mind his studies and his pennies."

His father soon gave up the Blood's Depot farm and moved south a few miles to Howard, where he ran the Bishop Hotel, while Mrs. Gannett cooked for the patrons. After a year and a half, he moved to another hotel, at Wallace, where Frank peddled newspapers and books, and, with a group of boys collected and sold berries. Once again, when Frank was fifteen, his father moved to another hotel in another town, Bolivar, near the Pennsylvania border.

When his family moved once more, this time to Oneonta, Frank stayed on in Bolivar to go to school, living at the home of the principal and doing chores in the Newton House. Among his chores was acting as relief man to the regular bartender.

"After watching booze ruin men," Gannett said later, "I made up my mind that if I ever got a chance I would fight it."

In his early self-education, Frank Gannett accentuated the practical. He learned bookkeeping by correspondence in Bolivar and shorthand and typing the next summer in Oneonta. With money saved on a bookkeeping job in Bolivar and with the aid of a scholarship that paid his tuition, Gannett entered Cornell in 1894.

He worked his way through college, doing all kinds of jobs: delivering laundry, waiting on tables, ushering at chapel. Specializing in political economics, he came under the influence of Professor Jeremiah Jenks, remembered today by associates principally for his deaconlike personality and his mild criticisms of the *status quo,* his distinctions between "good trusts" and "bad trusts."

At Cornell Jacob Gould Schurman took a personal interest in Gannett. In 1899, a year after Gannett's graduation, when President McKinley appointed Dr. Schurman head of the commission to recommend a program for the government of the Philippines, Gannett went to the Islands as Dr. Schurman's secretary.

Gannett's first-hand view of colonial problems convinced him that the United States should pull out of the Philippines and this made him, according to Williamson, intensely anti-imperialistic. Gannett refused reappointment to the secretaryship when William Howard Taft, then an Ohio judge, succeeded Dr. Schurman as head of the commission.

While in the Islands, Gannett, at Schurman's request, translated from the Spanish Jose Rizal's novel, *Nolé Me Tangere,* an exposé of Spanish misrule and clerical oppression. The translation was published in the States as *Friars and Filipinos* and Gannett was careful to note in his preface that the indictment should not be taken as a reflection on the Roman Catholic Church as a whole.

After the Philippines stint Gannett turned his full attention to launching a newspaper empire. He was not again moved to enter the political field until about the time Franklin D. Roosevelt became President in 1933.

Frank Gannett's newspaper career stemmed from Cornell. He had been campus correspondent for the Republican *Ithaca Journal* and when he came back from the Philippines he was hired at fifteen dollars a week as news editor of the rival Democratic *News* by a Cornell professor who had just bought it. (Several years later Gannett acquired and combined the two Ithaca papers and also became a Cornell trustee.)

In 1906, after he had left Ithaca to try his luck on journalistic jobs in New York and Pittsburgh, he returned to nearby Elmira and, with $3,000 in carefully guarded savings and $17,000 in bank notes and character loans, bought a half-interest in the *Elmira Gazette.* This deal formally started Gannett on his career of buying already established papers (he never created one) and established his financial pattern for expansion. Some years later he told a group of young Gannett employees:

> I am frequently asked how I became a newspaper owner. The only way is to save your money and at the same time establish credit. On graduation from college one should take out as much life insurance as he can. This helps establish credit on which one can borrow money to buy a paper outright. Money must be borrowed, and without credit and confidence, borrowing is impossible.

While Gannett concentrated on the editorial side, the other half-owner, Erwin R. Davenport, ran the business office. After Gannett and Davenport absorbed the rival *Star* in Elmira, the liquor interests, sinister in Gannett's eyes, started the *Herald.* In its brief and successful fight-to-the-death with the *Herald,* the *Star-Gazette* refused to accept liquor advertising, a policy that the Gannett papers followed ever after.

Deciding that there was not enough money in the Elmira venture to support the owning families fully, Gannett and Davenport looked afield for further income. They talked with Charles Langdon Knight about buying the *Beacon-Journal* in Akron, Ohio, but when Knight decided to run for Congress, he called off the deal in order to keep the paper for his campaign.

Then they turned to Rochester, where they bought a Republican and a Democratic paper and merged them into the *Times-Union*. That year Gannett moved to Rochester. That culture-conscious city, which owed so much of its development to George Eastman of Kodak fame, was thenceforth Gannett's home and the capital of his empire.

In Rochester Gannett looked up a distant cousin, William Gannett, minister of the Unitarian Church, which was not fashionable with the "best people" of Rochester (and father of Lewis Gannett, later widely known as book critic for the *New York Herald Tribune*). Frank Gannett, reared a Methodist, became a Unitarian and remained a leader of that church in his adopted hometown, although when he wintered in Florida, he found the local interpretation of the church's creed too strong for his conservative tastes.

In 1920, Gannett, then forty-four, married Caroline Werner, twenty-seven-year-old daughter of the late Justice William E. Werner of the New York State Court of Appeals. She was a native of Rochester, educated abroad and at Rosemary Hall in Greenwich, Connecticut. Gannett's marriage was looked upon as a step upward for him in Rochester's self-conscious society. Mrs. Gannett took an active interest in education and became a member of the State Board of Regents.

All through the twenties Gannett was bidding for and buying newspapers. On one of these deals he came a cropper.

Newsprint manufacturers had begun investing in newspaper preferred stock in return for long-term newsprint contracts.

The International Paper Company, a subsidiary of the International Paper and Power Company, lent Gannett $2,000,000 for the purchase of the *Brooklyn Daily Eagle,* took $450,000 in stock as collateral for another loan to Gannett for the purchase of two Albany papers, and helped him refinance the *Ithaca Journal-News.*

In 1929 Senator George W. Norris charged on the floor of the Senate that such purchases illustrated "the campaign on all over the country by the power trust to get control of the generation and distribution of electrical energy." The Hearst press, with which Gannett was competing in Rochester and Albany, took up the cry and accused the "power trust" of trying to buy up the free press.

When the Federal Trade Commission undertook an investigation of the power company's holdings, Gannett was called to Washington to testify. He insisted that his deal had been a straightforward business transaction and that his papers had never printed a word about the power question. On the way home from the hearings he left the train at Philadelphia and made arrangements to divorce himself at once from the International Paper Company tie.

He borrowed from a bank to repay the paper company in full and then offered preferred stock to employees of his newspapers and organized a campaign to sell stock to outsiders. More than 700 employees bought $1,000,000 worth of preferred stock and sold another $1,000,000 worth, enough to pay back Gannett's loan from the bank.

Gannett had hoped to buy a Manhattan evening paper and combine it with the *Eagle,* and to make Brooklyn his home and headquarters but he had not counted on the difficulties he ran into there. Manhattan publishers refused to sell, and the *Eagle*'s financial structure was maddeningly complicated. Gannett built an expensive new plant and installed new presses. The juggling of funds required in clearing his name of the "power trust" implications hit head-on into the depression. Wet Brooklyn didn't welcome a dry publisher with repeal of the Prohibition Amendment coming on. Furthermore, Gannett's training in conservative, unchallenging upstate communities had not been the best kind to equip him for the keen competition the *Eagle* faced from the powerful press across the East River.

Taking a customary walk over the Brooklyn Bridge one evening in 1932, Gannett suddenly made up his mind to return the *Eagle* to its executives, write off as a million-dollar loss his one and only venture into the metropolitan big time, and go back to Rochester.

Concentrating on winning a clear track in Rochester—there had been five newspapers there when he first arrived—Gannett engaged with Hearst in what has been called "one of the weirdest trades in American newspaper history." In Albany they exchanged the morning and afternoon fields and Gannett gave up the Sunday field to Hearst; in Rochester Gannett bought Hearst's presses and equipment to keep out any newcomers, and Hearst retired from the scene after a fifteen-year struggle in a city that had never taken to his jazz journalism. The other papers had previously folded or been absorbed, and Gannett came out of it all with his morning *Times-Union* and afternoon *Democrat-Chronicle*.

Meanwhile, firmly established in single-ownership and group-paper publishing, Gannett had embarked upon a political crusade in the conviction that he was called upon to save the Constitution and the country from ruin.

Gannett was in Miami in 1935 when he read President Roosevelt's statement that the Supreme Court decision outlawing the National Recovery Act was a throwback to the "horse-and-buggy days."

As Gannett recalled the occasion later, he turned to his wife and said, "Carrie, this is the end of the Constitution, the end of our government as we know it; I have to go North."

The first man Gannett saw in Washington was Senator William E. Borah of Idaho. Borah consented to run for the Presidency when Gannett agreed to go on the ticket with him.

But the Borah-Gannett ticket lost its test vote in the Ohio primaries, and the Cleveland Republican convention chose Alfred M. Landon and Frank Knox.

Gannett's misgivings about the state of the nation were galvanized when President Roosevelt presented his program for the reorganization of the judiciary in 1937. Some of Gannett's friends who had been with him in the Borah campaign met in a New York hotel to plan a course of action; among these friends was Dr. Edward Aloysius Rumely.

Dr. Rumely, whose connections with the German-financed *New York Evening Mail* in 1915 had resulted in wartime charges and conviction under the Trading With the Enemy Act and an eventual pardon from President Coolidge, had first met Gannett when both were active in the Committee for the Nation, an organization campaigning for basic changes in the monetary system.

Gannett advanced $50,000 to underwrite a program to fight the Roosevelt "court-packing" plan, and the National Committee to Uphold Constitutional Government was formed, with Gannett as chairman and Rumely as executive secretary.

In the next six months the committee mailed out 10,000,000 pieces of literature against the court proposal, and inundated Congressmen with telegrams. The Senate recommitted the court plan to the Judiciary Committee, where it died. The flag that flew over the Capitol that day was sent to Gannett as a treasured trophy, and the Gannett committee began to publicize its success in what it called "mail-order government."

The court fight over, the Gannett committee trained its guns on the President's program for reorganizing the executive branch of the government, calling it a bid for dictatorship, and thereafter kept up a constant fire against the New Deal.

A Senate lobbying investigating committee tried without success to subpoena the Gannett committee's correspondence and financial records in the spring of 1938. A Federal jury in Washington on April 18, 1951, however, found the sixty-nine-year-old publicist, Rumely, guilty of wilfully refusing to tell the House lobby committee who contributed large sums for the distribution of material published by his organization. Jail penalty was withheld because of the accused publicist's advanced age. The conviction was appealed to the Supreme Court on the ground that the First Amendment protects a publisher's right to withhold circulation data. Among the publishers who supported the appeal the most prominent were Robert R. McCormick of Chicago and Norman Chandler of Los Angeles.

The Gannett group's name had meanwhile been shortened to The Committee for Constitutional Government, and Gannett had relinquished the chairmanship to Samuel B. Pettingill, former Indiana Congressman who had bolted the Democratic Party in 1936. Pettingill centered the committee's efforts in the fight against a third term while Gannett's eyes turned toward the White House.

Under the direction of C. Nelson Sparks, former mayor of Akron, Ohio, Gannett made 150 speeches from coast to coast, inveighing against bureaucracy, planned economy, and government intervention in business affairs. Gannett employees financed a bust of their "chief" by Gutzon Borglum, the sculptor who had carved the heroic heads of Washington, Lincoln, Jefferson, and Theodore Roosevelt on the granite face of Mt. Rushmore in the Black Hills of South Dakota. The bust stood for a while in the Gannett's living room but was relegated to the basement because Mrs. Gannett didn't think it fitted the residential decor.

Sparks set the scene for Gannett extravagantly at Philadelphia. The convention headquarters of Gannett, crusading dry, were by all accounts, and without his knowledge or consent, the wettest spot in the city. Sparks had imported at considerable expense several elephants from a private zoo in New York state; they created something of a problem when it was discovered belatedly that proper arrangements had not been made for their care and feeding.

On the first ballot Gannett got 33 votes; 17 from the New York delegation and the rest scattered. After that his support faded away but he did not withdraw his name. On the fifth ballot and on the sixth, which nominated Wendell Willkie, a lone Georgia delegate held out for Gannett.

The next fall a few upstate New York Republican leaders suggested running Gannett for the Senate against Robert F. Wagner, but the move collapsed. Gannett was appointed assistant chairman of the Republican National Committee in September 1942 but resigned two months later. Gannett, no longer a young man, apparently therewith foreswore further personal political ambitions and returned to the advisory board of the Committee for Constitutional Government.

In 1943 E. P. Dutton and Company published a book called *Under Cover,* written under the pseudonym of John Roy Carlson by Arthur Derounian and undertaking to expose the activities of American superpatriots, nightshirters, and Nazi agents. It dealt in some detail with the activities of the Committee for Constitutional Government and its allied organizations and individuals. Soon after the book appeared, Dutton's charged that an organized attempt was being made to prevent its distribution by means of a letter circulated through the Committee for Constitutional Government, addressed to both wholesale and retail booksellers. Each letter was accompanied by a copyrighted letter bearing Frank Gannett's signature and placing the publishers "on notice" that they might take "whatever steps are required" to minimize alleged libelous statements in the book. The publishers charged intimidation and interference with freedom of the press, and Gannett dropped the subject.

During the *Under Cover* controversy, Gannett joined with a number of Senators, farm organizations, and food commissioners to call a National Food Conference in Chicago, which *Time* described as "perhaps the most concentrated collection of New Deal denouncers possible to imagine . . . with an irresponsible overworking of the terrible word famine."

As the 1944 election approached Gannett was reported as a frequent side-door visitor at the executive mansion in Albany to counsel with Governor Thomas E. Dewey, the Republican candidate for president. Gannett later remarked that Dewey took little of his advice.

At the height of the campaign, President Roosevelt said in a New York speech: "I am proud of the fact that this Administration does not have the support of the isolationist press. . . . I mean, specifically, to take the glaring examples, the McCormick, Patterson, Gannett and Hearst press."

Gannett promptly telegraphed a reply to the White House, stating:

> In calling the Gannett Newspapers isolationist, you are guilty of a gross misrepresentation which I resent. Not one of these papers could by any stretch of the imagination be correctly characterized as isolationist. The intimation that I, as head of this group of newspapers, am an isolationist is likewise unjust and utterly false.

Gannett's papers and committee continued to attack the Administration, but when President Roosevelt died in April 1945 Gannett wrote a signed tribute in his *Times-Union* which called the late President "a great leader, a great person, a friend of mankind whose name will be written large in the annals of history," with "fortitude seldom surpassed or equaled" who "paid with his life as much as if he had died on the battlefield."

When President Truman took office, Gannett expressed a feeling of relief and hope that under his administration the nation might get back to "sound government principles." But when President Truman submitted his legislative program to Congress, Gannett was chilled once more.

Among the measures in the Roosevelt-Truman program that Gannett and his committee denounced as socialistic were bills for expansion of the health and social security programs, for small business finance, for Federal education, for general housing.

Disagreement over leadership in the New York State Republican Party, as well as over policies and personalities, brought Gannett to an open break with Dewey in 1950, and the publisher refused to support the governor for reelection. The majority of the Gannett newspapers, however, continued to back Dewey. This fact was widely publicized by the Gannett papers as evidence of the independence of the individual members of the group from central control and dictation. That independence had also been manifested in other ways. The Rochester papers have long favored construction of the St. Lawrence Seaway but the Gannett papers in the southern tier of New York state have opposed the project. The *Hartford Times* in Connecticut, one of the three out-of-state papers in the chain, for instance, had remained through the years under the management of Francis S. Murphy, nominally an independent Democratic organ, as had the Sunday *Advance-News* in Ogdensburg, New York, under Franklin R. Little.

In hiring a New York public relations firm to explain to the general public what the Gannett papers stand for, the owner listed as the guiding principles of his papers: competitive enterprise, freedom of the press, public service, democratic government, good citizenship, fair play, tolerance, the American way of life.

In the eyes of one commentator on the press, Oswald Garrison Villard, other press critics do not stress adequately that the Gannett chain publishes clean and decent papers, both in the news and advertising columns. "They play down murder, sex and divorce stories," Villard said, adding that they were "as a whole not among the most distinguished in America" and that there was "little originality in their handling of the news."

Frank Tripp of Elmira, Gannett's salty general manager, often said that the Gannett papers were "as local as the town pump."

Unlike so many other press empires, the Gannett Newspapers are not a family dynasty. The Gannett Foundation was incorporated in 1935 to "assure continuation of our newspapers in the interest of the widest possible service rather than for the largest possible profits" and "to provide that most of the profits will be applied to public welfare and not to piling up a fortune for any individual."

Established as a charitable institution, the tax-exempt foundation was not to achieve full operation until after Gannett's death, but it made a few preliminary benefactions, including one to Cornell for dietetics research and grants to several other colleges in the state.

After establishing the foundation, Gannett turned over to it control of the common stock. His will provides that his shares of the common stock will be added, his family being protected by a preferred stock trust. The properties are not to pass on to members of the family, although Mrs. Gannett is on the foundation's board. The two Gannett children, Sally and Dixon, have never identified themselves with the newspapers.

Nine of the foundation's original self-perpetuating board of eleven directors, all of whom had to hold at least $10,000 in preferred stock, were executives, largely on the business side.

"I am not going to attempt to run these papers after I pass out of the picture," Gannett once said. "You just can't do that. The hand of death is—well, it's fatal. I am getting my affairs in the best possible shape for the inevitable that comes to all men. They have got to be on a sound financial basis. They are under no obligation that would hamper their freedom. I am very happy that they have reached this strong, independent position."

With the day-to-day management of his papers in competent hands and their continuity cared for, Gannett's interest turned to promoting and developing new printing methods in the confidence that they would revolutionize the indutsry and ease its mounting economic burden. The Rochester Institute of Technology took over the local printer's school that Gannett had founded and, with a $300,000 endowment from him, undertook extensive research and experimentation with offset printing, plastic color plates, and other technological innovations.

This work he liked to consider in his declining years as perhaps his greatest contribution to journalism. Looking back upon his long and busy life, Frank Gannett's chief lament was that the burden of taxes made it impossible "for a boy to start out today as I did and do what I have done."

While the Scripps-Howard papers claimed the distinction of being the nation's original chain and had, since 1937, outnumbered their chief rival, the Hearst press, by mid-century both Gannett and John Holliday Perry had passed them in number of individual chain units.

However, the latter chains were limited largely to the states of New York and Florida respectively and therefore were less noteworthy nationally. Furthermore, Perry's papers were mostly smalltown weeklies.

Born in Port Royal, Kentucky, in 1881, John H. Perry began his professional life as a lawyer after attending Hanover College in Indiana and the University of Virginia. He was national counsel for the early Scripps newspapers, the United Press, and Newspaper Enterprise Association and was connected with the James G. Scripps western papers until 1918.

Arriving in Florida in 1920 in the midst of the real estate boom, he invested in the *Jacksonville Journal,* bought land and buildings as well as papers, and campaigned for better highways in the state.

On the national scene Perry's prominence as "Boilerplate King" overshadowed his role as publisher. His Western Newspaper Union, with headquarters in Chicago, took control of the weekly syndication field with its purchase of the American Press Association in 1917. The American Press Association subsequently became exclusively an advertising agency and was sold by Perry in 1949 to its publisher stockholders.

In a civil suit filed in Jacksonville in the summer of 1951 the Department of Justice charged that the Western Newspaper Union did a $15,000,000 business in 1950 in the distribution of pre-print material and printing equipment among 8,000 weekly newspapers with aggregate circulation of 17,000,000 copies and was therefore subject to action under the antitrust laws.

"In excess of 90 per cent of all these rural printers purchase some or all of their supplies and services from the defendants," the complaint charged. "WNU is the dominant distributor in the United States of ready print and mats and stereotypes to rural printers." (WNU discontinued its ready-print service in March 1952.)

A year or so earlier, Farwell W. Perry, son of the publisher, had assumed the presidency of the Western Newspaper Union and the father had become chairman of the board.

John H. Perry Jr., the elder son, was groomed to pursue the other family interests. Born in Seattle in 1917, he went to Hotchkiss, Yale, and the Harvard School of Business Administration. Then he became vice-president of the Western Newspaper Union, vice-president and director of the American Press Association, and took an active part in his father's other interests, including operation of the 3,000-acre Glenwood Farms at Perry Park, Kentucky. After serving as a pilot in the U.S. Army Air Corps during the second World War, John Jr. returned to direct the family radio operations.

With his brother Farwell and William J. Higgins of St. Petersburg, Florida, John Jr. was instrumental in developing the photo-engraving process through which, by use of flexible magnesium plates and self-justifying typewriters, stereotyping and linotype machines could be dispensed with on small newspapers.

The elder Perry, except for laying down general policy principles, made even more of a point than did Gannett of the individual independence of his papers and did not attempt to assume personal direction of them.

"If I stayed only four days on each property," he once said, "it would take me a year to complete the rounds. I'd never stop traveling."

Perry displayed no undue sensitivity to criticism expressed in such liberal weeklies as the *New Republic* and the *New Leader* that he and his papers and syndicate were factors in the increasing centralization and standardization of the American press and a resulting "mass mediocrity."

Just as John Cowles defended monopoly for the big-city daily, John Perry defended it for the small-town weekly.

"You know there are very few competing newspapers in towns under 100,000 and I believe it is a good thing," he was quoted by Thomas Whiteside in the *New Republic* as saying. "Why, if there's just one newspaper in a small town, it's apt to be wealthy enough to withstand pressure from advertisers. But when you have competition, one paper is always much the weaker. That's when the editor begins pulling news stories to suit the taste of advertisers—in fact, when he gets weak, he has to, to survive."

As his chief editorialist, with headquarters at the *Palm Beach Post-Times,* Perry engaged Charles Francis Coe, a lawyer and clubman who brought to the expression of his conservative views on social and political issues the techniques he had acquired as a writer of stories and articles on crime and punishment.

In recent years Coe's editorials and other Perry activities have been promoted by national advertising, but, until then, despite the wide range of his operations, Perry was one of the least publicized of major American publishers.

Similarly Samuel I. Newhouse managed to collect a considerable number of newspaper properties without attracting much attention to himself personally, except when he clashed with the American Newspaper Guild over labor policies. But when, late in 1950, he bought the century-old *Portland Oregonian,* largest paper in the Pacific Northwest, students of journalism began to look for something more about him than the meager two lines that he grudgingly gave in *Who's Who.*

In the first magazine article ever published about publicity-shy Newhouse, "who has no office except his briefcase," Collie Small wrote in *Collier's:*

Perhaps the most remarkable thing of all about Newhouse, however, has been his adroitness in avoiding the limelight while assuming such an important place in the American newspaper picture. Not long ago, he was lunching at a New York hotel when his name was brought up at the next table. The people in the adjoining party, unaware that the bantam publisher was perched at their elbows, discussed him at some length before paying their checks and leaving. As they got up and filed out, Newhouse turned to his companion and said, contentedly, "That's the advantage of being a shrimp. Nobody notices you."

Newhouse's first break came in 1917, when he was an eighteen-year-old office boy at two dollars a week in the plant of the *Bayonne* (New Jersey) *Times,* studying law at night. The *Times* went bankrupt and the receiver put young Newhouse in charge. The paper was back in the black within a year. Investors were properly impressed, and Newhouse soon got ready backing for the purchase of the *Staten Island Advance, Long Island Press* and *Star Journal* and the *Jamaica Press,* all suburban New York dailies. Purchase of the *Newark Ledger,* a morning tabloid, took Newhouse back into New Jersey, where he later acquired the building, presses, and title of the *Newark Star-Eagle,* a failing afternoon paper.

In Syracuse, in upstate New York, Newhouse first bought interests in the *Herald,* then the *Journal* and *Sunday American,* and combined them under the *Herald-Journal* banner of the only evening paper in Syracuse. He added a radio and television station to the property. There, and in Harrisburg, Pennsylvania, he achieved monopoly ownership. Less fortunate was his joint ownership with the Dear family of the *Jersey Journal* in Jersey City, which forced him to spend much time in courts proving ownership of his half of the paper. In July 1951 a Jersey justice broke the deadlock by ordering the Dear corporation dissolved, and three months later Newhouse gained full control. The following month he bought the *Jersey Observer* in Hoboken and merged it with the *Jersey Journal* to establish a county-wide newspaper with the largest evening circulation in New Jersey except for the *Newark News.*

Short, stocky and round-faced, Newhouse was fifty-five when he bought the *Portland Oregonian,* ownership of which had been scattered among four family groups who were heirs of the founders. Newhouse paid $5,250,000 for the *Oregonian,* a record in newspaper cash deals.

"Most of my papers were sick when I got them," Newhouse said. "The *Oregonian* is the first that is at the height of its power and prestige." To the *Oregonian* as to his other papers, Newhouse applied his stated policy of letting the papers, mostly listed as independent Republican, retain their local character, political color, direction and staff, although he listed himself as a Democrat. Newhouse's brother, Theodore, and his two sons, Samuel Jr. and Donald, all have lent a helping hand on the Long Island papers.

When *Time* suggested that purchase of the *Oregonian* meant that Newhouse was trying to link together a nation-wide chain, Newhouse said, "That would be a pretty ambitious operation." But, *Time* added, newsmen thought that Sam Newhouse looked like a mighty ambitious man. In any case, Newhouse was one of the few chain operators who was still branching out. Chains, both in total numbers and in the numbers of units in each chain, had apparently passed their peak with the depression.

Editor & Publisher's annual listing of newspaper groups—that word was used because a good many owners of more than one newspaper do not like the connotations of the word chain— ranges all the way from Harry F. Byrd's two in Virginia and Arthur Capper's two in Kansas to Merritt C. Speidel's fourteen disparate and loosely linked publications scattered all the way from Poughkeepsie, New York, to Salinas, California. Few of these groups, however, were bound together by the impress of strong personalities as were the Scripps-Howard, Hearst, and other pioneer chains. Most of the remaining memorable figures in American journalism were men who grew up where their careers began and who mirrored in themselves and in their papers the image of a particular community or a particular region.

Fathers and Sons
in Philadelphia

NOWHERE IN AMERICA DID THE DISAPPEARANCE OF DAILY NEWS-papers occur so drastically and so dramatically as it did in Phila-delphia. Once Philadelphia boasted sixteen dailies; by 1947 it had but two big newspapers, with a small tabloid running a poor third. In the nation's third largest city and the birthplace of its first daily, many names had been added to the roster of journalism but only those of McLean and Annenberg remained after all the rest had passed.

The year 1925 marked the beginning of the end of lively competition in the Philadelphia press. Up to that time the *North American* laid claim to being the oldest daily newspaper in America, tracing its own history back to 1771 and direct descent from the *Weekly Pennsylvania Gazette* founded in 1723 by Benjamin Franklin. In its great days under Thomas B. Wanamaker, with E. A. Van Valkenberg as editor, the *North American* had fought vigorously against predatory interests and special privilege. The night that the "Old North" died in 1925 reporters took up their typewriters and tossed them out of the fourteenth-story windows in protest.

The more restrained and reserved journalism that ultimately survived in Philadelphia traced its lineage back only as far as 1895, when William Lippard McLean borrowed $72,000 to buy the forty-eight-year-old *Evening Bulletin*. McLean had sold newspapers as a boy in Pittsburgh and had been business and circulation manager of the *Philadelphia Press* for seventeen years.

According to David Wittels, writing in the *Saturday Evening Post,* "McLean deliberately made the *Bulletin* as typical of Philadelphia as its anachronistic City Hall, spraddling obstinately in the path of the two main streets; the quiet dignity of Independence Hall; the monotonous miles of row houses filled with solid, unspectacular workers; the lovely, childlike quality of its Mummers' Parade; the Quaker-garbed statue of Billy Penn, and scrapple."

McLean explained his editorial policy by saying that the newspaper was a visitor in the home, and that it should not give offense through bad taste or impropriety.

In 1895 the 6,000 circulation of the *Bulletin* was the lowest of the city's thirteen newspapers. By 1905, when the number of papers had been reduced to ten, the *Bulletin* led with a circulation of 220,000.

The *Bulletin* pioneered particularly in its circulation and mechanical departments. It was the first to put in automobile trucks for paper delivery. The *Bulletin*'s success prompted Harry Highland, an advertising agent, to suggest to McLean the slogan: "In Philadelphia Everybody Reads the Bulletin."

The publisher characteristically protested that the statement wasn't true.

"Well," said Highland, "nearly everybody does."

"All right," McLean replied, "say that."

Although McLean did not crusade and refrained from telling his readers how to vote, the paper gained influence. The story is told of a Philadelphia county sheriff who for many years, over the continued protests of the other papers, applied his extensive office fees to his political party uses. Finally the *Bulletin* printed a short editorial suggesting that payment of a regular salary to the sheriff would be a more orderly process. The sheriff, who had seen nothing wrong with the system up to that point, gave in when his wife insisted, "You must be wrong; the *Bulletin* says so."

The *Bulletin* supported reform movements in Philadelphia politics. It stood against the City Hall "organization" and the "gas house gang," which operated at the turn of the century on the site from which the *Bulletin* is now published.

McLean trained his sons, Robert and William, in the way he wanted his paper to go, and when he died in 1931, the *Bulletin* continued on its charted course under them without interruption.

"The smartest thing I ever did was to choose my parents," said Robert McLean, who kept his father's name at the top of the *Bulletin* masthead after succeeding to the presidency of the paper.

Robert McLean was born in Philadelphia October 1, 1891. After graduation from Princeton, where he studied history, politics, and economics, he started to work on the paper. There, he took a turn in almost every department, even stereotyping, where he mashed two fingers trying to turn out a matrix in a hurry. His widest experience was in circulation but he did some reporting briefly.

"The city editor was tender with me," he remarked.

Young McLean went to the Texas border with the first troops of the Philadelphia City Cavalry in 1915, returned to the Field Artillery Camp at Fort Niagara, and became a major.

"I fought the war at Fort Sill," said McLean, who was to remain "Major" from then on to his *Bulletin* associates.

After the first World War he married Clare Randolph Goode, a Southern girl, and became vice-president of the *Bulletin* Company. They had two children, Donald and Jenepher. Donald later began his career in journalism at college on the staff of the *Daily Princetonian,* and after post-college military service, looked toward a career on the *Bulletin*. His cousin William L. McLean III was already employed there.

McLean established a home in suburban Fort Washington,

joined the Union League Club, and turned to shooting and fishing when he could find the time. He developed an interest in dog-raising and became vice-president of the National English Springer Field Trial Association.

Visitors to the *Bulletin* office remarked upon the quiet confidence shown by the paper's tall, wiry, sandy-haired, and husky-voiced executive.

After his father's death Robert McLean adhered closely to the pattern so successfully set by "The Chief," and when he did make changes, he made them with cautious deliberation. Once when the paper undertook a face-lifting with the use of livelier and more modern type and makeup, the old-fashioned look was not allowed to disappear all at once, but bit by bit, day by day, in order not to startle readers into thinking that anything out of the ordinary was happening to their paper. Such typical features as the daily joke at the bottom of the front page and the "Ethical Problems" department remained in their regular spots untouched.

Moderation was the keynote of the editorial page as well as of the news columns. McLean wrote to an advertising agency in explanation of this policy:

Understatement that carries conviction (because the mind of the reader feels in it the sense that it is right) may carry with it a lesser effect . . . at the moment, but it will never subject us to the misfortune of being doubted or discredited. Scrupulous attention to moderation in statement, is one of the things which it is our constant effort to maintain in the daily news and editorial contents of the *Bulletin*.

By such temperate practices, the *Bulletin* came to be known as "The Old Lady of Filbert Street" and also as "the biggest and best small-town newspaper in the United States."

McLean modernized the building at the corner of Filbert and Juniper Streets that the rich, smug *Bulletin* had occupied since 1908. Paneled partitions, glass brick, a great world map with a battery of time clocks for each time belt, weather gauges, made the first-floor business office shining and inviting. Air-conditioning, metal furniture, locker and shower rooms converted the news floor into one of the most up-to-date in the country.

McLean brought to Philadelphia for news executive posts first Wisler Gable Zeamer from Memphis, Dwight Stanley Perrin from St. Louis, and then Walter Lister from New York. Meeting Ralph W. Page, son of Walter Hines Page, diplomat of the first World War, McLean was impressed by Page's defense of New Deal ideas and hired him as a *Bulletin* columnist.

After hiring Howard W. Stodghill from Hearst to revitalize the circulation department, McLean installed Richard Slocum, shrewd and suave lawyer with good social background, who had had some success in labor negotiations, as general manager. Slocum won credit for keeping the *Bulletin* one big happy family.

"The *Bulletin* is an enigma to outsiders because it doesn't follow a standard pattern," Publisher McLean once explained. "Philadelphia is essentially a community of communities and neighborhood news has a close personal interest. We try to handle it without sensationalism."

The safe and sane qualities of the *Bulletin* were the essential qualities of the Associated Press, to which, like most other newspapers, the *Bulletin* belonged. It was only natural that, when Frank B. Noyes of the *Washington Star* retired from his longtime presidency of the cooperative news agency in 1938, he should be succeeded by McLean. Perennially reelected, McLean became a familiar figure throughout the country at the frequent regional and national meetings of the AP.

The healthy survival of the *Bulletin* under McLean and of its only real rival, the *Inquirer,* came about only after a succession of complicated maneuvers and clashes among vivid personalities.

The *Bulletin* was one of eight important dailies still flourishing in Philadelphia in 1913 when Cyrus H. K. Curtis, who had made millions of dollars with his magazines, bought the *Morning Public Ledger* from Adolph S. Ochs for $2,000,-000. Curtis started an evening edition of the *Ledger* the next year. He bought and killed the *Press* to get its newsprint contracts; bought and killed the *Evening Telegraph* to get its Associated Press membership; bought and killed the *North American* to get its library.

In 1925 Curtis started the tabloid *Sun* to compete with the *News*, which had just been started by Lee Ellmaker. Ellmaker had been secretary to William Vare, Pennsylvania politician. Bernarr Macfadden, who was having a fling with the tabloid *Graphic* in New York, took over the *News* for six years, retaining Ellmaker as vice-president and manager. Ellmaker got his paper back in 1932 and kept it until his death in 1951 when it passed to his widow.

Curtis's tabloid venture proved less hardy and died within three years, but Curtis continued his effort to build a newspaper empire.

When Colonel James Elverson, playboy publisher of the *Inquirer*, died in 1929, Curtis bought the majority stock in that paper from the heirs.

Curtis died in 1933, but the contraction of the Philadelphia press continued. The *Morning Public Ledger* was merged with the *Inquirer* and shortly thereafter the consolidated paper was turned back to the Elverson heirs.

The blight put upon daily journalism by Curtis had meanwhile been countered somewhat by the appearance upon the scene of a figure who was to enliven the city's press and politics for the next several years. He was J. David Stern Jr., a native Philadelphian who had left home, after starting out as a cub reporter on the *Ledger*, to sharpen his editorial and business wits by working on papers in Seattle and Providence, by buying the *Brunswick Times* in New Jersey for $2,500 and selling it for ten times that amount, and by running the *Springfield News and Record* in Illinois. In 1919 he had acquired the *Camden Courier* in New Jersey and combined it with the *Morning Post*. Then, in 1928, Stern bought from Wanamaker the weakling *Record* in Philadelphia, across the Delaware River.

Stern hired and sparked a good staff and gave the *Record* a metropolitan flair. "For Roosevelt before Chicago"—one of that group that supported the New York governor for the Presidential nomination prior to the 1932 Democratic convention—he introduced New Deal liberal ideas into the machine-run Republican stronghold and began to play an active role in party politics himself.

Sympathetic with the labor legislation of the New Deal, the *Record* was the first newspaper in the United States to sign a contract with the newly organized union of editorial workers, the American Newspaper Guild. Subsequently Stern resigned his membership in the American Newspaper Publishers Association in protest against what he called its "unfair attitude" toward the Guild.

The year 1936 introduced another colorful character to the cast of the Philadelphia story and marked the opening of an intense personal and political feud. He was Moses L. Annenberg, head of a racing information empire that yielded him millions in profits each year.

"Moe" Annenberg, born in East Prussia, had come to the United States with his family when he was seven, attended public schools in Chicago, been a newsboy, Western Union messenger, grocery clerk and circulation manager for Hearst's *Chicago Evening American*.

In 1907 he had moved to Milwaukee where he was distributing representative for all the Chicago newspapers and briefly published the *Wisconsin News* for Arthur Brisbane. In 1920 he became director of circulation for all of Hearst's newspapers and magazines. He resigned from the Hearst organization in 1926, acquiring the *Daily Racing Form* and the *New York Morning Telegraph* and formed the Cecelia Company, named in tribute to his wife, as a holding company for operation of the *Nationwide News Service*. This service was described by Annenberg as "a sports news-gathering organization which is to the field of sports in large measure what the Associated Press or any other comprehensive news service is to general news."

Annenberg also owned *Radio Guide, Screen Guide, Official Detective Stories,* and other publications.

"He had toyed with the idea of retirement, for he was worth millions—no one knows how many," John T. Flynn wrote in *Collier's.* "But a new idea had entered his head. It was to prove a fatal one, but it captivated his fancy. He wanted to put on the garments of respectability. The millions made . . . serving the daily business-information needs of the bookies and the horse players were safely in the vaults. But they needed re-gilding. He wanted his fortune reminted with the image of a more respectable world upon it. He had a son. He wanted to leave a monument behind him."

Already owner of the *Tribune* in Miami, Florida, Annenberg bought the eminently respectable but tottering *Philadelphia Inquirer* in 1936 for $13,000,000. He came into immediate conflict with J. David Stern, socially, professionally, and politically.

Annenberg had supported Franklin D. Roosevelt elsewhere, but after the 1936 election, he announced that the *Inquirer* would be independent of any traditional political or economic thought. Six months later the *Inquirer* repudiated the New Deal.

Annenberg meanwhile sold his Miami paper and threw himself into the Pennsylvania fight. He turned the *Inquirer's* guns on the Democratic state administration of Governor Earle, who had been put into office by Stern and the *Record.*

In 1938 Annenberg endorsed Judge Arthur H. James as Republican candidate for Governor. James was tagged as Annenberg's man, and Annenberg himself was named as one of the triumvirate that was running Republican politics in Pennsylvania.

Senator Sherman Minton denounced Annenberg on the floor of the Senate. Secretary of the Interior Harold L. Ickes went to Philadelphia and told the public about Annenberg's early days in Chicago.

Annenberg retorted with a blast that "The New Dealers Can't Muzzle the *Inquirer*," declaring:

This newspaper will continue its battle for decency, efficiency and honesty in government. I will not be intimidated, nor will I be swerved by personal slander or abuse from performing the full duties of my trusteeship to the public.

In 1939 Annenberg was indicted by a Federal Grand Jury for evasion of income taxes, for running lotteries, and for attempted bribery. Convicted on the income tax indictment, he made a civil settlement with the government to pay $8,000,000 back taxes with $1,500,000 interest. He also disbanded his racing and wire services. Nonetheless he was sentenced to three years in the Federal Penitentiary at Lewisburg, Pennsylvania.

Annenberg sought parole twice in 1941 and was refused. In 1942, however, he was granted one because he was ill. After his release on June 3, 1942, he went to a hospital in Philadelphia. From there he was removed to the Mayo Clinic at Rochester, Minnesota, where he died on July 20, 1942 at the age of sixty-four. He left his property to his widow, his six daughters, and his only son, Walter Annenberg.

Pleasant-voiced and good-looking, with small dark eyes and dark hair, the younger Annenberg was said to resemble his mother in manner more than his father. Moe Annenberg strutted and postured, had a flair for the dramatic; Walter was quiet and ingratiating.

Born in Milwaukee on March 13, 1908, Walter was taken East with his parents when his father was given a job as general circulation director for all of Hearst's publications. The Annenbergs lived in Great Neck, Long Island, and young Walter was sent to Peddie School at Hightstown, New Jersey, and later to the Wharton School of the University of Pennsylvania.

After his father bought the *Inquirer*, Walter became his assistant, taking the title of editor and publisher early in the 1940's when the elder Annenberg's troubles with the government began.

The ornate office that Moe Annenberg had established in the *Inquirer* building on Broad Street was maintained as a virtual shrine to his memory after his death. Walter spoke to visitors with reverential awe of "my dad," whose portrait looked down over the room. "I regard his presence as an inspiration," the son would remark. Unquestioningly the father was in the eyes of the son a martyr to political persecution.

Walter Annenberg expanded and strengthened the *Inquirer,* establishing himself and the paper so firmly in the community life that he repeatedly received awards and recognition from civic organizations. The *Inquirer* took over the Philadelphia Forum, one of America's distinguished intellectual and artistic organizations, which had been founded by Edward W. Bok, for many years editor of the *Ladies' Home Journal.*

The *Inquirer* also sponsors the Philadelphia Music Festival and an All-Star Football Game for charity, a Science Fair, and book luncheons. The M. L. Annenberg Foundation contributes scholarships to the University of Pennsylvania and Temple University.

Calling the Annenbergs, father and son, "an editor's dream," John J. Fitzpatrick, Hearstman from Boston who became the *Inquirer*'s managing editor in 1938, said, "Either of them would let you charter a steamship or an airplane if necessary to get the news."

Under Walter Annenberg the *Inquirer* experimented with facsimile reproduction. The first regular transmission of a facsimile newspaper was made late in 1947 over its station, WFIL—FM.

Community-minded but not particularly gregarious, Walter Annenberg lives unostentatiously. Following a divorce, in September 1951 he married Mrs. Leonore C. Rosenstiel of Beverly Hills, California, and Greenwich, Connecticut.

In the November 1951 elections the *Inquirer* for the first time in its 123-year history, supported the victorious candidacy of a Democrat for Mayor of Philadelphia. This action underlined the determination of Annenberg to give his paper an independent character in a city where variety of viewpoint was steadily becoming more and more constricted.

By the time Walter Annenberg took over from his father, the Curtis newspaper empire, which had been worth $50,000,000 when Curtis died in 1933, had collapsed entirely. (In the interim, the *New York Post* had passed from Curtis to his fellow Philadelphian, J. David Stern Jr., who kept it going along with his Camden and Philadelphia papers until he, in turn, sold it to George Backer in 1939).

John Charles Martin, a son-in-law of the second Mrs. Curtis, had published the *Evening Public Ledger* since Curtis's death. He was forced out of control in 1939, and Cary W. Bok, Curtis's grandson, took over. Bok brought in Stanley Walker, a brilliant craftsman from New York. Walter livened the *Ledger,* but circulation and profits failed to mount.

At the end of 1939, the Curtis-Martin interests sold the *Evening Public Ledger* to a company headed by Robert Creswell, treasurer until then of the *New York Herald Tribune.* After an anxious year, the *Ledger,* bankrupt and entangled in a cumbersome financial structure, filed a petition to reorganize. Efforts to find new capital or a buyer failed.

On January 4, 1942, in a Federal District courtroom jammed by many of the 1,300 men and women whose jobs were at stake, the *Public Ledger* was ordered to suspend publication. It had died of hardening of the financial arteries.

Then there were four papers left.

Through it all the *Bulletin* and the *Inquirer* flourished, shrewdly guided by inherited circulation talents; and the *News* somehow managed to exist, even though at one point it was forced to pay its employees in stock. The *Record,* however, was heading into serious trouble.

First Stern refinanced his three newspaper properties in Philadelphia and Camden against which there were liens for $2,500,000, so that he could buy radio station WCAU, the Columbia Broadcasting System outlet. For his combined new loan of $5,500,000 he had to pay the high interest rate of 4.5 per cent.

Meanwhile the *Record*'s 1945-46 contract with the American Newspaper Guild had not been signed. Neither had the *Inquirer*'s, but the *Inquirer* had put into effect the benefits written by the Guild into the unsigned contract, while the *Record* had not, although Annenberg had been nowhere near as friendly to the Guild as Stern had been. The *Bulletin,* in the afternoon field, had never had a contract with the Guild.

The Guild originally asked the *Record* for a $100-a-week minimum for experienced reporters but subsequently scaled down its demands to $88. The company offered a $68 minimum and later raised it to $75, while offering a 5 per cent differential against the Guild's 10 per cent demand. Stern said that the company offer amounted to a 12 per cent increase in the scales and would have amounted to $10 a week more for those making more than $75 weekly.

The Guild also asked a five-day, thirty-five hour week, instead of forty hours; four weeks vacation for employees of three years service or more; length of service increase of 5 per cent or three dollars a week, whichever was larger, for each year, and severance pay upon resignation.

The Guild accused Stern of stalling and moved to take a strike vote. Stern accused the Guild of putting a gun to his head. In a letter to Guild members he charged that they had served on him a "no contract, no work" ultimatum that left no room for a compromise, adding: "You know, after you have looked down a gun barrel for several years you become impervious to threat. You finally get to thinking that perhaps the easiest solution is to let the other fellow pull the trigger. . . . I want to be fair. But I will not be coerced. If this business cannot be operated on a reasonable basis of give and take, then it is not worth operating."

On November 7, 1946, the editorial employees of the *Record* and the *Courier-Post* went out on strike. The *Record* continued to publish with a skeleton staff of executives working overtime.

Vituperation and violence increased. The Guild put out its own paper, the *Real Record*. The cry of communism was raised, but Arthur Riordan, local Guild leader, had become an all-out anti-communist, and the national Guild president, Milton Murray, who had been elected on an anti-communist ticket, went to Philadelphia to support the strikers.

Suddenly, on January 31, 1947, Stern announced that he was suspending publication and that he had sold the assets of the *Record* Company, including the radio station WCAU to the *Bulletin*. On the front page of the *Record*'s last edition appeared a statement by Stern:

> The strike against the *Record* by the American Newspaper Guild, involving more than 400 people, has gone on for nearly three months. It has been impossible to obtain a fair settlement which would assure this newspaper of its ability to discharge its obligations to the public.
> This is not only because of the Guild's excessive demands. Guild policy has acted to restrict the rights of management to a degree where it has become too great a burden to operate a completely independent press. I will not attempt to give the reason for this strange attitude of Guild leadership. I only know that the *Record,* Philadelphia's liberal newspaper, has been chosen by this one union as a target for its unusual theories.
> No other of the numerous unions with which the *Record* has had relations for so many years has adopted such an attitude.

It was reported that Stern got $13,000,000 for the papers and the radio station. In his sworn statement to the Federal Communications Commission as part of the sale of WCAU to the *Bulletin,* the net profit of the Philadelphia *Record* Company for 1946 was given as $796,670 and of the *Camden Courier-Post* for the same period as $173,452.20.

Later, before the House Labor and Education Committee in Washington, the nervous, stocky sixty-year-old publisher described himself in a high-pitched voice as a "broken old man" and made a "public confession" that he had made a "grave mistake" in recognizing the Guild.

In an interview with Edward T. Folliard of the *Washington*

Post, Stern recalled that, in granting the Guild its first contract in the United States, he thought of it as an organization that would raise the newspaper business to the status of a profession. He added that his idea of the Guild at that time was that it would not only improve salaries and working conditions, but would have a program to elevate the newspaper business.

"I made an offer to pay for university courses for young reporters," he said. "I also offered to pay some of the older men for lecturing the younger ones at forums—$25 a night, as I remember it. We actually got those forums started, too.

"Then I got tied up with the *New York Post.* I saw Heywood Broun, and found out that the Guild was to be changed from a craft union into an industrial union. I felt that this was a big mistake, since it would put the editorial people in the minority."

Stern said that he felt like a father who found that the more he did for his children, the worse they treated him. He insisted that the Guild was uncompromising and sought to drive him out of business. The Guild countered with the charge that Stern was uncompromising and was bent on wrecking the union.

Arthur Riordan, former assistant telegraph editor of the *Record,* stated:

What has happened bears out the Guild's charge that Stern was guilty of bad faith. Even while he was negotiating with the Guild for a new contract, he was carrying on negotiations with the *Bulletin* for the sale of the *Record.*

Richard Strouse of the *New Republic* concluded in an article in that magazine:

If a complicated psychological situation can be summarized in a phrase, Stern sold his properties because the emotional burden of the strike and the financial burden of his extended position rocked against each other and chafed him until they broke his spirit.

National Guild President Murray issued a statement that Stern could rest no blame on the Guild because "in no other city, even where strikes have occurred, has it been impossible, with competent negotiators on both sides of the table, to reach a mutually satisfactory agreement."

The statement added:

It is tragic to 580 courageous employees who went on strike to achieve economic goals which have been won without conflict in other cities.

It is also tragic to the citizens of Philadelphia and Camden who see their newspapers engulfed in the increasing trend of American newspaper monopoly.

The gaunt white building that the *Record* vacated stood like a specter on Broad Street. Stern kept offices there for a while, and there was talk of new ventures that he and his son, David Stern III, had under way, but Stern's agreement in selling the *Record* provided that he would not start another newspaper within ninety miles of Philadelphia.

In 1949 the family's money and enterprise found its way to New Orleans where David Stern III became president and publisher of the *Item,* purchased from Ralph Nicholson.

In Philadelphia, with all real opposition out of the way, Robert McLean and Walter Annenberg had things largely to themselves.

Eight days after the *Record* died, the *Bulletin* produced its first Sunday edition, but, for the succeeding years, remained far behind the *Inquirer* in Sunday circulation. The two papers ran closely together in daily circulation, the *Inquirer* in the morning and the *Bulletin* in the evening.

What had happened in Philadelphia had happened, with less fireworks, in many another American city. In Baltimore, as a single instance, the field had been left to Hearst and to the heirs of Arunah S. Abell, who had carried the penny-paper idea there after helping to found the *Public Ledger* in Philadelphia. The "Baltimore Sun papers," as the Abell properties came to be called, took their place among the most brilliantly written in the country, with the names of Henry L. Mencken, Frank Kent, and Gerald Johnson standing out. Since 1918 the publisher of the *Sun* had been Paul Patterson, who made an enviable record as city editor under Hearst and Munsey.

Cities differ and if the Philadelphia story is symptomatic it is not necessarily typical. David G. Wittels, summing up in his *Saturday Evening Post* article the qualities that made "The Old Lady of Filbert Street" such a successful representative of Philadelphia, told of the time many years ago when General Taylor, creator of the modern *Boston Globe,* visited his good friend, William L. McLean, who made the *Bulletin* what it remained.

Finding the *Bulletin* unexciting, he demanded: "McLean, how in hell do you sell this thing? I couldn't get away with something like that in Boston."

McLean, his eyes twinkling behind his spectacles, did not take offense.

"Well," he replied, "neither could I. But I wouldn't try to sell the *Philadelphia Bulletin* in Boston."

Erwin Canham and Boston

BY THE END OF THE NINETEENTH CENTURY, BOSTON, WHERE THE free press of America was born, had become, journalistically, a bold-face, big-type town. It was, as well, a city torn by tensions and traditions, pressures and paradoxes.

That is what General Charles H. Taylor meant when he said that he could never get by in Boston with a paper like the *Philadelphia Bulletin.*

Taylor, who had been a printer's apprentice and had served in the Civil War and in politics, acquired the year-old morning *Globe* in 1873. Four years later he cut the paper's price from four cents to two, established an evening edition, and went over to the Democratic Party. He used sensational news methods, played up crime, and printed readers' names by the thousands.

General Taylor early established the *Globe*'s editorial-page policy of not offending anyone, quoting the hoary maxim, "You can attract more flies with honey than you can with vinegar." His biographer, James Morgan of the *Globe,* pictured General Taylor as a kindly and tolerant man who practiced this policy in his private as well as his professional life.

Many years ago somebody asked General Taylor whom his paper would support in the coming election and he replied,

"The *Globe* is going to try hard to continue to support the Taylor family."

First Republican, then Democratic, the *Globe* classed itself as independent politically after 1896. In 1916 the paper's cautious impartiality paid off. Almost alone among the nation's major papers, it did not concede the Presidential vote to Charles Evans Hughes the day after election. The next day the returns from California elected Woodrow Wilson.

General Taylor died in 1921, and his son, William C. Taylor, who had worked on the *Globe* for almost thirty years, became president of the paper and trustee for the estates of Charles H. Taylor and Eben D. Jordan, co-founder of the Boston department store of Jordan-Marsh. Three Taylors of the third generation took business and editorial posts on the paper.

Early in the 1940's the *Globe* put out a promotion brochure entitled, "Confessions of America's Most Exasperating Newspaper." According to the booklet, the *Globe* stood first among twenty-three leading newspapers in the number of readers it had per page. The *Globe* was "exasperating" because so many stories started on one page and were continued on another, compelling the reader to turn through many advertisement-laden pages to get all the news. The reader's annoyance was the advertiser's advantage.

The news columns fell under the genial guidance of Laurence L. Winship, a Harvard graduate who rose to the top through the Sunday department and under the tutelage of the paper's ageless editorial mentor, James Morgan, whose wise and kind old eyes looked upon every President from Cleveland to Truman.

While the *Globe,* morning and evening, sought to remain all things to all men, the conservative old *Herald* was taken over by a group of New England industrialists and, in 1912, bought the *Traveler* as its evening edition. In 1940, Robert B. Choate, also a Harvard man, was put in charge as publisher of both papers. "Beanie" Choate, son of a Boston lawyer who had helped reorganize the *Herald* and owned considerable stock in it, had worked his way up on the *Herald* from office boy, through Washington correspondence, to the managing editorship.

"None of the owners interferes on the paper," Choate once told an interviewer. "Of course my own views may be colored by my associations, but I don't often come in contact with the directors. It is natural that as sound business interests own the paper we shall reflect their point of view."

When Frank Buxton, Pulitzer prize-winning editor of the *Herald,* retired in 1946, Choate appointed as his successor John Henshaw Crider, who had gained most of his eighteen-year journalistic experience on the *New York Times.* Two years later Crider himself won the Pulitzer prize for distinguished editorial writing. In November 1951 Crider resigned from the *Herald* in protest against Choate's refusal to print Crider's criticism of Senator Robert A. Taft's Presidential campaign book on foreign policy.

Neither the *Globe* nor the *Herald* and *Traveler* caught on as quickly in modern Boston as did the *Post* and the Hearst press.

In 1891, Edwin A. Grozier, son of a whaling captain, erstwhile private secretary for Joseph Pulitzer, and an editor of the *World,* brought to Boston the "yellow journalism" then rampant in New York. By emphasis on local crime and disaster, he made the *Post* "the great breakfast-table paper of New England."

The *Post* attracted Clifton B. Carberry, a graduate of Andover and Harvard Law School, who became managing editor. Carberry built the paper's circulation until by the first World War it had more readers than any other morning paper in the United States. After 1945, however, it began to fall off.

While the *Post* was growing, Grozier's only son, Richard, worked in all departments of the paper, though he had wanted to be an engineer. By the time the elder Grozier died in 1924 and was succeeded by his son, all the paper's stock had come back to the Grozier family. Richard Grozier stayed around the shop until the late 1920's, when he went into retirement in his Cambridge home, tinkering in his mechanical laboratory. The staff heard or saw little of him from then until his death, sending him each Christmas a bunch of American Beauty roses and getting back a note of thanks.

Published in a rabbit-warren that occupied several adjoining buildings and burrowed seven stories below the street surface, the *Post,* indifferent to change, went on cramming its front pages with a greater number and larger variety of stories than any other paper, always remembering to include some about animals and babies.

In answer to persistent reports in 1951 that the *Post* was about to be sold—among the rumored buyers was Joseph B. Kennedy, former Ambassador to Great Britain—W. F. Carley, general manager, retorted wryly that he understood that the *Pilot,* Catholic diocesan paper, and the *Christian Science Monitor* were about to be merged.

Soon thereafter Mrs. Helen D. Grozier, widow of the publisher, appointed Henry J. Gallagher managing director. Gallagher, who had joined the company in its mechanical department, was plant superintendent and co-executor of the Grozier estate.

It was the arrival of the Hearst press in Boston, with the establishment of the *American* in 1904, that probably precipitated the creation of the one newspaper published in Boston that gained lasting prestige and respect in the nation and the world.

Shocked by the sensationalism of most of the papers she saw, Mary Baker Eddy, founder of the Christian Science Church, said in a note to her church board of trustees: "It is my request that you start a daily newspaper. Let there be no delay."

Money poured in until the trustees called a halt to the donations, declaring that funds for all their needs filled the treasury.

In a short editorial in the first issue of the *Monitor,* on November 25, 1908, Mrs. Eddy wrote: "I have named all Christian Science periodicals. I named this one the *Monitor,* to spread undivided the Science that operates unspent. The object of the *Monitor* is to injure no man, but to bless all mankind."

The line under the editorial page banner read: "First the blade, then the ear, then the full grain in the ear." This meant, Mrs. Eddy explained, that "Man must be patient: With the growth of man: With the child: The Foreigner, the new nation emerging into the light."

In accordance with the church's philosophy of mind over matter, and its tenets that death, disease, and evil are errors, the news columns ignored or merely touched upon casualties, scandal, and the seamy side of life. Taboos deprived the public of the details of much of what it had come to regard as legitimate news. Public figures did not die; they "passed on." The *Monitor* refused advertisements for medical articles, coffee, tea, cigarettes, liquor, firearms, tombstones, and other products it regarded as unwholesome, thereby sacrificing a million dollars of possible annual income. Although it shunned content of mere entertainment value, the *Monitor,* however, showed an interest in many areas: music, athletics, poetry, chess, the home, history and travel.

Mrs. Eddy's venture was greeted with widespread skepticism. Said the *New York Times,* "It will be a miracle if she makes the paper pay."

In its first anniversary edition, the *Monitor* took pains to explain editorially:

> It is not to be understood that the *Monitor* has stooped to a censorship so narrow or opinionated as to render its news service inadequate, inefficient or incomplete. Far from it. Whatever is of public importance or affects the public welfare, even though it be news of what is ordinarily reckoned as crime or disaster, is printed in the *Monitor* in completeness sufficient for information without unnecessary embellishment or sensational display. The emphasis, however, is reserved for the helpful, the constructive, the encouraging, not their opposites.

The *Monitor* was distributed partly through Christian Science reading rooms and became familiar to non-Christian Scientists through the encouraged practice of leaving used copies in railroad stations and other public places.

Four years after Mrs. Eddy's death in 1910, Frederick Dixon, whom she had designated, was brought from England and made editor. Dixon's first order started the *Monitor* on a new tack, which was to be one of its greatest distinctions. It was: "Send out correspondents. Send them throughout the world. Teach them the ways of all men—all nations."

Under Dixon, the *Monitor* urged American entry into the first World War, a course that struck many both within and without the faith as inconsistent with the teachings of the church.

In an intramural controversy, Dixon joined with three trustees of the Christian Science Publishing Society to ignore the authority of the five directors of the First Church of Christ Scientist in Boston, known as the Mother Church. Both sides turned to Mrs. Eddy's Church Manual to support their arguments. Basing an opinion upon an independent reading of the manual, the Supreme Judicial Court of Massachusetts in 1922 ruled for the directors. Dixon and the trustees supporting him were dismissed.

Although this was purely a family affair based on theological differences, it disrupted the smooth operation of the paper and cost the *Monitor* heavily in circulation. An editorial hailing the end of this "unrighteous factional disturbance" declared that in the future the *Monitor* and other periodicals put out by the publishing society should have "the fostering care and loving guidance of the Board of Directors of the Mother Church."

The board named as editor Willis J. Abbot of New York, descendant of New England scholars and divines, whose newspaper experience had included working for Hearst. Under Abbot many of the paper's original taboos were relaxed, bureaus were established in foreign capitals, and lost circulation restored.

This was the paper to which Erwin Dain Canham (see photograph 12) came as a cub reporter in 1925 and upon which he carved a career that established him in the front ranks of the responsible national and world press.

Born in Auburn, Maine, on February 13, 1904, Canham early acquired the faith and facilities that were to lead him along that particular road. His father, Vincent Walter Canham, was a typesetter and reporter on the *Lewiston* (Maine) *Sun,* and his mother, who had been Elizabeth May Gowell, also wrote for the paper.

One of Canham's most lasting memories was of George W. Wood, editor of the *Sun,* a Democrat, isolationist, and free trader. Wood's opinions challenged if they did not shape those of the boy who saw him at work in his black silk skullcap, tugging at his typewriter, which he had arranged on a pulley so that he could push it out of his way when he wasn't using it.

Canham also remembered vividly riding with his father in the family buggy to gather news for the paper and later, at the family farm, penciling notes given to him over the phone by a local correspondent.

The elder Canhams were originally Methodists but they were converted to Christian Science when Erwin was a child and he was reared in the church.

When Erwin was ten, his father became editor and publisher of the *Sanford Star-News,* a weekly established by a group of State-of-Mainers who wanted a liberal outlet. Canham recalled that the plant had no linotype and relied mostly on boilerplate. Every Wednesday he would fold the four inside pages, and every Thursday he would fold them inside the four outside pages. Then he would go out to sell the paper. Admitting years later to an interviewer that the story was a "tear-jerker," Canham found it a pleasant introduction to newspaper business.

After two years at Sanford, the elder Canham was editor and publisher for another two years of the *Reporter-Journal* in Gardner. For the next five years he was compositor in the ad alley of the *Lewiston Sun* and ran his own print shop and farm on the side. Then he became agricultural editor of the *Lewiston Sun,* now combined with the *Journal.* Every day after school, on weekends and in summers, young Erwin worked on the paper as an office boy. He filled in as a reporter during the manpower shortage of the first World War, but after the armistice, he went back to work on galley proofs and bill collecting.

In 1921 Canham entered Bates College in his home town. His second summer vacation he served as counselor in a boys' camp, and by the end of his third year he was editor (and complete staff) of a small paper, *The Hilltop,* in Poland Springs, bringing his earnings up to $100 a week by corresponding at the same time for papers in Boston, Portland, Philadelphia, and New York.

At Bates, Canham won his Phi Beta Kappa key and led the college Outing Club, but debating was his forte. He was a member of the team that met the Oxford University debaters on their first visit to America. The subject was the entry of the United States into the League of Nations and, unfortunately, in the light of his eventual activities in the field of international cooperation, Canham's team drew the negative side of the question.

As a senior, Canham went abroad with the Bates team which competed with representatives of seven British schools. Later he became a Rhodes Scholar at Oxford.

Canham's intellectual and journalistic interests, as well as his religion, inevitably attracted him to the *Christian Science Monitor* and he applied for a job. In his cub-reporter days he shared an apartment with Roscoe Drummond of the *Monitor* who thought something more informal than "Erwin" was called for and took the inappropriate nickname "Spike" right out of the underworld. Canham was "Spike" from that day on.

In 1929 he returned from covering the League of Nations in Geneva for the *Monitor* to follow the American tour of Ramsay MacDonald, British Prime Minister. Returning again from three months at the London Naval Conference in 1930, Canham married Thelma Hart of Cape Cod, a girl on the *Monitor* staff he had met during his first year with the paper. They had two daughters, Carolyn and Elizabeth.

For two more years Canham reported the League of Nations

from Geneva. Then in 1932 he was sent to Washington as chief of the *Monitor*'s bureau there. From Washington he went forth from time to time on assignments that nourished his global viewpoint, to the London Economic Conference with the American delegation in 1933, to the inauguration of the Philippine Commonwealth Government in 1935.

Meanwhile, the Christian Science Church had erected opposite the Mother Church, at One Norway Street in Boston, a new four-million dollar structure for all its publications. The *Monitor* was housed on the second floor of the palatial block-long building, in pristine and spotless luxury. Smoking, drinking, swearing, and loud talk were frowned upon and a cathedral-like hush pervaded the precincts. The landscaped gardens and private offices were shut off from the outside world, but tourists were encouraged to visit the first-floor Mapparium, where, standing on a transparent bridge, they could see the whole world spread out around them, inside out, bright and glossy colors in baked glass setting off its areas.

Established in the new quarters, the *Monitor*'s editorial board, on the occasion of the paper's twenty-fifth anniversary, published a statement of aims and achievements:

Published in the United States, the *Christian Science Monitor* endeavors to go news-gathering in many countries with an understanding so patient and a sympathy so genuine as to arouse neither in itself nor in others any sense of being outside its own borders. . . .

There is no narrow nationalism in the *Monitor*. It has as its ideal a universal view of men and things. In its long experience the *Monitor* has found nothing impracticable in esteeming and treating the diverse human family as a unit. . . .

The *Monitor*'s treatment of its news involves looking below the surface of events in the shaping in order that something more than often misleading surface appearances may be presented to the reader. . . .

The value of this method of news treatment is shown in the reporting of anti-social news, whether it be political, economic or criminal. . . . By linking such effects to their actual causes, unmasking the fallacies that crime can long escape punishment or can bring prosperity or lasting satisfaction, or that it is necessary and to be expected, the *Monitor* divests crime of the false glamor that is likely to mesmerize the shocked reader and the often balked officer of the law.

The *Monitor* does not avoid crime news, as has sometimes been misstated, but in going into unconstructive situations it does so with a constructive intention. . . .

Willis Abbot had given up the editorship of the *Monitor* in 1927, and an editorial board had taken over while he roamed the world, bringing back genial tales from remote places of the *Monitor*'s farflung influence. Abbot passed on in 1934, after writing a book of reminiscences that bore the same title as his column in the *Monitor,* "Watching the World Go By."

On September 4, 1934 the editorial board printed a promise that it was "the goal of the *Monitor* to give to its readers a newspaper which will be vital, realistic and comprehensive, which will give to the good news, the encouraging news, and to the constructive news the prominence it rightly deserves." The board also pledged itself at the same time to ignore nothing "essential to the penetrating understanding of those aggravated social conditions to which the readers of the *Monitor* particularly can give healing attention."

In 1939 Erwin Canham was recalled to Boston to become the *Monitor*'s general news editor, and a year later he was made managing editor. There had been a number of managing editors between Abbot and Canham, among them Roscoe "Bulldog" Drummond, who came from the London office where he had directed the European staff, and who subsequently headed the Washington staff. Canham took over his new duties at about the time the revered old *Boston Transcript* was going through its death throes.

The *Transcript,* from its start in 1830, had maintained a reputation as the respectable, literate—and often reactionary— organ of the Brahmins, the cultured old Bostonians. As such, it was the butt of stories that are remembered as newspaper classics. One concerned the butler who announced to his Beacon Hill master: "Two reporters and a gentleman from the *Transcript.*" Another concerned the letter that came to the office: "Please cancel our subscription. Grandma just died."

In 1938, its circulation down to 30,000, the *Transcript* was forced into bankruptcy. Young Richard N. Johnson refinanced it, departmentalized it, streamlined its pages, and promoted it with ballyhoo. While staff veterans in shiny alpaca coats looked on in wonder, new blood was pumped in and lively progressive features introduced. Advertising increased a little, but circulation fell off to 15,000, and the paper gave up on April 30, 1941.

In the farewell issue, Luther Conant Jr., a *Transcript* columnist who had been given a free hand in combating Boston's racial and religious conflicts, wrote:

> There have been long and arid periods but for the last few years the paper was like the old *Transcript*—not the *Transcript* of legend, of T. S. Eliot, of the tattered story of the butler, the two reporters and the gentleman, of purple windows, but a paper that raised its voice for sanity and tolerance.
> For there was a staff on the *Boston Transcript* in these last few years as to make it the envy of city editors throughout the country.
> They were men and women of conviction—and they would be heard.
> At a time when the sparks of intolerance were burning brighter in Boston it was the *Transcript* that dared risk criticism and misunderstanding from one pressure group or the other, from a creed, from an advertiser.

Gentlemen from the *Transcript* scattered on Boston's other papers and most of them continued to talk nostalgically and affectionately about the *Transcript* as a high-minded and fine old institution. Others in Boston remembered the *Transcript* mostly as hidebound, class-conscious and reactionary—except in its frenetic last fight for life—addicted largely to antiquities and genealogy.

Although the *Monitor* had a national circulation around 150,000 it sold in Boston no more copies than did the stricken *Transcript*. When the *Transcript* disappeared, the *Monitor* made an open bid for its readers through an advertisement in the final issue. The *Monitor* was the logical heir to at least one of the *Transcript*'s traditions—that of dignity and refinement.

Admirers of the *Monitor* were not surprised when the paper sought to salvage what it could from the wreckage of the *Transcript,* but they were surprised when it made an out-of-character gesture in the direction of Bill Cunningham, Boston's most highly paid and widely read writer.

A week before the Presidential election of 1944, and the day before the *Monitor* formally came out for Thomas E. Dewey, it reprinted from the *Boston Herald* a typical anti-New Deal blast by Cunningham. Use of Cunningham's column brought a flood of protests from both *Monitor* readers and staff members, not alone because of its specific content but because of what Cunningham had come to represent in Boston journalism.

Cunningham's name had first made news in 1941 when he switched from the *Boston Post* to the *Herald* at $26,000 a year. Syndication of his column to other newspapers, radio broadcasts, speech-making, and magazine articles brought his income well above that amount.

"Nobody ever told me I was a columnist," Cunningham, a Texan who played center on Dartmouth's football team, once explained. "It started in a strange way. Clifton B. Carberry, mentor of the *Post,* realized that the paper was beginning to slip and wanted to liven it up. He decided to run a two-column head over the lead story on the sports page and set the story in larger type. After three or four years my stories appeared regularly in this space and I became a columnist. I was the original of these columnists and I don't give a damn who makes any claims to the contrary."

After Carberry died in 1939, Cunningham began to feel that the *Post* had become "the ghostship of American journalism." Robert B. Choate, of the *Herald* called Cunningham to his office and offered him a contract.

Early in his career on the *Herald* Cunningham raised a rumpus with a Sunday column that ridiculed postwar planners, suggested that they be "suspended for the duration, preferably by the neck, if no gentler means will suffice." Harvard professors protested the column. Publisher Choate replied that "some of you gentlemen in the higher seats of learning are wholly out of touch with what the man in the street thinks" and submitted some of Cunningham's fan mail as evidence.

This one attitude of Cunningham's and his method of expressing it would be enough to set him apart from the philosophy and personality of Erwin Canham, who was rapidly emerging as one of national journalism's outstanding representatives of international idealism expressed with reserve and moderation. Actually the decision to run Cunningham's column to support the *Monitor*'s political stand was not Canham's, but the church board's.

It was not until the next year, at the age of forty-one, that Canham was appointed editor of the *Monitor,* a title the paper had not used in eighteen years, in executive editorial charge of the paper but responsible on matters of business policy to the *Monitor* business manager and the board of trustees of the Christian Science Publishing Society and on editorial policies to the board of directors of the Mother Church.

It was fitting and characteristic that one of his first jobs as editor was to attend the organization meeting of the United Nations at San Francisco, referring to himself in the reports he sent back as "our man."

On his way home from San Francisco, Canham stopped in Los Angeles to receive the Helms Athletic Foundation award in recognition of the *Monitor*'s noteworthy achievements in the realm of sports. Canham took occasion to say that it was the purpose of the *Monitor*'s sport pages to tell the world that it is possible to compete keenly without bitterness or hatred.

Installed in an office that opened on the big, modern news room, Canham took to coming to work through the back door so that he could whiff printer's ink as he passed through the hospital-clean composing room.

A trained newspaperman with a respect for practicalities as well as ideals, and sensitive to criticism of his own paper as well as of the press in general, Canham looked for ways of bringing the *Monitor* closer to earth without compromising any of its standards.

For a period he kept a basket of apples beside his desk. At the morning editorial conference the news editor producing the snappiest anecdote to enliven the front page was given an apple as an award.

Searching for precedents for realistic reporting, Canham found that Mrs. Eddy, in the *Christian Science Sentinel,* another church publication, had included a news summary with reports of the Spanish-American War that gave totals of dead and wounded. At the height of the second World War the *Monitor* had printed a picture of a Normandy beach after D-Day. The photograph as used by other papers showed a corpse in the foreground, but the *Monitor* carefully retouched the corpse to make it look like a log. Questioned about the incident, Canham made no attempt to justify such overzealous application of the church's teachings; had he been consulted he would have printed the picture as it was or left it out altogether.

Canham, highly regarded among his colleagues as a competent and conscientious journalist, faced problems that most editors did not face. The *Monitor* had to make its pages seem timely to the great mass of readers outside Boston who received the paper anywhere from two to thirty days late, all the while keeping up with its local competition in Boston.

Eighty-five per cent of the *Monitor*'s circulation was outside Boston, and the paper was said to find its way to half a million readers in ninety-six countries. Its impact and influence were out of all proportion to its actual sales. About 90 per cent of the subscribers were Christian Scientists, with the largest blocs of readers in the Central States and the Far West, but the paper was read, cited, and quoted by countless others who had no connection with the church.

Canham had to see that the contents of the *Monitor* passed theological as well as journalistic tests, not always, in the eyes of those outside the faith, reconcilable. It was not part of his task, however, to proselytize. The paper confined its religious message to a single daily article, which was contributed by church members outside the staff and printed, along with a translation into some foreign language, on the Home Forum page. On the same page appeared a reproduction of some recognized work of art, with a brief expert description and a light literary essay or sketch.

A certain timelessness and leisureliness casts its spell over the *Monitor*. In the midst of war news, the reader might see a picture of cows grazing in Derbyshire and suggestions for a camping trip through rural England.

Professionally the *Monitor* got kudos—the Ayer award for typography, the Maria Moors Cabot award for distinguished service in inter-American relations, the University of Missouri award for distinguished service, among others.

Critics of a subsidized press complained that the *Monitor* enjoyed undue advantage because its church-owned property was tax-free. In a tax dispute with the City of Boston, the State Supreme Court ruled that the *Monitor*'s equipment was exempt because its dominant purpose was "to serve the religious cause of Christian Science."

As a Christian Scientist himself Canham continued to serve that cause in his personal as well as his professional life. He conducted a Sunday-school class at the "Mother Church" in Boston, and many of his public utterances carried a religious overtone.

Slim and broad-shouldered and of medium height, square-jawed, with iron-gray wavy hair, Canham like most of the men seen around the *Monitor* precincts, was healthy, smooth-shaven, and clean-cut, serious, serene, and scholarly in appearance and subscribed wholeheartedly to the abstemiousness imposed by the church.

"This may sound dramatic," he told Mary Braggiotti in an interview for the *New York Post*, "but we believe in the individual's right to be free—and not the slave to any particular habit that pushes him around."

In the postwar years Canham's name could be found on almost every committee, every forum, and every organization devoted to recognizing merit and to improving domestic standards of journalism and international understanding through the mass media of communication. Wherever he appeared, his undramatic manner, impressively straightforward and simple, gave weight to his words. He went to London in 1945 as a member of the Governor's Committee to bring the United Nations to Boston. He went to Geneva as United States representative at the United Nations Freedom of Information conference and later to Paris as a delegate on the Human Rights Commission. He served on the United States Advisory Committee on Information, which gave the State Department's Voice of America a clean bill of health at a time when it was under attack in Congress. He served on the *Editor & Publisher* responsibility panel and addressed meetings of editors and of journalism teachers, of industrialists and clubwomen. With it all he found time to broadcast weekly on the *Monitor*'s radio hour.

Convinced that the press had reached a crisis in public confidence, Canham dedicated himself to the achievement of a better understanding of its functions, on the part of its producers as well as its readers.

In the emotional aftermath of General Douglas MacArthur's relief of his Far Eastern command by President Truman in 1951, readers of the *Monitor,* like the readers of so many other papers, displayed their bewilderment. Some of them accused the *Monitor* of slanting the news, of interpreting events according to its own preconceived ideas, even of tendency toward "smear" tactics.

Editor Canham replied with a series of six articles on the front page of the *Monitor* entitled "How to Use Your Newspaper" in which he set out to explain press practices in general as well as the *Monitor*'s particular approach to the news.

Pointing out that, in much of the free world, newspapers in the past forty years had been evolving away from the violently partisan, biased organs they were during the nineteenth century and still were to some degree, he explained that there was an increasing effort to keep opinion or prejudice—though not interpretation—out of the news columns.

He continued:

The bare news event can be so misleading as to be false. For example, it is a customary editorial assumption that if an important man says it, it's

news. But what if the important man says something that is essentially a
lie? This happened often in the days of Herr Hitler and Doctor Goebbels.
It happens nowadays, and not only in Moscow. If we print only the press
association story of such a statement, we are flagrantly misinforming readers. It is not enough to catch up with the lie on the editorial page, a day
or two later.

We believe the balancing fact should be attached directly to the misleading assertion, if possible when it is published for the first time. We
think this is more important than hasty headlines. So we do not hesitate
to hold up a misleading story, until we can link it with the necessary
fact. . . .

News interpretation, with all its hazards, often is safer and wiser than
printing the bare news alone. Nothing can be more misleading than the
unrelated fact, just because it is a fact and hence impressive. Background,
motives, surrounding circumstances, related events and issues all need to
be understood and appraised as well as the immediate event. . . . But
interpretation requires integrity and knowledge and understanding and
balance and detachment.

News interpretation is all too readily misunderstood. Whenever the interpretations differ from the preconceived notions of the readers, misun-
derstanding is likely to creep in. Objectivity is a very elusive thing. It
usually means, to the individual, agreement with his own views.

However lightly such problems weighed on the consciences of
other Boston editors, they were the recurrent preoccupation of
successive groups of working newsmen who gathered year after
year at Harvard University, just across the Charles River.

These men were the beneficiaries of a foundation established
in 1937 by a bequest from Agnes Wahl Nieman in memory of
her husband, Lucius W. Nieman. For more than a half-century,
Nieman had been the "guff"-hating publisher of the *Milwaukee
Journal,* whose professional principles and concepts of staff
participation were effectively perpetuated on the paper after
his death by his long-time associate, Harry J. Grant.

The stated aim of the Nieman Foundation was "to promote
and elevate the standards of journalism in the United States
and educate persons deemed especially qualified for journalism." Among the first group of nine brought to Harvard was
Louis M. Lyons, topflight reporter on the *Boston Globe,* who
succeeded Archibald MacLeish the second year as "curator" of
the foundation. Working side by side with Arthur Meier Schles-

inger, Harvard's wise and mellow social historian who interested himself in the project from the start, Lyons guided Nieman Fellows at the rate of about a dozen a year thereafter. On leave of absence from their papers at a stipend approximating their regular salaries, the Fellows experienced nine months of class attendance in their chosen field, "hair-down" conferences with scholars and press leaders, mutual exchange of experience and contemplation among themselves and the Harvard faculty.

From his own experience, Lyons had become convinced that the important thing was that this should be a year of complete freedom of choice within the resources of the university. It shaped up as a highly individual experience. In newspaper shops throughout the land, Nieman Fellows today testify to the project's rewards and stimulation, and there can be little question that they have carried back to their day-to-day jobs a high conception of their calling.

Lyons himself, with his piercing eyes and Yankee twang, his keen mind and soft heart, humor and humility, was held in affectionate esteem by the newspapermen who came to know him, and his voice, like that of his neighbor Canham across the river, was heard wherever press discussions were conducted on a high plane. The intangible effect of his quiet influence, sifted into a hundred or more city rooms, established him as a maker of modern journalism as justifiably as those editors and publishers who had imposing plants and fortunes to show for it.

If Lyons and Canham were almost voices in the wilderness of their immediate surroundings—Boston's highly competitive and professionally spotty press—not far from Boston the conscience of the press had other outlets.

In Providence, Sevellon Brown and his sons built the *Journal,* with its evening *Bulletin,* into "The Bible of Rhode Island." The elder Brown, articulate like Canham in national press councils, was largely instrumental in establishing the American Press Institute, similar to the Nieman Foundation but more limited in time and less qualitative, which brought newspapermen to Columbia University in New York City for periods of intensive study and discussion about their practices and problems. In Hartford, Connecticut, Herbert Brucker helped John R. Reitemeyer revitalize his *Courant,* claimant to the distinction of being the country's oldest daily in continuous existence.

Meanwhile the famous old *Springfield Republican,* which was one of the nation's great independent newspapers of the nineteenth century under Samuel Bowles, had all but disappeared, its talents and traditions dissipated by his descendants.

The freedom for which the eighteenth-century New England editors fought was, on the whole, put to better use by twentieth-century editors in other farflung parts of the country.

23

Editors of the New South

SEVERAL EDITORS OF NATIONAL REPUTATION TODAY DOMINATE A South that once could boast of only two journalistic giants. These editors testify to the regional resurgence of which Henry W. Grady and Henry Watterson were the chief prophets.

Ralph McGill gave Grady's *Constitution* new vigor and stature that survived its mid-century combination with the *Atlanta Journal;* Barry Bingham and Mark Ethridge (see photograph 14) made Marse Henry's paper one of the most highly regarded in the nation at large even if Watterson did sever his connection with it three years before his death, disgusted with its support of President Wilson and the League of Nations.

The story of other Southern papers is worth telling, too, but that of the *Louisville Courier-Journal* easily comes first.

Judge Robert Worth Bingham, member of an old North Carolina family of longtime educators, who had turned to law and served as mayor after moving to Louisville, bought the morning *Courier-Journal* and the afternoon *Times* in 1917. He paid for the papers out of a fortune left to him by his second wife, the widow of Henry Flagler of Florida real estate and hotel renown.

In 1933 President Roosevelt appointed Judge Bingham Ambassador to Great Britain, and the papers were left in the hands of uninspired executives who were more impressed by the

profits on the *Times* ledger than they were by the tradition and
prestige of the *Courier-Journal*. Judge Bingham determined
that the sentimental and historical values of the *Courier-Journal*
must be preserved. On the lookout at home, Barry Bingham,
the Judge's son, liked what he heard about Mark Ethridge of
the *Richmond Times-Dispatch* in Virginia. Headed for Virginia Beach with his wife to meet the returning Judge, Barry
stopped off at Richmond, Mary Bingham's home town, and
persuaded a friend to invite Ethridge to dinner with them.
Ethridge accepted, not knowing that he was being looked over.
Proceeding from Virginia to the White House, Judge Bingham
remarked to the President, "I have come home to reorganize
my papers; I've got to get a new general manager and I'm
thinking about a young fellow down at Richmond, Mark Ethridge." President Roosevelt replied, "You couldn't do better."

The circumstances that brought Barry Bingham and Mark
Ethridge together resulted in one of journalism's most mutually
satisfying unions.

Born in Louisville on February 10, 1906, George Barry
Bingham was sent to Middlesex School in Concord, Massachusetts, and then to Harvard, where he was graduated *magna
cum laude* in English in 1928. At Cambridge he met Mary
Clifford Caperton, who was student correspondent of the *Christian Science Monitor* for Radcliffe and who played feminine
leads opposite him in college theatricals. They were married
in 1931.

After college Barry Bingham started to work as a police reporter on the *Louisville Times*. As part of his newspaper
apprenticeship he later served in the Washington bureau of the
Courier-Journal under Ulric Bell; worked on the paper's radio
station, WHAS, winning a Columbia Broadcasting System
award for the station's assistance in river-flood relief; and wrote
editorials. He conducted a personal investigation of Kentucky's
hospitals for the insane, which resulted in a series of articles
and a campaign for reform in the state's program of mental

care. The series led to an institutional system of construction and staffing.

While Barry Bingham continued learning the newspaper ropes, Ethridge, who was ten years older than young Bingham, set out to build up the paper and to establish himself in Louisville.

"Ethridge as a personality blends readily with the community," *Fortune* said. "If his thinking is hard, his drawl is soft; his hand curls gracefully around a julep glass, and in repose he is the picture of the shaggy, southern editor."

Ethridge was Southern clear through. Born in Meridian, Mississippi, in 1896, Mark was one of nine children in the family of a lawyer who had educated himself during the Reconstruction days. The elder Ethridge was, in the words of his son, "politically interested, a liberal for his day and one of the early advocates of public ownership of waterworks." Both parents were voracious readers, and young Mark had plenty of stimulation to read and to talk politics. One remark of the father's impressed the son strongly: "Nothing that embarrasses anybody is ever funny." That was one reason, Mark Ethridge realized later, that he was never able to enjoy jokes at the expense of Negroes.

While Mark was in school, his father gave him a horse and helped him get started on a paper delivery route. The elder Ethridge died in 1910 but Mrs. Ethridge lived on at Meridian into old age.

As a schoolboy, Mark Ethridge wrote sports stories for the *Meridian Dispatch* and a column called "Baseball Bubbles," which he signed Fanny. After graduation he worked for a year on the *Meridian Star*. He attended the University of Mississippi for a year but had to leave (when his money ran out because of the financial panic of 1915) and go to work as a reporter on the *Enquirer-Sun* in Columbus, Georgia.

"I wanted to learn every darn thing about the newspaper business," he recalled, "and I sought out the people I wanted to work for."

In Georgia he heard much about the progressive policies of the editors of the *Telegraph* in Macon. He got a job there, under a famous young editor, George Long, and the even more famous editor who succeeded Long, Colonel C. R. Pendleton.

"The consciousness of my inadequacy probably forced me to study a good deal more than I might if my preceptors had been mediocrities," he said.

Ethridge renewed his college studies for another year at Mercer University in Macon but was interrupted again in 1917, this time by America's entry into the first World War. Ethridge was never graduated, but Mercer gave him an honorary degree in later years in recognition of his achievements in journalism and in public life.

After serving in the Navy during the war Ethridge went back to Macon as city editor of the *Telegraph*. On the staff when he returned was a feature writer named Willie Snow, a spirited and dark-eyed Georgia girl with a quick sense of humor, whom he had met before the war. He used to take her out on his assignments and bring her back to sit around the office while he finished writing his stories. In Mark's absence at war, she had studied journalism at Wesleyan College in Macon, where one of her best friends was Mei-ling Soong, who later became the wife of Chiang Kai-shek, Generalissimo of the Chinese Nationalists. In 1921 Mark Ethridge and Willie Snow were married. The next year they went to New York where Mark worked for the *Sun* and the Consolidated Press for two years before returning to Macon. Mrs. Ethridge went on with her writing at home while rearing a family of four children, and produced a series of intimate, chatty diaries in book form as well as a novel set in the Southern textile mills.

Willie Snow Ethridge wrote for the *New York World* the first story to be published about the Warm Springs, Georgia, retreat for infantile paralysis victims and the site of the little White House where President Roosevelt died. It was Warm Springs that first brought Ethridge and President Roosevelt together. George Foster Peabody, Georgia banker and philanthropist, interested Roosevelt in going to the springs for the healing waters. Tom Loyless, columnist for the *Macon Telegraph,* who had taken over the springs, persuaded Roosevelt to write an occasional column for him, particularly on the subjects of erosion and conservation. Loyless invited Ethridge, along with a number of other guests, to dinner at Warm Springs with Roosevelt and a mutual admiration grew out of the meeting.

Ethridge's developing convictions, which paralleled many of Roosevelt's, had been deepened by the things he had seen happening around him. He began to wonder "why the hell you had a system that paid farmers five cents a pound for cotton that they produced at two or three times the cost." He saw a university in the South fall from about 1,000 students in one year to 200 the next year as a result of the price of cotton.

"You can chart pretty much the rise of tensions and prejudicial organizations in terms of economics," he told an interviewer once. "I saw more than 100 banks go busted one day in Georgia at the height of the Coolidge market boom. I became interested in what could be done about that and it naturally led to advocacy of guarantees of deposits and a stricter national bank system.

"The point I am making is that I think any liberal position I have taken has proceeded out of my own curiosity as to how and why things happen and if they are bad what can be done about them. I have no emotional bitterness about anything; I was never poor or mistreated."

In a speech entitled "Capitalism on the Defensive," made in the fall of 1931 before the civic clubs of several Georgia cities, Ethridge said:

In this country people go hungry because there is too much wheat; ragged because there is too much cotton; homeless because too many homes have been built; penniless because too much money lies idle in the banking vaults of the Nation; jobless because there are too many people willing to work. American capitalism has the greatest genius for obtaining production but it has made a monumental and disgraceful failure of obtaining distribution.

Uttered a full year and a half before inauguration of the New Deal, these words sounded the theme for the Democratic campaign and blueprinted some of the legislation introduced by President Roosevelt.

His interests expanding, Mark Ethridge went abroad in 1933 on an Oberlaender Trust fellowship to study the workings of the Versailles Treaty. When he got back to the *Macon Telegraph* a second time, he found that the paper had reversed its policies and he left there "by mutual consent." He then worked for a while for the Associated Press, but, in his own words, "I was beginning to lose my illusions and found that the AP had no soul." The *Washington Post* under Eugene Meyer was at the time endeavoring to regain its soul; Ethridge went there first as associate editor and then as assistant general manager.

In 1934 Ethridge transferred to Richmond to become general manager and publisher of the *Times-Dispatch*. It was there that Barry Bingham discovered him and induced him to go to Louisville as vice-president and general manager of the papers.

A year later when their sole rival, the *Herald-Post,* shut down, Ethridge waived exclusive rights to the Associated Press franchise to clear the way for any possible contenders. That year the elder Bingham died, and Barry, who had been made publisher before his father's death, worked hand-in-hand with Ethridge in restoring the paper's independent and progressive spirit.

Bingham and Ethridge permitted the afternoon *Times* to keep much of its original character of noncommittal provinciality, under the able editorship of Tom Wallace. Wallace, lean and dry descendant of pioneering Kentucky farmers, admirer and biographer of Colonel Watterson, was the papers' living link with their past. Beyond Louisville, he distinguished himself personally by his persistent promotion of conservation and Latin-American neighborliness, by his sharp rebukes to fellow editors for their subservience to syndicated columnists and for their conception of freedom of the press "as the right of a circulation truck to go through a red light."

When Barry Bingham was ordered to London by the Navy in 1942, he relinquished the title of publisher of the Louisville papers to Ethridge. Since 1946 he has been editor of the *Courier-Journal* and president of the newspaper corporation.

Bingham served thirty-nine months of overseas duty, first as public relations officer for the U.S. Naval Forces in the European theater, later as press officer at advance headquarters of the Pacific Fleet. He witnessed the Japanese surrender on the U.S.S. *Missouri* in 1945. He was discharged that year with the rank of commander and the Bronze and Silver Stars.

After his return to Louisville he broke ground for the expensive new plant of the two papers, Station WHAS, and other enterprises. In 1947 Bingham toured occupied Europe with other American editors, and in 1949 he was named chief of the Economic Cooperation Administration's mission to France, where he served for a year.

Ethridge, too, had been on constant call to serve his government in one capacity or another. He was first chairman of the Fair Employment Practices Committee created by President Roosevelt to handle cases of discrimination in the defense industries and an adviser for the Office of War Information. Secretary of State Byrnes sent him to Bulgaria, Russia, and Rumania on a reportorial mission in preparation for the Moscow conference of December 1945. The report he brought back led the State Department to inform the Moscow-dominated Bulgarian government that a new administration elected under the existing undemocratic conditions would not be recognized by the United States.

Two years later President Truman named Ethridge as American representative on the United Nations Commission to investigate disorders along the Greek border.

When either Ethridge or Bingham left Louisville on a public errand, the other would take over the duties of editor and publisher. After his return from service, Bingham served as active editor, writing more editorials than anybody on his staff.

Mary Bingham sits in on editorial councils when Barry is

away and has written some of the paper's most free-swinging, hard-hitting editorials. Mrs. Bingham, blonde and blue-eyed, with chiseled features, concentrates for the most part on her job of running the book page. Most staffers find Barry and Mary Bingham readily accessible.

At a Kiwanis Club luncheon one day Mary Bingham accepted for the *Courier-Journal* a plaque honoring the paper's community service. After a few words about what the paper strove to accomplish, she interrupted herself, in shy surprise, with the remark, "But I'm beginning to talk like a publisher myself."

The Binghams made a comfortable home for their five children on a large estate off the River Road a few miles east of Louisville and not far from the Ethridges.

Ethridge, who, by his own volition, owned no stock in the papers he published, kept in the forefront of public opinion by his independent, outspoken utterances, and often proved a thorn in the side of his more orthodox fellow publishers. In one speech he discussed reasons for much of the public's apparent distrust of the press. He attributed it partly to the fact that some publishers regarded freedom of the press as the right to be as vicious as they wanted to be and as a special privilege exempting them from any legislative action.

Most American newspapers, Ethridge charged, were organs of business, not run from the editorial side, and "cannot talk about a rounded America because they cannot understand what is going on in the minds of organized labor, of the white collar worker and the farmer." He admonished his colleagues to "give up their dreams of being big shots wielding political power" and to "root policies in a philosophy rather than in economic or political alliances and prejudices."

Ethridge's name came first in a tribute to liberal Southern editors written for the *Chicago Sun* by Carroll Kilpatrick, a thoughtful reporter from Alabama.

"Today Ethridge is universally regarded as one of the most forceful, intelligent and progressive newspapermen in America," Kilpatrick wrote. "He is a vigorous, hard worker, a zealous believer in democracy and an editor who is constantly alive to the responsibilities which freedom of the press implies."

For the monopoly publisher those responsibilities were heavy.

"I believe Louisville is the second-largest single ownership city in America, exceeded only by Kansas City," Barry Bingham once said. "I do not envy Roy Roberts the honor of leading that parade. . . . Monopoly forces a newspaper management to think over its course of action with painful care, to generate within itself ever rising goals of public service."

Although Ethridge and Bingham gave every evidence of recognizing monopoly's obligation in the marketplace of fact, their construction of opinion—outside of their own editorial candor—could be questioned, and was.

Among the syndicated columns the *Courier-Journal* published were those of Marquis Childs, a progressive of the New Deal school, with whom it often concurred editorially, and of Westbrook Pegler, a violent reactionary, with whom it wholly differed. To pose Pegler's out-of-key diatribes against Childs' thoughtful liberalism seemed to critics to put too heavy a burden upon the reader; rather than giving balance, it weighed frenzied emotion against calm questioning; it seemed as great a disservice to honest conservatives as it was to honest liberals. Bingham countered, however, by increasing the columnar confusion. He brought in the column of George Sokolsky, an angry Pegler-style writer, rather than substituting for Pegler—as critics had hoped—a quieter conservative spokesman like David Lawrence.

Recognizing Ethridge's role as the nation's "reluctant monopolist," *Fortune* noted that the *Courier-Journal* was distinctive for its intense reportage and high cultural content as well as for its strong-voiced editorial page, and added:

. . . it is important to underscore the fact that the *Courier-Journal*, though its heart is certainly in the city room, does not lack brains and ambition for the counting house. The *Courier-Journal* was one of the first papers to put out a locally edited type of gravure supplement, and its big plant prints fifteen such magazines for other newspapers. It also prints the *Police Gazette,* numerous trade papers, and two million copies weekly of the syndicated newspaper supplement, *Parade.* It is easy to see why no gentleman of the press, either amateur or pro, has accepted Marse Ethridge's chivalrous invitation to compete.

While Mark Ethridge was applying elsewhere the talents he acquired in Georgia, Ralph Emerson McGill had risen to the premier editorship of that state.

Ralph McGill was born of Scotch-Welsh descent on a farm near the Tennessee town of Scoddy on February 5, 1898, the son of Lou Skillern McGill and Benjamin Franklin McGill. He went to the private McCallie School in Chattanooga and to Vanderbilt University, where he played star tackle on the football team and "profaned about the periphery" of the literary group of "Fugitives." After serving in the Marine Corps in the first World War, he returned to Vanderbilt, where he got into trouble with the administration there.

In his editorial column in the weekly *Vanderbilt Hustler,* McGill accused the administration of embezzlement, using for other purposes a fund that a bachelor professor had bequeathed for the establishment of a students' lounging room. McGill was suspended as editor and placed on probation.

McGill had a part-time job on the *Nashville Banner* and, with two other student-reporters, had dance invitations printed to duplicate those sent out by a fraternity that was politically strong on the campus. The invitations got into the hands of unlikely guests, including inmates in institutions in what was called "the restricted district."

"I am not particularly proud of this, although in those salad days, it seemed like a great idea," McGill recalled later. "This, coming on top of the other events which had put me on probation, caused the Chancellor and me to part company."

Leaving Vanderbilt without graduating, McGill went to work full-time on the *Nashville Banner,* where his fellow alumnus, James Stahlman (later publisher and quondam president of the American Newspaper Publishers Association) was then city editor. He wrote politics until the sports editor left and then was put in the latter's place "until we can find someone else."

The hours were better, the pay was better, he had more freedom to come and go, and so McGill stayed in sports. While on the *Banner,* McGill wrote a folksy humor column called "I'm the Gink," which was syndicated for about five years.

Late one night the father of the girl who was to become McGill's wife saw him in a row in a "dog wagon," a sandwich shop on wheels. McGill took the part of a Vanderbilt freshman who was being bullied by a drunk in the place. "When I began to call on Mary Elizabeth Leonard," McGill once said, "it is fair to say that her parents had a dim view of me."

McGill remained with the *Banner* until 1929 when he moved to Georgia to write sports for the *Atlanta Constitution,* the powerful organ of three generations of the Howell family. Two years later he became sports editor, taking as his model in the field of sports the hearty prose of W. O. McGeehan of the *New York Herald Tribune.*

All the while McGill did features for the paper on his own time. His series on share-cropping and farm-tenant conditions attracted the attention of the Rosenwald Foundation, and in 1937 he was given a $1,700 fellowship for travel and study of small cooperative and marketing methods in Scandinavia.

About six months after McGill's arrival in Europe, Hitler marched into Austria and McGill went in right behind the Germans. "Never until I saw there in Austria the physical disappearance of freedom of the press," he remarked, "did it become something vital. Not until then did I become coldly angry to see it abused and prostituted in the United States."

Upon his return to Atlanta in 1938, McGill was made executive editor of the *Constitution.* He took over the full editorship in 1941, maintaining the policy established for the paper in the 1880's by Henry Woodfin Grady of an outspoken, signed editorial column.

McGill, big and energetic, husky-voiced, assumed leadership of the fight against Eugene Talmadge and managed the successful campaign of Ellis Arnall for the governorship. The Ku

Klux Klan marched around the *Constitution* building threatening violence.

When a veterinarian from Indiana, James A. Colescott, was chosen Imperial Wizard of the Klan, McGill wrote: "For the first time the Klan has chosen a proper man, a veterinarian skilled in dealing with dumb animals."

Despite McGill's fight, in which the *Atlanta Journal* and other Georgia newspapers joined, "Ol' Gene" Talmadge and later his heir, Herman, won back the governorship, but the campaign against the Klan won out. Governor Herman Talmadge was eventually forced to sign a bill passed by the Legislature banning the wearing of masks and hoods and other terroristic practices of the Klan.

The American Society of Newspaper Editors named McGill chairman of a committee to study the status of the world's press and to seek equality of access to news all over the world. After a globe-circling tour with the two other members of the committee, McGill produced a 50,000-word report. The Truman Administration sent him on a flight to Europe and the Middle East to study the problem of displaced persons. Later he became chairman of a committee of educators, editors, publishers, and civic leaders to further legislation for the State Department's overseas information program. In that role, McGill took a stand, unpopular with the run-of-the-mill editor and publisher, in sharp criticism of the refusal of the Associated Press and the United Press to cooperate fully with the government in that program.

Through the years, and more recently under the ownership of James Cox and the editorship of Wright Bryan, the rival *Atlanta Journal* had outclassed the *Constitution* in circulation and news coverage. The two papers were merged in 1950 under the joint ownership of Cox and Clark Howell, but continued to publish separately, with Bryan as editor of the *Journal* and McGill as editor of the *Constitution*.

The merger left McGill's personal status and influence unchanged. It did, however, place Atlanta in the growing list of

American cities with a single-ownership press like Louisville's.

So, too, with Richmond, Virginia, the city that Ethridge had left in 1936, to the keen disappointment of the reporters for whom he had raised salaries and encouraged colorful writing. The Richmond newspapers, controlled by the family of D. Tennant Bryan, contributed not one, but two, distinguished names to Southern journalism.

Until his retirement from the evening *News Leader* in 1949 at the age of sixty-three, after a service of thirty-four years, scholarly Douglas Southall Freeman, bald and bespectacled, was an industrious editor, more widely known to the nation as a Pulitzer prize-winning historian.

Freeman had said that he always yearned to list himself in *Who's Who* as a tramp newspaperman, but the listing actually is notable for its recording of a succession of honorary degrees, of teaching, of public service, and of important books. Freeman became convinced early that "newspaper work is just writing in the sand" and, donning a black skullcap, set down his studies in permanent form, particularly a four-volume *Robert E. Lee* and a six-book project on the life of George Washington. Cutting out social activities and budgeting his time to the minute, even for breakfast, he managed at the same time to continue his newspaper work, giving a morning newscast, and conduct a "Lessons in Living" radio program on Sundays.

On Richmond's other paper, the *Times-Dispatch,* the editor since 1936 (the year that Ethridge left there) had been Virginius Dabney, tall, broad-shouldered, and brown-eyed. Like Barry Bingham, Dabney came from a background of Southern scholarship, and like Ethridge, he advanced his own studies in Europe on an Oberlaender fellowship. His father, Dr. Richard Heath Dabney, was for forty-nine years professor of history at the University of Virginia. Virginius was born, on February 8, 1901, and brought up in the shadow of the Lawn at Charlottesville. The only boy in a family of three, he was taught at home by his father and a great-aunt before being sent, at thirteen, to Episcopal High School in Alexandria. He was editor of the school paper there and completed his course at sixteen, the youngest graduate in the school's history. He got his bachelor's and master's degrees at the University of Virginia, where he helped edit the school annual and played on the tennis team.

Dabney taught algebra and French at Episcopal High School before becoming a reporter on the *Richmond News Leader* in 1922. He joined the editorial staff of the *Times-Dispatch* in 1928 and became chief editorial writer in 1934, tilting, according to Gayle Waldrop, author of *Editor and Editorial Writer*, "at almost every Southern household god." In 1947 his editorials won him a Pulitzer prize.

Southern editors rarely satisfied Northern reformers in their stand on racial questions and, on that score, Dabney was no exception. Of President Truman's civil rights program he said: "The President is trying to make us swallow too much at once."

He no more opposed segregation of Negroes and whites, for instance, than did any other Southern editor but, along with Ethridge, he opposed the poll tax, which deprived so many Southern citizens of the vote, and he sought better educational and health facilities for all.

Yet another editor who personified the spirit of the New South, Jonathan Daniels of North Carolina, got his newspaper start in Louisville, on the *Times,* soon after Judge Bingham took over. Like Barry Bingham and so many other American editors, he inherited the newspaper urge. His father, Josephus Daniels, more generally known as statesman, author, and President Wilson's Secretary of the Navy, set high journalistic standards for his son to meet.

Josephus Daniels, born in Washington, North Carolina, in 1862, went to work as a printer's devil before he was twelve. At eighteen he was editor of the *Wilson Advance,* a tricounty Carolina weekly. His mother mortgaged their home to let him buy out his partners on the *Advance,* and later he and his brother established the *Free Press* in nearby Kinston. Then he acquired the *Raleigh State Chronicle* and the *Farmer and Mechanic,* which he merged.

Josephus Daniels sold the *Chronicle,* started the weekly *North Carolinian* and then bought the *Raleigh News and Observer,* consolidating the others with it.

Jonathan, his third son, was born in Raleigh on April 26, 1902. He went to the old Centennial School there and to the University of North Carolina, where he edited the university newspaper, getting an A.B. degree in 1921 and a master's the following year. After that he went to the Columbia Law School in New York and was admitted to the North Carolina bar, though he never practiced.

His childhood was made memorable by the excursions he took with his father, who believed that an editor's business was "moving as much as writing." After marrying Elizabeth Bridgers of Raleigh and serving out his reportorial apprenticeship in Louisville, Jonathan went to Washington as correspondent for his father's paper in Raleigh. His wife died in 1929, and he went abroad alone on a Guggenheim Fellowship, traveling in France, Germany, and Italy. He wrote a novel, *The Clash of the Angels,* based on hedonist-moralist conflict, before joining the editorial staff of *Fortune* in 1930. Two years later he married Lucy Billing Cathcart of Leonia, New Jersey, and returned to Raleigh to become associate editor of the *News and Observer.*

In 1933, when President Roosevelt appointed Josephus Daniels Ambassador to Mexico, Jonathan took over the editorship of the paper, while his brothers, Josephus and Frank, ran the business departments. He commented, tongue in cheek, that he had expected that his father, with his penchant for politics, would have settled all the usual editorial problems, but Jonathan Daniels found plenty left to do.

He campaigned against the Duke Power Company when it opposed the installation of power plants by the Public Works Administration. He campaigned to close North Carolina tobacco warehouses when the market was glutted and prices low, and he conducted a crusade that resulted in the closing of the warehouses until a plan for crop control and price supports could be worked out. He drove 3,000 miles through the South, visited the Tennessee Valley Authority, cotton plantations, the Delta country, and industrial centers to get material for a widely hailed book, *A Southerner Looks at the South.*

After Josephus Daniels returned from Mexico in 1941, he resumed the editorship of his paper, relieving Jonathan to go into wartime government activities. Jonathan served first as assistant director in the Office of Civilian Defense, and then became one of President Roosevelt's six secretarial assistants, the group that the President said he hoped would have "a passion for anonymity." Jonathan Daniels remained close to the White House after President Roosevelt's death and out of his intimacy with President Truman produced the book, *The Man of Independence,* a frank and unofficial, but admiring, portrait.

Following the death of Josephus Daniels in 1948, Jonathan went back to running the paper, a task made challenging by the character his father had given it. Known to its foes as the "Nuisance and Disturber," the *News and Observer,* for which the Daniels family had refused Hearst's offer of a million dollars, was operated on the principle voiced by Josephus Daniels that "Dullness is the only crime for which an editor ought to be hung."

Farther down in the Deep South, a new name had emerged in less traditional fashion than the names of Bingham and Daniels. Hodding Carter, educated at Bowdoin, Columbia, and Tulane, started the *Daily Courier* in his birthplace, Hammond, Louisiana, in 1932, at the age of twenty-five, after gaining his initial journalistic experience on press associations and newspapers in New Orleans.

Four years later he founded the *Delta Star* in Greenville, Mississippi, and became editor and publisher of the *Delta Democrat-Times* there in 1939. He left his paper in charge of associates to go to Harvard as a Nieman Fellow. From there he went to New York where he briefly edited the press page of the newborn newspaper *PM.*

After serving through the war with the Army Bureau of

Public Relations in Washington and as editor of the Middle East editions of *Yank* and *Stars and Stripes,* he was retired as a major, with a War Department citation, and returned to Greenville. Almost immediately he began to win for himself and his newspaper professional awards and nation-wide publicity. Editor Carter, *Time* said, was "a determined but unfanatical liberal who believes the South can best solve its own problems" and "has concentrated on building up respect between races and between religions."

In 1951 Carter and his general manager, John T. Gibson, spread out from Greenville and bought the two-and-a-half-year-old *Natchez Times.* In a lead editorial, he wrote: "We want [the *Times*] to be a mirror in which the community can see its full face. If the face appears smudged sometimes it will not be the fault of the newspaper. . . . We won't seek controversy for the sake of controversy or shun it for the sake of peace."

In speeches, articles, books, and his syndicated column, which appeared in sixteen other papers, Carter challenged Northern critics.

Without fanfare, and with varying techniques and success, other Southern editors dedicated their papers to helping the South to understand itself and interpret its problems to the rest of the nation.

24

Editors of the New West

IN TEXAS TED DEALY COULD TURN FOR INSPIRATION TO THE BRAVE
words of his father, engraved in huge letters across the slab-
front of the new plant of the *Dallas Morning News*:

> Build the *News* upon the rock of truth and righteousness, conduct it
> always upon the lines of fairness and integrity, acknowledge the right of
> the people to get from the newspaper both sides of every question.

Or, W. P. Hobby, one-time Governor, could point proudly to
the national swathe cut by his wife, Oveta Culp Hobby, wartime WAC colonel and the real power of the *Houston Post*.

William R. Matthews, a publisher who remained a reporter,
could give thanks for the lucky circumstance that prevented
him from boarding the plane carrying a dozen other newspapermen to their deaths in India in 1949 and permitted him to
return to his *Tucson Daily Star* in Arizona.

Santa Rosa could point to something new, brought to California small-city journalism with quiet dedication by William
Townes from his experience accumulated in Cleveland, Carolina, and Spokane.

Bigger publishers round about sat up and took notice when
Houston Waring made the name of the *Independent* mean
something in Littleton, just outside Denver.

From the Great Plains to the Coast, from Puget Sound to
San Diego, others like them could be spotted, but nobody

typified the passing of the frontier and the taming of the West more graphically than did Palmer Hoyt (see photograph 13) of Oregon and Colorado.

Although it still startled strangers with flaming red headlines on pink paper, the polished *Denver Post* of "Ep" Hoyt was as far a cry from the crude *Post* of Tammen and Bonfils as Gene Autry was from Jesse James.

Large and shuffling, heavy-lidded and gruff-voiced, Hoyt brought his sleepy looks and aggressive action to the *Post* in 1946 from Portland, Oregon, where he had carved out his career. Hoyt early dropped the name Edwin, given to him by his mother and Baptist-pastor father at birth, March 10, 1897, in Roseville, Illinois. He was taken by his parents to New England when he was a small boy. They lived in Massachusetts and later in Vermont, then moved to Montana. Palmer went to grade school in Vermont and Montana and prep school at William Jewell in Missouri.

At twenty Hoyt was sent to France with the American Expeditionary Force and advanced from private to sergeant-major. Discharged in 1919, he went back to school, enrolling in the University of Oregon. While a student, he married Cecile De Vore, and on his graduation day in 1923 his first son, Palmer, was born.

Hoyt entered newspapering in the cattle round-up town of Pendleton, where he was telegraph and sports editor of the *East Oregonian*. Then he moved to the metropolis of the state, Portland, where he became a copyreader on the *Oregonian*.

The oldest West Coast paper in continuous publication, for many years the *Oregonian* remained in the hands of Henry Lewis Pittock and Harvey W. Scott, who was the best known West Coast editor of his generation. Since Scott's death in 1910, the paper had been without the guiding hand of a strong personality and Hoyt found the way ahead clear.

Writing wild west fiction on the side—several novels and some fifty short stories—Hoyt rose steadily from reporter to drama editor, to night city editor, to executive news editor, to managing editor. Earthy and unaffected, he got to know people easily, went golfing and fishing with them.

In 1938 Hoyt became publisher of the *Oregonian* and kept it ahead of its opposition by dressing up its typography, revamping its departments, emphasizing pictures. A stickler for separation of news from opinion, he also insisted upon editorial nonpartisanship, although the *Oregonian* and Hoyt himself were almost inextricably associated with Republicanism.

After Gardner Cowles Jr. left the Domestic Branch of the Office of War Information in the Spring of 1943, Director Elmer Davis, needing for balance another Republican who had the confidence of the publishing world, called upon Hoyt. Even while Hoyt was traveling from Portland to Washington on a six months' leave from his paper, the House was voting to wipe out the domestic activities of the OWI. Hoyt appeared before Congress soon after his arrival and made a conciliatory speech in which he promised to release the fullest possible news as quickly as possible, to avoid propaganda, pamphleteering, and sugar-coating of military setbacks, and pledged the agency to yield to no political pressure and serve no political interests. The Senate reversed the House action and the OWI got its funds.

Hoyt appointed an advisory committee that included editors who had been hostile to the OWI and speeded up coverage of military engagements.

His OWI stint completed, Hoyt went back to Portland but didn't stay there long. The *Oregonian* still prospered, but its stock was scattered among four families, none of them engaged in its actual operation and all anxious to sell.

In Denver, since the death of Tammen in 1924 and Bonfils in 1933, the *Post* had lost much of its fire and its circulation had fallen, although it remained the largest in the Rocky Mountain States. In 1946 William C. Shepherd, the old Tammen-Bonfils managing editor who had been directing the paper, was seventy-one and ready to retire. E. Ray Campbell, lawyer-president of the concern and the Bonfils heirs, asked Hoyt to take over.

Given a free hand, Hoyt revived the vigor of the editorial page without its old venality, retaining the motto, published daily, "There is no hope for the satisfied man," and giving the editorial-page line "So the People May Know" an uncynical sincerity it had not known under its old operators. He increased local and regional coverage, sharpened news leads, gave more space to interpretation, features, and pictures.

The *Post,* with its glaring headlines, gaudy colors, and circus makeup, was a Denver habit, however, and Hoyt did not change that all at once. Modified somewhat, it still looked like the old *Post.*

With the old "Bucket of Blood" on Champa Street left far behind, Hoyt, in May 1950, opened the new $6,000,000 plant of the *Post* in downtown Denver, with its big new presses and its electrically heated sidewalk outside for melting the snow.

The prominent part played in the ceremonies by Helen Bonfils was the only reminder of the paper's past. Miss Bonfils, daughter of the co-founder, is treasurer and, with Hoyt and E. Ray Campbell, one of the three directors of the corporation that owns the *Post.* Her major interest lies with the theater and the benefactions established by her father.

Soon after moving to the new plant, Hoyt decided that it was "time to pause, recapitulate and prepare to recommence." He reduced the number of assignments of correspondents in Europe and in other cities in the United States, cut overtime work to a minimum, instituted other economies. Hoyt was obviously harassed by labor negotiations, newsprint costs, and the other problems that beset the modern publisher-editor, but to those who knew him and his record, the pause on the *Post* resembled one of those catnaps "Ep" had been observed taking on public platforms as a means of conserving energy for a new spurt.

The very week that Hoyt announced the shakedown he started a big new magazine called *Empire,* to be delivered, like the daily, by bicycle, burro, and plane throughout all the thirteen Rocky Mountain Empire states, which Hoyt had adopted as his domain.

In Hoyt's personal life as well, the move to Denver meant a new beginning. He moved into the penthouse of the once fabulous, still glamorous Brown Palace, where cattle kings and cowhands stride about in hats and spurs and dine coatless if they choose, and remarried.

Hoyt's elder son, Edwin Palmer, went to work for the *Post* soon after his father took over but resigned after a short time to go to San Francisco as night city editor of the *Chronicle*. Later when the editorial page editorship on the *Post* was vacant because of the death of Fred Colvig in a Bombay plane crash, Edwin Hoyt was the applicant to whom the editorial board gave the job. In 1951, when the International Typographical Union began to set up its own press, Edwin Hoyt went to the ITU paper in Colorado Springs. His younger brother, Charles Richard (Dick) was employed in the advertising department of the *Cheyenne* (Wyoming) *State Tribune*.

Supplementing the story he had told four years earlier in the *Journalism Quarterly* about the energizing "chinook" that had blown through Champa Street, Gayle Waldrop wrote in 1951:

> The "Voice of the Rocky Mountain Empire" has replaced "The Best Newspaper in the United States" in the *Post*'s nameplate. The reborn newspaper has achieved in large measure its new aspiration; the old one, in exuberant frontier fashion, had set itself an unattainable goal.
>
> Some years before 1946 the newspaper was not averse to being known as "the paper with a heart and soul." Since its rebirth five years ago it has achieved recognition as a newspaper with a head, and a sense of social responsibility. The old slogan is more colorful and quotable but the *Post*'s new character is more in keeping with today's needs. . . .
>
> Hoyt has kept the vigor of the old. He has stamped the new with his vitality, which is motivated strongly by the ideals of Sigma Delta Chi, of which he has been national president, and of which in 1949 he was elected a Fellow.

Farther west, in San Francisco, the retirement of Chester Rowell to the seclusion of a corner of the editorial page until his death at eighty in 1948, and the emergence of young, red-headed, freckle-faced Paul Clifford Smith as editor in 1935 bridged the gap between past and present and launched a new era for the *Chronicle,* easily the worthiest major newspaper on the Pacific Coast.

Smith's restless questing and ambition had carried him far and wide before he settled on the *Chronicle,* and once there, he refused to stay put, either in mind or body.

Smith's father, who was in the brokerage business in New York, died some months before Paul's birth in Seattle, Washington, on November 24, 1908. Paul spent most of his early childhood in Victoria, British Columbia, where he was privately tutored. Then he moved south to Pescadero, a fishing village on the California coast, because he had friends who lived on a ranch nearby. He finished high school there precociously at fourteen.

More interested in seeing the world than in going longer to school, Smith got a job in the Saskatchewan wheat fields and then rode the freights eastward through Canada to Ontario, where he looked in vain for gold. He came back west by freight again to go logging in British Columbia before he went on another futile search for gold, this time in the hot Mojave Desert of Southern California. Then, as a coal-digger, he ranged all the way from Utah to Pennsylvania. Next, he progressed to a white-collar job in Eugene, Oregon, where he ran a sporting goods store and taught golf on the side to promote his sales, although his own game wasn't good.

In the late twenties, in the face of the market crash, Smith's interest turned to the financial world. After being a bond trader for a while in San Francisco, he became resident manager in New York for the Anglo-California bank, and then returned to California to put his money-training to use as financial columnist for the *Chronicle.* He took time off from this job at the depth of the depression to go to Europe on a borrowed $500 and get interviews with Mussolini and Hitler.

When Herbert Hoover went home to Palo Alto from the White House in 1933, a defeated and bitter man, he read in Smith's column criticism of New Deal measures and of Roose-

velt's "baloney dollars," and he liked what he read. Hoover
and Smith became acquainted, and the former President urged
the young columnist to be his personal secretary. Smith declined, but a close personal friendship continued through the
years, cemented by association at the annual Bohemian Club
outing in the Northern California forest, where they were
members of the same camp.

It was one of the paradoxes of Smith's character that his two
heroes of the time were Hoover and Lincoln Steffens, whose
divergent philosophies few others were able to reconcile.

San Francisco's general strike in 1934, precipitated by a dispute between shipowners and the longshoremen's union, found
the *Chronicle* lined up with the other papers—even to the
extent of reprinting Hearst editorials along with the Hearst-
owned opposition—in a concerted effort to break the strike. It
was an uncompromising struggle on both sides that led to a
boycott against the *Chronicle* and other papers by union labor.

Paul Smith, who was on good terms with longshoremen's
leader, Harry Bridges, did much to heal the scars. The following year, when a strike broke out in the Salinas lettuce fields to
the south, Smith arranged for complete coverage and printed
a series of articles called "It Can Happen Here," which attracted national attention to the fascistlike factors of the fight
to stem the strike.

The *Chronicle*, to which sound businessmen had regularly
turned for counsel, printed a front page editorial by Smith
summarizing the issues at stake and suggesting that the strikers
might have a basis for their demands. When the strike was
finally settled, Smith got much of the credit.

After Smith was promoted to general manager in 1937, ship-
ping in San Francisco Bay was again tied up for weeks by a
longshoremen's and warehouse workers' strike. When Smith,
on the front page, demanded that both sides make peace, both
employers and workers told him to mind his own business. The
Chronicle retorted editorially that it made it its business "to
stick its nose into any so-called private row which affects broad

public interests." Smith was named mediator in the strike and got an agreement after twelve days.

When Herbert Hoover toured Europe in 1938 and interviewed world leaders, Smith went along with him. After he came back to San Francisco he was petitioned to run for mayor but he stayed on the *Chronicle,* saying "a conscientious newspaperman can be of real service to his country."

As the world teetered on the brink of war, Smith made a tour of the country and wrote four articles, "The Way Out for America," in which he suggested an all-America council with twenty-five leaders as diverse as Eleanor Roosevelt and John L. Lewis, Charles Evans Hughes and William Green.

Wendell Willkie caught Smith's fancy, as he did that of so many other Republican editors who were not content with the Old Guard's choices, and in April 1940 he launched a California campaign for Willkie, with the aid of Bartley C. Crum and Oren J. Root.

All the while the *Chronicle* had been broadening its horizon and reflecting the searching instincts of its editor. Smith turned over a page of the paper to a Monday Meeting, in which authorities in all fields discussed freely the problems of the day.

Smith made a five weeks' trip to England in 1941 at the request of the State Department to observe British defense efforts. He came back doubting that England could be invaded and convinced that the Atlantic was the crucial area.

As a naval reserve officer, Smith left the *Chronicle* after the United States entered the war to serve as lieutenant commander. He was immediately appointed to a press post. He transferred from there to the Office of War Information to be chief of the news bureau.

After a few months in the OWI, Smith made another of those unpredictable moves that characterized his whole career. He had given up a $25,000-a-year job to come to Washington and now he tossed over his $9,000-a-year job there to enlist in the Marines as a private. Smith said that he was starting at the bottom "to learn something about the anonymity and subordination that a hell of a lot of people have got to learn to win this war." He must have realized, too, that such a gesture would be no handicap to an ambitious young man in the postwar period.

After his boot-camp training, where he admittedly wasn't happy, Smith served as second lieutenant in the Pacific war theater and was in combat action at Bougainville, the Solomons, and Guam. Ordered back into the Navy as Commander in December 1944, he served with the staffs of Admirals Mitscher, Turner, and Spruance at Iwo Jima, Okinawa, and Japan, winning the awards of the Silver Star, Legion of Merit, Bronze Star, and three Presidential unit citations.

When the war ended, Smith returned to his editorship and general management of the *Chronicle*. Local leaders and staff members came to his shiplike home on Telegraph Hill, looking out over the sea—he is unmarried—to enjoy the food prepared by Clifford, his master cook and the talk led by the fiery little master talker.

Although the *Chronicle* in its editorial stands on major issues kept to a well-charted course of conformity, under Smith as editor and George T. Cameron as publisher it experimented boldly in news presentation, headline, and makeup techniques. When it did take up a cause, such as, for instance, academic freedom, it went all out in news handling and editorial follow-up.

The "gaudy century" of which the *Chronicle*'s John Bruce wrote had passed, and San Francisco's press, like Denver's had gained in sobriety and stability. As long as Paul Smith was around it would still have some of its spice.

Down the Coast, in Los Angeles, Manchester Boddy's rise to national recognition paralleled in some respects Paul Smith's in San Francisco. In 1949 his picture was one of twenty-three Westerners selected to hang in the "Editors of America" shrine of the San Francisco Press Club.

Elias Manchester Boddy, the second of five sons, was born on an unproductive forty-acre homestead at Lake Tapps, Washington, on November 1, 1891. After his first year in high school

Manchester left home to help earn a living for himself and his parents.

He made thirty dollars a month and board as a milker for a while on a dairy farm, then he became salesman for a self-heating flatiron. Soon he left home for good. He finished high school in Harrington, Washington, where he clerked in a grocery store and cooked breakfast and dinner for the store owner. While studying at Washington State College in Pullman, he worked as salesman for aluminum pots and pans. Transferring to the University, he waited on table and swept out the law library, while he camped on nearby Rattlesnake Creek. Hired by the president of Montana University to recruit students, Boddy was left stranded and broke in Sandpoint, Idaho, when the president lost his job. He went to work in the mines and moved from one job to another in the direction of New York City.

His success in selling the *Encyclopaedia Britannica* in such unlikely places as the Bowery and Harvard Yard was such that he was made New York City sales manager. On his rounds he met blonde Berenice Maud Klotz from Winnetka, Illinois, in Gimbels bookstore and married her on January 1, 1918, the day before he sailed for Europe as a second lieutenant in the infantry. Gassed a few days before the Armistice in the battle of Argonne Forest, he was sent home disabled and spent months in the hospital.

When he recovered, he started job-hunting again and finally contracted to train a staff to sell bound back copies of *Current History,* telling the story of the war, for the *New York Times.* When the *Times* bought up his contract, Boddy and his wife took a tent to the Maine woods to live. Broke again, Boddy sold the tent to get back to New York and started the very day of his return, at a salary of seventy-five dollars a week, selling *Current History* along with *Midweek Pictorial.*

A siege of double pneumonia that winter sent Boddy to California in search of sunshine. He and his wife arrived in

Los Angeles with only thirty-five dollars. There he set out to
sell books to school librarians.

As Frank J. Taylor told the story in the *Saturday Evening
Post*:

> One noon, following several men into an elevator and off at the second
> floor he discovered he had crashed the luncheon of the Commercial Board
> of Los Angeles.
> "That's all right; stay and eat," said the man at his right, when Boddy
> confessed his mistake. It was to be the luckiest mistake he ever made.
> The bumbling chairman of the meeting introduced the guest speaker,
> Will Rogers. After the meeting, everybody but Boddy rushed to shake
> Rogers' hand. Feeling sorry for the forgotten chairman, Boddy stepped
> up and congratulated him. Grateful, the latter induced Boddy to take
> out a membership. Boddy did, then asked if any member could help him
> set up an accounting system. The chairman promised to send over a
> member who specialized in that field. The bookkeeping expert who ar-
> rived, it developed, had inherited a white elephant, a little publication
> called *Smiles, the Magazine of Good Cheer*. Before the man left, Boddy
> had bought *Smiles,* for fifty dollars—on the cuff.
> Boddy hustled over to the office of the chairman of the Commercial
> Board and offered *Smiles* as the club's official house organ. The offer was
> accepted. In four furious hours, Boddy had established himself in the
> publishing business.

After obtaining rights to the discontinued *Mexican Yearbook*
from a British firm, Boddy uncovered a few trunks full of
valuable research on Mexico, originally financed by the Doheny
Foundation and left unused in the basement of Occidental
College. He engaged Robert G. Clelland of the faculty to do
the editing. Later he persuaded Harry Chandler, publisher of
the *Los Angeles Times,* to buy it. This led to the creation
of the Times-Mirror Book Publishing Company, specializing in
Southern California historical and biographical works, textbooks, and lives of movie stars, with Boddy in charge. Boddy
left the *Times* to become managing director and later president
of the Commercial Board.

Meanwhile the attempt of Cornelius Vanderbilt Jr. to establish a chain of conservative tabloids had given birth to the
Illustrated Daily News in Los Angeles. Vanderbilt spent $3,000-
000 on his venture before it went bankrupt. Chandler of the

Times, along with George Young of Hearst's *Examiner* and Edward Dickson of the *Evening Express,* made a joint bid of $150,000 for the *News,* stipulating that the plant should be abandoned. Boddy drew up a plan of operation and through a New York bank induced the Vanderbilt family to sign over to a receivership committee a $1,000,000 note; stockholders put up an additional $30,000 to meet the payroll for one month. With the canceled note, Boddy upped the bid and won the reluctant consent of a federal judge to his appointment as publisher.

Boddy's friends in the Commercial Board organized a syndicate which lent him $116,000 at 8 per cent with which to buy controlling interest in the paper and gave him six months to make good. His first major campaign "liberated" a blighted area of the city from the stigma of being a red-light and honky-tonk district. A grateful property owner repaid the Commercial Board syndicate and provided temporary financing for the struggling paper.

In the *News* Boddy undertook at once to expose municipal graft and corruption, and the underworld fought back by charging that the paper was owned by power companies. As a result of the crusade the Mayor was recalled, the Chief of Police removed, and the notorious Albert Marco sent to prison.

As part of an attempt to harass Boddy and the *News,* he and his city editor, Joel Rickman, were arrested for printing, along with the other papers, a United Press report of the Kentucky Derby in technical violation of an old ordinance against publication of racing news. They were released after they went on for a short time editing the paper from jail.

When the city council undertook an investigation of the *News,* Boddy, in turn, accused certain councilmen of graft in connection with the sale of a gravel pit to the city and contracts for selling city-collected garbage to hog ranchers. The investigation collapsed after one member demanded: "Is this committee investigating Boddy, or is he investigating us?" Convictions against guilty officials followed.

The *News* attracted a spirited staff. Duncan Aikman brought from El Paso to its editorial columns his fine scorn for the false and pretentious; Hal Rorke and Matt Weinstock brought to its news columns life and laughter.

In the winter of 1932 the *News* discovered headlines in economics, whereas its rivals stuck to the old formula, filling their pages with the latest sensation, the Aloha Wanderwell yacht-murder mystery. The *News* turned to technocracy, using valuable frontpage space and banner headlines to herald the advances of fiscal theories of Howard Scott of New York's Greenwich Village. Everybody began talking about technocracy and circulation boomed, but advertisers began to worry. Boddy's theory was that, in times of depression, economic panaceas were news, but to advertisers technocracy held out little promise.

As the technocracy fad died down, Boddy gave Social Credit the full treatment. At one time he had a regular lecture circuit including twelve communities; at each meeting he promoted circulation. Then he got interested in the visionary schemes of Upton Sinclair. Sinclair, the old time socialist and muck-raker who later turned exclusively to novel-writing, had rolled up considerable support for the Democratic nomination for Governor against George Creel of World War I propaganda fame. Liberals found Sinclair's End Poverty In California (Epic) scheme unrealistic, but they knew Creel would have hard going against Sinclair's popular appeal among the panacea-seeking and cult-conscious who had come to California hoping to find there the promised land. Also they could not stomach the Republican alternative, Frank Merriam, reactionary disciple of "Sunny Jim" Rolph.

Boddy planned to get into the campaign actively. First he considered running for Governor himself, then he planned to "knock some sense into Sinclair" and get behind him. Finally he decided to stick with his paper and wait to see what happened.

Sinclair won the nomination. But after several conferences Boddy found that Sinclair could not be "brought down to earth" and reluctantly switched to Merriam, who won the election.

Boddy's daily "Thinking and Living" column showed such ready receptivity to new ideas that hostile critics called him erratic and such a fondness for prediction that staffmen called his office the "crystal-ball department."

"I doubt if anything I advocate, urge, promote or espouse makes much difference," Boddy said. "But I am a firm believer in Fact, the Dictator."

The movie-conscious community, seeing lean, jaunty Boddy moving briskly about town or headed for his 165-acre ranch at La Canada in the foothills north of Los Angeles, where he lived with his wife and two sons, Robert Manchester and Calvin Jay, said he looked like Adolph Menjou. Newspapermen said he resembled a taller version of Roy Howard.

Boddy acquired the profitable *Huntington Park Signal* in 1934. In 1935 he sold the *Signal* and bought out his chief competitor, the old Scripps *Los Angeles Evening Record*. He merged it with the *News,* dropping the word *Illustrated* from the paper's title. As the circulation of the *News* rose to match that of its opposition, Boddy observed, "The readers vote for you every day; if you don't put their nickels in the box, you're out."

In 1948 Norman Chandler of the *Times,* son of Boddy's one-time boss, entered into direct competition with Boddy and with Hearst's afternoon *Herald and Express* by starting a new tabloid, the *Mirror.*

Chandler installed the *Mirror* in a brand new building and turned it over completely to Virgil Pinkley, former United Press European manager, as publisher. After the first issue, the *Mirror* abandoned the tricky device of printing the cover-page lengthwise like a standard-sized paper, obliging the reader to turn the paper around to read the smaller-sized inside pages, but it kept its run-of-the-paper color, its heavy quota of features, and its flashy makeup.

The *Herald and Express,* sounding like the "good old days," greeted the *Mirror* by accusing its staff of spying in the rival shop and purloining news.

Whatever the truth of the Hearst charge, the *Mirror* was a strangely brash product to issue from the ultraconservative precincts of the stodgy old *Times*.

Bland, wavy-haired Chandler, whose *Times* was neck-and-neck in the morning and Sunday field with Hearst's *Examiner,* observed that "Los Angeles had grown into an industrial and manufacturing community during wartime and that a tabloid paper of the *Mirror*'s type might appeal to the new elements of our population more than the *Times*."

Union men among the oldtimers and the newcomers would not easily forget that the nation's bitterest fight between unions and newspapers had occurred on the *Times*.

Harrison Gray Otis, who bought the *Times* a year after it was founded in 1881, a former colonel in the Civil War and general in the Spanish-American war, had strong views. An International Typographical Union strike directed against all Los Angeles newspapers in 1890 finally centered on the *Times*. The International Printers' Protective Fraternity, a conciliatory organization formed to aid publishers in altercations with the older ITU, supplied the *Times* with printers to replace the strikers, and Otis, in turn, directed Fraternity printers to publishers of other West Coast papers in order to strengthen his own open-shop position. After the local union had failed to budge the *Times* from its attitude by boycotts, it exerted pressure on subscribers and advertisers and diverted public printing from the *Times* to other plants. Hearst, then labor's friend, started his *Examiner* in 1903 at the instigation of ITU officials.

Early on October 1, 1910 the *Times* plant was dynamited, killing a score of men. The American Federation of Labor, Eugene V. Debs, the Socialist Party, and others suggested that "Old Walrus" Otis had wrecked his own plant to discredit the unions, but the McNamara brothers—John Joseph and James Barnabas—of the Iron Workers Union were caught in Indianapolis, brought to Los Angeles, tried, and finally confessed to the bombing.

The *Times* remained an open-shop paper in a largely open-shop city, and thereafter General Otis protested to the American Newspaper Publishers Association every time he saw any signs of cooperation with unions.

Control of the *Times* passed to Harry Chandler, who had married Otis's daughter Marion. Upon the latter's death in 1945 it went to the five Chandler children with forty-six-year-old Norman becoming publisher.

Norman Chandler had been on the *Times,* working in every department, ever since his graduation from Stanford University in 1922 and his marriage that same year to a classmate, Dorothy Buffum. He had served as his father's assistant from 1929 on.

Chandler's *Mirror* was noteworthy, if for no other reason, because it ventured forth bravely at a time when newspapers all over the country were giving up. Only one or two other new metropolitan dailies had been born—and had survived—in more than twenty years.

Marshall Field
and His Fortune

THE *CHICAGO SUN* ROSE FOR THE FIRST TIME ON DECEMBER 4, 1941. Three days later the Japanese dropped destruction on Pearl Harbor and robbed the *Sun* of part, but by no means all, of its reason for existence. Editorially, the *Sun* was Marshall Field's challenge to the isolationism of Colonel McCormick's *Chicago Tribune,* and the war enlisted the *Tribune,* however grudgingly and temporarily, along with everybody else in cooperative international effort.

The *Sun,* off to a bad start, would yet find a solid role for itself in the journalism of the Middle West, and other publishers would yet admit Marshall Field (see photograph 15) to their roster, no matter how balefully some of them may have greeted the man and his millions in the province where they had staked out a prior claim and where they granted him no right to poach.

Marshall Field III was a sport in journalism; his story combines the search of one man for salvation of his soul with a soul-seeking of the press itself.

Field began life under severe psychological handicaps. A doting mother supervised his education and his conduct from the cradle to adolescence, and an equally doting grandfather, founder of the Chicago department store fortune, superseded in the boy's life the melancholy and ailing Marshall Field II, who committed suicide. When the youngster was ill early in 1905, it was old Marshall Field who sat by the bed and shared the nursing chores with the mother. Business, hitherto all-important to him, had to wait until his grandchild turned the corner in his illness.

Immediately after his father's suicide, young Marshall's health became so much worse that his mother took him to Lakewood, New Jersey, where he stayed until his grandfather's fatal illness brought the family together again in New York.

At twelve, young Marshall, now the richest boy in the world, with a three-fifths interest in his grandfather's $130,000,000 estate, was packed off by his mother to her smart London town house. Field went to Eton where he was exposed for the first time to the conflict of ideas, both in great books and in school life. Athletics there and later at Cambridge repaired his precarious health. He rode to hounds, had his own racing and hunting stables, and took on the patina of an English country gentleman.

When he reached his majority in 1914 he was called back to the United States to take over the trusteeship of the Field estate. A ship companion on the return trip was Evelyn Marshall, a New York girl whom he had already met in London and whom he married a year later.

Field enlisted in the first World War as a buck private in the 1st Illinois Cavalry ten days after the United States entered the conflict. In France he was promoted to captain and saw action at St. Mihiel and the Meuse-Argonne, coming home to Chicago a hero.

In the first two postwar years he served as associate director of the city's "bureau of justice," getting jobs for ex-servicemen and helping organize community centers for Chicago youngsters. When the bureau completed its work, Field started selling bonds and then set himself up in a severely plain office to help the other four trustees manage the Field estate. He opened an investment banking business of his own and formed a partnership with two other young bankers.

Meanwhile he had moved to New York with his wife in 1921. There he began the fabulous life, in a fabulous era, that stamped him in the eyes of his enemies as a playboy.

After building a home in New York City, he created, on 1,750 acres of Long Island wasteland, the wonderland called "Caumsett." The Fields and their guests sunned themselves and bathed on a private beach along the Sound, cruised occasionally on the steam yacht *Corisande,* motored on about twenty-five miles of private roads, played tennis and polo, rode, shot pheasant, fished for trout, and flew in an amphibian. It took a staff of eighty-five to run the establishment, which operated like a small community with its own electrical and water supply and fire-fighting apparatus, gardens for the kitchen as well as more formal flower gardens, twenty tenant houses to accommodate the servants, and modern barns with the latest devices for storing hay and corn.

Field organized his estate as though it were a business, and, in the process, he exhibited some of his grandfather's characteristics for the first time. He had no patience with inefficiency; erring employees were likely to be fired on the spot. He also showed that he had the older Field's capacity for detail, and there were few matters on the estate that escaped his attention. He saw to it that surplus milk and wood were sold profitably, and his cattle brought substantial prices on the market.

He kept some horses in his stable at Caumsett, but the best in the string were divided among Newmarket, Belmont Park, and Kentucky. Field was elected to succeed the late Payne Whitney as a director of the Saratoga Racing Association in 1928.

Surrounded by luxuries, he never relaxed. His business days in Wall Street were filled with the details of his investment firm and his responsibilities as director of a dozen corporations. At Caumsett he hurried from one sport to another as though to appointments on a business day. While others lolled on his yacht, Field would board a speedboat and thread his way breathtakingly through East River traffic until he reached the

River Club, where the end result of the trip might be no more than a casual luncheon date.

After a few years of this life Field knew that he was not happy any more, as he had been in Chicago immediately after the war. He and his wife, parents of a son and two daughters, were divorced. Field was married again in the same month, to Audrey Janes Coats, a goddaughter of Edward VII, and a London beauty who was seen everywhere with the gay young set that included the Prince of Wales.

After their marriage, they embarked on an African expedition where they shot a lion and sent it to the Field Museum in Chicago, and escaped death when their plane crashed in the Sudan. Audrey was a crack shot like her husband and she vied with him in flying airplanes and racing boats. The Fields went hunting in England and yachting on the Mediterranean with the international set from the south of France; they rehabilitated an ancient Virginia plantation to its ante-bellum splendor; and once they even leased a ranch in Wyoming for a single house party. Then Audrey and Marshall were divorced in 1934.

A year later Marshall Field turned to psychoanalysis as a means of straightening out the pattern of a life that no longer made sense to him. After a year's treatment with Dr. Gregory Zilboorg, his first act was to quit the investment banking and brokerage business and his second was to marry Ruth Pruyn Phipps, in 1936. She came to Caumsett with her two sons, Robert and Harry, and took a lively interest in her husband's activities, an interest that sharpened as Field began to shape the creative course he now intended his wealth to take.

Field organized the New York Citizens' Committee on Children and gave new buildings, equipment, and personnel to children's agencies. By the time he was ready in 1940 to organize the Field Foundation, which channeled his social philanthropies, he had become one of the best informed laymen in the child welfare field. He had also become deeply concerned with the field of race relations. With a board of specialists, Field guided Foundation grants primarily into child welfare and better race relations, to research groups or agencies working to find and eliminate causes rather than superficial cures. The psychological impact of his father's death led Field to aid Dr. Zilboorg financially in setting up a committee for the study of suicide.

Then, in the spring of 1940, Louis Weiss, Field's attorney, told him of the dummies of a projected newspaper Weiss had seen in the adjoining office of his law partner, John Wharton. The paper was the dream of Ralph Ingersoll, who had left his job at *Time* to raise money for it. In form, the paper would scrap meaningless conventions and stereotypes of the orthodox press; in content, it would implement the principles of dynamic democracy; it would find the truth behind the surface news; it would be against "people who pushed other people around." Field, immediately interested, bought $200,000 worth of stock; up to that time the largest single investor had been Mrs. Marion Stern (who later, as Mrs. Max Ascoli, financed the fortnightly *Reporter*).

The plan for the paper had been in the back of Ingersoll's mind from the day in 1923 when the New York dailies, during a pressmen's strike, combined in producing a capsule eight-page daily. At that time, fresh from the mines of California, Arizona, and New Mexico, two years out of Yale's Sheffield Scientific School, and going on twenty-three, Ingersoll was a cub reporter on Hearst's *New York American*.

Off the *American* in a fight over the mishandling of one of his stories, Ingersoll became successively a reporter, then managing editor for the *New Yorker;* associate editor, then managing editor of *Fortune;* vice-president and general manager of all Luce publications; then publisher of *Time*.

In 1937 Ingersoll outlined his "Proposition to Create a New Newspaper" and the next year formed, with Edward Stanley of the Associated Press, Publications Research Inc. Ingersoll's decision to leave *Time* the next week was, in the words of a penetrating profile of him in the *New Yorker,* "at least partly dictated by a prejudice against obscurity. Nearly forty, he found himself an editor making $45,000 a year and practically unknown."

The word quickly got around the newspaper world that a new paper was in the making. It stirred curiosity, rumor, and opposition. Ingersoll sifted 9,402 applications for editorial jobs.

Ingersoll broke with Stanley before publication, but meanwhile he had been talking over his ideas with his writing friends and had gathered a group of unpaid writers in an office in the *Time-Life* building to work out an experimental dummy. Most of them cooperated anonymously and without commitment because of their current connections, but at least three remained close to Ingersoll in the actual preparations: Dashiell Hammett, detective story writer; Lillian Hellman, playwright, and Elizabeth Hawes, book-writing fashion expert.

Most of the preliminary work was financed by a loan of $25,000 from Daniel Gillmore, publisher of the magazine *Friday*.

Another name that appeared prominently in the early talks and then disappeared was that of Nelson Poynter, editor of the *St. Petersburg Times* in Florida. Ingersoll gave Poynter full credit for fixing in his mind the idea to publish a daily without advertising.

Later Ingersoll signed William Benton of the Benton and Bowles advertising agency and then assistant to the president of the University of Chicago (later Senator from Connecticut), and his one-time boss, Harold Ross of the *New Yorker,* to work with him during the three-months' prepublication experiment and rehearsal.

The newspaper was named *PM,* because it was to appear in the afternoon and because the initials could stand for "picture magazine." As managing editor, Ingersoll chose a seasoned Scripps-Howard editor, George H. Lyon. The original staff was largely recruited from three main sources: the field of experts and writers on special subjects who had little or no technical newspaper background, and who might be called the nonprofessional intellectuals; the field of orthodox technicians from the training schools of the Associated Press and the Scripps-Howard chain, who might be called the nonintellectual professionals; the men trained in Henry Luce's "new journalism" or fresh from a year at Harvard as Nieman Fellows, who might be called the professional intellectuals. These loose categories overlapped and, of course, there were others who just happened along.

June 18, 1940, publication date, arrived inauspiciously. The Nazis had marched into Paris a few days before, Hitler was meeting with Mussolini in Munich to gloat and plot, Congress was passing plans for a billion dollars' worth of warships, and the State Department was looking anxiously toward French possessions in the Western Hemisphere.

Morning broke thickly over Brooklyn. In the murky light of a loft over an engraving plant close to the Long Island railroad yard, men and women leaned stickily over desks and typewriters. An hour or so before the page forms were to be locked up, smoke began to filter into the already stifling city room, where chairs were backed against chairs to accommodate the staff, swollen to 200 by last-minute hirings. Fire engines screeched to a stop in the street below. Helmeted firemen carrying axes stalked into the room, hunting the source of the smoke. Few of the staff looked up from their typewriters or left their desks. The blaze was soon out.

Nine days earlier Ivan Annenberg, brother of the noted Max, had called the city's newsdealers together and told them that the *Daily News,* for which he was circulation manager, did not want *PM* on the stands and that if they sold the new paper it was probable that the *News* delivery truck would not serve them.

Ingersoll went to Captain Patterson, publisher of the *News* and was told: "I'm going by what happened to me. When I came to this town my circulation was a hell of a lot smaller than yours, and the *New York Times* predicted that the *News* would fold up. That was twenty years ago. Look where the *Times* is now—just about where it was then—and look where my paper is. I'm not taking any chances, Ingersoll. I don't want it to happen to me."

When *PM*'s circulation trucks went out one morning and were able to place the paper on only a few stands, Ingersoll asked Mayor F. H. LaGuardia for protection for his trucks. LaGuardia promised to help, but Patterson gave up fighting the new paper when he soon saw that the prospect of serious competition was remote. The *News* then joined the other papers in treating *PM* with condescension rather than open hostility.

After the first flurry of curiosity circulation that went to 400,000, sales fell off, other distribution problems developed, bitter critics attacked the paper, boycotts and pickets appeared at the plant, intra-office bickering began, staff changes came rapidly. The honeymoon was over.

The first issues were handsome, the fine quality pages stapled together like a magazine, with superior photography and reproduction, superb war maps, and unequaled radio coverage. Carrying no paid advertising, *PM* published, as a reader service, a digest of the offerings presented by stores in other papers. Yet the paper was a severe disappointment to many of those who made it as well as those who read it. Ingersoll's eloquent prospectus had stirred people's dreams of what a paper could do beyond the capacity of *PM* to fulfill them. As *Newsweek* commented, "The unprecedented prepublication flood of free and paid-for publicity, stamping it as a newspaper which would revolutionize the printing business, proved more of a handicap than a help."

Launched in a period of political tension, *PM* was plagued from the start by charges of communism. It was inevitable that *PM* should have attracted men and women with strong convictions about their work and the world. The *New Yorker* called them "a bunch of young fogies." In political orientation they ranged all the way from dead center to far left (few if any were on the right). The staff was a microcosm of the factionalism of the times. These differences were dramatized by the fact that two opponents in the American Newspaper Guild's internal controversy held equally prominent posts on *PM*: Kenneth Crawford, who succeeded Heywood Broun as national president of the Guild, was chief of the Washington bureau; Carl Randau, chairman of the New York City Guild, was chief of the foreign desk.

Nevertheless, it was not the clash of politics so much as the conflicts of personality and professionalism that interfered with the smooth functioning of the paper in its early days.

Frustrated staff members began to complain of the "bottleneck" of seven assistant managing editors—largely literal minded and technically inflexible—through whom it was difficult to reach Ingersoll or to implement their own ideas.

In its first few months, partly because of defense priorities and shortages, *PM* abandoned some of its most distinctive features: run-of-the-paper color, page-stapling, instant-drying ink, high quality paper, detailed radio listings, the artist-as-reporter. And it dropped or modified many of its original departments like the press commentary and the digest of advertising.

During the summer, as circulation failed to approach the break-even point, all but one of the score of stockholders expressed their doubts about the policies and prospects of the paper and indicated they were ready to withdraw. That one stockholder was Marshall Field.

Field did not know enough about the newspaper business to judge the paper from professional standards, but he was for many of the things it was for—Roosevelt, labor, intervention abroad—and he thought it ought to have a chance. Field offered to buy out the other stockholders for twenty cents on the dollar. That would leave them a 15 per cent nonvoting interest in the common stock of the new corporation thus formed. The stockholders accepted eagerly and Marshall Field became sole owner.

Field announced that the paper would proceed without interference from him, a pledge he kept scrupulously. Nevertheless he found himself under constant attack, although he did not originate, and often was not even aware of, *PM*'s policies until after publication.

In 1942, when Ingersoll's draft board called him up, Marshall Field wired General Lewis Hershey, Selective Service Director, without Ingersoll's knowledge, asking that the editor be deferred because he was in a position essential to public morale. Meanwhile Ingersoll accepted his classification and reported, but not before writing a 6,000-word letter, which he published in *PM,* accusing the draft board of calling him because they didn't like his paper and challenging the board for a clear ruling on the status of newspapermen. Having stated his case, Ingersoll promptly enlisted in the Army.

In Ingersoll's absence, John P. Lewis (now publisher of a lively, prize-winning, small-town paper in Franklin, New Hampshire) took over as acting editor and under him, for one year, in 1944, the paper made a profit.

Ralph Ingersoll returned from the war, and from writing books about it, at the beginning of 1946 and made a few abortive efforts to revamp and reestablish the paper, which was losing money again.

Trouble had been brewing in the Washington bureau. A few years earlier Kenneth Crawford had accused Editor Lewis of censoring and suppressing his stories from North Africa and had left to join *Newsweek.* James Wechsler had become head of the bureau, and Milton Murray, then national president of the American Newspaper Guild, had joined him there. When Ingersoll asked Wechsler to fire Murray and two other members of the bureau "for economy" or transfer them to the New York office, Wechsler stepped down as bureau head rather than carry out the order. After the fight had become a Guild issue as well as a clash between brash and stubborn personalities, five members of the Washington bureau resigned, issuing a statement in which they accused Ingersoll, among other things, of catering to communist elements inside the staff and out.

Politics aside, it had been apparent for some time that Ingersoll's heart was no longer in the paper. After Marshall Field decided to open *PM*'s pages to advertisers in the fall, Ingersoll took the occasion to resign, stating that he was convinced that no attempt should be made to sell advertising until public acceptance of the paper had been established beyond dispute.

Early in 1948 Marshall Field let it be known that he no longer intended to pour money into the venture. Douglas McKinnon of San Diego offered to buy the paper, but when the local Guild protested that McKinnon's labor record was inconsistent with *PM*'s generous labor policies, the offer was withdrawn. Then Bartley Crum from California, one-time Hearst lawyer and "Republican-for-Roosevelt," together with Joseph Barnes, scholarly, liberal-minded foreign editor of the *New York Herald Tribune,* persuaded Marshall Field to lend them enough money, along with what they had been able to scrape together themselves, to take the paper over and keep it going.

Crum and Barnes took charge in May 1948 and in July changed the name of the paper to the *Star,* hoping thereby to remove the stigma of biased news reporting that had clung to the paper under its old name, while retaining its liberal editorial policies. In the 1948 Presidential election the *Star* was the only daily in New York that supported the candidacy of Harry S Truman and therefore was not caught in the embarrassment that engulfed the great bulk of the nation's press in its confidence of a Dewey victory.

Nevertheless, time was running out for the paper. Barnes and Crum were unable to effectuate all their plans soon enough. Marshall Field withdrew his support for good and all, and the paper ceased publication abruptly on January 28, 1949, after a hectic eight-and-a-half years.

The paper's death caused grief in some quarters but hardly shock. Much of its life had been a process of decline broken by occasional rallies—robust criticism degenerated into mere carping; all-out crusades tapered off in whining parochialism. The dream that fired *PM*'s founders, its staff and readers flitted tantalizingly into occasional issues, offering a hint of what the paper might have been. Clinically, the *Star* operation succeeded "but the patient died." The *Star* alienated *PM*'s un-questioningly loyal little band of followers before it won over the larger and less emotional following it sought. Perhaps *PM* did not actually fail. Potent intangibles remained. Other news-papers, though few of them said so, were affected by its coverage and content. Investigations pioneered and conditions un-covered by *PM* resulted in reform action that the big dailies had to recognize. Reporters on other papers, irritated by *PM*'s self-conscious "do-gooders," were nonetheless stirred and prodded. Many thoughtful Americans cherished their *PM* files and went on believing that what *PM* set out to do could yet be done.

An aftermath of the *PM-Star* debacle, but without direct con-nection, was the birth of another New York newspaper, the *Compass,* after a remarkable sequence of events. Dorothy Backer, heiress to the Schiff banking fortune, followed her divorce from George Backer, with whom she had bought the *New York Post* from J. David Stern Jr. in 1939, by marrying her editor, Theodore O. Thackrey, and making him co-pub-lisher. In the pages of the *Post* during the 1948 Presidential campaign, Thackrey, in signed columns, supported Henry A. Wallace; editorialist and columnist Samuel Grafton upheld Truman; Columnist Frank Kingdon came out for Norman Thomas; and Mrs. Thackrey, at the last minute and with some reluctance, announced on the editorial page that she was going to vote for Dewey. The staff, in published statements bearing signatures, lined themselves on one side or another—mostly as pro or anti-Wallace.

After the election Mrs. Thackrey went to Europe and on her return removed her name from the masthead, announcing that she was turning direction of the paper entirely over to her husband. A few months later, just as suddenly, she reappeared in the masthead, under her maiden name, Dorothy Schiff, and Thackrey's name disappeared, with the announcement that his policies, particularly his opposition to the Atlantic Pact, had become intolerable. James A. Wechsler, late of *PM,* assumed the editorship, and stimulated circulation with a heady brew of sex shockers and literate liberalism.

Ted Thackrey immediately got enough cash from aging Anita McCormick Blaine, cousin of Chicago's Colonel McCormick and a backer of Henry Wallace, to start within six weeks, in May 1949, a new tabloid in the plant vacated by the *Star.* Mrs. Blaine's initial gift ran out and, having been declared legally incompetent, she could give no more. The *Compass,* partly staffed with *PM-Star* alumni, notably I. F. (Izzy) Stone whose spirited news-digging and comment had won him fame; Jennings Perry, columnist; and Tom O'Connor, reporter and writer, trimmed to the bone and struggled on.

Marshall Field, meanwhile, turned his full attention—journalistically, at least, for the Field Foundation and its extensive philanthropies took much of his time—to his Chicago venture. The *Sun* had obviously been his main concern and more satisfactory outlet since its founding a year and a half after *PM* was born.

The *Sun* was one of the most hastily organized newspapers in history. It had actually been conceived at a luncheon conversation in New York between Silliman Evans, publisher of the *Nashville Tennessean,* Field, and Charles G. Cushing, a former Chicago investment banker who had become Field's financial counselor. The occasion that brought them together was Cushing's espousal of *Parade,* a picture-text Sunday supplement derived from *PM* material (which was to achieve faster and more general approval than any of Field's journalistic enterprises and wide syndication among newspapers throughout the country). Cushing had solicited Evans to sign up as *Parade*'s first subscriber, and Evans had flown to New York to have a look at it.

At the luncheon Field began to talk about a Chicago newspaper, and before he was through, Evans agreed to take a leave of absence from the *Tennessean* to be its publisher.

A $10,000 prize contest was opened to name the project. More than 220,000 people responded, and a majority of them

suggested the *Sun* as a proper title, but the first prize went to
Russell Trenholme, for his argument: "Well, it seems to me
when morning comes you look for two things to make your
world right; you look for the sun and sunlight, and you look
for your morning paper for the truth of what's going on in the
world."

Evans had never won public acclaim as a holder of liberal
views, in spite of the fact that he had supported Roosevelt, and
the executives he picked to operate the *Sun* were, by and large,
scarcely the kind one would expect to find on a liberal newspaper. He did, however, name Frank Taylor, ex-managing
editor of the *St. Louis Star-Times,* as assistant to the publisher
and surprised the newspaper world by signing Turner Catledge,
ace of the *New York Times* Washington staff, to become corre-
spondent-at-large.

Looking over the city staff, some observers remarked that it
seemed as though the *Herald-Examiner* had been reincarnated,
there were so many familiar Hearst faces.

For its reporting of the eventful days ahead, the *Sun* made
a pledge to its readers in the masthead: "The news columns
shall be fair and accurate; the editorial columns shall be honest
and just in the expression of conscientious opinion." In brief,
it would be everything that McCormick's *Chicago Tribune* was
not. The *Sun* further promised: "No fictional reporting. Not
in one single news story will there be any bias, any prejudiced
viewpoint, any imaginative conclusion."

On the morning the *Sun's* credo appeared, the *Tribune's*
front-page banner shrieked: FDR'S WAR PLANS. Under it
ran the now famous story that provoked Secretary of War Stimson, a man of McCormick's own political party, to exclaim
indignantly, "What would you think of an American General
Staff which in the present condition of the world did not investigate and study every conceivable type of emergency which may
confront this country and every possible method of meeting the
emergency? What do you think of the patriotism of a man or

a newspaper that would take those confidential studies and make them public to the enemies of this country?"

For the general public, accustomed to more forthright reporting and editing than the *Sun* presented in its early issues, the *Sun* seemed objective past the point of interest. It had not begun to attain the cohesiveness of an established newspaper; in its groping toward the proper formula it seemed to be shooting off in a dozen different directions. But at least the familiar *PM* criticism could not be leveled at it. It was a *news*paper in the accepted sense of the word, with 170 columns devoted to editorial content—more than any other paper in town. Besides the news it had a wide variety of features, although many of them were completely new to Chicago and had to wait for acceptance.

Expected circulation troubles began soon after the first day's issues were out. The *Sun* had been lulled by the *Tribune*'s apparent decision to ignore its new rival. The newsstands in the Loop abruptly refused to carry the Sunday *Sun*. Anticipating this move, the *Sun* had built two thousand wooden stands, but found itself up against a city ordinance requiring steel stands.

There were innumerable other difficulties. Files of undelivered papers were discovered not infrequently in manholes and under sidewalk gratings. Some were even found floating in the river. The deliverers—those the *Sun* was able to apprehend —said that they had been paid to throw away the paper.

Home deliveries were extremely difficult, particularly in the suburbs. There were plenty of potential customers, but dealers told them they were still "trying to get" the paper, even while large unopened bundles lay at their feet. It took time and trouble to solve these problems.

Nor did the *Sun*'s news columns appear to justify the high-priced talent that was putting them together. The editorials were uninspired; local stories were adequate but lacked color. Strongest criticism of the *Sun* did not come from the likely quarters. Unlike *PM* it drew more fire from the liberal element than it did from the conservative, for being "insipid" and for lacking "originality and independent news judgment."

The *Sun* began to clear away the clouds around it and show brightness as 1942 wore on. On the editorial side, there was almost a complete turnover of top executives. Turner Catledge took over as acting editor and Frank Taylor was promoted to executive assistant.

By the time the *Sun* was a year old, it had begun to assume more character. It was on the air over WJJD with an every half-hour news summary. Its columnists were attracting more readers, including some *Tribune* habitues who could hardly get used to the idea of finding commentators with such diverse viewpoints as Frank Kent and Samuel Grafton in the same newspaper.

Field and Evans imported Eli Zachary Dimitman, former executive editor of the *Philadelphia Inquirer,* to take over the same job on the *Sun.* Dimitman made several changes in the city staff, put some life and direction into the news policies, and improved the appearance of the paper with bigger and blacker type. For the first time the *Sun* began to look like the bold, forthright paper it should have been from the beginning. Dimitman demonstrated that it was possible to tell the news fairly and at the same time make it readable.

Catledge resigned and went back to the *Times* and later Evans returned to Tennessee. Marshall Field, who had been learning a great deal about the newspaper business, assumed Catledge's title as editor, directing the editorial page and writing an editorial himself now and then.

In 1945, after a long fight, the *Sun* rounded out its national and foreign coverage by obtaining the daily file of the Associated Press, a service that the great majority of American newspapers could not do without.

The bylaws of the Associated Press provided that in an area where there was already an AP member-paper, a new applicant could be admitted only on the payment of 10 per cent of the total assessments by the AP in that area since its reorganization under the New York laws in 1900—which in the *Sun's* case amounted to $334,250—unless the existing member waived the payment. This, Colonel McCormick refused to do.

The *Sun* protested that the bylaws restricted fair competition in news service and appealed to the Roosevelt Administration. The Department of Justice instituted action in New York against the Associated Press for violation of the Sherman Anti-Trust Act in August 1942. Colonel McCormick led the fight against the government's action, but the federal court in the Southern District of New York on October 3 directed the AP to change its bylaws to prevent a member from barring the election of a competitor. This "summary judgment" was appealed to the Supreme Court of the United States the following January. On June 18, 1945 the verdict of the lower court was upheld on the ground that "freedom of the press from governmental interference does not sanction repression . . . by private interests" and that the "First Amendment affords not the slightest support for the contention that a combination to restrain trade in news and views has any constitutional immunity."

At a special meeting in November, with Colonel McCormick still 'fuming, the Associated Press amended its membership rules to conform to the decision, and admitted the *Chicago Sun*.

Unable to build a plant for the *Sun* because of war shortages, Field had been restive while his paper was being printed in the plant of the *Daily News,* where it was subject to the demands of John S. Knight. The only way Field could get a plant of his own was to buy one already in operation; so in August 1947 he purchased the *Chicago Times,* an evening tabloid, from the heirs of Samuel E. Thomason for $5,339,000. He made the *Sun* a morning tabloid two months later. Richard J. Finnegan, a white-haired, dynamic, Chicago-wise Irishman who looked something like a priest, remained as editor and publisher of the *Times.*

In February 1948 the two tabloids were combined as the *Daily Sun and Times,* with round-the-clock operation like that of the *Times-Herald* in Washington and the *Globe* in Boston.

Field put his son, Marshall IV, in charge of daily operations, to work side by side with Managing Editor Milburn ("Pete") Akers.

By mid-century Marshall Field III had sunk an estimated $25,000,000 in his newspaper undertakings. Besides the *Sun-Times* and *Parade,* his communications empire included four radio stations; Quarrie Corporation, publishers of World Book Encyclopedia; Simon and Shuster Pocket Books, in a financial arrangement by which the publishers shared in the profits; and the *Southern Farmer,* edited by New Dealer Aubrey Williams. The *Sun-Times* was selling more than 600,000 copies a day and Field was ready to relax.

In October 1950 the title of publisher passed from Marshall Field III to Marshall Field IV, although the father remained president. Akers became executive editor and Thomas Reynolds, Washington bureau chief, was moved up to the managing editorship.

Field Jr. had been carefully groomed for succession. After serving in the second World War, he gave up the law career for which he had studied at Harvard and the University of Virginia and returned to Chicago to learn about newspapers from the bottom, riding the circulation trucks. In 1947 he broadened his education by a tour of duty outside the *Sun.* He worked for a month on the paper's Washington staff, spent another month with the London staff, and went back to New York for a period with his friend, "Whitey" Reid on the *Herald Tribune.*

The fourth Marshall Field combines the temperaments of his father and his great-grandfather. Like his father, he is warm-hearted, intensely interested in making the world a better place in which to live and in the uses of wealth rather than the further accumulation of it. On the other hand he has something of Marshall I's cold, steady judgment, an ability to assess other people accurately, and a certain conservative tempering of his liberalism. Although he admires his father, he thinks him too much an idealist in some respects.

Even as this latest of newspaper dynasties was in the making,
the process that led press observers like Oswald Garrison Villard to talk about the "Disappearing Daily" was accelerating.
Somewhat offsetting the toll taken in newspaper ranks, other
men had come forth to open new channels for getting news to
the people.

Luce, Wallace,
and Their Magazines

Since 1920 total readership of American newspapers has increased steadily, although the number of newspapers has declined; but also since 1920 a whole new area of journalism has opened up, adding to the millions of daily newspaper readers hundreds of thousands of weekly news magazine readers.

The $130,000,000 corporation known as Time Inc., which publishes *Time, Life,* and *Fortune,* is the end result of a revolutionary journalistic development brought about in the twenties by two brilliant partners not long out of Yale, Briton Hadden and Henry Robinson Luce (see photograph 16). Hadden died in 1929, six years after the founding of *Time,* and Luce carried on alone.

Henry Luce was born April 3, 1898 at Tengchow, in the Shantung Province of China, where his father, the Rev. Dr. Henry Winters Luce, was a Presbyterian missionary. Luce's parents were not well-to-do but they had influential church and family connections. The elder Luce was a descendant of the Henry Luce who was among the first settlers an Martha's Vineyard in 1643, and Mrs. Luce was, before her marriage, Elizabeth Middleton Root, related to Elihu Root, Republican statesman of World Court fame.

Until he was ten, Henry Luce's days were spent almost entirely with his parents and sisters, Elizabeth and Emmavail, and the families of the British and Americans who made up the missionary compound, a self-contained settlement in the plains of North China.

The gray brick house in which they lived was severe and forbidding, along formal American lines, with small dark rooms that the mother, with a sense of color and decoration, somehow managed to make attractive. Economies were rigid; any extra cash went for books and travel. The family library was well stocked, and Luce read, rapidly and avidly, everything from G. A. Henty's boys' tales to Gibbons' *Decline and Fall of the Roman Empire*.

The family spent long evenings, after early suppers at home, reading or singing, with the mother at the piano. Mrs. Luce read aloud a great deal, from the Bible, Shakespeare, and Dickens. Henry—he was Henry to the family but became Harry to those who knew him well in later years—dictated ideas to his mother before he was able to set them down himself. Later he started a hand-written boys' newspaper in the compound. He was good at the guessing games they played, called "clumps," based on words and passages in the Bible, as well as at chess and tennis.

"The gang was always at our house," Henry's sister Elizabeth recalled later (after she became Mrs. Maurice T. Moore, wife of the chairman of the board of Time, Inc.). "They played a game with big blocks on the nursery floor and we never touched the blocks when they left them; it was Henry's war."

Sometimes they went outside the compound to a show set up in the fields, to a festival or a parade. In the summer they took a cottage at Tsing-tau, a resort colony on the seashore of the same province.

Always America was glorified, the Fourth of July dramatically celebrated; they built up a passionate devotion for the distant homeland, kindled for Henry when he made a couple of childhood trips there with his father. Luce later sometimes regretted that he had not been brought up in a more cultural

Chinese background so that he might have been closer to the people and their arts.

When he was thrown upon his own resources he used to get one of the donkeys kept in the compound and ride out over the plains.

"I was at home in the countryside," he said later. "I knew the proper things to say to the Chinese when they saw that little foreign white devil coming along."

Luce's chances for continued close contact with the Chinese in his childhood were limited. At Chee-Foo, the strict British boarding school for the sons of missionaries in North China to which he was sent when he was ten, all communication with the Chinese was forbidden as a disciplinary measure to make it easier for the teachers to control the students' activities and health. Luce was younger than the average member of the class and had a hard time keeping up. By "the most terrific concentration" he managed to come out third or fourth in the school form of about twenty.

At fourteen Luce set out alone to travel from China to America, using his missionary allowance and a little extra to take him the long way around. After studying briefly at St. Albans in England, Luce enrolled at the expensive and exclusive Hotchkiss School at Lakeville, Connecticut, on a scholarship.

Hotchkiss classmates remembered him as a serious-minded student who didn't go out for the athletics of which the school made so much and who waited on table and swept out classrooms to help earn his way. In the spring of 1915 Luce and Erdman Harris, later head of the Shady Side Academy in Pittsburgh, were elected editor and associate editor of the Hotchkiss *Literary Monthly,* a rather unpopular publication, filled with schoolboy poetry and immature essays. They sat out under the trees and dreamed up ways of improving it, with pictures, interpretative reporting even of athletics, and articles from prominent men, including Theodore Roosevelt.

Editor of another school publication, the *Record,* was Briton

Hadden, another precocious lad who, like Luce, had first evidenced journalistic leanings by dictating thoughts to his mother and who had furthered those leanings at Brooklyn Polytechnic High School. A friendly rivalry developed at Hotchkiss between Luce and Hadden.

They went on to Yale, where, as close companions, the competition continued. Both were editors of the *Yale News* and were tapped for Skull and Bones. Luce was voted the most brilliant of his class and Hadden most likely to succeed.

When the first World War came, Luce and Hadden, after basic training on the campus, were second lieutenants together in the Student Army Training Corps at Camp Jackson, South Carolina. They crunched along over the sands on evening walks and talked about the paper they would some day start.

After returning to graduate from Yale, Luce used his share of *News* profit to go on to Oxford; Hadden went to New York and headed for the *World*. As Herbert Bayard Swope, *World* editor, told it:

I was sitting at my desk one evening just after the editorial conference on the next day's paper when, suddenly, I became aware of a shadow on my desk. Someone was standing there. I had given strict orders that no one was allowed in my office except one or two of my editors. I took it for granted that it was one of them. When I looked up, I saw a young man I could not recall having seen before.

I said: "Who are you?"

He said: "My name is Briton Hadden and I want a job."

I said: "How did you get in here? My secretary has orders not to let anyone in."

"I waited till she left her desk."

"And how did you get past the managing editor's desk?"

"I waited until he went into the city room."

"We don't do things like that. Go out again and send in your name properly tomorrow. I don't want to talk to young men I have never met before."

"Mr. Swope, you have met me before."

It turned out that he had me there. I had made a talk at some event in New Haven and later met some members of the board of the paper, when he was the editor. Nonetheless, I told him again that he would have to leave.

"Mr. Swope," he said, "you're interfering with my destiny."

Well, that was something new to me. I asked him to explain how I would be interfering with his destiny.

He told me that his destiny required him to work on the *World* for a year in order to get experience to help him start a paper of his own. I asked him why the *World*. His answers seemed to make a lot of sense. By the end of a few minutes I felt convinced that he had something. We had a rule just then against giving these young college kids jobs on the paper. Most of them expected to be columnists. I could see that whatever Hadden had in mind at the time, it wasn't that. He was serious and sensible in his talk. I said: "All right: you have a job." *

While Hadden wrote animal stories on the *World* and came to know the glamorous crew that inhabited the place in those days, Luce returned to America and went directly to Chicago. Mrs. Edith Rockefeller McCormick, a devout woman of good works, had shown an interest in him and he had fallen in love abroad with a Chicago girl, Lila Ross Hotz. Mrs. McCormick, who, as Luce never failed to point out, was of the *Harvester,* not the *Tribune,* McCormicks, wanted him to go into the ministry, a choice that his minister-father had never imposed, but Luce felt no call to the cloth.

Still anxious to help, Mrs. McCormick got the family to find a spot for Luce in the Harvester firm. When he discovered that an opening was being made just for him at a time of wide unemployment, Luce set out to look for a newspaper job instead. His repugnance for the journalism of McCormick and Hearst (a feeling that was to be aggravated and reciprocated) narrowed his field and so he went to work for the *Daily News*. There he legged for Ben Hecht's column of daily drama. The job soon palled and Luce was transferred to the cityside.

Luce missed his one chance to make a name for himself as a sixteen-dollar-a-week reporter. He didn't find the body when he was sent out to cover the disappearance of a Northwestern University student. Instead, he packed off to Baltimore in response to a letter from Walter Millis of the *World*.

Millis, a Yale classmate, had sent Luce and Hadden identical

---

* From *Briton Hadden,* copyright 1949, by Noel F. Busch, with the permission of the publishers, Farrar, Straus and Young, Inc.

messages telling of Frank Munsey's quest for new blood to staff the *Baltimore News*. Hadden scrawled a note to Luce: "If we're ever going to start that paper, this looks like our chance."

In Baltimore they went on talking where they had left off and prepared a prospectus for a publication, which first was to be called *Facts* but became *Time*. It said:

Although daily journalism has been more highly developed in the United States than in any other country in the world—

Although foreigners marvel at the excellence of our periodicals, *World's Work, Century, Literary Digest, Outlook,* and the rest—

People in America are, for the most part, poorly informed.

This is not the fault of the daily newspapers; they print all the news.

It is not the fault of the weekly "reviews"; they adequately develop and comment on the news.

To say with the facile cynic that it is the fault of the people themselves is to beg the question.

People are uninformed BECAUSE NO PUBLICATION HAS ADAPTED ITSELF TO THE TIME WHICH BUSY MEN ARE ABLE TO SPEND ON SIMPLY KEEPING INFORMED.

TIME is a weekly news-magazine, aimed to serve the modern necessity of keeping people informed, created on a new principle of COMPLETE ORGANIZATION.

TIME is interested—not in how much it includes between its covers—but in HOW MUCH IT GETS OFF ITS PAGES INTO THE MINDS OF ITS READERS.

Soliciting from Yale friends and their families, Luce and Hadden raised $86,000 of the $100,000 they sought; the biggest chunks came from Mrs. William Harkness, her son, and her daughter. Paying themselves thirty dollars each a week and planning to alternate each year as editor and business manager so that both would know both sides of the enterprise, Luce and Hadden gathered the nucleus of a small staff from fellow collegians. The first issue of *Time,* tightly departmentalized, appeared on March 2, 1923.

Its arrival, in the view of Noel F. Busch, Hadden's biographer, fitted into the decade perfectly:

Time itself was something new, started by two members of the controversial younger generation. Its purpose was to enable everyone to find out, in a new way, just what this marvelous new world was all about. *Time*'s invention, its growth and, especially, its style were all expressions of the period. The magazine did more than portray and reflect the era. It exemplified it.

The twenties produced many heroes of all sorts but its spirit, to judge by recent interpretations, seems to have been concealed. *Time* may have been, in a sense, exactly that. If one had to select, as a symbol for the era, a single individual who summed up and epitomized its positive and productive genius, its wild love of competition, its faith and its foibles, it might be hard to find a better one than Hadden.*

It was Hadden who created the idiom that came to be known as "*Time* style" and was so widely imitated—often badly—that it can justly be said to have revolutionized the journalistic writing of a generation. Cumulative descriptive adjectives like eagle-eyed, lantern-jawed; ellisions and telescoped words like cinemactress; coined words and refurbished old ones like tycoon, which became part of the language; reverse word order and inverted sentences. ("Backward ran sentences until reeled the mind," said Wolcott Gibbs in a neat *New Yorker* parody.)

After Hadden's death of streptococcus infection, a plaque in the Hadden Memorial Building at New Haven declared, "His genius created a new form of journalism." And the living monument that was *Time* became, under Luce, the nucleus of an empire so big and bright and strong that it frightened some as much as it inspired others.

A year after Hadden's death, Luce started the slick, elaborately researched and polished *Fortune,* which sold at the then-startling price of a dollar a copy. *Fortune* was officially launched to "give business a literature." It was designed, according to Luce, "to represent an interest that had never been represented in an imaginative way, in conversation, in dramatic form; people talked about business, yes, but in the smoking car, in terms of the stock market, not in the parlor, in terms of the steel industry, say, in itself."

Fortune hit into the decade of the depression, some of its

* From *Briton Hadden,* copyright 1949, by Noel F. Busch, with the permission of the publishers, Farrar, Straus, and Young, Inc.

sharp articles seemed almost radical in the light of later developments, but it soon struck its stride and prospered.

About that time, Mariner Eccles, early New Dealer with whom Luce was "surprised" to find himself in agreement, called Luce's attention to the fact that the main line of attack against the depression would be in housing. *Fortune* had been started as a magazine for general business, and Luce now wanted a magazine for a particular industry. To that end, he bought the *Architectural Forum* but did not at once realize his ambitions for it. It became a stepchild of Time Inc. and only began to make a profit in 1948 after it had been changed to the *Magazine of Building*. In January 1952 the *Magazine of Building* was split into two magazines to come out alternately, one every two weeks: the brand new *House & Home* and the rejuvenated *Architectural Forum*.

Luce unloaded two other magazines, *Tide* and the *Saturday Review of Literature*, after a brief fling at running them. He then branched out into other media with striking success, developing the radio March of Time and the film March of Time.

Then Luce plunged his staff—it had grown into the hundreds by now, including an army of researchers and checkers new to journalism—into elaborate experimentation upon a picture magazine. After a year of dry runs, unseen by the public, Luce bought for $100,000 the name of an old humor magazine, *Life,* and the new *Life,* big and bright and shiny, appeared in November 1936. Advertising rates had been established for a circulation of 250,000. The demand for the magazine exceeded all expectations and circulation quickly passed the million mark. In satisfying the demand, the expensively produced magazine lost $3,000,000 in its first year, until advertising contracts for the second year were adjusted to the circulation figures. As *Life* grew and prospered, it balanced its pictorial matter by more and more printed text. Its development of the reporter-photographer was an outstanding contribution to journalism.

While *Life* was in the making, Luce had met Clare Boothe, a glamorous blonde writer on the staff of the smart and sophisticated *Vanity Fair*. Miss Boothe had been divorced since 1929 from George Brokaw, a wealthy clothing firm heir. Almost at once, Luce and Miss Boothe began to exchange ideas about how magazines should be run. When she went off on a trip to Europe, Luce, now divorced from his first wife after twelve years of marriage, followed. Upon their return, and coincidentally with the uncelebrated opening of Miss Boothe's first play, *Abide With Me,* they were married. Subsequently she wrote three more successful plays, *The Women, Kiss the Boys Goodbye,* and *Margin for Error.* In 1942 Connecticut Republicans elected her to Congress. After two terms as Representative, Clare Luce became a widely publicized convert to Catholicism and retired from public political life.

After his second marriage, Luce's social life broadened and he mixed more, being seen often in the Big Name society that Elsa Maxwell, social catalyzer, party-giver, and erstwhile columnist, collected to her bosom.

Luce, a tall spare man whom his own magazines might have described as balding, beetle-browed, did not go in for creature comforts or lavish living. Almost ascetic in dress, manner, and habits, he did not approve of heavy drinking and rarely finished a cocktail, though he did smoke a great deal. In the living room of their Connecticut home, guests would see Luce pick up his briefcase at ten o'clock in the evening, no matter who was present, and go off to his room, saying, "See you at seven in the morning." And he would mean seven.

Once Luce went for five years without a vacation. In 1943, he had just returned from a rare respite in California, with his wife and her daughter, Ann Brokaw, when word came of the girl's death in an automobile accident on the Stanford University campus where she was a student. Luce flew back to California the same day and then went to their 7,000-acre plantation at Monck's Corner, near Charleston, South Carolina, where Ann was buried from a little chapel on the estate. The following June Luce delivered the commencement address to the Stanford class with which his stepdaughter would have been graduated.

Henry Luce III, elder of Luce's sons by his first wife, joined the Washington bureau of *Time* in 1951 after Yale, World War II service, and an apprenticeship on the editorial staff of the *Cleveland Press*. His younger brother Peter Paul went from Brooks School at North Andover, Massachusetts, to the Massachusetts Institute of Technology, and then into the Air Force.

Personally established in family and fortune, Luce discovered that his professional and public role raised questions of profound concern both to himself and to the vast audience reached by his publications.

In search of some of the answers, Luce appropriated $200,000, to which the *Encyclopaedia Britannica* added $15,000, for an inquiry into the state and prospects of freedom of the press in America, with Robert M. Hutchins, then chancellor of the University of Chicago, as chairman. A dozen outstanding scholars and public leaders, who had no personal stake in the press, interviewed reporters, editors, readers, and analyzed papers and surveys before issuing their conclusions, in 1947, in a supplement to *Fortune* and in book form under the title, *A Free and Responsible Press.*

The commission found freedom of the press in danger because its development as an instrument of mass communication had decreased the proportion of the people who could express their opinions and ideas through the press, because the few who were able to use its machinery had not provided a service adequate to the needs of society, and because society would inevitably undertake to control or regulate the press if practices that it condemned were not corrected. Government action, the commission warned, might prove more disastrous than the ills it sought to cure.

Specifically, the commission decried precisely the kind of concentration of power represented by the pervasive Luce interests.

Luce never made any official statement concerning the commission's finding nor has he ever voiced any fixed formula for his magazines. Associates said he "edited by ear," and remarked that a special set of antennae was needed to pick up Luce's wave-lengths. His mind, given voice, raced, stalled, detoured, and backfired. Often he stopped midway in a sentence or even a word, started over, and stuttered a little. He gave the impression at times that his mind was going too fast for his words to keep pace, at others that he was groping for just the right shade of meaning. Profound thoughts and inarticulate expression left a blur for the unaccustomed listener.

Luce's magazines reflected a strange dualism in his approach to life. He worshipped facts and for that reason might regard the profession of journalism as amoral, with no social obligation but to inform. At the same time, he inherited the qualities of missionary and crusader, a call to teach and reform and to make the facts speak for him as well as for themselves. From the walled Chinese compound of his boyhood to the penthouse tower atop the luxurious *Time-Life* building in New York City, little of his life had been spent in direct contact with the man in the streets and in the fields.

From their heights, which impart a superior know-it-all quality to what they write, Luce and his editors have struggled with the concept of objectivity.

"No article will be written to prove any special case," *Time's* initial promotion said. "But the editors recognize that complete neutrality on public questions and important news is probably as undesirable as it is impossible, and are therefore ready to acknowledge certain prejudices which may in varying measure predetermine their opinions on the news."

The catalogue of these prejudices included:

1. A belief that the world is round and an admiration of the statesman's "view of the world."
2. A general distrust of the present tendency toward increasing interference by government.
3. A prejudice against the rising cost of government.
4. Faith in the things which money cannot buy.
5. A respect for the old, particularly in manners.
6. An interest in the new, particularly in ideas.

Since *Time* had no editorial page, Luce turned to the pages of *Life* for direct statements of his own thinking.

Almost a year before the United States entered the second World War, an editorial in *Life* bearing his signature and entitled "The American Century," declared: "America is at war. But we are not in a war to defend American territory. We are in a war to defend and even to promote, encourage and incite so-called democratic principles throughout the world." Luce saw "America as the dynamic center of ever-widening spheres of enterprise, America as the Good Samaritan, really believing again that it is more blessed to give than to receive, and America as the powerhouse of the ideals of Freedom and Justice." But, he wrote, we must learn to think in larger terms. "For example, we think of Asia as being worth a few hundred millions to us. Actually in the decades to come Asia will be worth to us exactly Zero—or else it will be worth to us four, five, ten billions a year."

Luce expressed surprise when critics attacked this concept as imperialistic and later became convinced that the substance of the American Century article had been largely justified by events.

On certain subjects with which he is personally concerned, Luce's editorial views carry over into the information columns of *Time* and *Life*. The result of his rejection of the thesis of objectivity, or, at least, his reservations about its practicality and his justification of printing the truth as he sees it, has been the presentation of opinion and conjecture as straight news, without qualification or attribution. To those who find themselves in agreement with Luce, this practice makes his magazine a strong force for "right-thinking"; to those who disagree, the practice makes his magazines a deceptively harmful influence in the democratic process.

These considerations give added significance to the concluding sentence of Wolcott Gibbs's *New Yorker* profile of Henry Luce, written at a time when his publishing enterprises, with their present 7,000,000 circulation, were still expanding: "Where it all will end, knows God."

The only direct competition of any consequence *Time* has ever had comes from the magazine *Newsweek,* established in 1933 by Thomas J. C. Martyn and reorganized in 1937, with Astor and Harriman family funds, under Malcolm Muir. In January 1935 the *New York Times* began to publish a "Review of the Week" section, supervised by Lester Markel, a practice that was followed by many other newspapers in response to the growing appetite for news summaries in weekly capsules.

Luce's spectacular success was paralleled by that of another magazine publisher-editor, DeWitt Wallace, who similarly parlayed a simple idea into an immensely profitable venture and came to be both respected and feared for the power he wielded.

Wallace's *Reader's Digest,* which by mid-century had a circulation of more than 15,500,000—all over the world in fifty-eight countries and eleven languages and in Braille and on records for the blind—ranks, along with Luce's *Time* and *Life,* as one of the most remarkable publishing wonders in all history.

The *Reader's Digest* is not, strictly speaking, journalism since it does not deal with news, but its "articles of lasting interest" exert an impact upon public opinion that entitles its creator to attention here.

DeWitt Wallace's father was Dr. James Wallace, president of Presbyterian Macalester College at St. Paul, Minnesota, who confronted his students with Xenophon's *Anabasis* and the nation with *The Great Betrayal,* a book that denounced the Senators who had blocked American membership in the League of Nations. Dr. Wallace continued to deliver lectures with vigor when he was in his nineties.

DeWitt Wallace was born in St. Paul, and, at a suitable age, went to Macalester College for two years. He then transferred to the University of California. That was in 1909. Without completing his course there, he returned to St. Paul where he worked three years for the Webb Publishing Company, then a few months as direct-mail advertising salesman for a firm of calendar makers.

Wallace met Lila Bell Acheson, daughter of another Presbyterian minister, one Christmas vacation while he was visiting her brother Barclay, whom he had known at college, in Tacoma, Washington. They met again later when she went to St. Paul to speak as traveling secretary for the Presbyterian Church in charge of facilities for migrant workers.

While Wallace fought in the first World War and was hospitalized as a result of wounds he suffered in the Verdun offensive, Lila Bell Acheson directed morale, safety, and recreation work in munitions plants for the Young Women's Christian Association.

Lying in an Army hospital and thumbing through magazine after magazine, Wallace began to feel that it took too long to read them and that there ought to be a quicker and easier way of keeping abreast of world thought. He began to practice tightening up the articles, penciling out phrases, sentences, paragraphs. After the war, when he was working in the foreign publicity department of the Westinghouse Electric Company in Pittsburgh, he kept up his trimming of magazine articles during his spare time.

Then, in the postwar depression, he lost his job. After spending three months in Pittsburgh promoting his project by mail, he went to New York with a sample copy of collected condensations. He looked up Lila Bell Acheson and interested her in the project. They rented a storeroom under a speakeasy in Greenwich Village and prepared to publish the magazine on $5,000 they had borrowed in bits from family and friends.

Wallace and Lila Bell Acheson were married in October 1921, while more circulars announcing their project were in the mail. When they returned from their honeymoon, they found enough subscriptions to pay the first month's printing bill.

The first *Reader's Digest* appeared in February 1922 and described its contents thus: "Thirty-one articles each month from leading magazines, each article of enduring value and interest, in condensed and compact form."

The Wallaces couldn't afford to buy all the periodicals from which they wanted to digest material, so they went to the New York Public Library day after day. Puzzled attendants, handing out first a copy of *Physical Culture,* then the *Yale Review,* then the *Woman's Home Companion,* and so on until closing time, looked upon the couple as a new kind of library nut.

By the end of its first year the *Reader's Digest* had a circulation of 7,000 and the Wallaces looked for better quarters. Lila Acheson Wallace had visited Pleasantville in Westchester County and liked it. When Pendleton Dudley, Manhattan public relations man who had an estate there, offered to rent them his garage and pony-shed for twenty-five dollars a month, they took it.

For three years they lived comfortably upstairs and worked in the pony stalls. Office equipment consisted of a big table, a desk, and a filing case. They had one girl for help, except in the Christmas rush.

By 1925 the *Digest's* circulation reached 20,000. The Wallaces bought a piece of land next to Dudley's, built a home on it, moved the *Digest* office into the ground-floor study and hired several girls. As subscriptions continued to pour in, the *Digest* took over successively two floors of one Pleasantville bank building, three floors of another, the upper floor and basement of the post office, and other space.

In 1929, when the *Digest* was going to 109,000 subscribers, the first serious competitor, *Fleet's Review,* appeared on the newsstands. Meanwhile Wallace had started to pay twenty-five and fifty dollars apiece for articles used, but editors of a few other publications had begun to worry. Some people were cancelling subscriptions because they could get the cream of the crop in the little magazine. Scribner's temporarily withdrew reprint rights.

Imitators began to spring up. To meet the competition—and to limit it—Wallace took two big steps: he put the *Digest* on

sale on newsstands and he instituted contracts with source publications. One by one he signed up most of the better known
magazines and some of the lesser, agreeing to pay them large
lump sums in exchange for exclusive reprint rights.

Later the *Digest* began to produce articles of its own. In
February 1933 for the first time a byline appeared among the
magazine credits in the table of contents. After that, pieces
written on order for the *Digest* showed up more and more frequently. Freelancers joined the *Digest* staff, devoting their full
time to writing for it.

The *Digest* could now afford to repay its "hosts" in kind. It
began to offer to other magazines free, articles that it had
ordered and paid for. To publications close to the financial
margin the gifts were manna; it allowed them to feature names
that their own budgets couldn't command. More solvent magazines also welcomed the windfall but some insisted upon sending their own checks to the authors, too, at their regular rates.

It wasn't easy to spot *Digest* gifts in other magazines because
they weren't labeled. Usually, but not always, they were reprinted later in the *Digest*. Normally they were condensed;
one or two even were expanded, "with additional notes by the
author," in their second printing. Sometimes they appeared in
the *Digest* simultaneously with or before their "original" publication. A number of publications became *Digest* "farms"
where articles were regularly planted.

All this time the *Digest* was making more money and finding
new ways to spend it.

A research staff was set up to work in the New York Public
Library and another at the Cleveland library—chosen because
of its open shelves, which made the researcher's work easier—to
check facts and to look for short fillers for the magazine.

By 1938 the *Digest*'s central staff was feeling crowded in its
scattered Pleasantville cubbyholes. The Wallaces wanted to
stay in the countryside, but no building in Westchester County
suited their needs. So they built a four-story plant on an eighty-

acre tract just outside Chappaqua. From there money flowed in a steady stream to editors, authors, publishers.

Writers whose pieces had been picked up by the *Digest* were often surprised to get checks for double and triple the amount first publication had brought.

In that same year the *Digest* entered the foreign field with a British edition in London that soon had the largest circulation of all monthly magazines there. Two years later the *Digest* entered South America and the Spanish and Portuguese language editions quickly became the most widely read magazines below the border. So far Wallace had sold no advertising in the pages of his little magazine, but the South American editions carried advertising.

Certain *Digest* articles reached audiences even larger than those represented by the circulation figures. On request the *Digest* reproduced in leaflets key articles for special distribution —by schools and other interested organizations and institutions.

The basic editorial formula for the *Digest* worked out by Wallace sought to make the magazine appeal alike "to an intelligent high school student and to a college professor." At first the editors tried to get into every issue something from each of a score of categories: science, medicine, social service, education, government, the art of living, international relations, biography and personality, movies, radio, sports, travel, humor, essays, labor, business and industry, Americana, nature, and agriculture. There was heavy emphasis on miracle and achievement stories. The *Digest* was frequently uninhibited in a refreshing way, touching on subjects that many established publications tabooed. Much of its content was noncontroversial but in the political heat of the late thirties, many readers detected in the *Digest* a strong emphasis upon the conservative point of view and sharp criticism of the activities of the Roosevelt administration.

This attitude prompted Senator Joseph Guffey of Pennsylvania to call the *Digest* a "world cartel," to accuse it of subsidizing other American magazines, and to talk of antitrust action. Nothing came of this threat but, at about the same time, the *New Yorker* refused to let the *Digest* use any more of its material, in protest against the *Digest*'s "reprint myth" and its "creative function, which is a threat to the free flow of ideas and to the independent spirit." The *New Republic* followed suit, objecting not so much to the *Digest*'s reprint practices as to its apparent political philosophy.

Subsequently, the *Digest* discontinued its exclusive reprint contracts with other magazines and began to charge for articles it offered for publication elsewhere.

Wallace brushed off the Guffey charges as New Deal nonsense, the *New Yorker*'s action as intellectual snobbery, and the *New Republic*'s protest as leftist propaganda. With attractive Lila Acheson Wallace at his side and with her brother, Barclay, running the foreign editions, he went right on building circulation, adding benevolent luxuries and comforts for the 1,300 employes in the idyllic plant at Chappaqua, increasing the army of roving editors, and paying freelance writers generously for what they wrote, even if it wasn't used. To visitors at the opulent *Digest* plant, artfully decorated under Mrs. Wallace's direction, De Witt Wallace seemed forever surprised at what had befallen him; his "little wonder" was a constant source of proud amazement even to its creator.

On the occasion of its thirtieth anniversary the *Digest* published an anthology of the best of all of the 12,960 articles and books it had printed or condensed. Meanwhile the *Digest* had added another popular and profitable sideline by issuing four times a year a volume of book condensations (supplementary to the monthly book condensations), which soon rivaled the output of the older book clubs.

The sophisticated *New Yorker,* so scornful of both Wallace's "capsule" theories and Luce's omniscient techniques, made a mark all its own on the journalism of its day. Founded, like *Time* and the *Reader's Digest,* in the topsy-turvy twenties, with the financial backing of Raoul Fleischmann, it developed under the editorship of a volatile genius from Colorado, Harold Ross, some of the finest and most polished reporting of all time. John Hersey's story of Hiroshima, to which the magazine once turned over its entire issue, shines as a classic example.

Besides profoundly affecting the pattern of American humor and fiction publications, the *New Yorker* developed specialized reporting in its penetrating biographical "Profiles," in its critical "Wayward Press" commentary, in its "Reporter at Large" pieces and its "Letters" from various capitals and world centers. Ross, the "shy egotist" whose dominating drive gave these features their high polish, died in Boston after a lung operation on December 6, 1951 at the age of fifty-nine. He was succeeded as editor by William Shawn, polite, tactful, quiet—unlike Ross in almost every way except in his devotion to precision.

27

Washington and the
Political Pundits

PRESS AND POLITICS GO HAND IN HAND, YET WASHINGTON, FOUNT
of American political life, has throughout its history been called
a journalistic graveyard. Although the eyes of the nation focus
on the capital, almost 600 newspapers and other periodicals
have lived and died there without so much as casting a shadow
beyond the seventy square miles of the District of Columbia.

Nevertheless, while New York has remained the capital of
journalistic enterprise, Washington because of the corps of
correspondents and syndicated columnists centered there, if not
because of its local newspapers, functions as the fountainhead
of the nation's news and editorial opinion.

The *Post,* alone of Washington's four surviving dailies, has
aspired to nation-wide prestige, but only since it was acquired
in 1933 by Eugene Meyer, stocky, high-browed, sharp-eyed and
gruffly amiable ex-banker with a long record of activity as a
public servant.

In 1946, at seventy, Meyer retired as publisher and turned
the job over to his thirty-one-year-old son-in-law, Philip L.
Graham, a studious, thoughtful, and slow-spoken lawyer just
out of the Army.

Under his management, the *Post* gained the highest readership among Congressmen, Cabinet members, and other national

policy-makers of any newspaper; it is the most frequently quoted in the *Congressional Record*.

The *Post* established itself as an organ of internationalism in 1937 when it applauded President Roosevelt's famous "quarantine-the-aggressor" speech in Chicago. Two years later it so accurately interpreted Roosevelt's Warm Springs remark—"I'll be back in the fall if we don't have a war"—that the President had the entire editorial included in the minutes of his press conference, calling it "very good, very clear, very honest."

The *Post*'s rapid rise in Washington is a story of regeneration.

Founded as a Democratic organ in 1877, well after the *Evening Star* had established itself, the *Post* was purchased in 1905 by John R. McLean, prosperous owner of the *Cincinnati Enquirer,* a principal stockholder in the Washington Gas Company, and one of the capital's leading bankers. Until then the only fame that had come to the paper was the dedication of the *Washington Post March* to it by John Philip Sousa.

On John McLean's death in 1916 control of the *Post* passed to his popular playboy son, Edward B. (Ned) McLean, a poker-table companion of President Harding and the ill-starred Secretary of the Interior, Albert Fall. McLean was said to have sold the zinc in the paper's morgue and emptied its tills of cash, leaving no funds to meet the payrolls. Circulation fell to 50,000. Sick and in bad repute, he left the paper and moved to Canada. The American Security and Trust Company, which had removed McLean from control for neglect of duty, put the paper on the auction block.

On June 1, 1933, Mrs. Evalyn Walsh McLean, estranged wife of Ned McLean, was in the crowd that gathered in front of the *Post* building. Through her attorney she bid up to $600,000 in an effort to keep the paper for her sons. It was reported that she offered to sell her jewels to raise the money. Failing to get the paper, she continued her role as Number One Hostess of Washington until she was succeeded by Mrs. Perle Mesta.

As the bidding for the *Post* continued, a Hearst representative offered $800,000 and then, for an undisclosed principal,

George E. Hamilton, made an offer of $825,000, which was accepted. Two weeks later it was announced that the buyer was Eugene Meyer, who four years earlier had been willing to pay $5,000,000 for the paper.

Meyer had resigned as governor of the Federal Reserve Board only the previous month, although President Roosevelt, who had come to office that year, had asked him to stay on. Meyer's extensive public service under four Presidents included drawing up the Reconstruction Finance Corporation bill for Hoover and serving as the RFC's first chairman.

Aged fifty-seven and without journalistic experience, Meyer went about rebuilding the *Post*. Change was almost immediately apparent. The latest pay-cut was restored, the staff enlarged, bylines appeared on the front page along with bigger type, brighter headlines, and better pictures. Felix Morley was brought in from the Brookings Institution as mentor of the editorial page.

Meyer and Morley meant from the start to make the editorial page the heart of the paper, at a time when many other editors seemed to be abdicating their prerogatives of political leadership in favor of the syndicated opinion columnists. At the same time, however, they sought to create a forum and in so doing loaded their pages heavily with the writings of those very columnists.

A feud soon developed between Meyer and Eleanor Patterson, who was then operating the *Times* and *Herald* for Hearst. They raided one another's staffs for prize writers and tried to outbuy one another on features. The *Post* published the Gumps, Dick Tracy, and other valued *Chicago Tribune* comic strips. Mrs. Patterson used her connections with Cousin McCormick of the *Tribune* to try to get them away from Meyer. When Meyer sued to stop her and won a court injunction, Mrs. Patterson, with invidious allusion to the character of Shylock in the *Merchant of Venice,* had her butcher wrap and send a pound of raw meat to Meyer.

When Meyer sought to buy the *Herald* to combine with the

Post in 1937, Mrs. Patterson was spurred into leasing it, along with the *Times,* from Hearst, with an option on purchase. Two years later she bought and combined the papers. The *Times-Herald* took to speaking contemptuously of "our venerable lady friend, the *Post"* and "our nasty-nice morning contemporary."

A procession of news editors marched through the *Post,* but by 1935 the paper hit its stride with the hiring of Alexander (Casey) Jones from Minneapolis. Without attempting to become a paper of record, the *Post* endeavored to reestablish itself in the community. It gathered news to support crusades for slum clearance, against the baby-adoption racket, for penny milk for schoolchildren, against gambling, and for police reform.

Felix Morley resigned in 1940 to become president of Haverford College, and Herbert Elliston, a native of Yorkshire, England, and former financial editor and columnist for the *Christian Science Monitor,* was named associate editor.

A little later, after the second World War involved the United States, Agnes E. Meyer, who took no active part in the control of the paper, proved herself one of its principal editorial assets. A graduate of Barnard College and a member of the staff of the old *New York Morning Sun* for a short time before her marriage, Mrs. Meyer surveyed the British home front, then made an extended tour of wartime America. She wrote a long, discerning, and carefully documented series, later collected into a book, *Journey Through Chaos.*

In April 1942, the day after a *Post* editorial had belabored Jesse H. Jones, Secretary of Commerce and publisher of the *Chronicle* in Houston, Texas, for failing to anticipate the rubber shortage, Jones ran into Meyer at a gathering of the Alfalfa Club. Jones, the bigger man, seized Meyer by the lapels and shook him until Meyer's pince-nez glasses dropped to the floor. Meyer, who had once studied boxing under James J. Corbett, came back with a haymaker that went wild, and other guests separated them.

While Meyer was thus aggressively asserting himself, the only one of the five Meyer children who indicated much interest in the paper was Katharine (Kay), who handled letters to the editor and worked in the circulation department before she married Philip L. Graham.

Graham was born in South Dakota and reared in Florida where his father, Ernest R. Graham, owned a large dairy herd. He went to Harvard and was editor of the *Law Review,* served as secretary successively to Supreme Court Justices Stanley Reed and Felix Frankfurter, and worked in the government's lend-lease administration. When the United States entered the war, Graham enlisted in the Air Force, was sent to the intelligence school at Harrisburg, later served at the Pentagon in Washington, then in Leyte and Manila. When the war ended he was a major.

When Eugene Meyer was appointed president of the International Bank for Reconstruction and Development in June 1946, he announced that he was severing all connection with the *Post*. He had his name removed from the masthead and designated Graham publisher, with Elliston as chief of the editorial page.

Six months later, satisfied that his work in getting the world bank started was completed, he resigned as its president and returned to his office as chairman of the board at the *Post* but not to day-to-day operational administration. A novel arrangement was set up, whereby voting stock in the *Post* (of which Graham owns a majority and his wife a minority) could not be sold except to a person approved by an independent committee of five.

Graham continued Meyer's established practice of giving editor and other executives free rein and deferring to professional know-how. The *Post* deliberately divided the editorial and news departments into separate domains with Elliston presiding over opinion and Casey Jones over fact. In 1947, when Jones became assistant to the publisher, J. R. Wiggins, who had been a St. Paul editor and assistant to the publisher of the

New York Times, was put in charge of the news department. Jones eventually moved to Syracuse, New York, to become executive editor of the *Herald-Journal* and, as a president of the American Society of Newspaper Editors, an influential figure in national journalism, and Wiggins continued his constructive role on the *Post.*

In mid-century the *Post* transferred from its musty old graystone building in downtown Washington into an ultramodern plant close by the equally modern Statler Hotel. It had come a long way in fifteen years. Its editors were sensitive to criticism of its hit-and-miss local coverage, its scholarly point of view, which may have missed the man in the street, but in a country whose capital, unlike other world capitals, had never produced a truly national newspaper, the *Post* filled a niche all its own.

Although Washington is the capital of the world's greatest power, a city where every day, matters are weighed that affect the fate of the world, it is also the provincial home of thousands of ordinary people, a city that has much the spirit of a small Southern town.

For a good many years provincial Washington has sworn by the *Evening Star,* stuffed with ads, services of all kinds, and news. It is a paper in which almost any reader can find some special feature geared to his interests. Far and away the most prosperous daily in the city, the *Star* boasts that it is a home newspaper—79 per cent of its circulation delivered at the door and 95.8 per cent within the city and the immediate trading area.

The capital's biggest and oldest daily, the *Star* is a surviving example of a rare journalistic phenomenon: For the greater part of a century it has remained in the control of the same families without mergers or links with any chain and with a record of steady profits.

Founded in 1852, the paper came into the possession of Crosby Noyes in 1867. On his death in 1908, one son, Theodore W., succeeded him; another son, Frank B., held the presidency of the concern from 1910 until he died in his eighties.

Frank Noyes' son, Newbold Noyes, was associate editor for twenty-three years.

One of Crosby Noyes' partners was Samuel H. Kauffmann, whose grandson of the same name succeeded to the presidency on the death of Frank Noyes. Members of the Newbold, Boyd, and Thompson families, related by marriage, have also held key positions on the paper.

Befitting its age and dignified position, the *Star* dresses itself in neat, restrained typography. The front page remains clean, quiet, unvaried, and unmarked by heavy black type. Big headlines are reserved for big stories. The hallmark on the front page for many years has been the Berryman cartoon, distinguished by its inoffensive goodwill, on which father and son, Clifford and James Berryman, used to alternate until the father's death. Since then the son has shared the stint with Gibson Crockett.

Most of the *Star*'s national and foreign news carries an Associated Press credit line; the *Star* uses more AP domestic news than most papers since its readers include people in Washington from every part of the country. The AP, always closely linked with the *Star*, is readily accommodated to the paper's solid, sober pattern. *Star* president Frank B. Noyes was one of the AP's founders and its president for thirty-five years, after which he served as honorary president until his death. The AP located its Washington headquarters in the *Star* building.

On its inside pages the *Star* covers Washington as if it were a small town, with attention to every aspect of life within the District of Columbia and with emphasis on the doings of the pipe-and-slipper readers at home before their fireplaces. Believing in the well-tested formula that "names make news," the *Star* records the lives of Washingtonians from their births straight through school, marriage, jobs, children, golden wedding anniversaries, and deaths.

The *Star*'s tradition of definite separation between editorial and business departments was established by Crosby Noyes in the nineteenth century; an old company bylaw places sole responsibility for policy in the editor, subject only to the board of directors.

Advertising linage of the *Star* has not suffered from that rule. For years the paper led the entire country in linage and remained at the head of the evening field. In addition to its volume of display advertising, the *Star* carries four to five solid pages of classified ads daily, and as many as fourteen on Sunday, broken up only by spot cartoons—and all of its classified advertising is unsolicited.

Sandy-haired Ben McKelway, the first person outside the immediate owning families to hold stock or a top executive position on the paper, at the age of fifty-one took over his seat behind the desk he inherited in 1946 from T. W. Noyes in the triangular corner office on the seventh floor, with its unused Victorian fireplace and narrow window looking out toward the Capital. He puffed at his pipe, peered at callers owlishly, spoke diffidently, and managed his staff with quiet caution and efficiency.

McKelway, whose father, the Reverend Alexander Jeffrey McKelway, edited the weekly *Presbyterian Standard* and wrote editorials for a short time in the *Charlotte News* in North Carolina and whose younger brother, St. Clair McKelway is a successful magazine and film writer, had worked for newspapers since 1916 and for the *Star* since 1920.

Listed as a Democrat in *Who's Who*, McKelway took pains to remind interviewers that he had lived in voteless Washington most of his voting life and did not regard himself as affiliated with any party, any more than was the *Star*.

McKelway saw the *Star*'s job as one of solid coverage and careful analysis of public questions, without attempting omniscient interpretations.

"The *Star* has always been interested in the development of the city as a capital and in anything affecting the welfare of the city," he remarked once. "One of the *Star*'s first campaigns was to get the Washington Monument finished, another was to get the railroads off the Mall. It has been campaigning steadily for the elimination of Washington slums since 1914, but Washington is handicapped by the lack of organized means of expression from the people."

McKelway became sensitive to suggestions, which have been made by *Time* and other upstarts, that the *Star* was a stodgy old lady.

"We have a tradition of responsibility to maintain," he has retorted, "and we can't go off at tangents. Stunts are fun in journalism but you can't get away with them on certain types of newspapers."

The Washington best known to the outside world is not so much the provincial Washington of the *Star* as it is the national, official capital composed of administrators, lawmakers, judges, and diplomats; of politicians, lobbyists, scientists, and scholars; of men whose work, by and large, is of national concern, whose aims, by and large, are serious, and whose doings are reported by the world's largest collection of press correspondents and columnists, many of whom are themselves national figures.

The Washington political column that has all but supplanted —or at least overshadowed—the homegrown editorial in a number of American newspapers is a distinct development of the early 1930's. It was germinated by the depression and the New Deal, to satisfy an appetite for explanation and clarification of perplexing economic and social issues and the deepening complexities of federal government.

This function was spelled out early in the game by one of the most level-headed and responsible of the Washington columnists, Kansas-bred, U.P.-trained Raymond Clapper, who died in 1944 in an airplane crash in the Pacific war theater. He said:

We found . . . that there was much to be told . . . that did not get into our news stories. . . . It just did not fit, for the straight news story is a formal, conventional thing. It broke over the somber and dignified convention of news writing. . . . But as a matter of public interest, newspaper readers like to know what the man close to the story actually thinks about it. . . . In other words, is not the steady increase in the number of columns the natural reaction from a formula of news writing that has grown too stiff, that fails to paint a fully rounded picture of life in its various departments? Are we not groping for some way in which—in this day of talking pictures, radio dramatization of the news, the strident picturization of news in the weekly news magazines—we can vividly and realistically reconstruct the news of the day in our newspapers?

One of the earliest and most influential, if not the first of the serious type of opinion columns that attempted to interpret the news, tell what it meant, and what the writer thought about it, was undertaken by Walter Lippmann. Although Lippmann did not start his stint in Washington, he made the capital the base of his operations soon after his column found its audience, for Washington was the place where the news that needed interpreting was being made.

Born in New York City on September 23, 1889, Lippmann as a boy studied in private schools and in summers went abroad with his father, a prosperous manufacturer of German descent. In his sophomore year at Harvard, the sight of the Chelsea slums in Boston where he had been summoned with other University students to help families made homeless by a fire, so shocked Lippmann that he turned to the kind of reading and study that led him to help organize a college Socialist club.

Writing for undergraduate magazines, Lippmann became a friend and disciple of the philosopher, William James. After completing his four-year course at Harvard in three years, Lippmann served as assistant to George Santayana in philosophy classes. As would seem almost inevitable for a youth of his leanings in those days, Lippmann was enlisted by Lincoln Steffens as a fellow muck-raker on the staff of *Everybody's Magazine*.

For a short while thereafter Lippmann was secretary to the Socialist mayor of Schenectady, New York. Then he retired to a cabin in the Maine woods to write his first book, *A Preface to Politics*.

When the liberal opinion weekly, the *New Republic,* was founded in 1914, Lippmann joined its editorial board. Three years later, President Wilson asked Lippmann to become special assistant to Newton D. Baker, Secretary of War, to handle labor relations in the construction of Army camps.

Wilson's aide, Colonel E. M. House, was impressed by a book Lippmann had meanwhile written, *The Stakes of Diplomacy*, and appointed him secretary of the staff to assemble data for the World War I Peace Conference. He was then commissioned a captain of military intelligence and sent overseas in 1918 to prepare propaganda for the War Department and serve as special agent of the State Department in studying and trying to correlate the peace plans of England and France.

Ten days before the Armistice, Lippmann was summoned to Paris and informed that the Germans were ready to surrender, on the basis of Wilson's Fourteen Points, which Lippmann had helped to draw up. Wilson appointed Lippmann to the staff of the Peace Commission, but when disillusionment with the progress of the settlement overcame Lippmann, he resigned and returned to the *New Republic*.

At the invitation of Frank I. Cobb, editor, Lippmann went to work for the *New York World* in 1921. Two years later Cobb died and Lippmann took his place. Lippmann's brilliant direction of the editorial page and its crusades was one of the predominant factors that gave such luster to the *World* in the twenties. On the side Lippmann continued to set down his ideas in book form. His classic on public opinion, in which he explored the concept of stereotypes in American thinking, took its place on library shelves as a perennial reference source.

When the *World* folded, Lippmann, politically independent but well to the right of the socialism of his youth, was called to the *New York Herald Tribune,* where he dropped the anonymity of the editorial page and came into the open with a signed column, "Today and Tomorrow." Syndication followed, with results best described by Frederick Lewis Allen in his *Since Yesterday:*

> For more orthodox men and women the consumption of Walter Lippmann's daily analysis of events was becoming a matitutinal rite as inevitable as coffee and orange juice. . . . Clear, cool and orderly in his

thinking, he seemed to be able to reduce a senseless sequence of events to sense; he brought first aid to men and women groping in the dark for opinions.

With the *Herald Tribune* tolerantly promoting Lippmann, for he was often in disagreement with the paper's editorial policies, he fulfilled his daily role almost without interruption until 1951, when he took time out to add another volume to the impressive shelf of books bearing his name.

More directly a product of the Washington scene than Lippman and just as truly a pioneer in political columning was David Lawrence.

While Lawrence was an infant his family moved to Buffalo, New York, from Philadelphia, where he was born on Christmas Day of 1888. Lawrence worked for the *Buffalo Express* in his spare time while he was still in high school. Later, at Princeton, he attracted the attention of Woodrow Wilson, then president of the university. Upon his graduation in 1910 he joined the Washington bureau of the AP. Quickly he won the confidence of the diplomatic corps to which he was assigned. Later the Madero and Orozco revolutions in Mexico gave him a workout in on-the-spot news coverage. Returning to Washington after Wilson became President, Lawrence was close to the ear of the administration and succeeded in outmanoeuvring the other White House correspondents.

Lawrence escaped from the rigid strictures and selfless anonymity of the Associated Press in 1915 to the staff of the *New York Post,* where he wrote the daily lead story out of Washington under his own byline. The shirt tail of interpretation that he added to his dispatches was a novelty for those days and as it caught on, his pieces came to tell more and more of the why and less and less of the who, what, when, where. When the *Post* began to syndicate these stories in 1916, it was the first time Washington dispatches other than those of the press associations had been distributed across the nation by wire. Encouraged by the *Post* to set up his own syndicate of news features, Lawrence organized in 1920 a telegraphic service known as the Consolidated Press Association.

Hoping to inform the people further about their government, Lawrence founded the *United States Daily* in 1926; changed the name to the *United States News* when it became a weekly seven years later; and seven years after that, in 1940, dropped the newspaper format for that of the magazine. In 1946 Lawrence started *World Report* and two years later combined it with his original periodical into a single publication. *U. S. News and World Report.*

Lawrence, an early exponent of Wilson's New Freedom, has always classified himself as a "conservative liberal." In his columns, which ultimately went to 190 newspapers, he favored passage of the minimum wage law, advocated the RFC as an intermediate banking system, defended the right of collective bargaining, and supported reciprocal trade treaties.

For several years Lawrence operated the Bureau of National Affairs, which supplied subscribers reference services, digests of court decisions, and the like. Releases of the bureau, which was turned over to its employes in the late 1940's, bore some resemblance to another twentieth-century development in Washington journalism—the news-letter. These relatively small, but potent, mimeographed or printed sheets of inside information are circulated at high subscription rates, without advertising, to limited audiences.

Homer Joseph Dodge claims to have established in 1913 the first of the Washington news-letters as they are known today. It was the Bankers' Information Service, an intermittent letter almost wholly confined to news of the establishment of the New Federal Reserve System. The letter developed into a daily service, carried by leased wire to New York and covering news of the federal government important to banks, industrial corporations, commercial establishments, law firms, and other interests.

The second Washington news-letter of wide interest was established by two Philadelphia newspapermen, P. H. Whaley and Henry M. Eaton in 1918. It was edited at mid-century by the aging but still active Whaley and Harry Eaton, son of the original partner.

The most widely circulated news-letter is that of Willard Monroe Kiplinger, a native of Indiana. After an apprenticeship with the Associated Press and the Bankers' Information Service, he established the *Kiplinger Washington Letter* in 1923. In 1947 Kiplinger established *Kiplinger's Magazine* to reach a wider and more general audience.

Interpretation and explanation distinguished the type of columns developed by Lippmann and Lawrence and the bevy of writers who followed them; revelation and sensation marked a second type of political column that erupted in Washington in the thirties. Just as Walter Winchell from New York made capital of the secrets and anticipated "blessed events" of Broadway, Drew Pearson (see photograph 17) and Robert S. Allen found a ready market for exposure of behind-the-scenes goings-on and predictions of things to come in Washington. By 1951 the column they started, now conducted by Pearson alone, led all the rest, appearing in 600 papers.

Pearson was baptized Andrew Russell after his birth, December 13, 1897, in Evanston, Illinois, where his minister-father, Paul Martin Pearson, was taking postgraduate work at Northwestern University. Paul Pearson later continued his studies at Harvard and became a professor of public speaking at Swarthmore. There he joined the Society of Friends and Drew was reared as a Quaker.

Drew attended Phillips Academy at Exeter, New Hampshire, and went on to Swarthmore. During vacations he worked on the Chautauqua circuit, first helping with the tents, then operating the motion picture machine, and finally appearing on the platform as a lecturer.

After graduation from Swarthmore in 1919, Pearson spent two years in European relief work for the British Red Cross and for the American Friends Service Committee. Putting aside for the moment his ambition to get into the diplomatic service, he took a job teaching industrial geography at the University of Pennsylvania on his return to the United States.

Using his collegiate connections, Pearson covered the Washington Disarmament Conference in 1922 for the Swarthmore student weekly, the *Phoenix,* and for the Intercollegiate Press Association, which he had founded as an undergraduate.

Then he prepared a circular entitled, "Around the World with Drew Pearson" and persuaded thirty-five editors across the country to buy the dispatches he planned to mail from abroad. To start his tour, he had his chest tatooed with the crescent and star, and bared it in hiring-halls to get a job as seaman. Jumping ship at Yokohama, he continued around the world on his own, sending his promised dispatches and lecturing as he went.

On a later trip Pearson got interviews with "Europe's twelve greatest men" for syndication by the United Publishers Corporation News Service in America, and on still another journey he visited the Gobi Desert.

After David Lawrence started his *United States Daily* he hired Pearson as foreign editor, a post that took him to the Geneva Naval Conference in 1927. Two years later Pearson moved to the Washington bureau of the *Baltimore Sun* and became diplomatic correspondent.

One day at a press conference with Secretary of State Kellogg, Pearson's attention was attracted to a cocky little reporter at the foot of the conference table who was demanding to know why the United States had sent Marines in Nicaragua, why Mexico had been "attacked," and why we were "picking on little nations."

That reporter turned out to be Robert S. Allen, who, like Pearson, had been trying in vain to get his paper, the *Christian Science Monitor,* to print the juicy out-of-the-ordinary bits of news he had been able to pick up about the Hoover Administration. The two men—rambunctious, hard-boiled, belligerent Allen and smooth, soft-spoken, cultured Pearson—were drawn to one another and became good friends.

In 1932 both official and unofficial Washington were startled by the appearance of a racy, gossipy, irreverent book entitled, "Washington Merry-Go-Round." When it became known that the authors of the book were Pearson and Allen, both lost their correspondence jobs. After Allen had been fired a second time in a policy dispute with the Hearst bureau, the two ousted writers got together a newspaper column in the same saucy, free-and-easy style as the book and began syndication of the "Washington Merry-Go-Round" with only six newspaper subscribers as a starter. Within a few years it was appearing in hundreds of papers with millions of readers.

In 1936 they collaborated on a book, *The Nine Old Men,* which was a forerunner of President Roosevelt's move to reorganize the Supreme Court and which prompted David Lawrence to retort with a book called *Nine Honest Men* in defense of the Court as it was then constituted.

When the second World War started, Allen went back into the Army where he had served nine years in his youth and became General Patton's intelligence officer. After the war, in which he lost an arm, Allen began a column of his own for the *New York Post* and Pearson continued alone with the "Merry-Go-Round."

By now Pearson had become one of the most colorful and controversial figures in the journalistic world. After a radio broadcast in which he had said that Secretary of State Cordell Hull wanted to see Russia "bled white," Pearson won the dubious distinction of being dubbed a "chronic liar" by President Roosevelt.

Both Pearson and Allen contributed to journalistic history in their private lives as well as their professional lives. Allen married Ruth Finney, astute Scripps-Howard writer and one of the most highly regarded women members of the Washington corps. Pearson married the Countess Felicia Gizycka, daughter of Eleanor Patterson, in 1925. They were divorced in 1928, but Pearson's relationship with Mrs. Patterson remained friendly, for a time at least. In 1936 when Pearson married the divorced wife of a *Times-Herald* staff member, George Abell, Mrs. Patterson installed the new Mrs. Patterson as her motion picture reviewer. Eventually, however, when Pearson and Allen withdrew their column, which supported Roosevelt's foreign policy, from the hostile pages of the *Times-Herald,* its publisher proceeded to berate them. Mrs. Patterson took to ridiculing her former son-in-law as "The Headache Boy."

In the midst of the controversy that swirled around Pearson —denials and contradictions of his tips and forecasts and threats of libel action—he could point to such confirmation of his important statements about corruption in high office as the conviction of Congressman Thomas Parnell and the investigation of the five percenters in government, which led to the conviction of John Maragon. A feud developed between Pearson and Wisconsin's Senator Joseph McCarthy, which brought them to blows in Washington's Sulgrave Club in December 1950.

When Adam Hats announced that it was not renewing its contract as Pearson's radio sponsor, other correspondents joined the fight. Westbrook Pegler, in thorough sympathy with McCarthy's methods, wrote of Pearson: "That lying blackguard is my man, just as Harold Ickes was in his time. Santa Claus brought him to me. Pearson is a liar and a rogue and I will belt him through the skylight as a service to my country and my honorable profession of journalism."

Pearson sued Pegler for libel, and other newspapers and newspapermen came to Pearson's defense. Calling McCarthy's charge that Pearson was a communist tool an "outrageous big lie," the Washington *Post* said: "McCarthy is able, by virtue of his Congressional immunity, to engage in unrestricted defamation of any radio commentator or newspaper columnist whose opinions displease him. . . . The public must demand an end to the kind of thought control that Senator McCarthy is creating through blackmailing advertisers."

Adam Hats denied, in a full-page ad in the *New York Times,* that it had dropped Pearson because of pressures and announced that it had previously notified Pearson it was switching into printed advertising.

Nonetheless two months later Pearson brought suit against McCarthy for libel and also asked $250,000 for being "painfully grabbed by the neck and kicked in the groin" by McCarthy in their December brawl. Pearson also sued Pegler, Fulton Lewis Jr., and others, charging they had conspired to hold him up to "public scorn and ridicule" and rob him of potential sponsors for his radio program.

Pearson had sued Pegler for libel twice before. He withdrew the first suit in 1946 after he and Pegler made a gentlemen's agreement to stop calling each other names. The second suit was filed after Pegler called Pearson a "lying blackguard."

The new personal journalism of the syndicated columnist, here at least, seemed to be recapturing some of the high old flavor of invective and vituperation that marked the old personal journalism of the eighteenth-century editors.

The stories of those few personal journalists that have been related here are a mere sampling of a subject about which books have been written. Lippmann, Lawrence, and Pearson, however, remain the pioneers who set the pace for those who followed them—Dorothy Thompson, Frank Kent, Marquis Childs, Thomas Stokes, the Alsop brothers, Doris Fleeson, Peter Edson, and the many, many others.

By mid-century the number of syndicated political columnists operating out of Washington numbered close to half a hundred, not to mention the regular correspondents for newspapers and press associations who swell the capital press corps to 1,500 men and women filing 700,000 words a day. Many of them often exercise their prerogative to express themselves editorially upon affairs of the day.

With a few notable exceptions such as the *New York Times, Christian Science Monitor,* and *Chicago Tribune,* scarcely a daily newspaper in the country with 25,000 circulation or more fails to print the writings of one or more of the syndicated columnists from three to six times a week. The *Times,* the *Monitor,* and the *Tribune,* of course, give their readers a similar

service through the opinions of their own writers like Arthur
Krock, and Roscoe Drummond, and Walter Trohan.

For many of these pundits of the press, the opening up of the
new fields of radio and television added another dimension to
their tasks and a wider range to their activities.

28

New Voices and New Faces

IN SEPTEMBER 1920 A LOCAL DEPARTMENT STORE ADVERTISED IN the *Pittsburgh Sun* that Dr. Frank Conrad was broadcasting experimentally and that by purchasing receivers (handmade locally) customers could join the select audience of the new scientific marvel—radio. Two months later some 500 persons put on earphones and heard Dr. Conrad and his station (now bearing the famous call letters KDKA) report the victory of Warren G. Harding over James M. Cox in that year's Presidential election. This was the nation's first scheduled news broadcast.

In January 1928 Dr. E. F. W. Alexanderson of the General Electric Company invited reporters to a house on Front Street in Schenectady, New York, to watch and hear on an instrument there the words and motions of a girl stationed several miles away. This was the nation's first public demonstration of television, but laboratory perfection of television equipment took a dozen more years.

In the summer of 1940, despite the small number of television sets yet in existence, the National Broadcasting Company turned four cameras upon the Republican National Convention in Philadelphia. This was the first public telecast of a news event.

From these beginnings a great new area of journalism has

developed, which has not yet reached the stage where its ultimate effect upon the earlier media of communication can be
accurately estimated. It has brought before the American public a whole chorus of new voices and an army of new faces
intent upon telling the news and interpreting it.

Who are the real makers of this most modern journalism of
sight and sound?

Are they the scientists whose researches made it all possible—
men like Grant and Conrad, Berzelius and De Forest, Einstein
and Marconi?

Are they the industrial and executive masters who financed,
capitalized upon, and developed the inventions—men like David
Sarnoff, Niles Tramwell, Frank Stanton, and Dr. Allen B.
Dumont?

All, of course, deserve a good share of the credit, just as Hoe
of the printing press, Mergenthaler of the linotype, and the
business and legal counsellors of the American Newspaper Publishers Association had a hand in the making of the earlier
journalism of the daily newspaper.

Within the context of this chronicle, however, the men with
whom we are primarily concerned are the men who saw the
news opportunities offered by the fresh channels and made the
most immediate and direct use of them to carry information to
the people.

While men like Paul White and A. A. Schechter remained
in the background seeing that the news got onto the air, other
men took the spotlight.

Straight news broadcasters were the more numerous and perhaps, in the final analysis, more important, but the commentators who spiced their presentation of facts with rumor or
speculation, prediction or interpretation, won the most listeners and became themselves news personalities.

In this category, by virtue of the size of his audience and his
unique contribution to the journalism of his day, Walter
Winchell comes first.

Winchellism was not spawned by radio but it came to its

fullest flower over the air, where its neologisms, Broadway boudoir whisperings, and cosmic overtones took on the added feverish excitement of a high-pitched voice, fast-paced delivery, and the staccato accompaniment of a clicking telegraph key.

Winchell's schooling in his native New York ended with the sixth grade when, at thirteen, he went on the stage with the Newsboys' Sextette in Gus Edwards' 1910 song revue.

In the first World War Winchell left the variety theaters where he was playing his own act to enlist in the Navy where he was promoted from apprentice seaman to third-class yeoman. After the war he appeared on the Pantages circuit in a singing, dancing, and talking act called "Winchell and Green." In an early display of his flair for coining words, he wrote a bulletin of professional gossip called the "Daily Newsense," which he posted on notice boards in the theaters where he played.

In 1922 Winchell went to work for Glenn Condon, editor of the *New York Vaudeville News,* published by the E. F. Albee circuit, as reporter, photographer, and advertising solicitor.

When Bernarr Macfadden started the New York tabloid *Graphic* in 1924, his editor, Fulton Oursler, hired Winchell as dramatic editor, critic, and columnist. In the milieu of tabloids, speakeasies, and racketeering, Winchell probed into the intimacies of the private lives of the famous and the notorious beyond the limits known to any "keyhole journalism" of the past. He told when Broadway notables were "infanticipating" even to the point of predicting the dates of coming "blessed events"; he revealed when popular couples "phfft" and when they planned to "Renovate." His phrase, "making whoopee," found a permanent place in the nation's lexicon; his other inspirations, like "middle-aisling," remained his own special trademark or the stock of the imitators who followed in his wake, and won for Winchell recognition from Henry L. Mencken, expert on the American language.

Sources for his tips included checkroom girls, nightclub waiters, taxi drivers, press agents, other reporters with stories their own papers wouldn't handle, and volunteers from all ranks.

In 1929 Winchell took his gossip to the *Mirror,* Hearst tabloid, from which it was distributed by the King Features Syndicate. He remained there, although the coming of Roosevelt and the New Deal and the second World War—with all of which he was in patriotic accord—found him often at odds with Hearst editorial policies. At one point The Chief warned his editors: "Watch Winchell, he's getting dangerous and careless." Besides needling his employer, Winchell engaged in a series of feuds with fellow columnists.

By now Winchell was on the air every Sunday night, in the vanguard of the radio commentators. The kidnaping of the Lindbergh baby gave Winchell his big opportunity to branch out from mere Broadway tidbits to matters of greater import. His knowledge of gangsterdom and his friendship with J. Edgar Hoover of the Federal Bureau of Investigation gave him a definite edge on the other reporters. After the conviction and execution of Bruno Hauptmann for the crime, Hoover thanked Winchell publicly for aiding the investigation by withholding for twenty-four hours his clear beat on Hauptmann's arrest.

For a while some of the tips too hot for his orthodox press and radio outlets appeared in a column that Winchell wrote for the upstart newspaper *PM* over the signature of Paul Revere II.

Winchell had been commissioned a Lieutenant Commander in the Navy in 1934 and he went into uniform a few weeks after Pearl Harbor. Continuation of his pro-Administration broadcasts drew fire from anti-Roosevelt Congressmen.

Back in mufti after the war, Winchell turned on the Reds the fire he had trained against fascist seditionists and stepped up the intensity of his exposés and alarums. He boasted of having twenty columns quoted in the *Congressional Record* within six months, of having uncannily predicted the death of gangster Vincent Coll on the assassination eve, of having brought about the surrenders of racketeers Lepke and Macri, of exclusive interviews with Frank Costello and other slippery newsmakers.

In October 1951 Winchell signed an exclusive lifetime contract with the American Broadcasting Company whereby, in return for his services as consultant for radio and television, he would receive about $520,000 a year in addition to shares of the company's and his sponsor's stock.

In his public and professional performance, as world crisis electrified the atmosphere, Winchell came more and more to encompass affairs of Washington and the world as well as of Broadway. His broadcasts took on the flavor of Messianic punditry, a field in which others had pioneered before him.

The undisputed "dean" of the radio pundits is Hans Von Kaltenborn, whose clipped pronouncements upon events of the day have been going out over the air ever since 1922. It was appropriate that, when television beamed its first coast-to-coast program from the Japanese Peace Treaty conference at San Francisco in September 1951, the running commentary was provided by Kaltenborn.

Kaltenborn spent his early boyhood in the small town of Merrill, Wisconsin, and worked in the woods as a lumberjack before he began writing for Milwaukee newspapers in both English and German at the age of nineteen. Looking for wider horizons, he set out for New York and worked his way to Europe on a cattleboat for what was to be the first of some thirty crossings. On his return from Europe he settled in New York and got a job on the *Brooklyn Eagle* by a device few modern editors would recommend: submitting poetry for publication. After two years on the *Eagle,* he entered Harvard University in 1905.

During a later transatlantic voyage, while a traveling tutor for Vincent Astor, he met the Baroness Olga Nordenflycht, daughter of the then German Consul General in Rio de Janeiro, and married her in Berlin in 1910.

Kaltenborn returned to work for the *Eagle* as a reporter but was soon called upon to edit the dramatic section and write editorials and interpretive articles; then to serve successively as head of the Paris bureau, managing editor, and associate editor.

Kaltenborn's radio debut in 1922 preceded the organization of the great coast-to-coast networks. (The National Broadcasting Company was founded in 1926, and the Columbia Broadcasting System in 1927.) He joined CBS in 1930 and remained there until 1940 when he switched to NBC.

Speaking several languages fluently, Kaltenborn became a world commuter and undertook to interpret Europe and Asia to the United States. He interviewed Chiang Kai-shek, "an altogether charming human being," at a back-province Buddhist monastery. When the Kaltenborns met Mussolini "he even treated us as important guests by rising from his chair and advancing to the front of his desk while we covered the interminable distance . . . across the immense room." He interviewed Hitler at Berchtesgaden in 1932 and found him "far more capable than people abroad give him credit for," adding that "it is a mistake to think that because a man wears a moustache he has no brains." He made frequent trips to Soviet Russia and broadcast over Moscow's powerful Comintern station.

In 1938 the Munich crisis and the approach of war in Europe gave both radio as a whole and Kaltenborn in particular their biggest boost as news purveyors. Up to that time Kaltenborn had been heard on the air once or twice a week at the rate of $100 a broadcast; thereafter his income from broadcasting, lectures, and books reached thousands of dollars weekly. During the German invasion of France he remained on the air about eighteen hours a day. Up to two days before Hitler invaded Poland, however, Kaltenborn had been convinced and so told his listeners, that war would be averted by further appeasement.

Once, while being interviewed by the glamorous radio-television man-and-wife team of Tex McCrary and Jinx Falkenburg, Kaltenborn told of teaching his son Rolf how to play deck tennis when the boy was ten. On a later cruise father and son met in the finals of a shipboard tournament. During the match Mrs. Kaltenborn whispered to her husband, "This match means a lot to the boy. Let him win. We must build up his self-confidence."

"No," H.V. replied. "It wouldn't be fair to the boy. When he beats me, by God, he'll have to win because he is the best player."

Rolf managed to win. Later, after attending both Harvard and Yale, he went to work for his father, checking news reports and preparing broadcasts.

That the elder Kaltenborn never lacked self-confidence was amply demonstrated by the tone of his broadcasts, by the sixty-eight lines he pre-empted in *Who's Who,* and by his autobiography, *Fifty Fabulous Years,* published in 1950 when he was seventy-two years old and still going strong.

Other pioneers, like Lowell Thomas, followed, but meantime a new kind of radio newsmaker was rising.

As radio came of age it developed its own practitioners as well as recruiting from the training ground of the press. Edward Roscoe Murrow exemplifies the pure radio product, having risen to prominence and prestige along with the new medium itself. Neither as excitable as Winchell nor as oracular as Kaltenborn, he typifies radio newscasting at its responsible best.

Paying tribute to Murrow's "almost poetic insight into the feelings of the war-stricken English . . . due to spending every available moment, day and night, talking to the clerks, shop-girls, munitions workers, pub-sitters, raid wardens and house-wives of the Island," Elmer Davis wrote in the introduction to Murrow's *This is London:* "We who work with Murrow are keenly aware of his excellence as a reporter of pure news; indeed, some of us—having, like most radio newsmen, learned our trade in another medium—are perhaps faintly scandalized that such good reporting can be done by a man who never worked on a newspaper."

Tall, lean, and dark, with chiseled features, Murrow has been described as "the only foreign correspondent who could play a foreign correspondent in the movies and give the role all the glamour Hollywood wants."

Wesley Price, describing in the *Saturday Evening Post* his "coppery baritone charged with authority" and his "all-American, beveled accent," reported that Murrow was at heart a moralist who wouldn't preach.

When Murrow was a boy, his family moved from his native North Carolina to the Puget Sound area on the Pacific Coast. Murrow went to Washington State University, where he concentrated on political science, speech, international relations, and dramatics.

For two years he served as compassman and topographer for timber cruisers in northwestern Washington, British Columbia, and Alaska.

From 1930 to 1932 he visited some 300 American colleges and universities and traveled in Europe as president of the National Student Federation. He organized a special student travel bureau for the federation and arranged the first international debates between American and European universities.

In 1932 he became assistant director of the Institute of International Education, financed by the Carnegie and Rockefeller Foundations, supervising personnel, finance, publications, and foreign affairs in London, Paris, Berlin, Geneva, and Vienna.

The Columbia Broadcasting System appointed Murrow director of its department of talks and special events in 1935. Murrow was on his way to Poland in March 1938 to arrange for a children's broadcast for the Columbia School of the Air when word came that Hitler had marched into Austria. Immediately Murrow chartered a passenger plane and got to Vienna in time to describe for Columbia listeners the entry of the Nazis. He followed up this historic broadcast with eye-witness accounts of Chamberlin's trips to Munich and the fall of Czechoslovakia.

"I averaged two hours sleep per day, I imagine, and I didn't dare risk any more," Murrow said. "You just had to be up and about every minute because events moved so rapidly that it would be impossible to catch up if you allowed yourself the luxury of eight hours' sleep."

As European director for CBS, Murrow assumed the responsibility of placing correspondents in key spots in Europe. Among the men he picked was William L. Shirer, whose broadcasts from Berlin placed him in the top ranks of radio reporters.

Murrow came back to the United States for a lecture tour and then, during the Battle of Britain, achieved lasting recognition for his calm but graphic broadcasts amid falling bombs.

"I can tell you from personal experience," his growing public heard him say, "that it's not pleasant to sit in a studio filled with the odor of iodine and antiseptics and talk to you at home while good friends are being carried on stretchers along the corridor outside the studio door."

And again: "Five times I've fallen flat on the pavement. . . . The individual's reaction to the sound of falling bombs cannot be described. That moan of stark terror and suspense cannot be encompassed in words."

Nevertheless Murrow spent nights on the studio roof practicing *ad lib* descriptions of the raids, drove in an open car with his colleague, Larry Leseur, to dine in Soho under an exposed skylight, broadcast morning and night, rode in every kind of military machine from submarine to bomber, served as fire warden and lost thirty pounds he could ill spare from his lean frame.

When CBS executives refused to sanction his project to take a cruise on a minesweeper, he asked for a vacation in the Kentish countryside, and came back on the air at the end of the week with a vivid first person description of life on a minesweeper.

His wife, who had been a New England girl named Janet Huntington Brewster, worked in London with him, sometimes substituting on his program when there were stories like the evacuation of the British children from London; made sandwiches and coffee for the guests who crowded their flat after midnight broadcasts; and directed the Bundles for Britain drive.

When he came home for a visit, Murrow was honored at a dinner given by William S. Paley, CBS president, attended by government officials, educators, editors, industrialists, and fellow broadcasters. Over a coast-to-coast network he gave his first uncensored report of the war.

The Murrows were invited to dine at the White House on Sunday, December 7, 1941. That afternoon, while Murrow was golfing, word was sent to the links that Pearl Harbor had been attacked. A little later Mrs. Roosevelt greeted her guests on schedule. The President did not show up at table but sent word for Murrow to stay on. After midnight, President Roosevelt called Murrow in, questioned him about conditions in London, and told him the story of what had actually happened at Pearl Harbor, a story that Murrow could not tell at the time.

Back on the job in Europe, Murrow was the man chosen to give the official flash on all networks on June 6, 1944 that D-Day had come.

In 1946, Murrow returned to the United States after having been abroad the greater part of nine years. After a 20,000-mile tour of his own country, Murrow sat down behind a desk in CBS headquarters as vice-president, director of public affairs, and a member of the board of directors.

"It's the big desk with the telephones," he commented after eighteen months at this task, "the IN basket and the OUT basket. Conferences, memos, budgets and firing people. Who am I to be firing people—the Almighty himself?"

On the air again, with an average of 5,000,000 receivers tuned in to hear him, whether he was offering hard news, an interview, a tape-recording, or a thoughtful analysis, Murrow observed: "It is much easier to report a battle or a bombing than it is to do an honest and intelligible job on the Marshall Plan, the Taft-Hartley Law or the Atlantic Pact."

The long list of prizes, awards, medals, citations, honorary degrees that came to Murrow, as well as the spontaneous tributes from his fellows, attested to the fact that if anybody was doing an honest, intelligible job on the air, this was Murrow.

Late in 1951, Murrow followed up his "Hear It Now" radio review by launching a television program, "See It Now," which at the outset was hailed by thoughtful communications critics as the new medium's supreme journalistic achievement to date. Planned and presented by Murrow and Fred W. Friendly, the program taxed Murrow's recognized talents to their utmost. It called upon him to keep a watchful eye on the clock, on the controls, on the script, much of the time in full view of the audience himself and all the while providing with apparent ease and assurance the analytical commentary, the dramatic sequence, the background and perspective necessary to give meaning to the wide-sweeping and quick-shifting shots of word and deed that flashed across the screen.

Responsible in the end for his own performance alone, Murrow was able to take advantage of the skillful aid of a corps of reporters and technicians and to adapt techniques developed by other pioneers in the field. John Cameron Swayze, for instance, had for some time presented a daily news program on the rival NBC network compounded of tape recordings, kinescopes, personal interpretation, and dramatization.

Just as radio required reporters to become vocal as well as verbal, television, by making them visual, added a further dimension to their role, gave them fresh opportunities and fresh problems.

John Crosby, whose *New York Herald Tribune* column keeps a sharp eye on radio performance and progress, writes:

Television hasn't yet produced a satisfactory substitute for a newspaperman—there are those who say that radio hasn't either—or for news . . . whoever reads the news, with which he is familiar, in front of a camera, with which he isn't . . . feels visible and this has left its mark. Already . . . these newsmen feel the urge to gesticulate, to . . . emote. When radio came we got an entirely new type of newsman. It wasn't enough to ferret out the facts, assess them and report them in something approximating English; it was necessary to have a voice. (In fact the other requirements were largely discarded.) We got Gabriel Heatter and H. V.

Kaltenborn. Bassoons, both of them, more appropriate to the Philharmonic than to the new field. . . .

We're going to see some great performances on television when the news comes on but it's going to be increasingly difficult to figure out what goes on in the world.

Television reporters like Douglas Edwards and John Cameron Swayze (who went from Wichita, Kansas, to New York as a youth to study dramatics) used movies and visual aids such as maps and diagrams to augment their journalistic and histrionic talents and get the news across. Television met its initial tests most effectively, not through its reporters, but through presenting actual events and real news-making personalities directly to the public. The 1948 political conventions in Philadelphia gave television its first full-scale workout. The Kefauver Crime Investigating Committee hearings in New York in 1951, sponsored by *Time* over a nineteen-city network (and broadcast unsponsored over many other stations) were seen by an audience estimated at 20,000,000 persons.

Quoting Crosby again in this connection:

Television . . . has contributed to popular enlightenment, but, more importantly, to public maturity. But we've still some distance to go before we can view such a hearing with anything like the cool skepticism and judicial impartiality it deserves. Television is a wonderfully potent instrument for arousing the populace, and in this case, it's arousing it against organized crime, a fairly noncontroversial thing. Next time, though, the question might not be anything so open and shut as our opinions on criminals; it could be a question such as foreign policy. Then we'll have to judge the proceedings not on the physical attractions or personal problems of the witnesses, but, of all things, on what they have to say.

Television imposes obligations upon the viewer almost as heavy as those it imposes on the producer and the performer. Now the voter may observe act by act and word by word how the men he puts in office go about their jobs.

After the televised Kefauver hearings precipitated the committee's counsel, Rudolph Halley, into the political limelight, some keen observations upon the potentialities of the new medium were made by Robert Ruark, a relative newcomer and rapid riser in the ranks of the columnists:

The immense potency of the television program cannot be underestimated from now on as a political weapon. Its easy approach to the listener, its huge command of audience, almost would make it possible for Milton Berle to win an election over a qualified but dull-gray opponent. . . .

The appeal of the medicine show, of the carnival barker, has never been denied as a vital approach to an essentially emotional public. . . .

The cracked voice, the jerked tear, the thunderous condemnation, have been used often in radio but never with the paralyzing effect of good lighting, good makeup, and a little careful consideration of timing and enunciation. . . .

We really have the bull by the tail in this television assist to campaigning. It augurs an almost impossible discipline on the voter, who must remember that he is not voting for Dagmar or Capt. Video but for men who will control his welfare, taxes and, maybe, even his death when once elected.

For the journalist as well as the politician, the merciless glare of the camera lights can project the good as well as it can expose the bad. It can also show up the reporter himself and let the public for the first time see newspapermen on duty, not as Hollywood would have it, but as they actually are.

Meet the Press, a program developed by Lawrence Spivak and Martha Rountree, offers a weekly demonstration and an object lesson for students of journalism, presenting reporters often at their best and revealing how well public figures can stand up under the probing of the press.

Whether the makers of video journalism will find themselves in the end competing or cooperating with the makers of the earlier types of journalism remains to be seen. It is a well-remembered bit of press history that newspaper publishers first ignored radio, then opposed it, then embraced it. Researchers found that new media, as they developed, seemed to help rather than hinder the older media; the more people listened to radio news, the more they read the newspapers.

The halfway point in the twentieth century marked a transition period in which each of the various outlets of fact and opinion groped for its proper place in the spectrum.

In a world where wider and wider areas were becoming stifled and blinded by censorship, suppression, and controlled propaganda, free Americans with access to typewriters, presses, microphones, and cameras faced a "rendezvous with destiny."

No better personification of this period of transition and challenge for the press could be found than Elmer Davis, a scholar with a sense of perspective, who progressed from the highest type of daily newspapering to the highest type of radio commentary, and then took on for his government the seemingly thankless task of trying to interpret America's aims to itself and to the world.

Striking in appearance, with bushy black eyebrows and snowy white hair, habitually wearing a black bow tie with a white shirt, Davis resumed his radio spot after the war, bringing to his "comprehensive commentary" a rich background of education and experience, a Hoosier twang that inspired confidence, a dry and quiet wit, and clear appraisal. In 1951 he won for the third time the Peabody Award, which is radio's equivalent for the Pulitzer prizes of the written word.

Son of an Indiana banker, he was printer's devil on the *Aurora Bulletin* as a boy. After teaching high school in his native state, he got his bachelor's and master's degrees at Franklin College and went on to Oxford as a Rhodes scholar. As a student of history and politics and the classics, he came to believe that the clues to many current ills lay in the philosophy of Thucydides, to turn to the poetry of Catullus and Horace in the original Latin for inspiration, to music and to the care and cultivation of cats for relaxation. During his student days in Paris, he met Florence MacMillan of Mount Vernon, New York, and they were married four years later.

After a year on the editorial staff of *Adventure Magazine* in New York, Davis joined the *New York Times* as a cub reporter in 1914. It was not long before he was writing political features, contributing editorials, and traveling as a correspondent.

At the 1920 Democratic convention in San Francisco, Davis created the newspaper character named Godfrey Gloom of Amity, Indiana, who played the role of Davis's alter ego at the next four national conventions until, bored with his creation, Davis put an end to him. Arthur Krock of the *Times* solemnly wrote Godfrey's obituary.

Davis became his newspaper's historian, and his volume about the *Times* served as the standard reference source until 1951 when, on the occasion of the paper's centenary, the *Times* assigned Meyer Berger to bring the record up to date with a new history.

In 1924 Davis wrote a warmly humorous newspaper novel with a New York speakeasy setting, *Friends of Mr. Sweeney,* which won him new friends. In all, Davis produced nine novels, three collections of short stories, and a book of essays.

While the Columbia Broadcasting System's ace commentator, H. V. Kaltenborn, was abroad covering the European crisis of 1939, CBS called upon Davis to take over Kaltenborn's spot on the home scene. His tempered, often skeptical, understatement, his shrewd and tolerant analysis, and his indications of substantial agreement with the Administration's attitudes led President Roosevelt to call upon Davis after the United States went to war.

Six months after Pearl Harbor the President combined four prewar agencies into the single Office of War Information and persuaded Davis to leave his $1,000-a-week job as one of the nation's favorite commentators to become director of the OWI at less than a fifth of his former salary.

In the previous war, both information and censorship had been combined under one man, George Creel; this time censorship was no part of Davis's job but was delegated to the Office of Censorship set up under a fellow Hoosier, Byron Price of the Associated Press, who shared Davis's deep dislike of any unnecessary curbs upon freedom.

Davis's assignment was to organize and direct the biggest news and propaganda distribution operation ever undertaken

by the United States. On the domestic front it included chan-
neling straight news on the progress of war activities from
government departments to newspapers and news agencies,
monitoring and analyzing foreign propaganda broadcasts, re-
solving differences and correcting inconsistencies in the output
of other agencies, conducting campaigns for salvaging war
materials, dispelling rumors, promoting victory gardens, recruiting efforts and war bond sales. Overseas, it meant collecting and
processing facts to be carried to the armed forces and propaganda that would encourage allies, attract neutrals, and dis-
hearten enemies.

"I hope nobody in this country is any longer scandalized by
the word propaganda," he told Arthur Krock in an interview
for the *Times*. "Propaganda may be either true or false, directed to worthy or unworthy ends. The most successful job of
propaganda and political warfare in history was that accomplished by Benjamin Franklin in the years following 1776. You
can't turn up a Franklin every time you need one, but we are
trying to do the same job he did, to the same end of American
victory."

Davis worked hard at prying loose legitimate news from the
military, many of whom would have preferred to keep the
whole war out of print. He was under constant fire from anti-
Administration Congressmen, publishers, and columnists who
charged that he was using his position to promote Franklin D.
Roosevelt and the Democratic Party.

"It does annoy me," he confessed once, "to have to spend two
or three months a year fighting John Taber [upstate New York
Representative who was ranking Republican on the House
Appropriations Committee] for the privilege of being able to
fight the enemy."

On another level, Davis had to overcome understandable
resistance led by still another native Indianan, Kent Cooper,
general manager of the Associated Press since 1925 and for fifteen years before that in various executive capacities.

It was Cooper's proud boast that he had released the great

international news service from its one-time ties with a world cartel of government-controlled agencies and he was now committed to the free flow of information throughout the world by private endeavor and without the stigma of government coloration. The wartime emergency, however, made it vital to reach the have-not nations that could not afford to pay for commercial news services. It was here that the government felt obliged to step in, taking care not to operate in direct competition with established private agencies. Reluctantly, and only as a wartime concession, Cooper permitted the Office of War Information to make limited use of the Associated Press file.

When the war ended, Davis promptly dissolved the OWI and returned to the radio, this time on the American Broadcasting Company network, now under the presidency of Robert Kintner, another newsman who had bridged the gap from the printed word to the spoken word.

The Voice of America, overseas shortwave service, which had been developed under Davis, continued as a function of the Department of State and became increasingly important as an arm in the cold war of words between the Soviet sphere and the democratic sphere.

Davis, back on the air, obviously still subscribed to the statement he had made long before his name became known around the world—a statement that could serve as well to underscore the postwar objectives of the Voice of America:

With the irrational optimism befitting an alumnus of the absurd age in which I came to the surface, I still believe that higher peaks of human felicity may be ahead; that our race, if it keeps on trying, might make quite a habitable place of the planet on which it resides.

What a large part of the planet still found difficult to appreciate was the fact that it was not Elmer Davis alone who spoke for the United States, nor Fulton Lewis Jr., nor Henry Luce, nor Robert R. McCormick, nor Helen Rogers Reid.

The discordant tones of idealism and cynicism, of selfishness and altruism, of sincerity and hypocrisy, of culture and vulgarity, of reaction and radicalism, of conservatism and liberalism, of hysteria and sanity—this is the din that democracy makes. It represents the very freedom of thought and expression for which the early editors of revolt fought and for which many modern editors still fight, a freedom that carries with it the risks of all freedoms—the dangers of license, betrayal, and excess —and the hope of all freedoms. It is the voice of America.

A Reading Bibliography

General

There are six standard histories of journalism. Of these, the only one of real value to students, from the standpoint of comprehensiveness, is Frank Luther Mott's *American Journalism* (rev. ed., New York, 1950). It has no equal in the field as a reference work, it is more reliable than any of the others, and it treats adequately the development of journalism in recent years.

Among magazine histories, Dr. Mott's *A History of American Magazines* (3 vols., Cambridge, 1938) is also unequaled and definitive.

Dean John E. Drewry has edited two collections of profiles of journalistic figures from the pages of the *Saturday Evening Post*, under the title *Post Biographies* (Atlanta, 1942 and 1947). These contain a wealth of information, not all of it accurate and some of it considerably biased.

Perhaps the most complete biographical source for newspaper and magazine personalities is the *Dictionary of American Biography*, whose well-written and scholarly essays are generally accurate, unprejudiced and very informative. Some of the chapters in this volume are based on these sketches.

Much sound historical insight into the lives and policies of great editors, along with samples of their work, are to be found in Allan Nevins, *American Press Opinion* (New York, 1928).

Highly opinionated but valuable sketches of editors and newspapers are contained in Oswald Garrison Villard's *The Disappearing Daily* (New York, 1944), a revision of *Some Newspapers and Newspapermen* (New York, 1923).

Even more biased are the estimates in *Lords of the Press,* by George Seldes (New York, 1938) and *America's House of Lords,* by Harold L. Ickes (New York, 1939).

Among the best sources for contemporary personalities and developments are the files of the trade weekly, *Editor & Publisher,* and the press sections of *Time* and *Newsweek.*

Chapter 1

The prime source book for colonial newspapers and their printers is Isaiah Thomas, *The History of Printing in America, With a Biography of Printers and an Account of Newspapers* (Worcester, 1810; rev. ed., Albany, 1874). Another valuable source is Joseph T. Buckingham, *Specimens of Newspaper Literature, With Personal Memoirs, Anecdotes and Reminiscences* (2 vols., Boston, 1850). There are also biographical sketches in George Emory Littlefield, *The Early Massachusetts Press,* 1638-1711 (2 vols., Boston, 1907).

There are no satisfactory book-length biographies of Revolutionary editors except Benjamin Franklin and Zenger. Perhaps the best account of Franklin's newspapers days is contained in James Parton's *Life and Times of Benjamin Franklin* (2 vols., New York, 1864), though the best modern biography of Franklin remains Carl Van Doren's *Benjamin Franklin* (New York, 1938). The most complete story of Zenger and his trial is in Livingston Rutherford, *John Peter Zenger* (New York, 1904).

A biography of Isaiah Thomas is Annie Russell Marble, *From 'Prentice to Patron* (New York, 1935).

Chapter 2

Philip Freneau's newspaper work is best described in *The Political Activities of Philip Freneau* (Johns Hopkins University Studies in Historical and Political Science, Vol. XX, Nos. IX-X).

The Life of William Cobbett, by G. D. H. Cole (London, 1925) remains the best study.

Benjamin Franklin Bache's story is told in Bernard Faÿ's, *The Two Franklins* (Boston, 1933).

Andrew Jackson's editors are treated partially in Marquis James, *The Life of Andrew Jackson* (Indianapolis, 1938) and in Arthur M. Schlesinger, Jr., *The Age of Jackson* (Boston, 1945). The only specific work of consequence is *The Autobiography of Amos Kendall* (Boston, 1872).

Chapter 3

There are two primary biographies of the Bennetts. One is contemporary, Isaac C. Pray's *Memoirs of James Gordon Bennett and His Times* (New York, 1855), published anonymously as written "By A Journalist," and undoubtedly authorized. The modern biography is Don C. Seitz, *The James Gordon Bennetts* (Indianapolis, 1928).

Chapter 4

The most recent and by far the best biography of Greeley is *Horace Greeley, Voice of the People,* by William Harlan Hale (New York, 1950). Others written in this century include Henry L. Stoddard, *Horace Greeley, Printer, Editor, Crusader* (New York, 1946); Don C. Seitz, *Horace Greeley* (Indianapolis, 1926); and William A. Linn, *Horace Greeley* (New York, 1903). The contemporary biography of consequence is James Parton, *Life of Horace Greeley* (Boston, 1872). Greeley's own book is *The Autobiography of Horace Greeley, or Recollections of a Busy Life* (New York, 1868). A scholarly but very readable study of Greeley's political life is *Horace Greeley and the Republican Party,* by Jeter A. Isely (Princeton, 1947).

Chapter 5

The two principal biographies of Dana are Candace Stone, *Dana and The Sun* (New York, 1938), and Charles J. Rosebault, *When Dana Was The Sun* (New York, 1931). The authorized biography is *The Life of Charles A. Dana,* by James Harrison Wilson (New York, 1907).

There are numerous articles about Godkin (see bibliography in *American Dictionary of Biography*) but only one book, *Life and Letters of Edwin Lawrence Godkin,* edited by Rollo Ogden (2 vols., New York, 1907).

Chapter 6

The standard biography of Pulitzer is Don C. Seitz, *Joseph Pulitzer: His Life and Letters* (New York, 1924). James Wyman Barrett, last city editor of the *World,* has contributed two colorful volumes, *The World, The Flesh and Messrs. Pulitzer* (New York, 1931) and *Joseph Pulitzer and His World* (New York, 1941). An intimate picture of the man is provided by Alleyne Ireland in *Joseph Pulitzer: Reminiscences of A Secretary* (New York, 1914). This book has also been issued as *An Adventure With A Genius*.

Chapter 7

At the time of Hearst's death in 1951, there were four biographies extant. Of these, the best is generally considered to be *Hearst, Lord of San Simeon,* by Oliver Carlson and Ernest Sutherland Bates (New York, 1936). Ferdinand Lundberg's *Imperial Hearst* (New York, 1936) is unfortunately too biased to be of substantial value. The authorized biography is *William Randolph Hearst, American,* by Mrs. Fremont Older (New York, 1936), which is just as biased in the opposite direction, but contains the most accurate and fullest information about the Hearst family. John K. Winkler's *W. R. Hearst, An American Phenomenon* (New York, 1928) is an amiable, anecdotal treatment, much outdated.

A new, full-length biography by John Tebbel has been scheduled for publication in the autumn of 1952.

Chapter 8

An excellent biography of Henry J. Raymond, *Raymond of the Times,* by Francis Brown (New York, 1951), has replaced Augustus Maverick's *Henry J. Raymond and the New York Press for Thirty Years* (Hartford, 1870), the only previous Raymond biography. For the interval between Raymond and Ochs, the best source is Fraser Bond's *Mr. Miller of the Times: The Story of An Editor* (New York, 1931). Gerald W. Johnson's *An Honorable Titan* (New York, 1946) is the authorized biography of Ochs, but an excellent study nonetheless.

Meyer Berger's *The Story of the New York Times* (New York, 1951) was published on the paper's hundredth anniversary. It is an authorized work, but definitive and extremely readable. Only twelve of its forty-seven chapters, however, are devoted to nineteenth-century *Times* history.

A short biography of Carr Van Anda, the *Times'* great managing editor, is *A Giant of the Press,* by Barnett Fine (New York, 1933).

Chapter 9

The best biography of Nelson is Icie F. Johnson's *William Rockhill Nelson and The Kansas City Star* (Kansas City, 1935); there is also a memorial volume by the *Star's* staff, titled *William Rockhill Nelson, the Story of a Man, a Newspaper, and a City* (Cambridge, 1915).

An authorized biography of Victor Lawson, which also relates the history of the Chicago *Daily News,* is Charles H. Dennis, *Victor Lawson: His Time and His Work* (Chicago, 1935). Melville Stone's autobiography, *Fifty Years A Journalist* (New York, 1921) is an anecdotal reminiscence which deals with the early years of both the *Daily News* and the Associated Press. These may be supplemented by Oliver Gramling's *AP: The Story of News* (New York, 1940) in which Lawson and Stone's part in the formation of the Associated Press is told from a naturally partisan viewpoint.

Chapter 10

Raymond B. Nixon's *Henry W. Grady, Spokesman of the New South* (New York, 1943) is an excellent modern biography of Grady. Henry Watterson told his story in *Marse Henry, An Autobiography* (2 vols., New York, 1919). An outside view, but one no less sympathetic, is provided by Isaac Marcosson in *Marse Henry* (New York, 1951).

Chapter 11

There is no modern biography of Joseph Dennie, or in fact, no full-length treatment. A scholarly examination of his life and writings may be found in H. M. Ellis, *Joseph Dennie and His Circle* (Bulletin of the University of Texas, Austin, 1915).

Ed Howe's autobiography, *Plain People* (New York, 1929) is almost unexcelled in its field.

William Allen White's *Autobiography* (New York, 1946) is detailed and valuable down to 1920. It should be read in conjunction with Walter Johnson's *William Allen White's America* (New York, 1947), which casts further light on the autobiography and brings the story down to White's death.

Chapter 12

A more factual account of the exploits of Bonfils and Tammen than Gene Fowler's *Timber Line* (New York, 1933) may some day be written, but it is unlikely that anyone will ever surpass this famous biography.

Fremont Older's *My Own Story* (New York, 1926) conveys the flavor of his personality and is valuable for its story of his crusades, but it should be read with *Fremont Older*, by Evelyn Wells (New York, 1936), a sympathetic biography that is more complete.

Chapter 13

Cyrus Curtis's only biographer has been Edward W. Bok, whose *A Man From Maine* (New York, 1923) is too admiring to be of considerable value but nevertheless provides a generally accurate account of the publisher's life. Bok's autobiography, *The Americanization of Edward Bok* (New York, 1920) is a modern classic in the field.

The only biography of Lorimer is *George Horace Lorimer and The Saturday Evening Post*, by John Tebbel (New York, 1948).

Chapter 14

The story of Joseph Medill and the McCormick and Patterson newspaper families is told in *An American Dynasty*, by John Tebbel (New York, 1947).

For an excellent account of the years between the Medill and McCormick regimes on the Chicago *Tribune*, see James Weber Linn's *James Keeley, Newspaperman* (Indianapolis, 1937).

The *Tribune*'s various biographies of itself contain a wealth of information, which is made unreliable by the paper's peculiar interpretation of its own and the nation's history.

Chapter 15

The beginnings of the Reid dynasty are most completely covered in the two volumes of *The Life of Whitelaw Reid*, by Royal Cortissoz (New York, 1921) and *The New York Tribune Since the Civil War*, by Harry W. Baehr Jr. (New York, 1936). Personalities in the paper's foreign venture are accurately and entertainingly described in *The Paris Herald: The Incredible Newspaper*, by Al Laney (New

York, 1947). Mrs. Helen Rogers Reid's story is told by Mona Gardner in the *Saturday Evening Post* (May 6 and 13, 1944) under the title, "Queen Helen." A vignette of Mrs. Reid, along with uncritical portraits of countless others on the distaff side of journalism, is presented in *Ladies of the Press,* by Ishbel Ross (New York and London, 1936).

Frank A. Munsey's relations with the Reids and the *Tribune,* as well as with the rest of the American press, are recounted fairly in *Forty Years, Forty Millions,* by George Britt (New York, 1935).

Chapter 16

It is advisable to read all three of the Scripps biographies—in spite of some inevitable repetition—to get a well-rounded view of the man: *Lusty Scripps,* by Gilson Gardner (New York, 1932); *E. W. Scripps,* by Negley Cochran (New York, 1933), and *Damned Old Crank,* edited by Charles R. McCabe (New York, 1951). A commonplace autobiography of Scripps' early partner is *Forty Years of Newspaperdom,* by Milton A. McRae (New York, 1924).

Chapter 17

Roy Howard is subjected to severe criticism in "From Scripps to Howard," by Robert Bendiner and James A. Wechsler in the *Nation* (May 13 and 20, 1939). Both "Press Lord," by Forrest Davis in the *Saturday Evening Post* (March 12, 1938), and "Publisher," by A. J. Liebling, in the *New Yorker* (August 2, 9, 16 and 23, 1941) are critical evaluations written by one-time Scripps-Howard employes. Marginal notes by Howard himself accompany the article on "Roy Howard, Newspaper Napoleon," by Leland Stowe, in *Look* (May 30, 1944).

"Rip Roaring Baillie," by Jack Alexander, in the *Saturday Evening Post* (June 1 and 8, 1946), is a good portrait of the president of the United Press.

For further light on the columnists discussed in this chapter, see *Heywood Broun,* by Dale Kramer (New York, 1949) and the chapter on Pegler in *The Columnists,* by Charles Fisher (New York, 1944). Many magazine articles have been written about Pegler but none of them really explains him.

A closeup of an outstanding Scripps-Howard editor mentioned in this chapter, Louis B. Seltzer, is given in "Mr. Cleveland," by R. L. Williams in *Life* (March 13, 1950).

Chapter 18

Further details on the career of John S. Knight may be found in "Up From Akron," by Jack Alexander in the *Saturday Evening Post* (August 18, 1945).

Journey Through My Years, by James M. Cox (New York, 1946) reviews Cox's more than fifty years of contact, as newspaperman and official, with public affairs.

Chapter 19

Not a great deal has appeared in print about the Cowles brothers beyond two articles by George A. Brandenburg in *Editor & Publisher* (February 6 and 13, 1943). The Cowles publishing ventures are briefly discussed in connection with other newspaper leaders in "The Prudent Publishers" in *Fortune* (July, 1950).

Chapter 20

Imprint Of A Publisher, by Samuel T. Williamson (New York, 1948) is the second authorized biography of Frank Gannett by the same writer. As the latter explains, the shorter first book "was turned out in considerable haste so as to be in the hands of the delegates and alternates to the Republican National Convention in 1940."

Publishing and syndication activities of John H. Perry are treated questioningly in "Boiler Plate Empire" by Thomas Whiteside in the *New Republic* (November 17, 1947), and "John H. Perry— Florida's Little Press Lord" in *The New Leader* (January 1, 1951).

"Little Publisher, Big Empire," by Collie Small, describes the career of Samuel I. Newhouse (*Collier's,* August 4, 1951).

Chapter 21

"The Paper That Was Tailored To A City," by David G. Wittels in the *Saturday Evening Post* (April 7, 1945) tells the story of the McLean family and the *Bulletin.*

The background of the *Inquirer's* publisher is uncompromisingly discussed in "Smart Money," by John T. Flynn in *Collier's* (January 13, 20 and 27, and February 3, 1940).

An interesting glimpse of the character of J. David Stern, Jr., and of the death of his *Record* is contained in "Let's Look at The

Record," by Richard Strouse in the *New Republic* (February 24, 1947).

Chapter 22

Many articles have been written about the *Christian Science Monitor,* including notably, "Journalism Without Jaundice" by Carol Hughes in *Coronet* (December, 1944) and "The Christian Science Monitor," by Marquis Childs in the *Saturday Evening Post* (September 15, 1945), but few have given much insight into the character of the *Monitor*'s editor, Erwin D. Canham.

Chapter 23

Josephus Daniels told his own story in *Tar Heel Editor* (Chapel Hill, 1939) and *Editor In Politics* (Chapel Hill, 1941).

Sketches of Mark Ethridge, Barry Bingham, Ralph McGill, Virginius Dabney, along with those of some other editors mentioned in this book, may be found in *Current Biography*.

An excellent picture of personal beginnings in Southern journalism is provided in *Chip Off My Shoulder,* by Thomas L. Stokes (Princeton, Princeton University Press, 1940).

Chapter 24

Palmer Hoyt's adventure with the Denver *Post* is described in "A Chinook Blows on Champa Street" and "Reborn Denver *Post* Has Prestige and Power," both by A. Gayle Waldrop, in *Journalism Quarterly* (June, 1947, and Summer 1951 respectively).

Manchester Boddy's story is told in "Man With A Borrowed Shoestring," by Frank J. Taylor in the *Saturday Evening Post* (December 2, 1944).

Chapter 25

A number of magazine articles have been written about Marshall Field, but the subject is covered completely in *The Marshall Fields,* by John Tebbel (New York, 1947).

Field has told some of his own story in *Freedom Is More Than A Word* (Chicago, 1945).

The most penetrating profile of Ralph Ingersoll is "A Very Active Type Man," by Wolcott Gibbs in the *New Yorker* (May 2 and 9, 1942).

Chapter 26

Briton Hadden: A Biography of the Co-Founder of Time, by Noel F. Busch (New York, 1949) and a *New Yorker* profile by Wolcott Gibbs (November 23, 1936), sharply portray the personalities behind Time, Inc.

De Witt Wallace's role in journalism is depicted in "The Reader's Digest," *Fortune* (November, 1936) and *Little Wonder,* by John Bainbridge (New York, 1948). It is also the subject of a cover piece in *Time* (December 10, 1951).

Dale Kramer's *Ross And* The New Yorker (New York, 1951) appeared just a month before the *New Yorker* editor's death.

Chapter 27

The best collective sources of biographical material about the Washington pundits are *The Columnists: A Clinical Survey,* by Charles Fisher (New York, 1944); *Molders of Opinion,* edited by David Bulman (Milwaukee, 1945) and *Dateline: Washington,* Cabell Phillips (editor) and the National Press Club (New York, 1949).

Chapter 28

Winchell and other radio commentators are covered in Fisher's *The Columnists.* Kaltenborn tells his own story in *Fifty Fabulous Years* (New York, 1950). "Murrow Sticks To The Facts" by Wesley Price in the *Saturday Evening Post* (December 10, 1950) is a worthy evaluation of one of radio's outstanding leaders.

Index